Microsoft®

OFFICE EXCEL 2007

Introductory

William R. Pasewark, Sr., Ph.D.
Professor Emeritus, Business Education, Texas Tech University
Scott G. Pasewark, B.S.
Occupational Education, Computer Technologist
William R. Pasewark, Jr., Ph.D., CPA
Professor, Accounting, Texas Tech University
Carolyn Denny Pasewark, M.Ed.
National Computer Consultant, reading and Math Certified Elementary Teacher, K-12 Certified Counselor
Jan Pasewark Stogner, MBA
Financial Planner
Beth Pasewark Wadsworth, B.A.
Graphic Designer
Robin M. Romer
Contributing Author

*Pasewark and Pasewark is a trademark of the Pasewark LTD.

by Pasewark and Pasewark*

COURSE TECHNOLOGY
CENGAGE Learning™

Australia • Brazil • Japan • Korea • Mexico • Singapore • Spain • United Kingdom • United States

Microsoft Office Excel 2007 Introductory
Contributing Author: Robin M. Romer
Authors: William R. Pasewark, Sr., William R. Pasewark, Jr., Scott G. Pasewark, Jan Pasewark Stogner, Beth Pasewark Wadsworth, Carolyn Pasewark Denny

Managing Editor: Donna Gridley

Product Manager: Jennifer T. Campbell

Editorial Assistant: Amanda Lyons

Content Project Manager: Heather Furrow

Copy Editor: Devra Kunin

Proofreader: Marc Masse

Indexer: Rich Carlson

Marketing Coordinator: Julie Schuster

Quality Assurance Testers: John Freitas, Christian Kunciw, GreenPenQA, Serge Palladino, Jeff Schwartz, Marianne Snow, Teresa Storch

Developmental Editor: Custom Editorial Productions, Inc.

Composition: GEX Publishing Services

Art Director: Bruce Bond

Cover Designer: Joel Sadagursky

Cover Illustrator: Neil Brennan

For product information and technology assistance, contact us at
Cengage Learning Customer & Sales Support, 1-800-354-9706
For permission to use material from this text or product, submit all requests online at **cengage.com/permissions**
Further permissions questions can be emailed to
permissionrequest@cengage.com

ISBN-13: 978-1-4239-0411-3
ISBN-10: 1-4239-0411-7

Course Technology
25 Thomson Place
Boston, Massachusetts 02210
USA

Cengage Learning is a leading provider of customized learning solutions with office locations around the globe, including Singapore, the United Kingdom, Australia, Mexico, Brazil, and Japan. Locate your local office at:
international.cengage.com/region

Cengage Learning products are represented in Canada by Nelson Education, Ltd.

For your lifelong learning solutions, visit **course.cengage.com**

Purchase any of our products at your local college store or at our preferred online store **www.ichapters.com**

Microsoft and the Office logo are either registered trademarks or trademarks of Microsoft Corporation in the United States and/or other countries. Course Technology, Cengage Learning is an independent entity from the Microsoft Corporation, and not affiliated with Microsoft in any manner.

Printed in the United States of America.
3 4 5 6 7 8 9 10 09

MESSAGE FROM THE AUTHORS

About the Pasewark Author Team

Pasewark LTD is a family-owned business with more than 90 years of combined experience authoring award-winning textbooks. They have written over 100 books about computers, accounting, and office technology. During that time, they developed their mission statement: *To help our students live better lives.*

Pasewark LTD authors are members of several professional associations that help authors write better books. The authors have been recognized with numerous awards for classroom teaching and believe that effective classroom teaching is a major ingredient for writing effective textbooks.

Award-Winning Books by the Pasewarks

The predecessors to this book, *Microsoft® Office 2000: Introductory* and *Microsoft Office XP: Introductory*, by the Pasewarks, won the Text and Academic Authors Association *Texty Award* for the best el-hi computer book for the years 2000 and 2002.

Acknowledgement:

Many thanks to my talented coauthors and the dedicated editorial team at Course Technology. Much love to my family for their constant support. A special thank you to Brian for your patience and endurance, and to Jake, who just turned 5, for your help in writing all the As, Es, Js, and Ks. - *Robin M. Romer*

About the Contributing Author

Robin M. Romer has been writing and editing computer textbooks for the past 20 years. Most recently, she coauthored *New Perspectives on Microsoft Office 2007* and edited *New Perspectives on Microsoft Excel 2007.*

TEACHING AND LEARNING RESOURCES FOR THIS BOOK

Student Online Companion

The *Student Online Companion*, available at www.course.com, includes the Data Files, MCAS mapping grids, and Key Terms. CourseCasts and PowerPoint presentations allow students to learn more about the topics.

Instructor Resources CD

The *Instructor Resources CD* contains many teaching resources, including Data and Solution Files, ExamView® tests, Instructor Manuals, and PowerPoint presentations for each lesson.

ASSESSMENT INSTRUCTIONS

SAM 2007 POWERED BY SAM

SAM 2007 helps bridge the gap between the classroom and the real world by allowing students to train and test on important computer skills in an active, hands-on environment.

SAM 2007's easy-to-use system includes powerful interactive exams, training or projects on critical applications such as Word, Excel, Access, PowerPoint, Outlook, Windows, the Internet, and much more. SAM simulates the application environment, allowing students to demonstrate their knowledge and think through the skills by performing real-world tasks.

SAM 2007 includes built-in page references so students can print helpful study guides that match the textbooks used in class. Powerful administrative options allow instructors to schedule exams and assignments, secure tests, and run reports with almost limitless flexibility.

ExamView®

ExamView is a powerful objective-based test generator that enables you to create paper, LAN, or Web-based tests from test banks designed specifically for your Course Technology text. Utilize the ultra-efficient QuickTest Wizard to create tests in less than five minutes by taking advantage of Course Technology's question banks, or customize your own exams from scratch.

SCANS

The Secretary's Commission on Achieving Necessary Skills (SCANS) from the U.S. Department of Labor is a list of workplace competencies and foundation skills that can be used to ensure that students achieve the level of skills required to enter employment. The workplace competencies are identified as (1) ability to use resources, (2) interpersonal skills, (3) ability to work with information, (4) understanding of systems, and (5) knowledge and understanding of technology. The foundation skills are identified as (1) basic communication skills, (2) thinking skills, and (3) personal qualities.

Exercises in which students must use a number of these SCANS competencies and foundation skills are marked in the text with the SCANS icon.

Microsoft Certified Application Specialist Certification

This courseware, when used in conjunction with our *Microsoft Certification Application Specialist Office 2007 Workbook*, covers all of the necessary skills to prepare for the Microsoft Certification Application Specialist (MCAS) Program exams for Word, Excel, PowerPoint, and Access. To learn more about the MCAS program, go to www.microsoft.com/learning/exams.

What is the Microsoft Business Certification Program?

The Microsoft Business Certification Program enables candidates to show that they have something exceptional to offer—proved experience in Microsoft Office programs. The two certification tracks allow candidates to choose how they want to exhibit their skills, either through validating skills within a specific Microsoft product or taking their knowledge to the next level and combining Microsoft programs to show that they can apply multiple skill sets to complete more complex office tasks. Recognized by businesses and schools around the world, over 3 million certifications have been obtained in over 100 different countries. The Microsoft Business Certification program is the only Microsoft-approved certification program of its kind.

What is the Microsoft Certified Application Specialist Certification?

The Microsoft Certified Application Specialist Certification exams focus on validating specific skill sets within each of the Microsoft® Office system programs. The candidate can choose which exam(s) they want to take according to which skills they want to validate. The available Application Specialist exams include:

- Using Microsoft® Windows Vista™
- Using Microsoft® Office Word 2007
- Using Microsoft® Office Excel® 2007*
- Using Microsoft® Office PowerPoint® 2007
- Using Microsoft® Office Access® 2007
- Using Microsoft® Office Outlook® 2007

*Use this book along with the *Microsoft Certification Application Specialist Office 2007 Workbook* to practice the certification skills for this exam.

GETTING STARTED

Start-Up Checklist

Minimum Hardware Configuration

✓ PC with Pentium processor

✓ Hard disk with 400 MB free for typical installation

✓ CD-ROM drive or access to network drive for downloading and saving Data and Solution Files

✓ Monitor set at 1024x768 or higher-resolution. (*if your resolution differs, you will see differences in the Ribbon, and may have to scroll up or down to view the information on your screen*)

✓ Mouse or compatible pointing device

✓ Printer

✓ Internet connection. If you are not connected to the Internet, see your instructor

Software

This book was written and tested using the following settings:

✓ A typical installation of Microsoft Office 2007

✓ Microsoft Windows Vista (running with Aero off)

✓ Microsoft Internet Explorer 7 browser

For Windows XP users

The screenshots in this book show Microsoft Office 2007 running on Windows Vista. If you are using Microsoft Windows XP, use these alternate steps.

Starting a program

1. Click the **Start** button on the taskbar

2. Point to **All Programs**, point to **Microsoft Office**, then click the application you want to use

Saving a file for the first time

1. Click the **Office Button**, then click **Save As**

2. Type a name for your file in the File Name text box

3. Click the **Save in** list arrow, then navigate to the drive and folder where you store your Data Files

4. Click **Save**

Opening a file

1. Click the **Office Button**, then click **Open**

2. Click the **Look in** list arrow, then navigate to the drive and folder where you store your Data Files

3. Click the file you want to open

4. Click **Open**

DATA FILES GRID

LESSON	DATA FILES	SOLUTION FILES
1	Frogs.xlsx, Homes.xlsx, Names.xlsx, Neighborhood.xlsx	Activity 1-1 solution.docx, Activity 1-2 solution.docx, Frogs Census.xlsx, Homeownership.xlsx, Last Names.xlsx, Neighborhood Estimates.xlsx
2	Balance.xlsx, Basketball.xlsx, Bird.xlsx, Budget.xlsx, Cell.xlsx, Mileage.xlsx, Phone.xlsx	Activity 2-1 solution.docx, Activity 2-2 solution.docx, Basketball Standings.xlsx, Bird Census.xlsx, Cell Bill.xlsx, Mileage Chart.xlsx, Nigel Budget.xlsx, Phone Shop.xlsx, Techsoft Balance.xlsx
3	Biology.xlsx, Booster.xlsx, Imports.xlsx, Inventory.xlsx, Pool.xlsx, Store.xlsx, Time.xlsx, Utilities.xlsx	Biology Grades.xlsx, Booster Club.xlsx, Chimpanzee Behavior.xlsx, Pool Attendance.xlsx, Store Assets.xlsx, Supply Inventory.xlsx, Time Record.xslx, Trade Imports.xlsx, Utilities Expenses.xlsx
4	Drink.xlsx, Formula.xlsx, Investment.xlsx, Prairie.xlsx, Results.xlsx, Zoo.xlsx	Activity 4-2 solution.docx, Drink Sales.xlsx, Formula Practice.xlsx, Investment Record.xlsx, Job Offer.xlsx, Prairie Development.xlsx, Results of Formulas.xlsx, Zoo Fundraiser.xlsx
5	Finances.xlsx, Functions.xlsx, Golf.xlsx, National.xlsx, Occidental.xlsx, Team.xlsx, Test.xlsx, Xanthan.xlsx	Basketball Stats.xlsx, Budget for Student Name.xlsx, Car Purchase.xlsx, Functions Worksheet.xlsx, Golf Tryouts.xlsx, National Bank.xlsx, Occidental Optical.xlsx, Test Grades.xlsx, Xanthan Promotion.xlsx
6	Botany.xlsx, City.xlsx, Compact.xlsx, Employee.xlsx, Expense.xlsx, Impact.xlsx, Oil.xlsx, Paper.xlsx, Rose.tif, School bus.bmp, School.xlsx, Stock.xlsx, Tax.xlsx, Top.xlsx	Activity 6-1 solution.xlsx, Activity 6-2 solution.xlsx, Botany Florist.xlsx, City Facts.xlsx, Compact Cubicle.xlsx, Employee List.xlsx, Expense Report.xlsx, Expense Report Web.mht, Expense Report 2003.xls, Impact Salaries.xlsx, Oil Production.xlsx, Paper Sales.xlsx, Roberts Statement.xlsx, School Bus.xlsx, Stock Quotes.xlsx, Tax Estimate.xlsx, Time Card.xlsx, Top Movies.xlsx
7	Alamo.xlsx, Annual.xlsx, Continental.xlsx, February.xlsx, Rainfall.xlsx, United.xlsx, Voting.xlsx	Activity 7-1 solution.docx, Alamo Amalgamated.xlsx, Annual Statement.xlsx, Continental Sales.xlsx, February Statement.xlsx, Rainfall Records.xlsx, United Circuitry.xlsx, Voting Tally.xlsx
8	Chico.xlsx, Concession.xlsx, Coronado.xlsx, Education.xlsx, Family.xlsx, Grains.xlsx, McDonalds.xlsx, Populations.xlsx, Red.xlsx, Running.xlsx, Study.xlsx, Triangle.xlsx	Chico Temperatures.xlsx, Concession Sales.xlsx, Coronado Foundries.xlsx, Education Pays.xlsx, Family Expenses.xlsx, Grains Sales.xlsx, McDonalds Restaurants.xlsx, Populations of Large Cities.xlsx, Red Cross.xlsx, Running Times.xlsx, Sounds Good.xlsx, Study and Grades.xlsx, Triangle Growth.xlsx
Unit Review	Club.xlsx, CompNet.xlsx, Computer.xlsx, Gas.xlsx, Java.docx, Organic.xlsx	Club Members.xlsx, Coffee Prices.xlsx, CompNet Expenses.xlsx, Computer Prices.xlsx, Gas Sales.xlsx, Java Menu.docx, Java Menu Revised.docx, Organic Financials.xlsx

TABLE OF CONTENTS

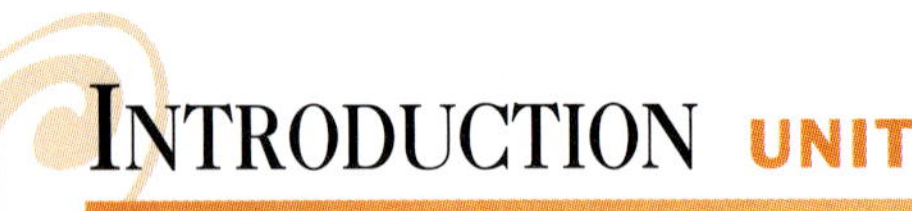

INTRODUCTION UNIT

MICROSOFT EXCEL UNIT

INTRODUCTION

Unit

Lesson 1   1 hr.
Windows Vista Basics

Lesson 1   1.5 hrs.
Microsoft® Office 2007 Basics and the Internet

Estimated Time for Unit: 2.5 hours

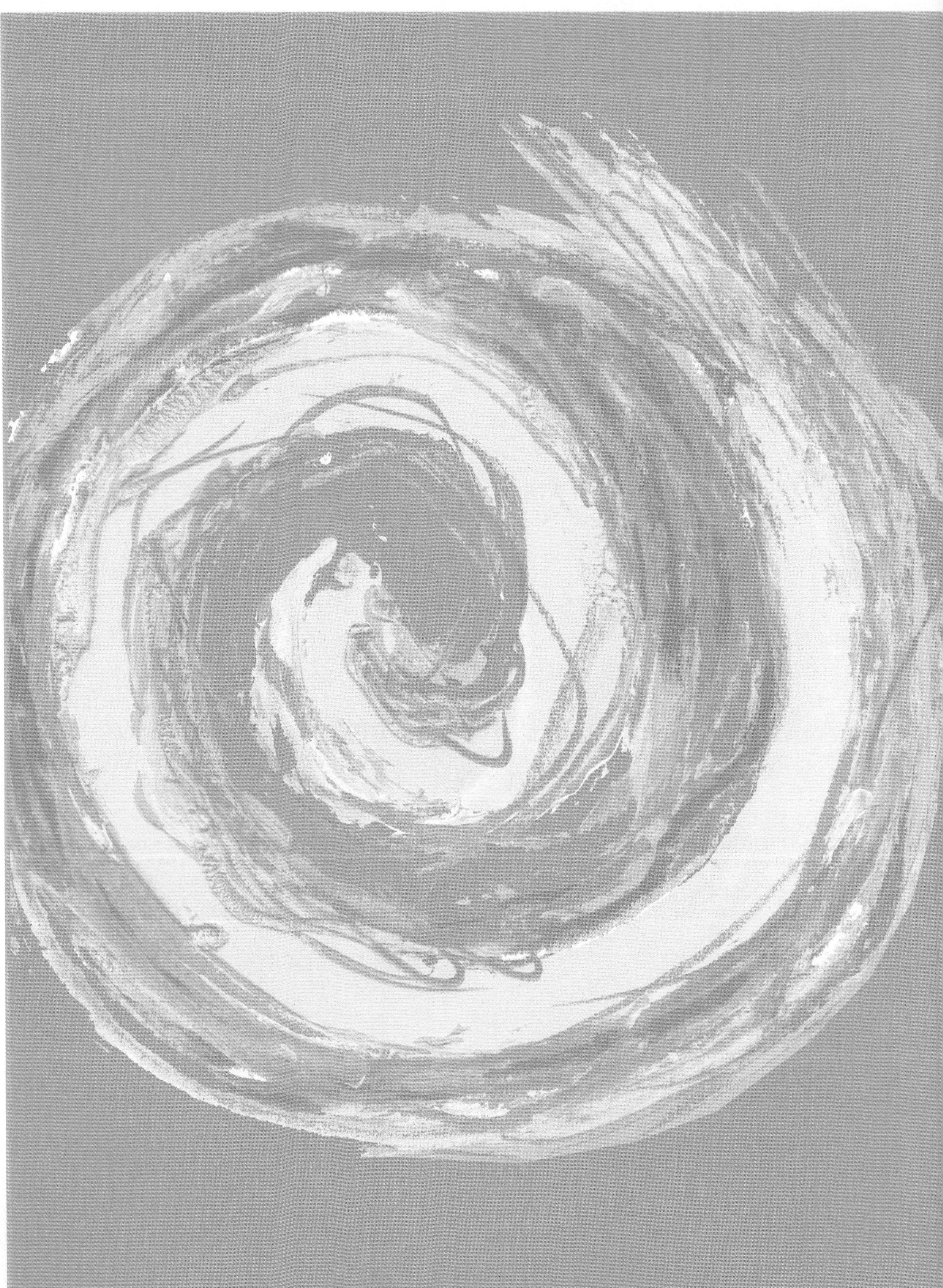

WINDOWS VISTA BASICS

This lesson will familiarize you with the Windows Vista operating system. An operating system is software that controls the basic operations of your computer. In this lesson, you will learn to control your computer's components, move around your desktop, and manage the files, folders, and other resources you work with every day. You will also learn about the Windows Help system and the basics of managing your computer.

Starting Windows

If Windows is already installed, it should start automatically when you turn on the computer. If your computer is on a network, you may need some help from your instructor. Remember that because there are many versions of Windows Vista available and not all educational institutions have hardware that supports all the Vista features, some tasks in this lesson may not be applicable, while other Vista features are intentionally not covered. For example, some editions of Windows Vista support Windows Aero, a graphic interface feature that gives a translucent quality to windows, dialog boxes, and other items. Aero allows you to see through one window to the next or scan through thumbnails and other miniatures in what is known as Flip or Flip 3D. For this lesson, Windows Aero is turned off.

S TEP-BY-STEP 1.1

1. Turn on the computer and the monitor, if necessary.

2. After a few moments, the Windows Vista desktop appears.

3. If prompted for login information, type your **username** and **password**, and then click the **Next** button.

4. If the Welcome Center opens, click the **Close** button in the upper-right corner of the Welcome Center window.

Using a Pointing Device

A **pointing device** allows you to interact and communicate with your computer. A pointing device can be a mouse, trackball, touch pad or screen, pointing stick, digital pen, or even a joystick. All pointing devices share the ability to point to and manipulate graphics and text on the screen. The **pointer**, which appears as an arrow on the screen, indicates the position of the pointing device. Table 1-1 describes the five most common mouse operations.

TABLE 1-1
Common pointing device actions

ACTION	DESCRIPTION
Point	Positioning the pointing device on a specific object on the screen
Click	Pressing and releasing the left button once while pointing to an object on the screen
Double-click	Quickly pressing and releasing the left button twice to initiate an action
Drag	While pointing to an object on the screen, pressing and holding the left button and moving the object to a new location; releasing the button completes the drag operation
Right-click	Pressing and releasing the right button to view file properties or a menu of functions

Understanding the Desktop

When Windows starts up, icons, windows, folders, and files appear on the desktop. Files and **folders**, directories that contain files or other folders, are displayed in a small work area known as a **window**. The **desktop** is the main work area in Windows. It contains Windows program elements, other programs, and files. Figure 1-1

Did You Know?

Douglas Engelbart invented the first mouse in 1967 and was inducted into the Inventors Hall of Fame in 1998.

illustrates a typical desktop screen when Windows is first installed. Your desktop may contain different icons, shortcuts, or the Windows Sidebar. An **icon** is a small picture that represents a file, folder, program, or program shortcut. You use shortcuts to open files and folders and start applications. You can also drag icons to a new location on the desktop, copy, or delete them. The **Windows Sidebar** is a transparent panel that is attached to one side of the screen and contains gadgets. The **taskbar** displays icons of the programs you have open or that run in the background. You can customize and organize your desktop by creating files, folders, and shortcuts.

FIGURE 1-1
Typical Windows Vista desktop

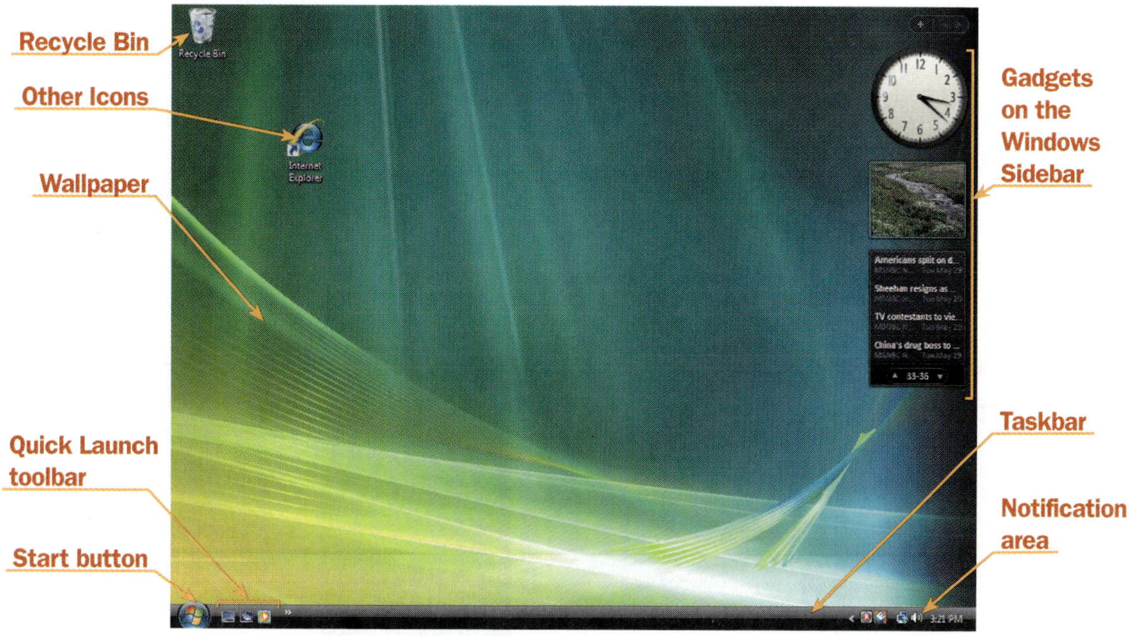

Recycle Bin
Other Icons
Wallpaper
Quick Launch toolbar
Start button
Gadgets on the Windows Sidebar
Taskbar
Notification area

The main features of the desktop screen are labeled on Figure 1-1 and discussed below:

1. The Recycle Bin stores the files you want to delete and allows you to restore them if needed.

2. Icons appear on the desktop and are visual representations of a program, file, or operation.

3. Wallpapers or themes use images, patterns, or colors as the background on the desktop.

4. The Start button brings up menus that give you a variety of options, such as starting a program, opening a document, searching for items on your computer, finding help, or shutting down the computer.

5. The Quick Launch toolbar on the taskbar contains buttons you can use to display the desktop or start frequently used programs.

6. The taskbar, located at the bottom of the screen, lets you access open programs and files.

7. Notification area task icons run in the background; you can use these to check the time and date, adjust speaker volume, and access other network or system features.

8. **Gadgets** on the Windows Sidebar are mini-programs that have specific functionality, such as displaying the time, weather, news feeds, slide shows, and other frequently accessed information.

Click the Start button to open the Start menu. The Start menu is divided into two panes. On the left, you can view recently opened programs, search for any file or folder, and easily access programs installed on your computer by pinning them to the menu. The right pane lists popular functions and features.

STEP-BY-STEP 1.2

1. On the taskbar, click the **Start** button. The Start menu appears in two panes, as shown in Figure 1-2. 

FIGURE 1-2
Start menu

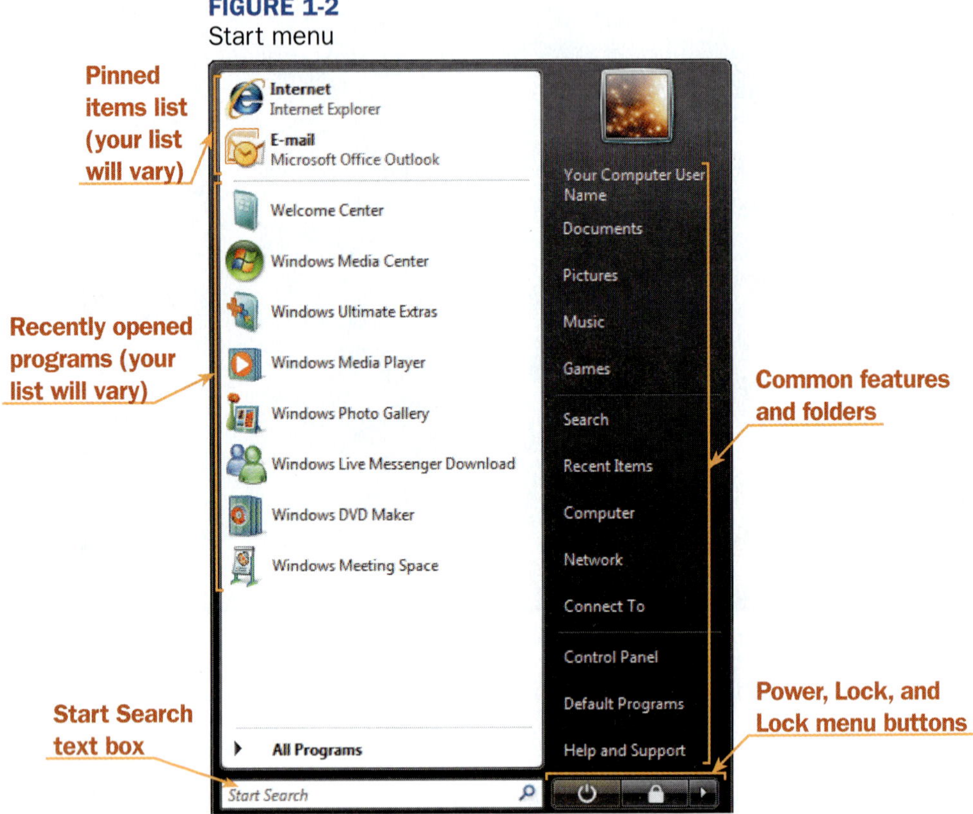

2. In the left pane, click **All Programs**. The list of programs installed on your computer appears in the left pane, as shown in Figure 1-3.

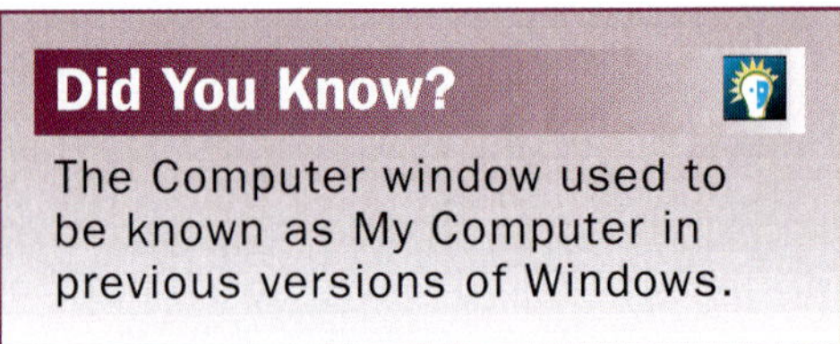
Did You Know?

The Computer window used to be known as My Computer in previous versions of Windows.

STEP-BY-STEP 1.2 Continued

FIGURE 1-3
Start menu showing list of All Programs

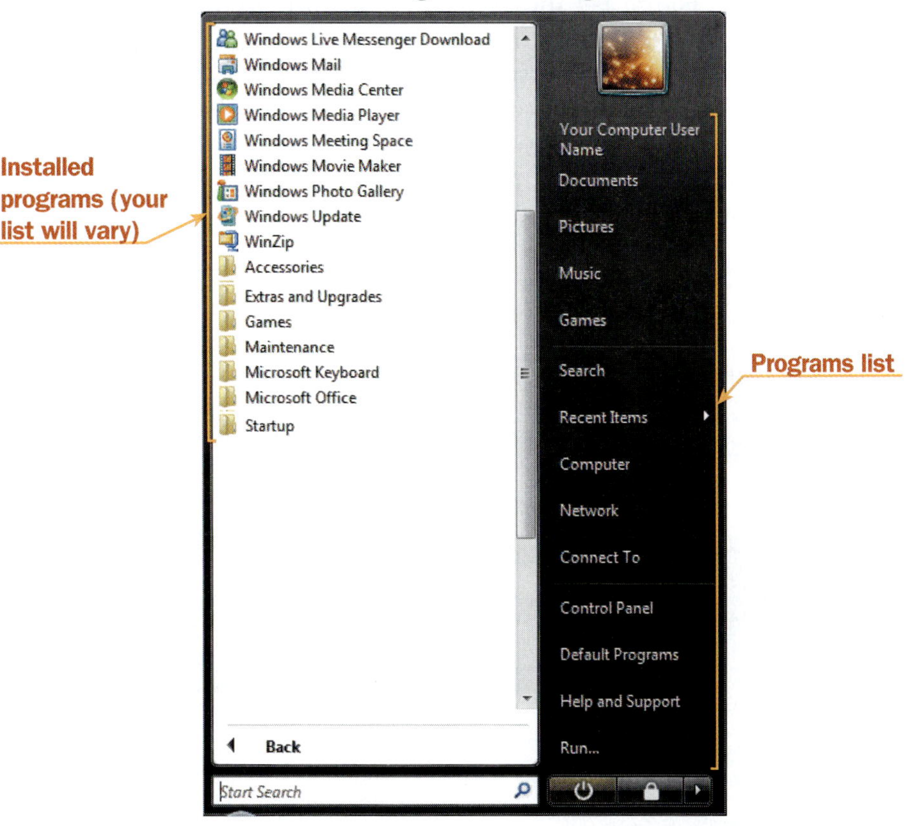

3. In the Programs list in the right pane, click **Computer**. The Computer window opens.

4. On the Quick Launch toolbar, click the **Launch Internet Explorer Browser** button. 

5. In the upper-right corner of the Internet Explorer title bar, click the **Close** button to return to the open window on the desktop. Leave the Computer window open for the next Step-by-Step.

Navigating in Windows

Windows offers many features that allow you to easily locate and open the files you need. **Explorer windows** are used to navigate to items on your computer. Most windows share common navigation tools such as a Navigation pane, Address bar, or toolbar, even if their specific function varies.

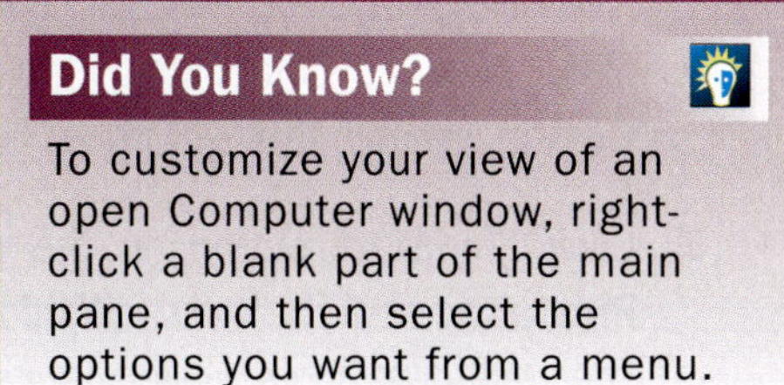

Switching to View Open Windows

Many windows you work with share common features, so you can work effortlessly and efficiently no matter the task you need to perform. Each window has a **toolbar** that contains functions specific to the window. Figure 1-4 shows common features in three different windows. You can move to an open window, program, or file by pressing and holding the Alt key, and then pressing the Tab key. As you press the Tab key, an icon representing the open window appears highlighted in a bar with icons of the other open windows. You can continue pressing the Tab key until the desired window is highlighted. When you release the Alt key, the selected window appears on the screen.

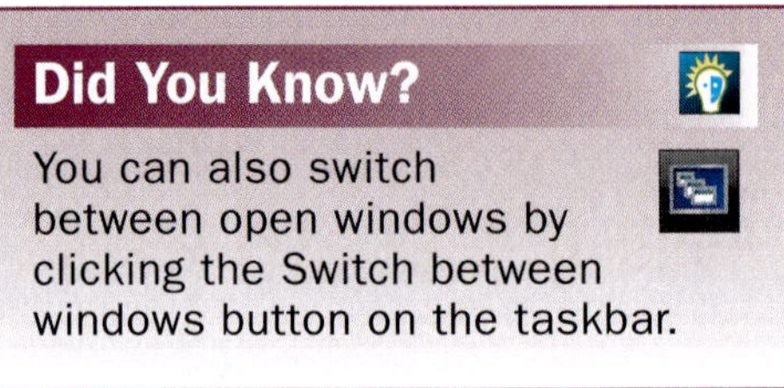

Did You Know?

You can also switch between open windows by clicking the Switch between windows button on the taskbar.

FIGURE 1-4
Viewing shared window features

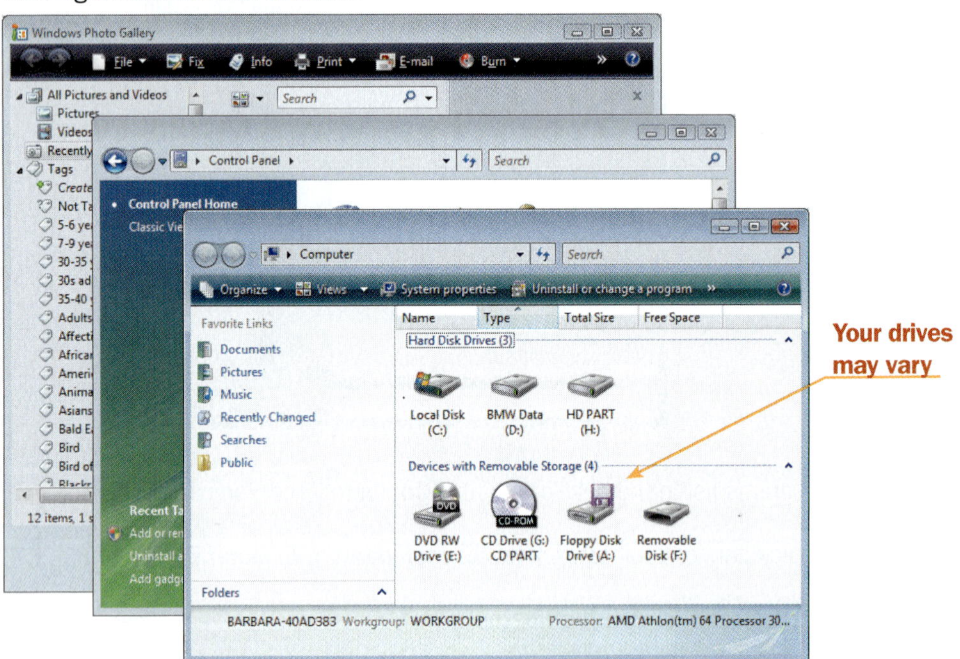

Your drives may vary

STEP-BY-STEP 1.3

1. Make sure the Computer button is on the taskbar, click the **Start** button, and then click  **Control Panel** in the right pane. The Control Panel window opens.

2. Click the **Start** button, in the left pane click **All Programs**, and then click **Windows Photo Gallery**. The Windows Photo Gallery appears on top of the Control Panel. All three windows are open, but they overlap each other, making it difficult to view them all at once.

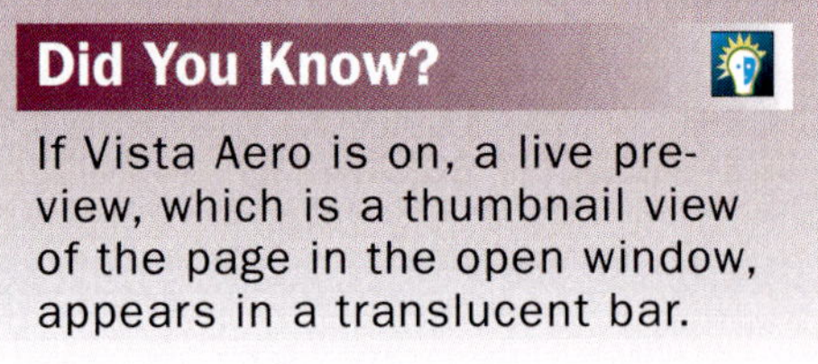

Did You Know?

If Vista Aero is on, a live preview, which is a thumbnail view of the page in the open window, appears in a translucent bar.

STEP-BY-STEP 1.3 Continued

3. Press and hold the **Alt** key, and then press the **Tab** key once. The Control Panel is on top.

4. Press and hold the **Alt** key, and then press the **Tab** key once. The Windows Photo Gallery is now on top.

5. Press and hold the **Alt** key, and then press the **Tab** key twice. The Computer window is on top. Compare your screen to Figure 1-5. Leave the windows open for the next Step-by-Step.

Did You Know?

Windows performs searches incrementally; it begins searching as soon as you type a character in the text box and refines the search as you add more text.

FIGURE 1-5
Viewing open windows

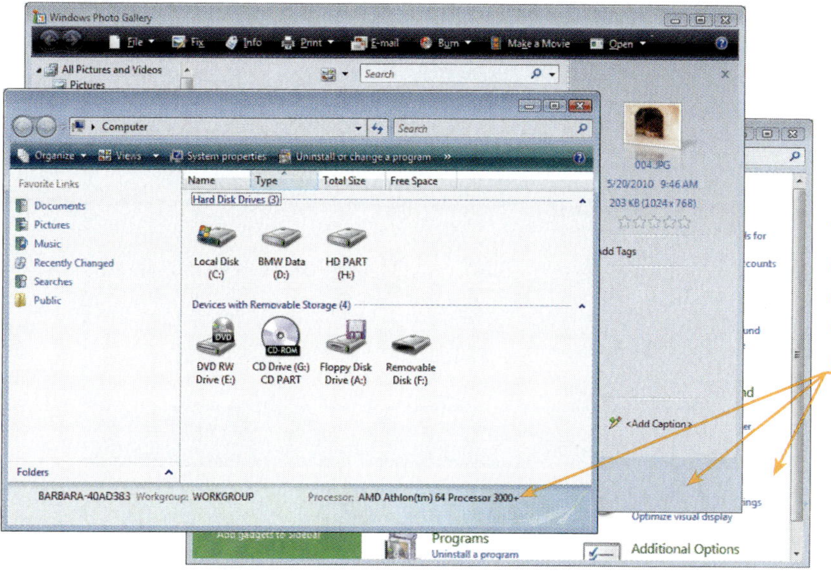

Navigating Using the Address Bar

The Address bar in Windows is a dynamic tool and shares some functionality with the Address bar in Internet Explorer. The **Address bar** identifies the path for the currently open folder, as shown in Figure 1-6. Each folder name in the path is a link that you can click to display that folder's contents, which is useful when working with subfolders within a main folder. To navigate to recently visited locations, click the Back button and the Forward button to the left of the Address bar. You can also view previous locations by clicking the Previous Locations arrow button at the end of the Address bar. The Search text box searches the contents of the open folder for the search term you entered.

FIGURE 1-6
Viewing a path in the Address bar

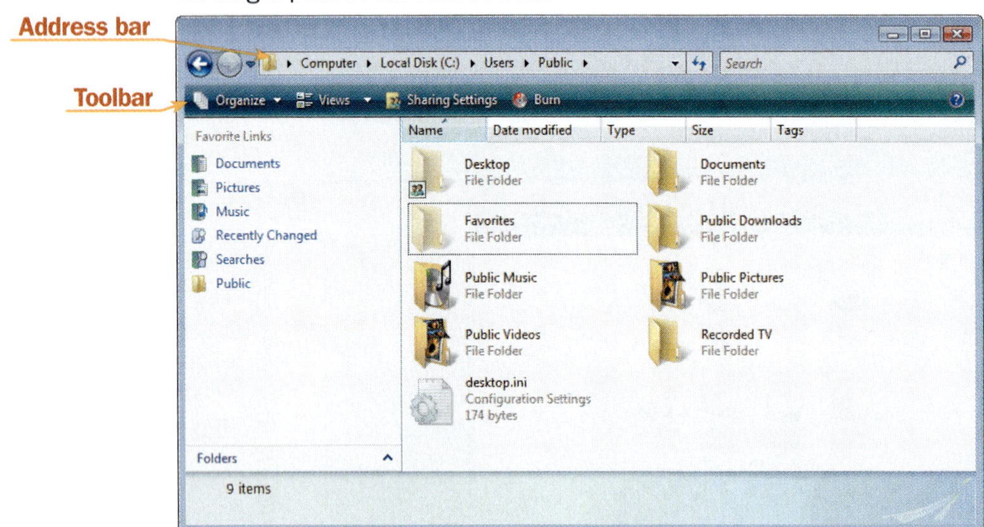

STEP-BY-STEP 1.4

1. Make sure the Computer window is open, and then double-click the **Local Disk (C:)** icon. (*Note*: Select another disk or device if this disk is not available. Because your computer setup may vary, read this Step-by-Step and complete as many steps as you can.)

2. In the Main pane, double-click **Users**, if necessary, double-click **Public**, and then compare your window to Figure 1-6. The Address bar shows the path to the Public folder.

3. In the Address bar, click **Computer**. The Main pane shows the disks and removable devices in the Computer folder.

4. Click the **Back** button next to the Address bar. The Main pane shows the files in the Public folder. 

5. Click the **Forward** button next to the Address bar. The Main pane shows the files in the Computer folder. Keep this window open for the next Step-by-Step. 

Navigating Using the Favorites and Folders List

Many Explorer windows have a Navigation pane to help you find your files, which you can also customize. The **Navigation pane** includes Favorite Links, which are links to folders containing the items you use the most, including recent searches. The Favorite Links contains popular default folders such as Documents, Pictures, and Music. You can add frequently used folders or files to the Favorite Links by dragging the file or folder from the Main pane to the Navigation pane. The Navigation pane also contains a Folders section that you can hide or show by clicking the Folders bar. Here you can view folders as a tree diagram, which provides an overview of the overall folder structure on your computer, as shown in Figure 1-7. You can display an individual folder in the Main pane by clicking it in the Folders section.

Did You Know?

You can further personalize the look of your Explorer window by clicking Organize on the toolbar, pointing to Layout, and then selecting the panes you want to be visible or hidden.

FIGURE 1-7
Viewing the Navigation pane

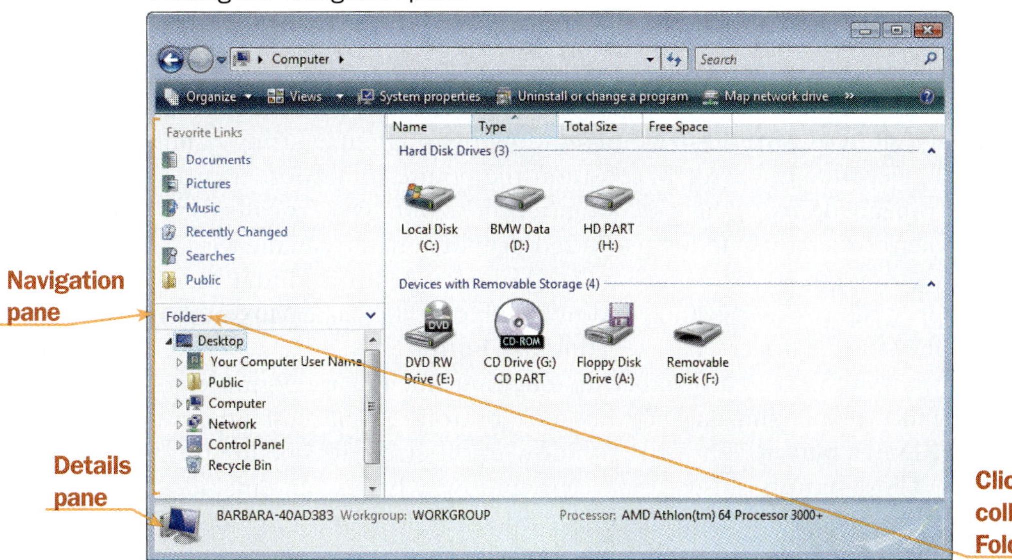

STEP-BY-STEP 1.5

1. Make sure the Computer window is open, and then in the Favorite Links section of the Navigation pane, click **Documents**. Files and folders in the Documents folder appear in the Main pane.

2. In the Favorite Links section of the Navigation pane, click **Pictures**, and then click a **photo** if one is available. Photos that you have downloaded to your computer appear in the Main pane, and a preview of the selected image appears in the Preview pane and in the Details pane, if those panes are visible.

Did You Know?

You can display a list of textual or graphic choices, known as a menu. To do so, click Organize on the toolbar, point to Layout, and then click Menu Bar.

STEP-BY-STEP 1.5 Continued

3. In the Navigation pane, click **Folders**, if necessary, and then click a folder to view its contents in the Main pane.

4. Click **Folders** to collapse the tree diagram, and then in the Address bar, click **Computer**. Close all open windows.

Using Windows

Windows are essential to using the Vista operating system. They display and store information and run programs. It is important to understand how to adjust and use them so you can optimize your efficiency.

Moving and Resizing Windows

Sometimes you will have several windows open on the screen at the same time. To work more effectively, you may need to move or change the size of a window. To move a window, click the title bar, the bar at the top of the window, and drag the window to another location. You can adjust the height, width, or overall size of a window by dragging a sizing handle on a window's border or corner. Depending where you position the pointer on a border or corner, the pointer changes to a two-headed arrow that is configured horizontally, vertically, or diagonally. When you adjust a corner border, the window is resized proportionately smaller or larger. You can also resize a window using the Maximize button, Minimize button, and Restore Down button, located in the upper-right corner of the window. See Figure 1-8. The Maximize button enlarges a window to the full size of the screen. The Minimize button reduces a window to an icon on the taskbar. The button on the taskbar is labeled, and you can click it any time to redisplay the window. When a window is maximized, the Maximize button is replaced by the Restore Down button. The Restore Down button returns the window to the size it was before the Maximize button was clicked. The Close button is used to close a window, which would include any file you have open in a program. If you are in a program, clicking the Close button will exit the program and you will be prompted to save or discard any changes in an open file.

FIGURE 1-8
Window resizing buttons

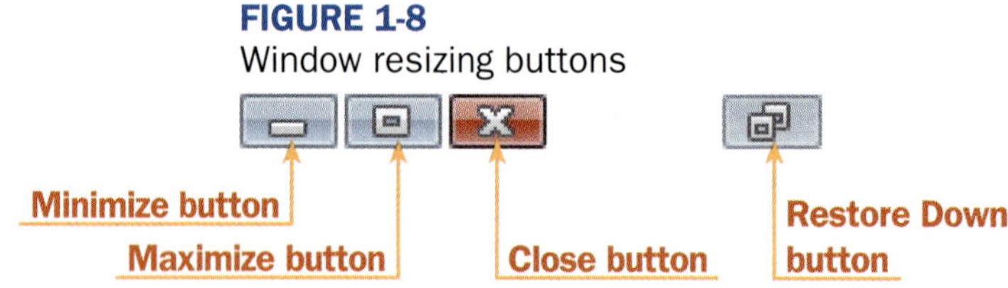

STEP-BY-STEP 1.6

1. On the taskbar, click the **Start** button, and then click **Control Panel**. The Control Panel window opens. 

2. Point to the title bar, click and hold the left mouse button, and then drag the **Control Panel window** until it appears to be centered on the screen. Release the mouse button.

3. Point to the border at the right side of the Control Panel window. When the pointer turns into a horizontal two-headed arrow, drag the right border farther to the right to expand the window.

4. Point to the lower-right corner of the window border. When the pointer turns into a two-headed diagonal arrow, drag the border up and to the left to resize both sides at the same time until the window appears similar to Figure 1-9.

FIGURE 1-9
Resizing a window

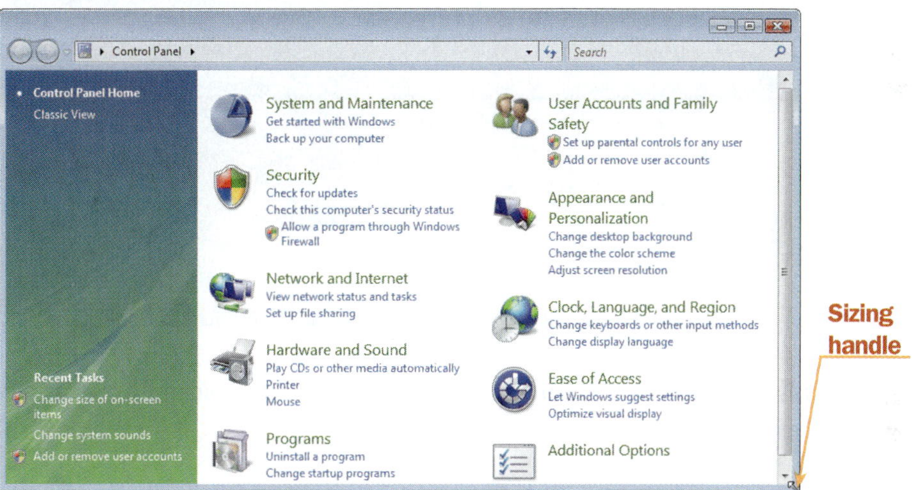

5. Click the **Maximize** button in the upper-right corner of the window. The Control Panel window is maximized and you cannot adjust its borders. 

6. Click the **Restore Down** button in the upper-right corner of the window. The Control Panel window returns to its previous size and approximate position on the desktop. 

STEP-BY-STEP 1.6 Continued

7. Click the **Minimize** button in the upper-right corner of the window. The Control Panel window is no longer visible on the desktop, but it is still open. The minimized window is shown as an icon on the taskbar, as shown in Figure 1-10. 

FIGURE 1-10
Minimized window

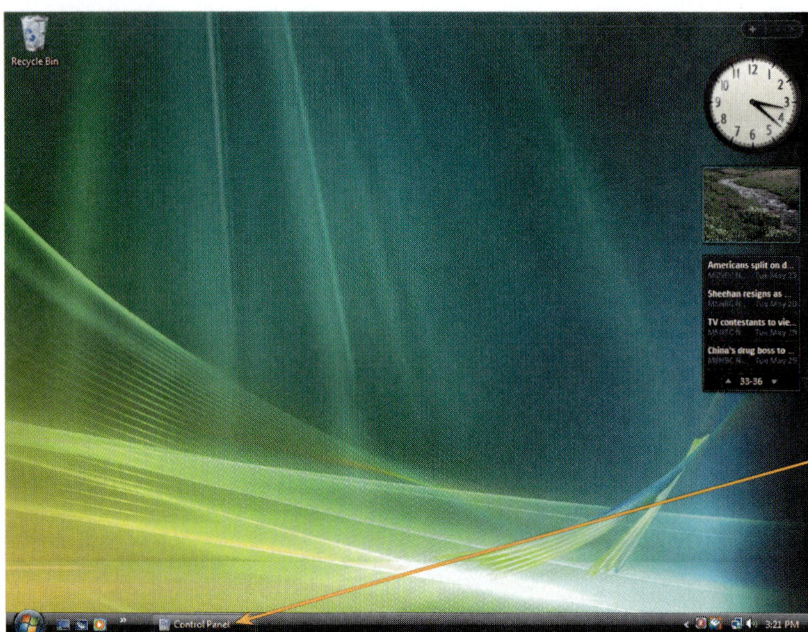

8. On the taskbar, click the **Control Panel** button to restore the window. Leave the Control Panel open for the next Step-by-Step.

Scroll Bars

A scroll bar appears on the edge of a window any time there is more content than can appear in the window at its current size, as shown in Figure 1-11. A scroll bar can appear along the bottom edge (horizontal) and along the right side (vertical) of a window.

Scroll bars are a convenient way to bring another part of the window's contents into view. The scroll bar contains a scroll box and two scroll arrows. The scroll box is a slider that indicates your position within the window. When the scroll box reaches the bottom of the scroll bar, you have reached the end of the window's contents. Scroll arrows are located at the ends of the scroll bar. Clicking a scroll arrow moves the window content in that direction one line at a time. You can move to the end of a window's content by clicking a blank area of the scroll bar on either side of the scroll box.

FIGURE 1-11
Scroll bar, arrows, and boxes

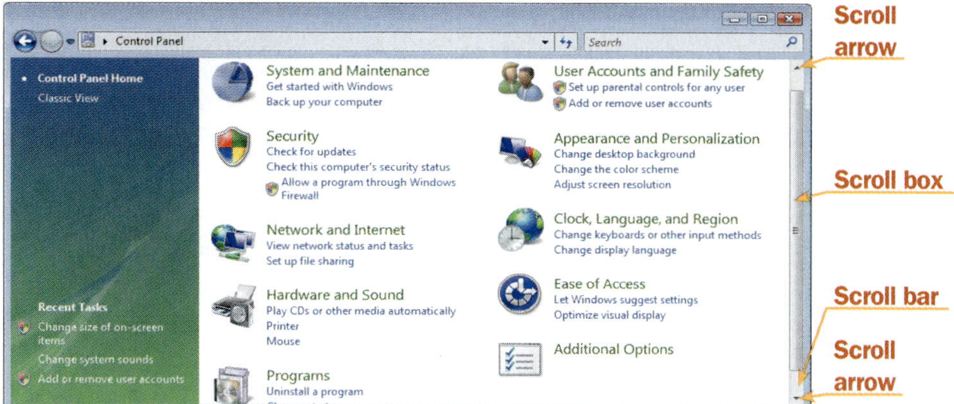

STEP-BY-STEP 1.7

1. Make sure that the Control Panel window is open, and then, if necessary, resize the window vertically until the vertical scroll bar is visible on the right side of the window.

2. On the vertical scroll bar, click the **down scroll** arrow twice. The contents of the window shift downward one line at a time, as shown in Figure 1-11.

3. On the vertical scroll bar, drag the **scroll box** all the way up, and then the all the way down. You can drag the scroll box anywhere in the scroll bar to keep certain content in view.

Did You Know?

To scroll quickly through a window, point to a scroll arrow in a window, and then click and hold the mouse button.

4. Click the blank space above the vertical scroll box. The contents scroll all the way to the top.

5. Resize the Control Panel window until the scroll bar is no longer visible. Click the **Close**  button in the Control Panel window.

Using Toolbars, Menus, and Dialog Boxes

You perform many tasks by clicking commands and buttons. These functions are usually contained on a menu, a toolbar, or in a dialog box. A toolbar contains buttons that execute a function or open a command menu. A menu contains commands for initiating certain actions or tasks. For example, when you click the Start button, a menu appears with a list of options. A dialog box, an interactive message window, appears when more information is required before the command can be performed. You may have to enter information, choose from a list of options, or simply confirm that you want the command to be performed. To back out of a dialog box without performing an action, press the Esc key, click the Close button, or choose Cancel (or No).

STEP-BY-STEP 1.8

1. On the taskbar, click the **Start** button, click **All Programs**, and then click **Windows Photo Gallery**. The Windows Photo Gallery window opens.

2. On the toolbar, click the **File** button. A list of commands appears, as shown in Figure 1-12.

Did You Know?

Instead of clicking commands, you can use a keyboard shortcut to perform a task, which is pressing a combination of keys on the keyboard. If available, a keyboard shortcut is shown to the right of the command, as shown in Figure 1-12.

FIGURE 1-12
Viewing a menu

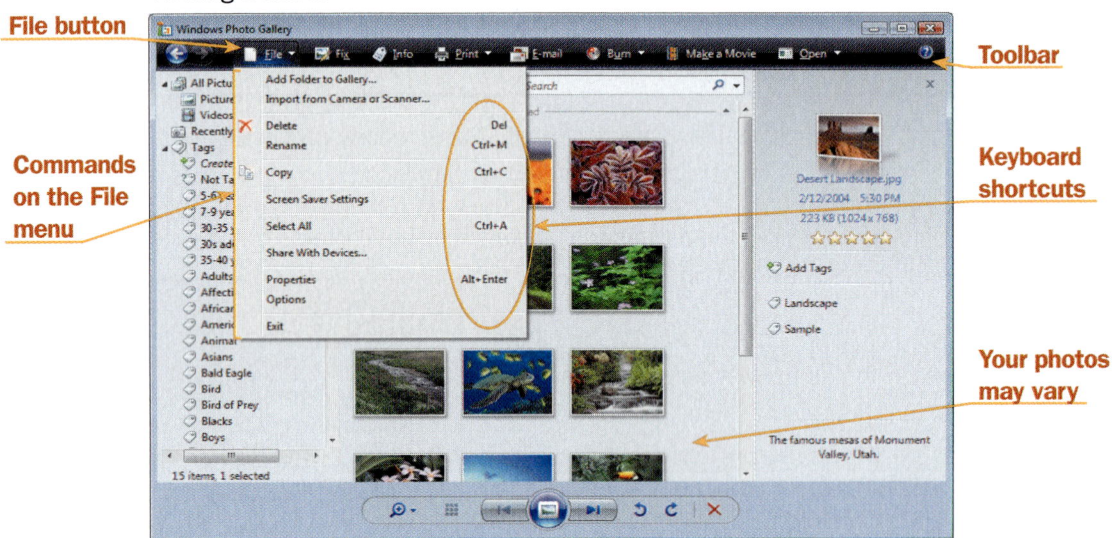

3. On the File menu, click **Options**. The Windows Photo Gallery Options dialog box opens, where you can change settings for managing photos on your computer, as shown in Figure 1-13.

STEP-BY-STEP 1.8 Continued

FIGURE 1-13
Windows Photo Gallery Options dialog box

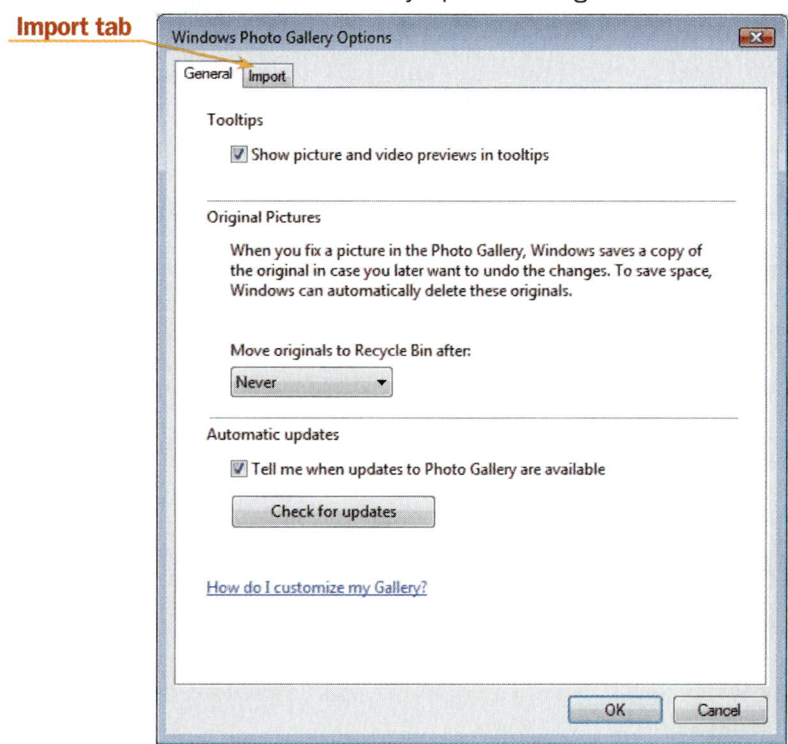

4. Click the **Import** tab, click the **Settings for** list arrow to view the available options, and then click **CDs and DVDs**.

5. Click **Cancel** to close the Windows Photo Gallery Options dialog box.

6. On the toolbar, click the **File** button, and then click **Exit**. The Windows Photo Gallery program closes.

Using the Control Panel

The **Control Panel**, shown in Figure 1-14, is the command center for configuring Windows settings. You can customize settings for appearance, sounds, and performance. The number of icons and categories can be overwhelming and may not be descriptive enough for you to find exactly what you want. To find the settings you are interested in, enter a word or search term in the Search text box. For example, to find settings associated with sounds on your computer, type "sounds" in the Search text box. You can search in ordinary language without knowing the official or technical term.

FIGURE 1-14
Control Panel

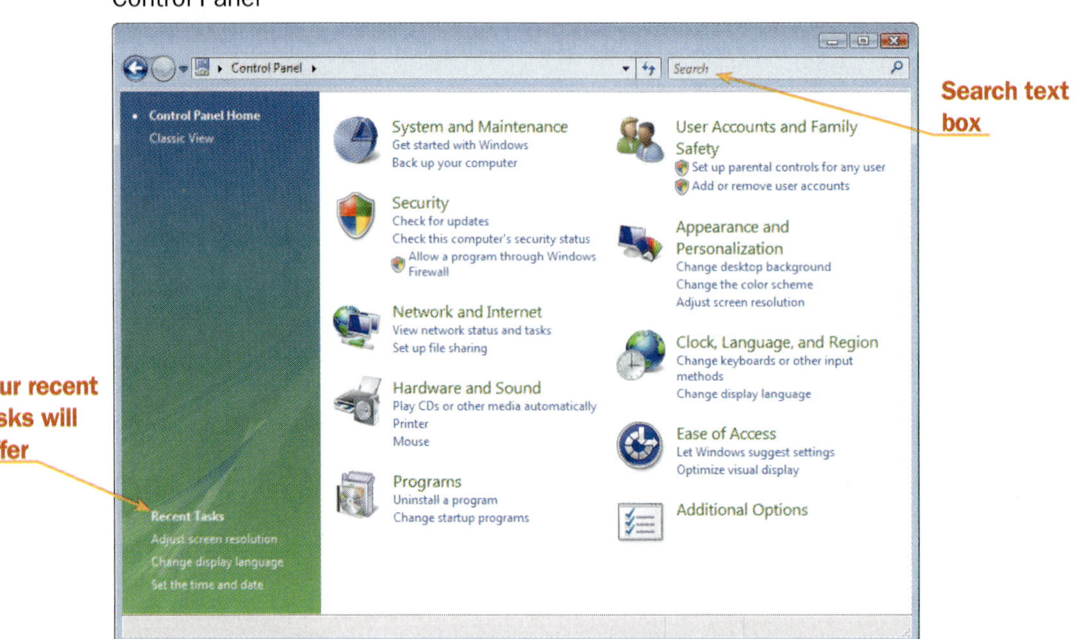

STEP-BY-STEP 1.9

1. On the taskbar, click the **Start** button, click **Control Panel**, and then resize the window so that the scroll bar is not visible.

2. Click **Appearance and Personalization**. Notice that topics pertaining to appearance and personalization appear.

3. In the Address bar, click **Control Panel** to return to Control Panel Home.

4. In the Search text box, type **sound**. Search results related to "sound" appear as you type the word, as shown in Figure 1-15. Your results may differ depending on your connection to the Internet.

STEP-BY-STEP 1.9 Continued

FIGURE 1-15
Viewing search results in the Control Panel

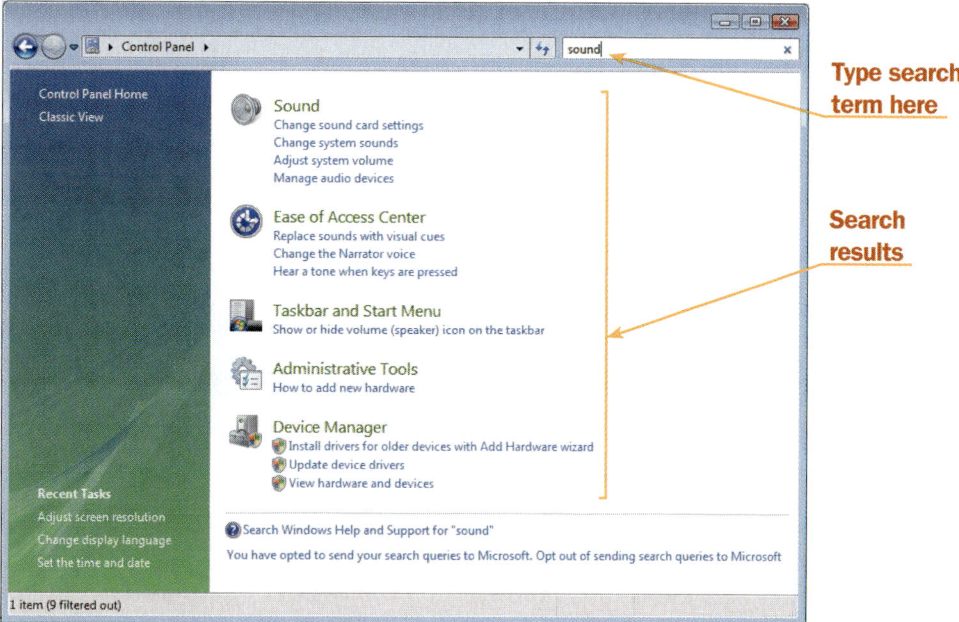

5. Click **Change system sounds**, review the options on the Sounds tab, and then click **Cancel** in the Sound dialog box to close it.

6. In the left pane, click **Control Panel Home**, and then click **Classic View**. The Control Panel changes to a collection of individual icons.

7. Scroll down, if necessary, and then double-click the **Sound** icon. The Sound dialog box opens, with the Playback tab active. Click the **Close** button in the Sound dialog box.

8. Close the Control Panel.

Managing Files and Folders

Windows Vista has several default folders, such as Music or Pictures. For example, the Computer folder is where you access hard disk drives, removable drives and media, CD and DVD drives, network locations, and other removable media such as cameras and scanners. The Documents folder stores the files you use for your projects, such as documents, presentations, and spreadsheets. Many programs use this folder as the default location for saving files. You use the Public folder to store the files you want to share with other users on the same computer or who are connected through a network. Note that you cannot restrict access to the Public folder.

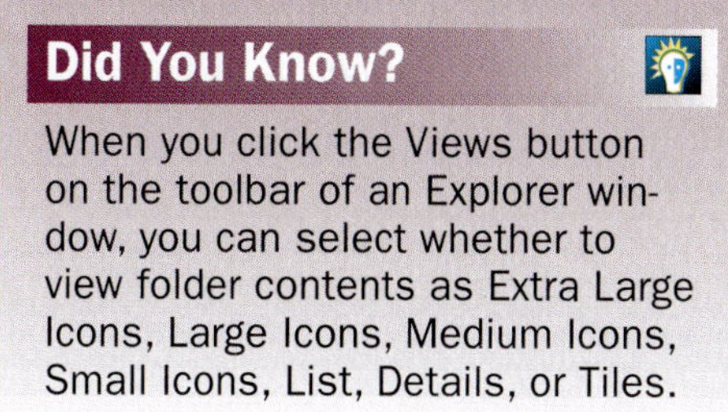
Did You Know?

When you click the Views button on the toolbar of an Explorer window, you can select whether to view folder contents as Extra Large Icons, Large Icons, Medium Icons, Small Icons, List, Details, or Tiles.

The **Personal folder** stores your most frequently used folders and is by default named with the name you used to create your computer account. It appears on the Start menu under that name.

STEP-BY-STEP 1.10

1. On the taskbar, click the **Start** button, and then click **Computer**. The Computer window opens. 

2. On the taskbar, click the **Start** button, and then click **Documents**. The Documents window opens, as shown in Figure 1-16.

FIGURE 1-16
Viewing folders in the Documents folder

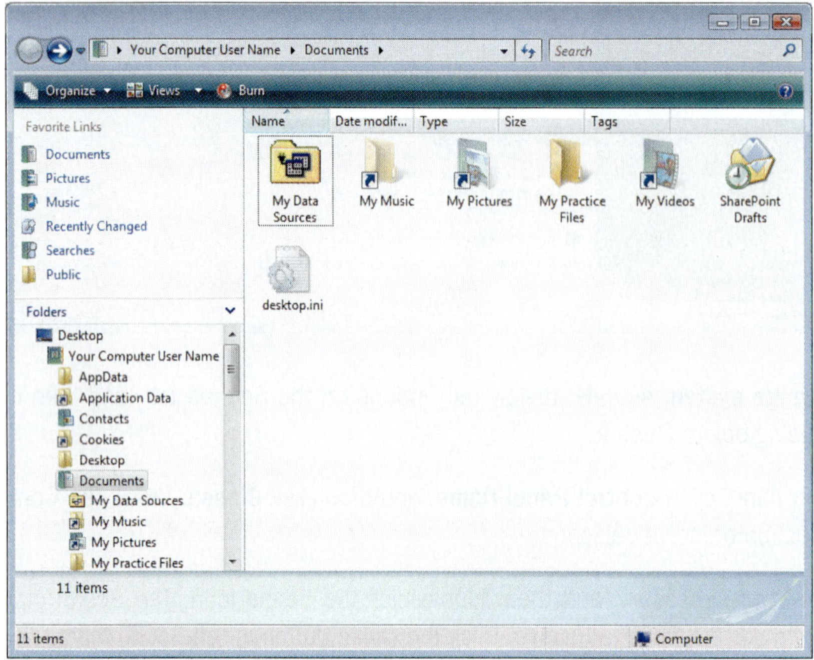

3. In the Navigation pane, click **Public** to display the Public folder and its contents.

4. Display the Folders section of the Navigation pane, scroll up, if necessary, and then click your **computer user name**. (*Note*: If you do not have an account on the computer, click the name that appears at the top of the folder list.)

5. Switch between each open window and note the contents of each folder window. When you are done, close each open window.

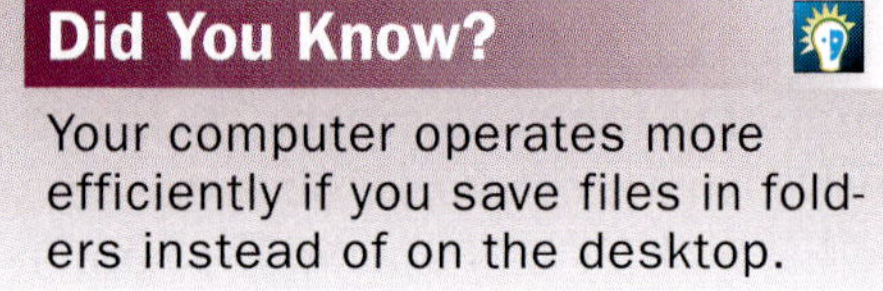

Deleting Files Using the Recycle Bin

As you work with different files, there will always be some you no longer need and want to delete. When you delete a file from a window, its name is removed from the window's content and the file is physically moved to the Recycle Bin, the wastebasket icon on the desktop. However, while the item is stored for deletion, it is not permanently deleted. The Recycle Bin icon changes depending on whether or not it contains files, as shown in Figure 1-17. To permanently delete files in the Recycle Bin, right-click the Recycle Bin icon, and then click Empty Recycle Bin from the menu. Fortunately, just like a regular wastebasket, you can retrieve items before they're gone for good. To restore a deleted item from the Recycle Bin, you first open the Recycle Bin by double-clicking the icon, select the file you want to restore, and then click the Restore this item button on the toolbar. Note that once you permanently delete an item by emptying the Recycle Bin, you cannot restore it using another Vista function, although you can purchase third-party software that may be able to recover deleted files.

FIGURE 1-17
Comparing the Recycle Bin when it
has items or is empty

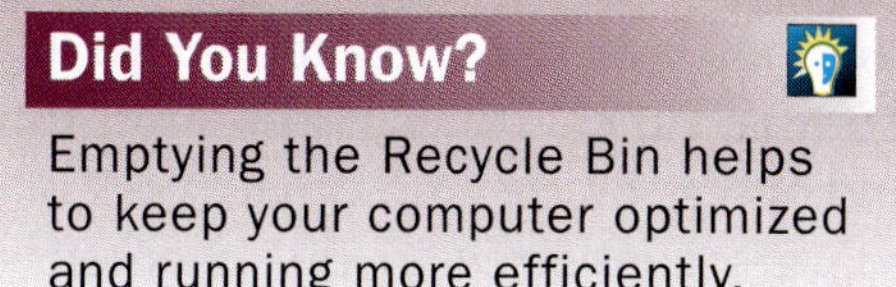

STEP-BY-STEP 1-11

1. On the desktop, double-click the **Recycle Bin** icon. If there are files in the Recycle Bin, it will look similar to Figure 1-18; if not, it will be empty.

FIGURE 1-18
Viewing an item in the Recycle Bin

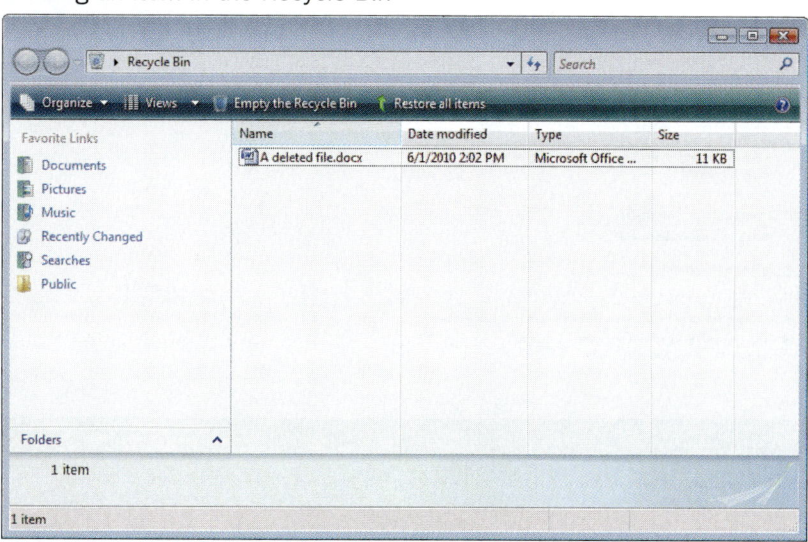

STEP-BY-STEP 1.11 Continued

2. On the toolbar, click **Empty the Recycle Bin** to delete the file, and then click **No** in the Delete File dialog box. (*Note*: Unless you work on your own computer, you should not make permanent deletions without first checking with your instructor or computer lab manager.)

3. Close the Recycle Bin.

Using Windows Help

This lesson has covered only a few of the many features of Windows. For additional information, Windows has an easy-to-use Help system. Use Help as a quick reference when you are unsure about a function. You can access Windows Help by clicking **Help and Support** on the Start menu. Then, from the Windows Help and Support window, you can choose a category in the Find an answer section, such as Windows Basics or Troubleshooting. You can continue to click topics or you can type a search term, just like you can in the Control Panel. You can also print topics, browse Help, and access online and other types of help. Note that if you are connected to the Internet, your searches can include Help results from the Windows Help online Web site. See Figure 1-19.

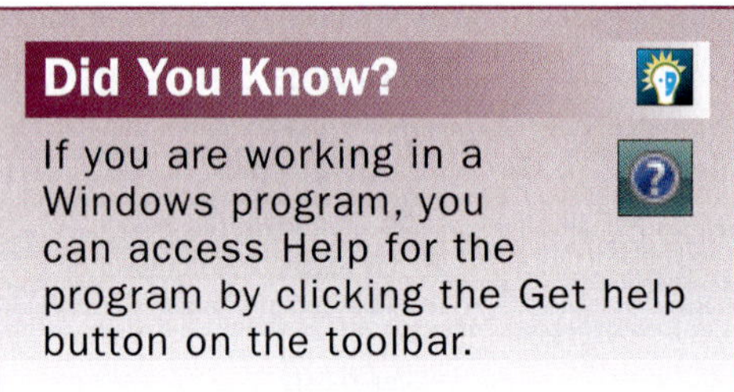

Did You Know?

If you are working in a Windows program, you can access Help for the program by clicking the Get help button on the toolbar.

FIGURE 1-19
Windows Help and Support window

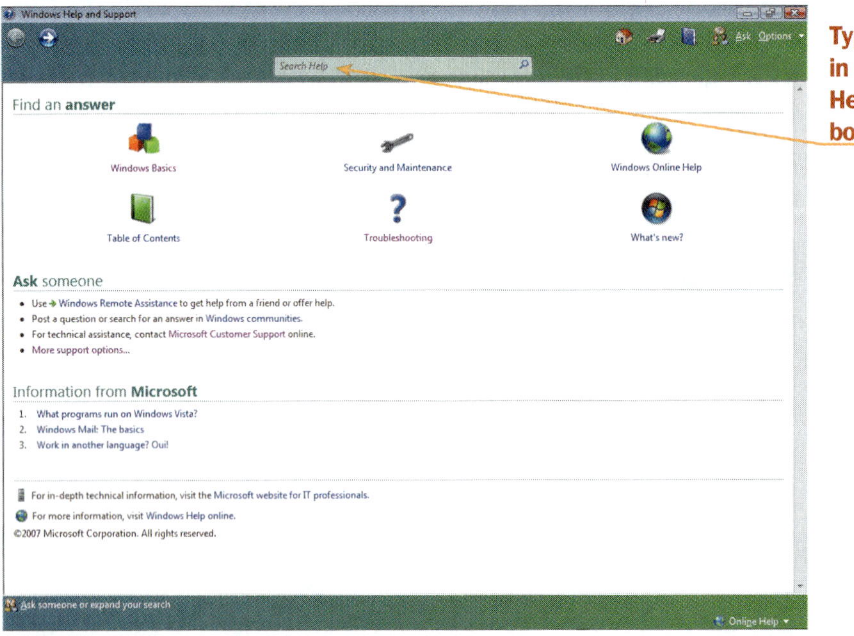

S TEP-BY-STEP 1-12

1. On the taskbar, click the **Start** button, click **Help and Support**, and then maximize the window, if necessary. The Windows Help and Support window opens, as shown in Figure 1-19. 

2. Click **Windows Basics**, on the Windows Basics: all topics page, scroll down, click **Exploring the Internet**, and then review the topic on the Exploring the Internet page.

3. Click the **Back** button twice to return to the main Help and Support page. 

4. Click the **Search Help** text box, type **print photos**, and then click the **Search Help** button. A list of search results appears for the keywords you typed, as shown in Figure 1-20. 

FIGURE 1-20
Viewing Help search results

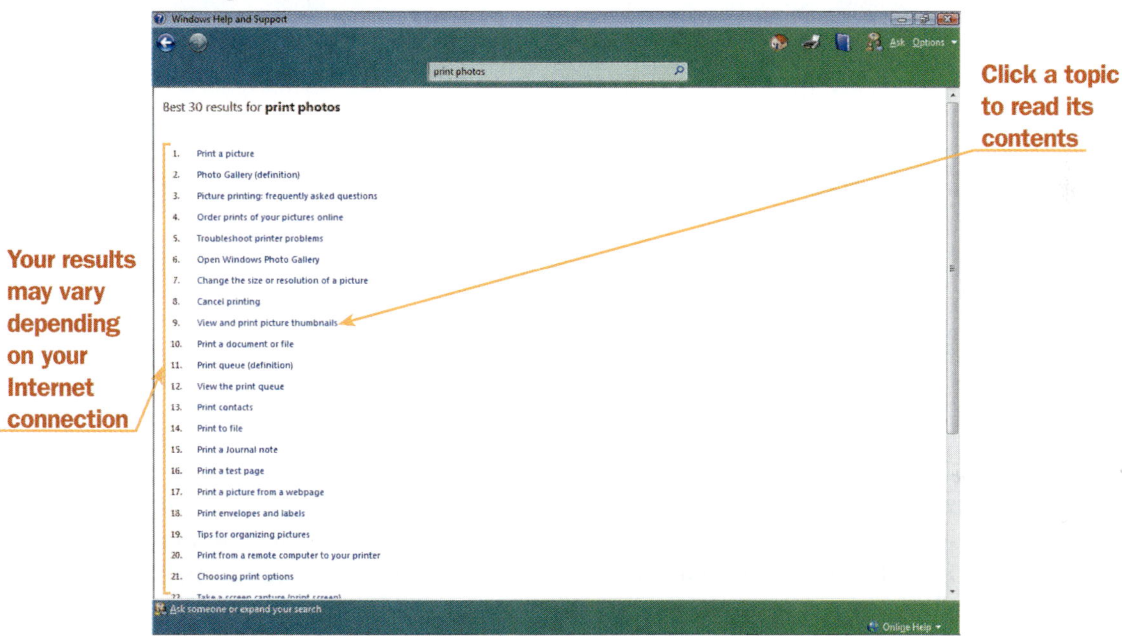

5. Click a topic that interests you, read it, and then close the Windows Help and Support window.

Managing Your Computer

Like any machine, a computer requires maintenance to keep it running smoothly. Windows provides utilities designed to keep your computer optimized and safe.

Using Disk Cleanup

A computer handles thousands of files to do its job. Reducing the number of files on your hard disk frees up space and helps improve your computer's speed. Windows provides Disk Cleanup, a utility that deletes temporary files created when you surf the Web, edit files, or perform other actions, such as opening e-mail attachments from the message window instead of first saving the attachment to your hard disk. To run Disk Cleanup, click the Start button, click All Programs, click the Accessories folder in the left pane, click the System Tools folder, and then click Disk Cleanup. You can choose to clean up the files in your account or clean up all the files on the computer, and specify which drive(s) to clean. Disk Cleanup describes the categories of files it can delete and you check the boxes of the files you want to include, as shown in Figure 1-21. Click OK to begin the cleanup, and then click Delete Files to confirm the action.

FIGURE 1-21
Disk Cleanup

Understanding the Windows Security Center

Windows Security Center monitors critical security components on your computer, such as the firewall, antivirus protection, spyware protection, and other features such as Windows updates and User Account Control. Protecting your computer from unauthorized access, malicious code, and software that collects information about your Web-surfing habits is essential. The components of the Windows Security Center are shown in Figure 1-22 and described in Table 1-2.

TABLE 1-2
Windows Security Center

COMPONENT	DESCRIPTION
Firewall	Monitors whether a firewall is installed and working properly
Automatic updating	Determines whether automatic updating is enabled and configured properly
Malware protection Antivirus Spyware	Verifies that your system is running antivirus software (third-party software) Verifies that your system is running antispyware software (Windows Defender or third-party software)
Other security settings Internet security settings User Account Controls	Determines whether Internet Explorer security settings are at recommended settings Requires explicit consent before allowing software changes to your computer

FIGURE 1-22
Windows Security Center

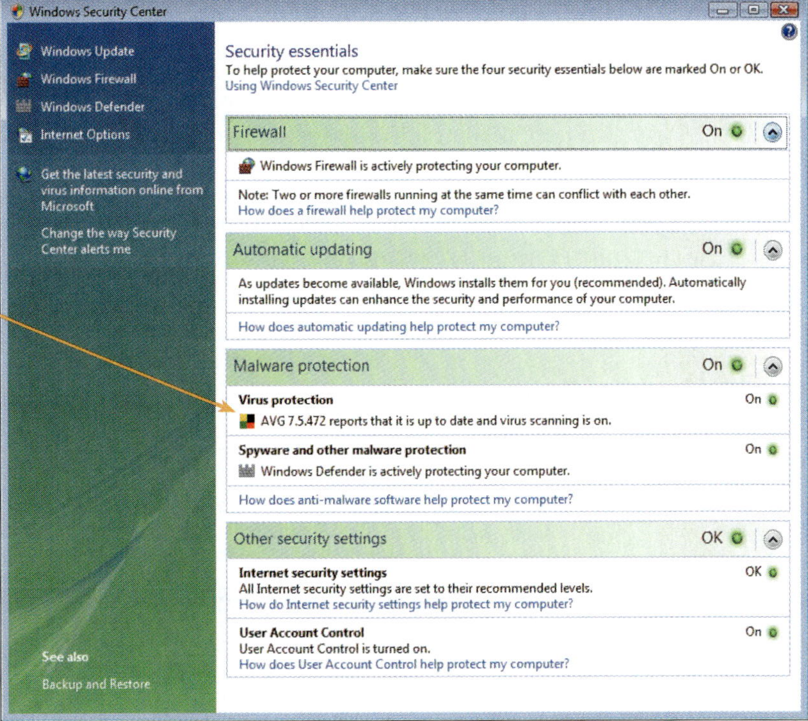

SUMMARY

In this lesson, you learned that:

- Starting Windows brings up the desktop, and possibly the Welcome Center window or other programs, depending on your settings. Several different versions of Windows Vista are available.

- A pointing device, such as a mouse, trackball, touch pad, or pointing stick, is a device you use to interact with and navigate your computer.

- The desktop is the main work area, and contains access to Windows elements such as files, folders, and programs, all of which are represented by icons. The main features of the desktop are the Start button, Recycle Bin, wallpaper or theme, Quick Launch toolbar, taskbar, notification area, and gadgets in the Windows Sidebar.

- Windows contain commands and buttons for a specific function. You can switch between open windows, open different folders by clicking folders in a path on the Address bar, and use the Navigation pane to open and organize favorite folders.

- Windows can be moved, resized, opened, and closed. If you are unable to display all the contents of a window as it is currently sized, scroll bars appear to allow you to move to the part of the window that you want to view. Windows can be maximized to fill the screen or minimized to appear as a button on the taskbar. You can use toolbars and menus in windows to perform tasks or actions, and input information in dialog boxes. The Control Panel contains searchable links for configuring Windows settings.

- Windows provides several default folders for storing and organizing files on your computer and for viewing similar files, sharing files, or accessing frequently used files.

- The Recycle Bin stores files you have deleted from your computer. You can restore deleted files that are placed in the Recycle Bin or delete them permanently from your computer.

- The Windows Help and Support window provides additional information about the many features of Windows. You can access the Help program from Start menu or from any Windows program.

- Windows provides several utilities you can use to clean up unnecessary files on your computer and check your computer's security settings.

VOCABULARY *Review*

Define the following terms:

Address bar	Icon	Restore Down button
Close button	Maximize button	Scroll arrows
Computer folder	Menu	Scroll bar
Control Panel	Minimize button	Scroll box
Desktop	Navigation pane	Taskbar
Dialog box	Operating system	Title bar
Disk Cleanup	Personal folder	Toolbar
Documents folder	Pointer	Window
Explorer windows	Pointing device	Windows Aero
Folder	Public folder	Windows Security Center
Gadgets	Recycle Bin	Windows Sidebar
Help and Support		

REVIEW *Questions*

TRUE/FALSE

Circle T if the statement is true or F if the statement is false.

T   F   **1.** You can view topics on adjusting your monitor in the Documents folder.

T   F   **2.** You can restore items moved to the Recycle Bin.

T   F   **3.** Pressing the Alt key and the Tab key minimizes all open windows.

T   F   **4.** You can use the path in the Address bar to navigate to a folder.

T   F   **5.** You can automatically share files in your Personal folder with other users.

WRITTEN QUESTIONS

Write a brief answer to each of the following questions.

1. What happens to a window when you minimize it?

2. Describe two ways you can find information in Windows Help and Support.

3. What does right-clicking a pointing device, such as a mouse, do?

4. How do you switch between open windows using the keyboard?

5. What is the difference between a toolbar and a menu?

PROJECTS

PROJECT 1-1

1. Start Windows.

2. Use the Start menu to open the Music window.

3. Use the Start menu to open Windows Calendar.

4. Make the Music window active, and then make Windows Calendar active.

5. Use the middle scroll bar to move to 11PM.

6. Minimize Windows Calendar.

7. Open the Pictures folder from the Music window.

8. Open the Control Panel from the Music window.

9. Close all open windows.

PROJECT 1-2

1. Open the Recycle Bin.

2. Double-click a file, if available, and then close the dialog box.

3. Restore the file.

3. Delete the contents of the Recycle Bin, if there are any, and if you are the sole user of the computer.

4. Use the toolbar to change the view to Details.

5. Close the Recycle Bin.

6. Exit Windows.

PROJECT 1-3

1. Open Windows Help and Support.

2. Find information about **print**, and then display search results for printing using Windows.

3. Print the page.

4. Open Windows Photo Gallery from the Start menu.

5. Search for photos using the term **ocean**. (*Hint*: Use another term if no ocean photos are available from the search.)

6. Right-click a photo, and then use the menu to rotate the photo counterclockwise.

7. Use the same menu to rotate the photo clockwise.

8. Open the Options dialog box from the File menu.

9. Cancel out of the dialog box, and then close Windows Photo Gallery.

CRITICAL *Thinking*

ACTIVITY 1-1

You want to add a photograph to your Web page, but first you need to edit the image. Use Windows Help and Support to find information about editing a photo and read several topics. Print the topic that lists tips for editing pictures.

ACTIVITY 1-2

Your supervisor has asked you to prepare a handout on how to create files and folders. Use Windows Help and Support to find a demo about Working with Files and Folders. Watch the demo, and then close the Windows Media Player window. Expand the transcript in the Help topic, and print the page.

ACTIVITY 1-3

You want to see how Windows can help you learn about burning a CD. Open Computer, Windows Help and Support, and the Control Panel. Search for "CD" in each window and write down the search results on a sheet of paper. Search for "burn CD" and compare the search results to the first search. Where possible, print the search results in each window.

MICROSOFT® OFFICE 2007 BASICS AND THE INTERNET

Introducing Microsoft Office 2007

Microsoft Office 2007 (or Office) is a collection of software programs. Word is the word-processing program. It enables you to create documents such as letters and reports. Excel, the spreadsheet program, lets you work with numbers to prepare items such as budgets or to calculate loan payments. Access, the database program, organizes information such as addresses or inventory items. The presentation program is PowerPoint. It is used to create electronic slides that usually accompany a verbal presentation. Outlook is the program used to send and receive e-mail messages and to organize information about people, appointments, and to-do lists. Publisher, the desktop

> ### Net Tip
>
> For more information on Microsoft Office and other Microsoft products, visit the Microsoft Web site at *www.microsoft.com*.

publishing program, helps you design professional-looking documents such as newsletters and brochures.

Office is available in many suites, each of which includes a different combination of programs. For example, the Professional suite includes Word, Excel, Access, PowerPoint, Outlook, and Publisher. Other Office suites include additional programs.

Because Office is an integrated program, the programs can be used together. For example, numbers from a spreadsheet can be included in a letter created in the word processor or in a presentation. This ability to share information between programs ensures consistency and accuracy. It also saves time because you don't have to reenter the same information in several programs.

> ### Did You Know? 
>
> Many people call any file created on a computer a *document*. In Office, a *document* is created in Word, a *workbook* is created in Excel, a *database* is created in Access, and a *presentation* is created in PowerPoint.

Starting an Office Program

To start an Office program, click the Start button on the taskbar, click All Programs, and then click Microsoft Office. A list of the Office programs available on your computer appears, as shown in Figure 1-1. Click the name of the program you want to start. 

FIGURE 1-1
Microsoft Office folder

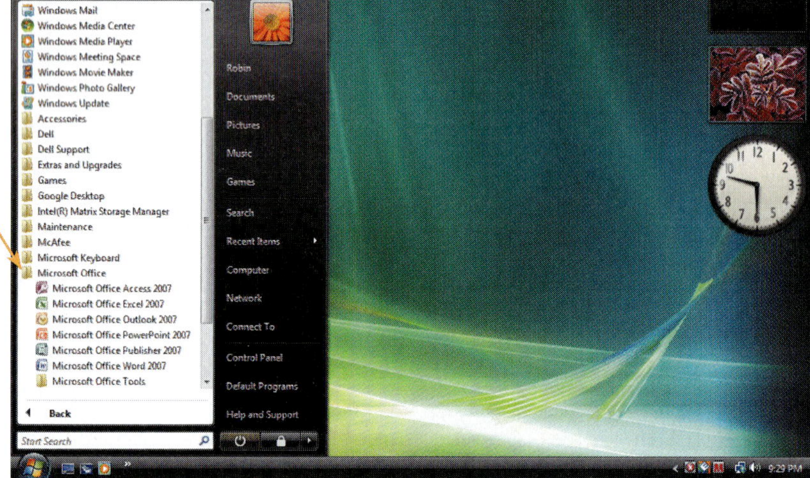

STEP-BY-STEP 1.1

1. On the taskbar, click the **Start** button. The Start menu appears. 

2. Click **All Programs**. The left side of the Start menu changes to show the All Programs menu.

3. Click **Microsoft Office**. The Microsoft Office folder expands to show all the Office programs installed on the computer, as shown in Figure 1-1.

4. Click **Microsoft Office PowerPoint 2007**. PowerPoint starts and opens a blank presentation.

STEP-BY-STEP 1.1 Continued

5. Click the **Start** button again, and then click **All Programs**.

6. Click **Microsoft Office**, and then click **Microsoft Office Word 2007**. Word starts and opens a blank document, as shown in Figure 1-2.

FIGURE 1-2
Blank document in Word

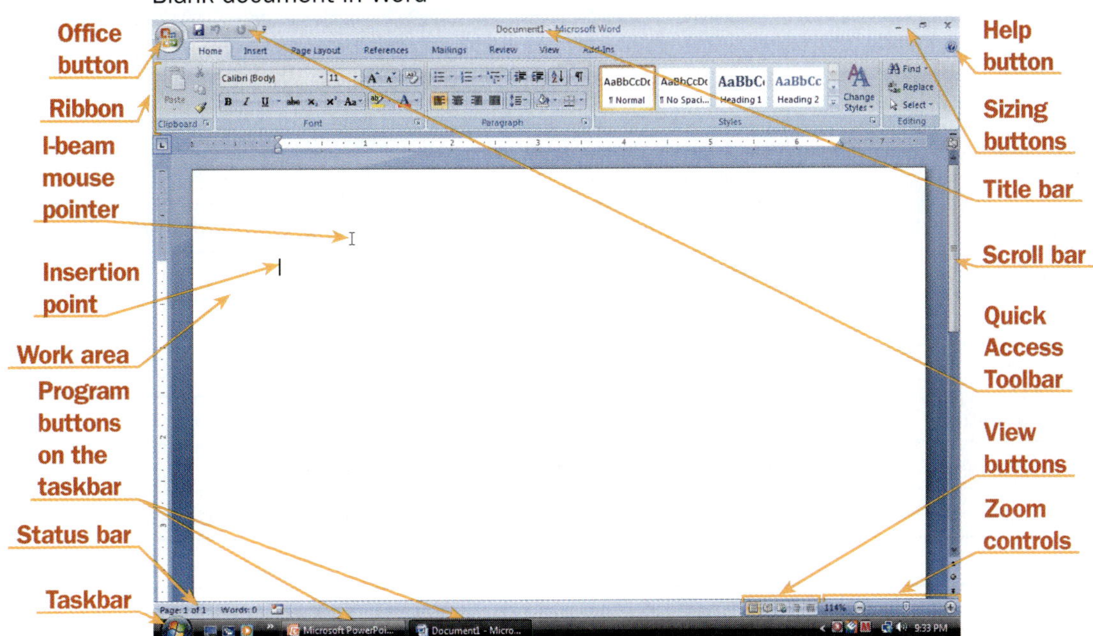

7. Leave Word and PowerPoint open for the next Step-by-Step.

Computer Concepts

When working in Office 2007 programs, you can open more than one file at a time. You can open multiple files in the same program. You can also open one or more files in different Office programs, such as Word and Excel. To move between the open files, just click the taskbar button for the file you want to display.

Careers

For help in choosing a career or college major, go to *www.careerkey.org*. You can take a test that measures your skills, abilities, talents, values, interests, and personality. A list of promising careers and jobs is identified based on the answers you provide.

Exploring the Program Window

A **program window** is the rectangle that contains the open program, tools for working with the file, and the work area. Look carefully at the parts of the Word program window labeled in Figure 1-2. These parts are similar in all of the Office programs and are described in Table 1-1.

TABLE 1-1
Items in the program window

ITEM	FUNCTION
Office Button	Contains commands for working with files, including commands for opening, saving, printing, and creating new files
Quick Access Toolbar	Provides access to commonly used commands
Title bar	Shows the names of the program and the current file
Sizing buttons	Change the size of the program window and exits the program
Ribbon	Contains tabs from which you can choose a variety of commands
Microsoft Office Help button	Opens the Help window for the program
Work area	Displays the file you are working on
Insertion point	Shows where text will appear when you begin typing
Scroll bars	Shifts other areas of the file into the work area
Status bar	Provides information about the current file and process
View buttons	Change how a file is displayed in the workspace

Using the Ribbon

The **Ribbon** is "command central" for the Office programs. The **tabs** on the Ribbon organize the commands into related tasks. The commands on each tab are organized into **groups**. Each group contains buttons that you click to choose a command. By clicking a **button** to choose a command, you give the program instructions about what you want to do. Each button has an **icon** (a small picture) or words to remind you of its function. Figure 1-3 labels the different parts of the Ribbon.

FIGURE 1-3
Parts of the Ribbon

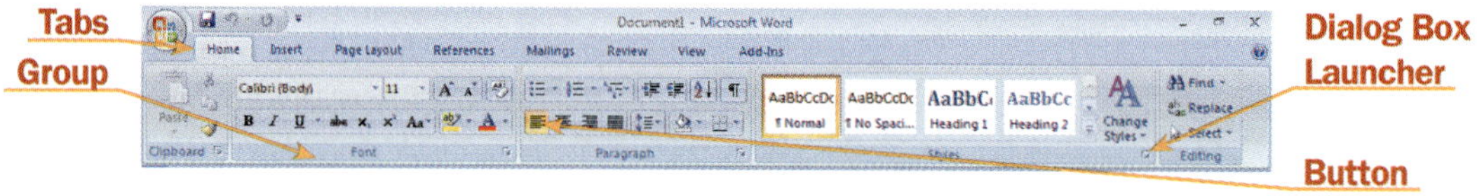

To use the buttons on the Ribbon, you need to click them. When a step instructs you to click a button or something else on the screen, it means to do the following: Move the mouse until the pointer is positioned on top of the item, press the left mouse button, and then release it.

Generally, when you click a button, something happens. Some buttons are like light switches: one click turns on the feature and the next click turns it off. This is often referred to as a *toggle*. Other buttons have two parts: a button that you can click to choose the command and an arrow that you can click to open a menu, or list, of other commands related to the button. Figure 1-4 compares these different types of buttons.

Did You Know?

You can shrink the Ribbon to one line that shows the tab names by double-clicking any tab. You can then see more of the work area. To redisplay the entire Ribbon, double-click any tab.

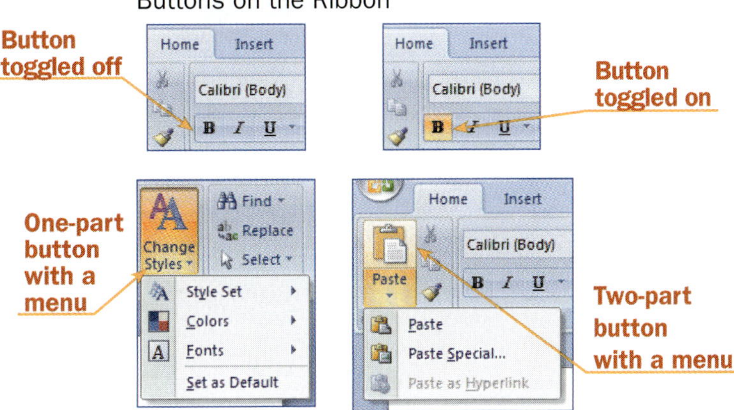

FIGURE 1-4
Buttons on the Ribbon

Did You Know?

If you do not know the function of a button, move the pointer to the button, but do not click. A ScreenTip with the button's name and a short description of its function appears below the button. You'll learn more about ScreenTips later in this lesson.

Some buttons open galleries. A **gallery** shows the options available for a command. Galleries can also appear directly on the Ribbon. If a gallery on the Ribbon has more options than can be displayed on the Ribbon, you click its More button to open the full gallery. **Live Preview** lets you see how a gallery option affects your file without making the change. Point to an option in a gallery, but do not click it. Your file shows the results of selecting that option. After you find the option you want, you click that option to make the change in your file. See Figure 1-5.

FIGURE 1-5
Text Highlight Color gallery

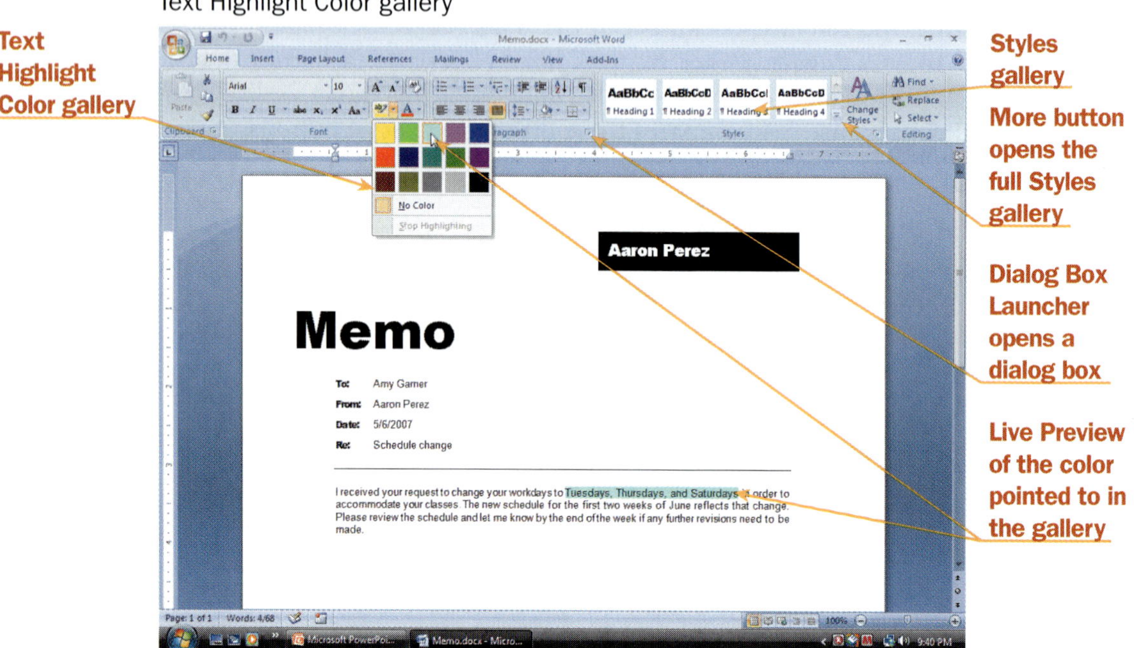

The Ribbon has one other type of button—the Dialog Box Launcher, which you click to open a dialog box or task pane to choose additional settings. A **dialog box** is a window that opens on top of the program window. A **task pane** is a pane, like a windowpane, that opens on the right or left side of the program window. The Dialog Box Launcher appears in the lower-right corner of any group that has a related dialog box or task pane. See Figure 1-5.

The buttons on the Ribbon change depending on settings in your computer and on how big the program window is. For example, the Home tab on the Ribbon in Word might look like the one shown in Figure 1-6a or the one shown in Figure 1-6b. If the Ribbon on your screen looks like the one shown in Figure 1-6b, you will need to make some adjustments as you follow the steps in this book. For example, look at the Editing group in both figures. A step might say "In the Editing group, click the Find button." If your screen looks like the one shown in Figure 1-6b, you will need to click the Editing button on the Ribbon first to expand the group, as shown in Figure 1-6b. Then you can click the Find button.

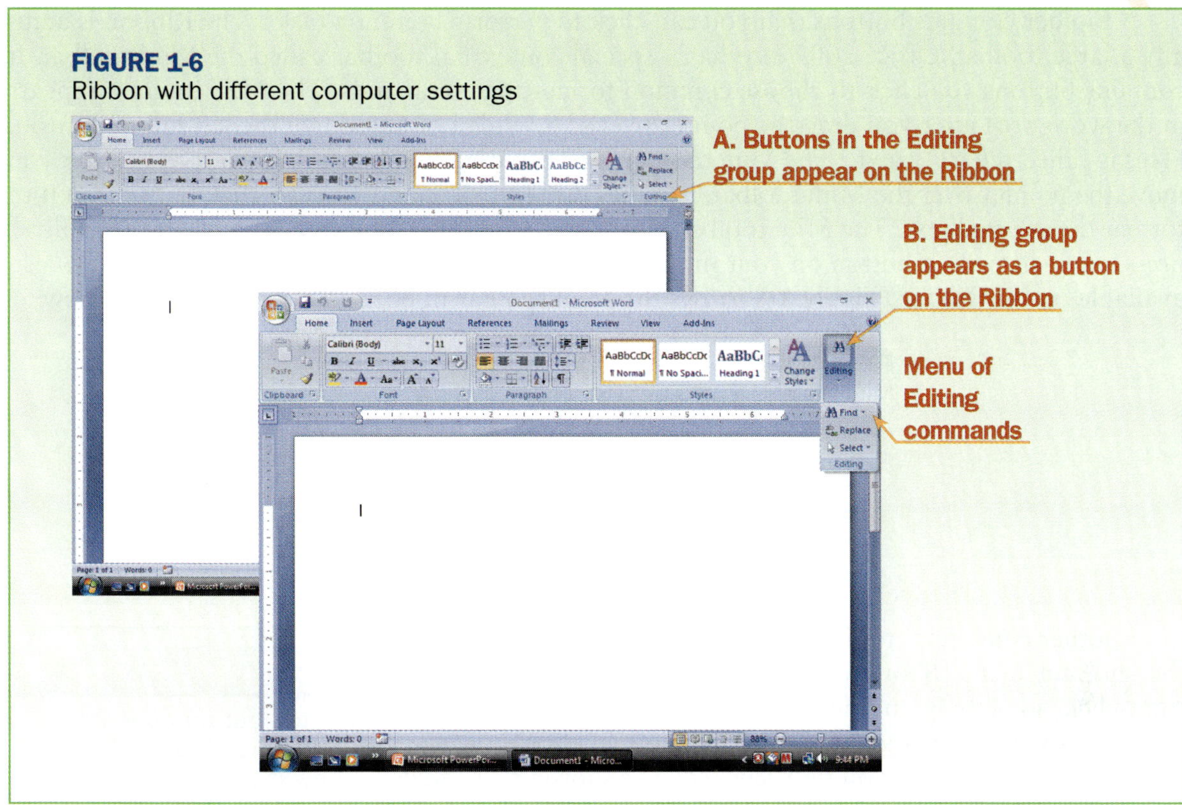

FIGURE 1-6
Ribbon with different computer settings

Understanding Contextual Tools

Some tools appear as you work. Because they appear only when you need them, the workspace stays neat and uncluttered. This type of tool is called a contextual tool.

Contextual tabs appear on the Ribbon only when you select certain items in a file, and they contain commands related to that item. The contextual tabs work the same way as the standard tabs, but they disappear when you click somewhere else on the screen. Figure 1-7 shows the Drawing Tools contextual tabs. In this case, there is only one—the Format tab. This tab appears when you click a drawing in a Word document.

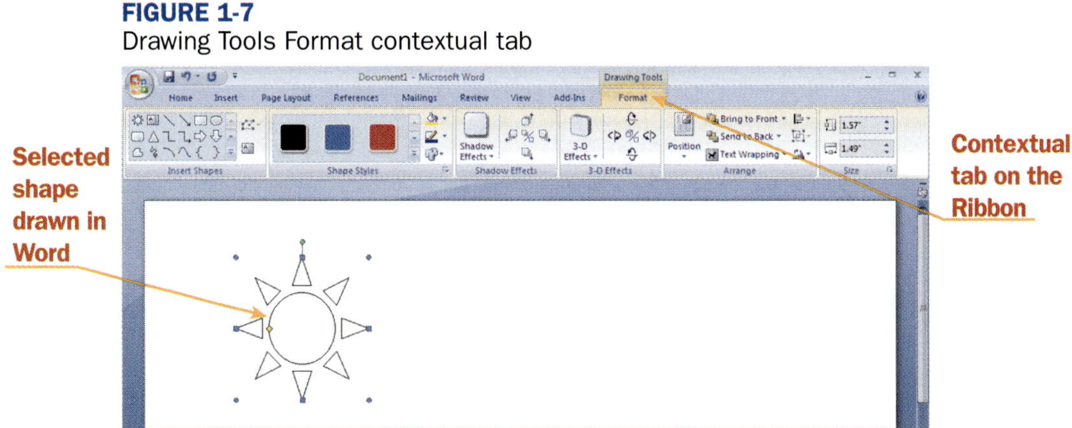

FIGURE 1-7
Drawing Tools Format contextual tab

A **toolbar** contains buttons that you can click to perform common tasks. The Ribbon is actually a large toolbar. Office 2007 also has a special contextual toolbar called the Mini toolbar. It contains buttons you click to choose common formatting commands. The **Mini toolbar** appears in the work area after you drag the pointer over text while holding down the left mouse button. (This is called *selecting* text.) The Mini toolbar is transparent when you first select text. After you move the pointer over the Mini toolbar, it comes into full view and you can click buttons on it to format the selected text. The Mini toolbar disappears when you move the pointer off the toolbar, press a key, or press a button on your mouse. All of the commands on the Mini toolbar are also available on the Ribbon. Figure 1-8 shows the Mini toolbar in both transparent and full view.

FIGURE 1-8
Mini toolbar

Transparent Mini toolbar　　**Full view Mini toolbar**

Another contextual tool available in Office 2007 is the shortcut menu. **Shortcut menus** appear when you right-click something in the program window. They contain lists of commands that you are most likely to use with the item or text you right-clicked. The shortcut menu can be a faster way to get to these commands than the Ribbon. Figure 1-9 shows the shortcut menu that opens when you right-click selected text. Notice that the Mini toolbar appears at the top of this shortcut menu. (It does not appear on all shortcut menus; only on those shortcut menus that appear when you right-click selected text.)

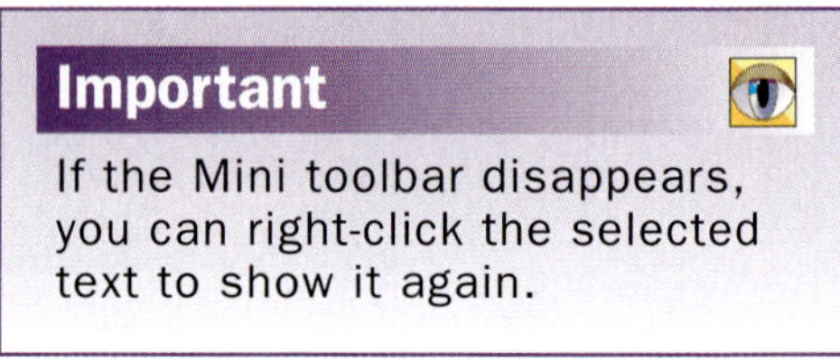

If the Mini toolbar disappears, you can right-click the selected text to show it again.

FIGURE 1-9
Shortcut menu with the Mini toolbar

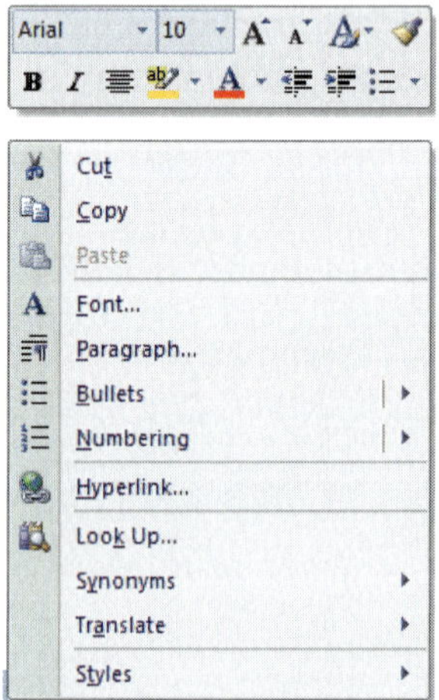

Using the Office Button to Open, Save, and Close Files

In all Office programs, you open, save, and close files in the same way—with the Office Button. *Opening* a file means loading a file from a disk into the program window. *Saving* a file stores it on a disk. *Closing* a file removes it from the program window.

Opening an Existing File

To open an existing file, you can click the Office Button to open the Office menu, and then click Open. The Open dialog box appears, as shown in Figure 1-10.

FIGURE 1-10
Open dialog box

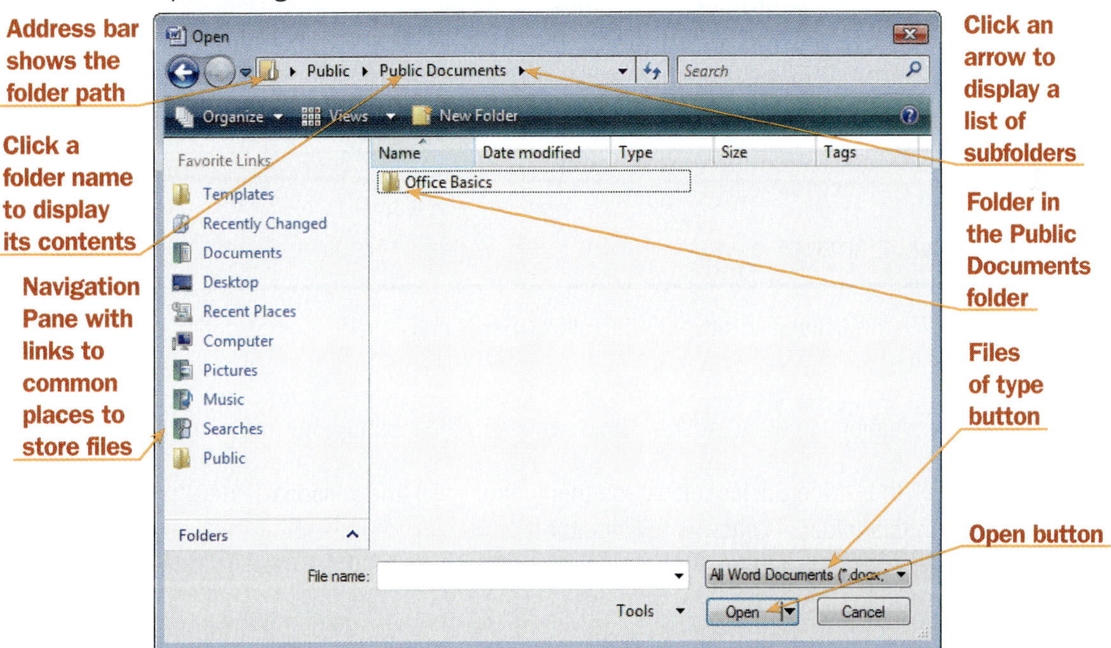

From the Open dialog box, you can open a file from any available disk or folder. You need to move to the location where the file you want to open is stored. The Address bar, near the top of the dialog box, shows the path of the drive and folders to your current location. Below the Address bar, a list shows the folders or files that are in the current location. The Navigation Pane, on the left side of the dialog box, provides links to common places on your computer to store files. To change the path, you can use a combination of the following methods:

Did You Know?

To create a new, blank file in any Office program, click the Office Button, and then click New. The New dialog box appears. Double-click the type of new file you want to create.

- Click a link in the Navigation Pane.

- Click a location in the Address bar to see the folders and files in that location.

- Click a location arrow in the Address bar to see a list of folders in that location, and then click the folder you want to see.

- Double-click a folder to see its folders and files.

The Open dialog box shows all the files in the folder that the active program can open. To see all the files in the folder, choose All Files from the Files of type button located above the Open button. After you have located the file you want to open, click the file to select it and then click Open.

Did You Know? 

In the Open dialog box, you can double-click a file to open it in the program without clicking Open.

The files you need for each lesson in this book are stored in a series of folders. The main folder shows the name of the program whose unit you are working on. For example, *Office Basics* is the main folder for this unit. The next folder lists the current lesson in the unit. For example, *Lesson1* is the subfolder for this lesson. Your instructor will tell you where to find the folders that store the Data Files you need for this book. The following Step-by-Step includes steps for moving to this location. All other lessons in this book instruct you to open the *File name* Data File.

S TEP-BY-STEP 1.2

1. In Word, click the **Office Button**, and then click **Open**. The Open dialog box appears, as shown in Figure 1-10. 

2. Use the Navigation Pane and Address bar to move to the location of your Data Files.

3. Double-click the **Office Basics** folder, and then double-click the **Lesson1** folder. The *Employees* folder is stored in this folder, as shown in Figure 1-11.

STEP-BY-STEP 1.2 Continued

FIGURE 1-11
Employees folder

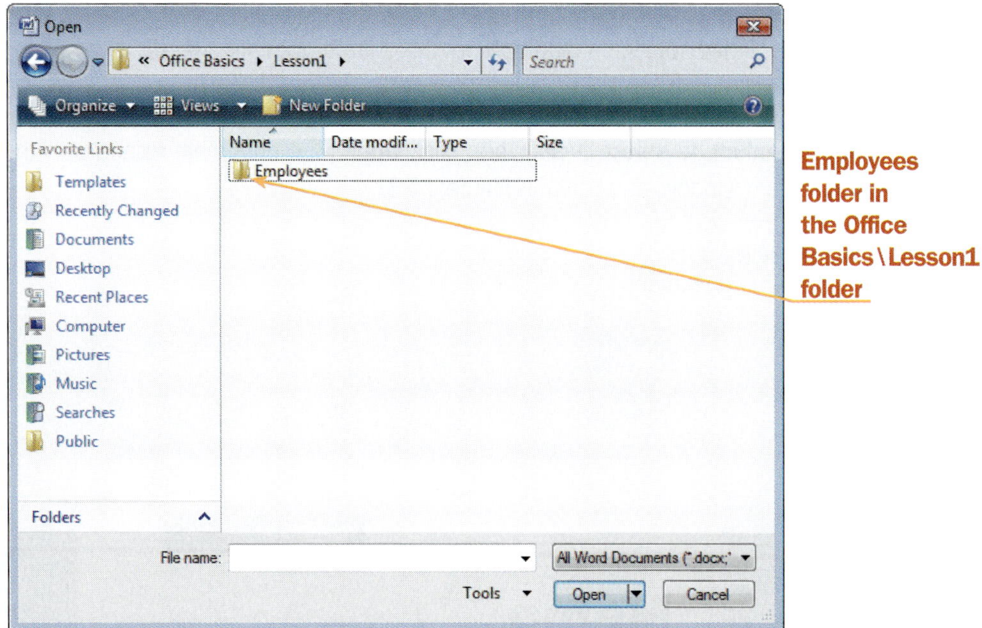

4. Double-click the **Employees** folder. The folders within the *Employees* folder appear, as shown in Figure 1-12.

FIGURE 1-12
Contents of the Employee folder

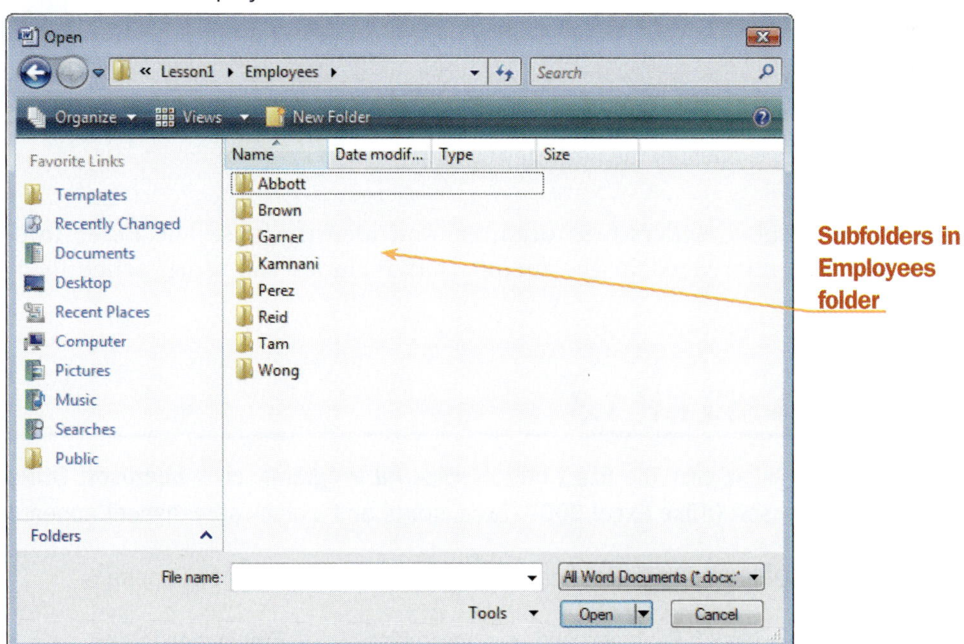

STEP-BY-STEP 1.2 Continued

5. Double-click the **Perez** folder. The Word document named *Memo.docx* appears in the *Perez* folder.

6. Click the **All Word Documents** button to display the list of file types. Click **All Files** to display all the files in the *Perez* folder. In addition to the *Memo.docx* file, there is also an Excel file named *Schedule.xlsx*.

7. Click **Memo.docx** to select it, and then click **Open**. The document appears in the work area of the Word program window, as shown in Figure 1-13.

FIGURE 1-13
Memo document

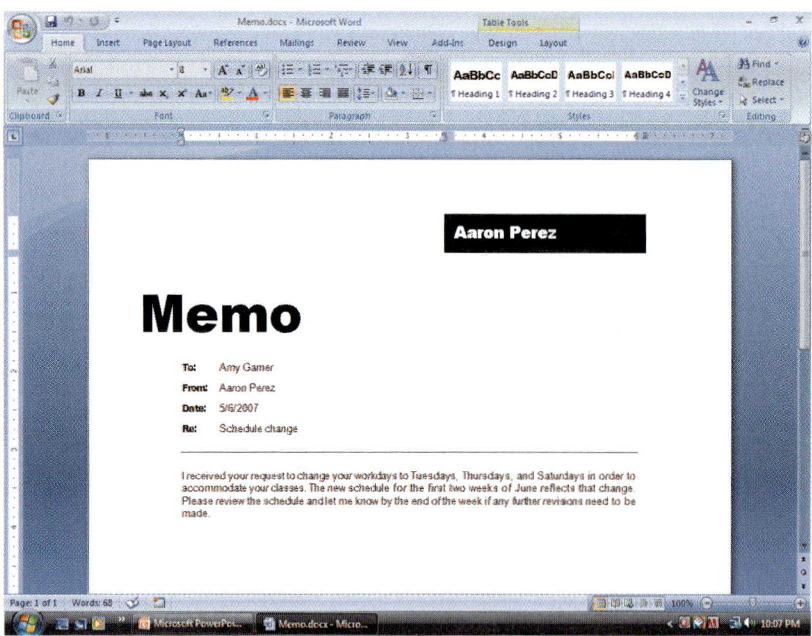

8. Leave the file open for the next Step-by-Step.

You can see how folders help organize and identify files. The *Perez* folder also contains the spreadsheet referenced in the memo that includes the work schedule for the first two weeks in June.

STEP-BY-STEP 1.3

1. On the taskbar, click the **Start** button, click **All Programs**, click **Microsoft Office**, and then click **Microsoft Office Excel 2007**. Excel starts and a blank spreadsheet appears. 

2. Click the **Office Button**, and then click **Open**. The Open dialog box appears. 

3. Use the Navigation Pane and Address bar to display the **Employees** folder.

4. Double-click the **Employees** folder, and then double-click the **Perez** folder.

STEP-BY-STEP 1.3 Continued

5. Double-click **Schedule.xlsx**. The *Schedule* workbook appears in the Excel work area, as shown in Figure 1-14.

FIGURE 1-14
Schedule workbook

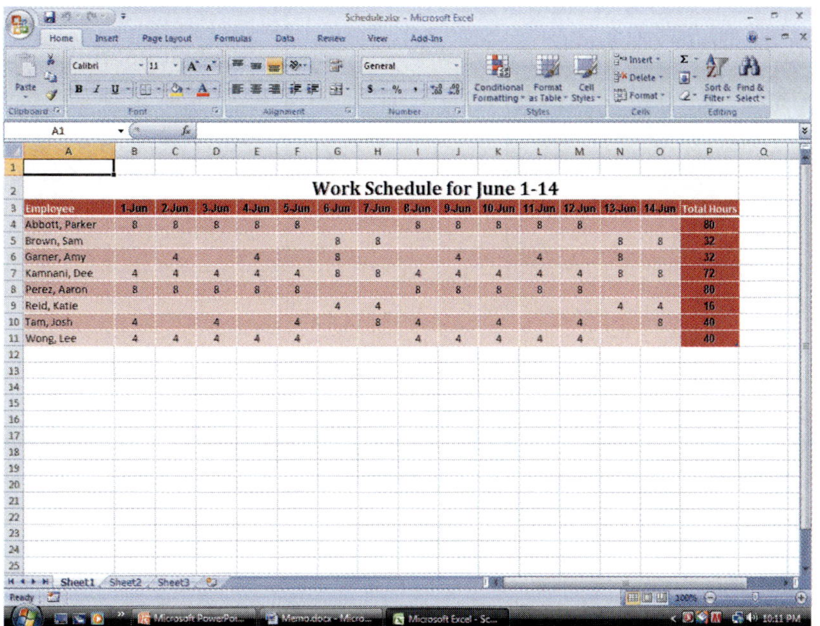

Employee	1-Jun	2-Jun	3-Jun	4-Jun	5-Jun	6-Jun	7-Jun	8-Jun	9-Jun	10-Jun	11-Jun	12-Jun	13-Jun	14-Jun	Total Hours
Abbott, Parker	8	8	8	8	8			8	8	8	8	8			80
Brown, Sam						8	8						8	8	32
Garner, Amy		4		4		8			4		4		8		32
Kamnani, Dee	4	4	4	4	4	8	8	4	4	4	4	4	8	8	72
Perez, Aaron	8	8	8	8	8			8	8	8	8	8			80
Reid, Katie						4	4						4	4	16
Tam, Josh	4		4		4		8	4		4		4		8	40
Wong, Lee	4	4	4	4	4			4	4	4	4	4			40

6. Leave the workbook open for the next Step-by-Step.

Saving a File

Saving is done using one of two methods. The Save command saves a file on a disk using its current name and save location. The Save As command lets you save a file with a new name. You can also use the Save As command to save a file to a new location.

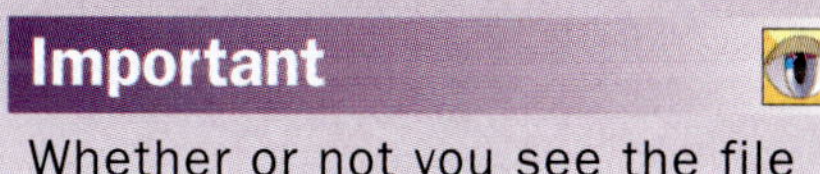

Important

Whether or not you see the file extensions, you do not need to type one when you enter the descriptive name for a file. If you do type a file extension, you will create a duplicate, such as *June Schedule.xlsx.xlsx*.

Each program has a different **file extension**, which is a series of letters Office adds to the end of a file name that identifies in which program that file was created. Table 1-2 lists the file extensions for the four main Office programs. Depending on how your computer is set up, you might not see file extensions.

TABLE 1-2
File extensions for the Office programs

PROGRAM	FILE EXTENSION
Word	.docx
Excel	.xlsx
PowerPoint	.pptx
Access	.accdb

Computer Concepts

Earlier versions of Office used different file formats. The file extension for Word documents was .doc. The file extension for Excel workbooks was .xls. The file extension for PowerPoint presentations was .ppt. And, the file extension for Access databases was .mdb. If you want a file created in one of the Office 2007 programs to open in a program from an earlier version of Office, you need to save the file in one of these formats.

STEP-BY-STEP 1.4

1. Click the **Office Button**, and then click **Save As**. The Save As dialog box appears, as shown in Figure 1-15. 

FIGURE 1-15
Save as dialog box

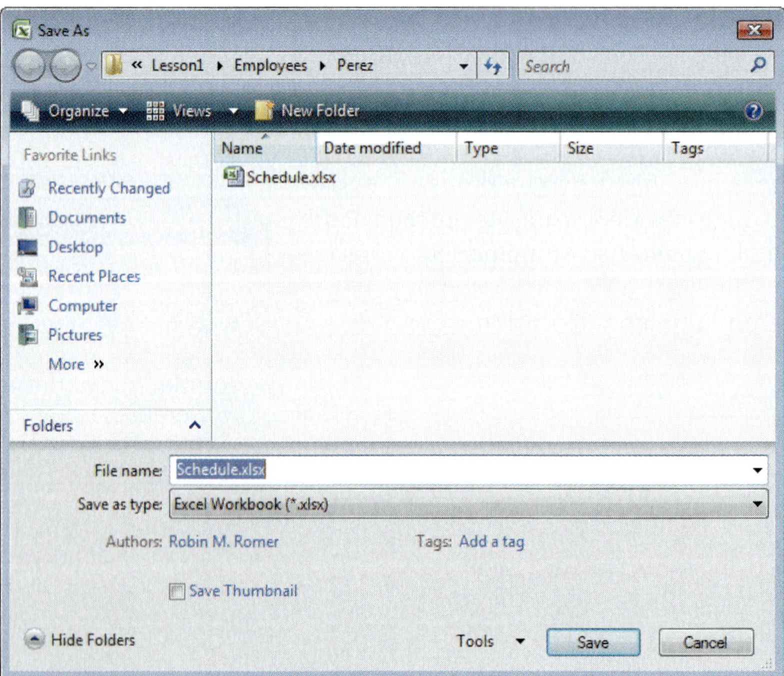

2. In the File name box, type **June Schedule** followed by your initials.

STEP-BY-STEP 1.4 Continued

3. In the Address bar, click the **Employees** location arrow. The list of folders in the *Employees* folder appears, as shown in Figure 1-16.

FIGURE 1-16
Employees subfolder list

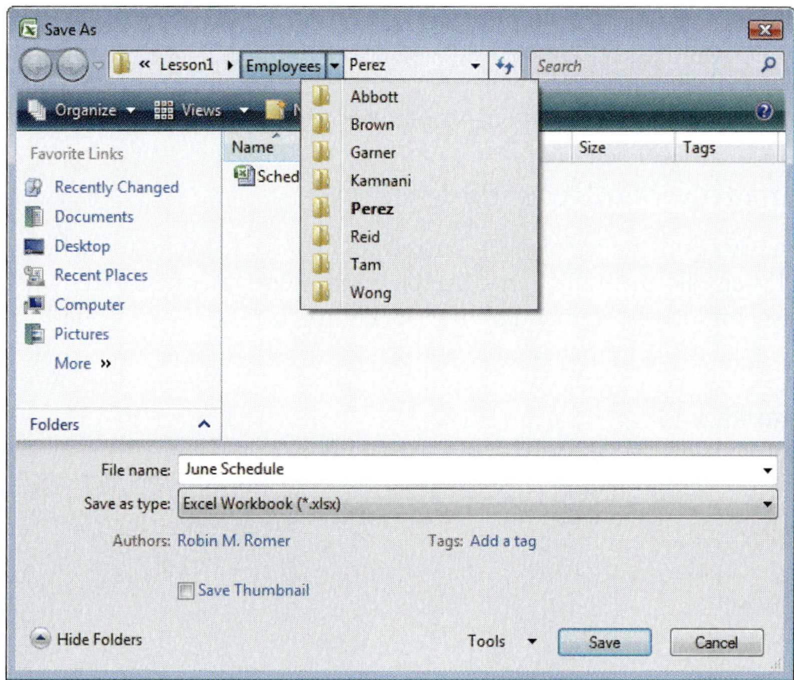

4. Click **Garner**.

5. Click **Save**. The workbook is saved with the new name in the Garner folder.

6. Leave the workbook open for the next Step-by-Step.

To save changes to a file using the same name and location, you can click the Save button on the Quick Access Toolbar.

Closing a File

You can close an Office file by clicking the Office Button and clicking Close. If you use the Close command on the Office menu to close a file, the program remains open and ready for you to work on another file. You can also close the file by clicking the Close button on the right side of the title bar. If you close a file with the Close button, and no other file is open in that program, the program also closes.

Did You Know?

If you try to close a file that contains changes you have not saved, a dialog box appears, asking whether you want to save the file. Click Yes to save and close the file. Click No to close the file without saving. Click Cancel to return to the program window without saving or closing the file.

STEP-BY-STEP 1.5

1. Click the **Office Button** to open the Office menu, and then click **Close**. The *June Schedule* workbook closes, and Excel remains open. 

2. Click the **Memo - Microsoft Word** button on the taskbar to make the window active. The *Memo* document appears.

3. Click the **Office Button**, and then click **Close**. The *Memo* document closes, and Word remains open.

4. Leave Word, Excel, and PowerPoint open for the next Step-by-Step.

Using Shortcuts to Open Recently Used Files

Office provides two shortcuts for opening recently used files. The first shortcut is to click the Start button, and then click Recent Items on the Start menu. A menu opens listing the 15 most recently used files, similar to the menu shown in Figure 1-17. To open one of the recently used files, click the file you want to open.

FIGURE 1-17
Recent Items list on the Start menu

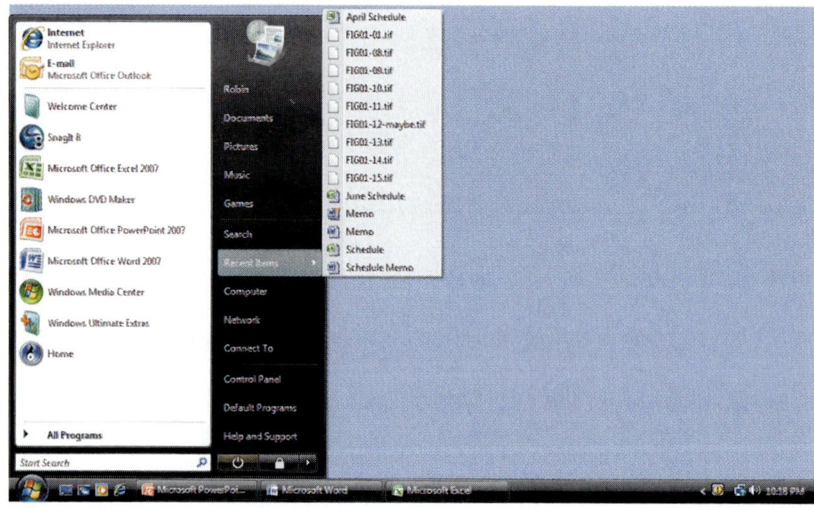

The second shortcut is to click the Office Button in any of the Office programs. The Recent Documents list appears on the right side of the Office menu and shows the file names of the 17 files that were most recently opened in that program. The most recently opened file appears at the top of the list, as shown in Figure 1-18. When a new file is opened, each file name moves down to make room for the new most recently opened file. To open one of the files, you simply click it as if it were a menu selection. You can click a pin next to a file in the Recent Documents list to keep that file "pinned" to the list. If the file you are looking for is not in the Recent Documents list on the Office menu, use the Open command to locate and select the file.

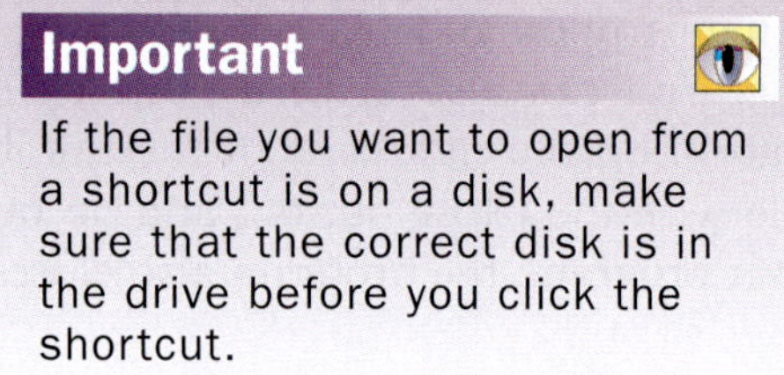

Important

If the file you want to open from a shortcut is on a disk, make sure that the correct disk is in the drive before you click the shortcut.

FIGURE 1-18
Recent Document lists on the Office menu

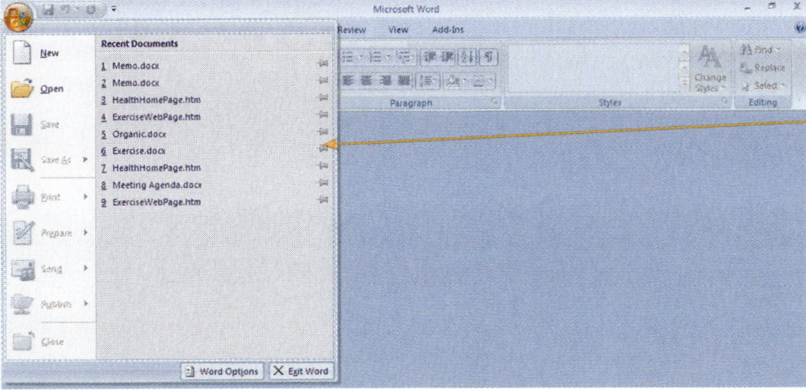

Getting Help in Office

This lesson has covered only a few of the many features of the Office programs. You will learn more about each of these programs in their individual units later in this text. But you can always learn more by using the Office Help system, which includes ScreenTips and the Help window.

Using ScreenTips

A ScreenTip is a box that appears when you point to a button. As shown in Figure 1-19, it contains the button's name and a description of its function. It can also include a link to more information and a keyboard shortcut if the command has one. To view a ScreenTip, you just point to a button—do not click it. If the ScreenTip includes a link to more information, you can press the F1 key to open the Help window with that topic displayed.

FIGURE 1-19
ScreenTip for the Show/Hide ¶ button

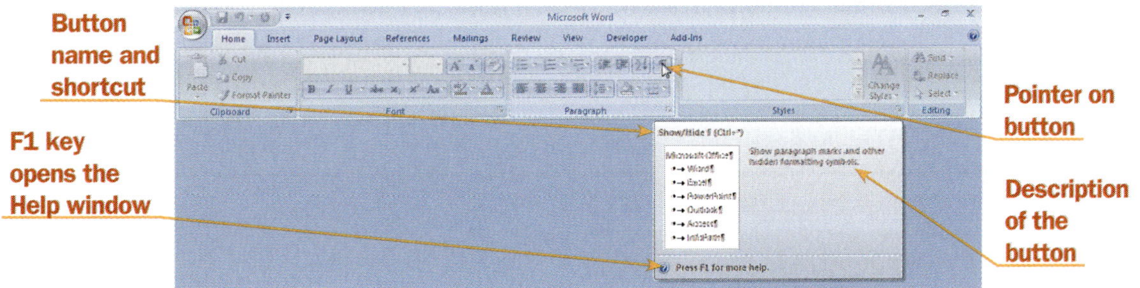

Using the Help Window

To get specific help about topics relating to the program you are using, you use the Help window, as shown in Figure 1-20. To open the Help window, click the Microsoft Office Help button located near the upper-right corner of the program window. Each program has its own Help window.

FIGURE 1-20
Word Help window with Table of Contents

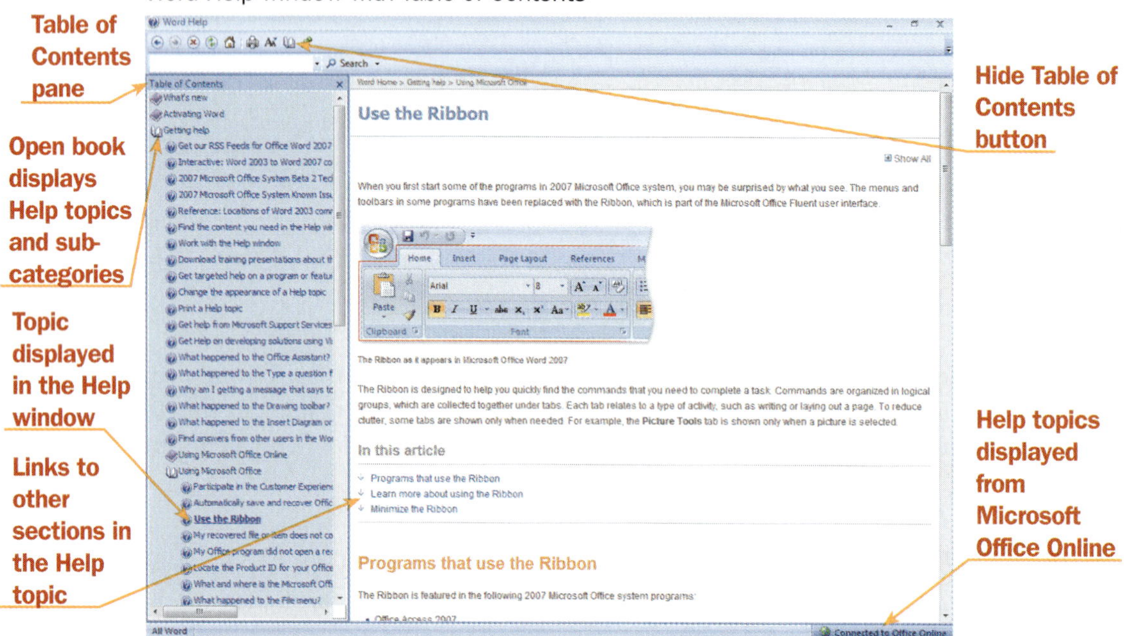

You can search the Help system using the Table of Contents or keywords. The Table of Contents lists the general categories of topics and subtopics in the Help system. This is organized similarly to a table of contents in a book. To see the information in a category, click the text.

When you want to search for help on a particular topic, you can type a word or phrase in the *Type words to search for* box. After you click the Search button, a list of Help topics that include the keyword appears in the Help window, and you can click a topic to display it in the Help window.

S TEP-BY-STEP 1.6

1. On the Ribbon, click the **Home** tab if it is not displayed.

2. In the Clipboard group, point to the **Show/Hide ¶** button, resting the pointer on the button. The button's ScreenTip appears, as shown in Figure 1-19. 

3. Read the button's name and a description of its function in the ScreenTip.

4. On the Ribbon, point to the **Microsoft Office Word Help** button and read its ScreenTip. 

5. Click the **Microsoft Office Word Help** button. If the Word Help window that appears does not fill the screen, click the **Maximize** button on the title bar. 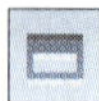

STEP-BY-STEP 1.6 Continued

6. On the Help window toolbar, click the **Show Table of Contents** button to display a list of Help topic categories. If you have Internet access, this information is downloaded from Microsoft Office Online rather than only the Help topics stored on your computer. 

7. In the Table of Contents pane, click the **Getting help** book, click the **Using Microsoft Office** book, and then click the **Use the Ribbon** topic. The topic appears in the right side of the Word Help window, as shown in Figure 1-20. If you are not connected to Microsoft Office Online, the list of topics and the topic content you see will differ.

8. Read the contents of the Help window.

9. On the Word Help window toolbar, click the **Hide Table of Contents** button to hide the pane. 

10. In the Word Help window, click the **Type words to search for** box.

11. Type **print**, and then click the **Search** button to display the list of search results shown in Figure 1-21. If you are not connected to the Internet, your list of search results will differ. 

FIGURE 1-21
Search results

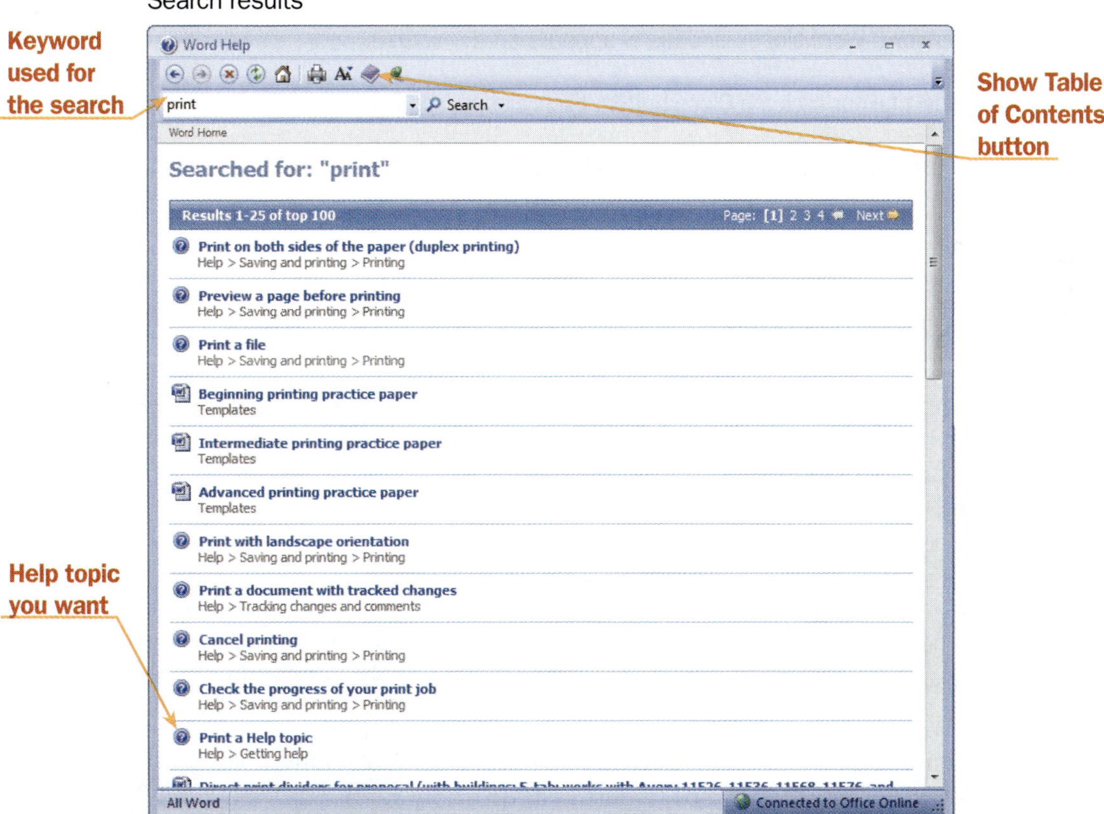

12. Search the list of results until you find **Print a Help topic**. Click it to display information in the Word Help window.

STEP-BY-STEP 1.6 Continued

13. Read the information, and then print the information by following the instructions.

14. On the Word Help window title bar, click the **Close** button. The Help window closes. 

Exiting an Office Program

The Exit command, which is located on the Office menu, closes the open Office program. If you have only one file open in that program, you can also click the Close button on the right side of the title bar. If you have not saved the final version of your file, a dialog box opens, asking whether you want to save your changes. Click Yes to save and close the file and exit the program. When you exit an Office program, the program window closes. 

STEP-BY-STEP 1.7

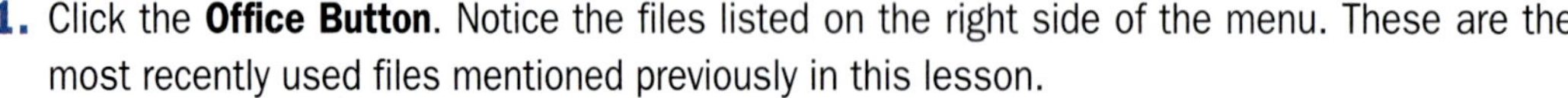

1. Click the **Office Button**. Notice the files listed on the right side of the menu. These are the most recently used files mentioned previously in this lesson.

2. Click **Exit Word**. Word closes and Excel appears on the screen.

3. On the Excel title bar, click the **Close** button. Excel closes, and PowerPoint appears on the screen. 

4. Click the **Office Button**, and then click the **Exit PowerPoint** button. The desktop reappears on the screen.

Viewing a Web Page

The Internet is a vast network of computers located all over the world and linked to one another. The Internet allows people around the world to share information and ideas using Web pages, blogs, and e-mail as well as other services. Connecting to the Internet requires special hardware and software and an Internet service provider (ISP). Before you can use the Internet, your computer needs to be connected, and you should know how to access the Internet.

The World Wide Web (or Web) is a system of computers that share information by means of links on Web pages. A link is text (often colored and underlined) or a graphic that you click to "jump" to another location or Web page. A Web page is a document specially formatted to be displayed on computers connected to the Internet. To find a Web page, the Web uses an address system. Just like you have a home address, each Web

Net Tip

You can connect your computer to the Internet in a variety of ways. You might use a regular telephone line (also called a dial-up connection) or a high-speed connection through your local cable company or a special telephone service called DSL. You might also connect without any phone lines or cables by using a wireless connection. The connection you have depends on your service provider, how much you are willing to spend, and the way your computer is connected to the provider.

page has an address on the Web. The fancy name for these addresses is **Uniform Resource Locators** (**URLs**—you pronounce each letter separately: U-R-L or U-R-Ls). Examples of URLs are:

http://www.senate.gov

http://www.microsoft.com

http://www.course.com

To view Web pages, you need special software called a **Web browser**. Internet Explorer is the Web browser that is packaged with computers that run Windows. Figure 1-22 shows a Web page using Internet Explorer as a browser.

FIGURE 1-22
Internet Explorer Web browser

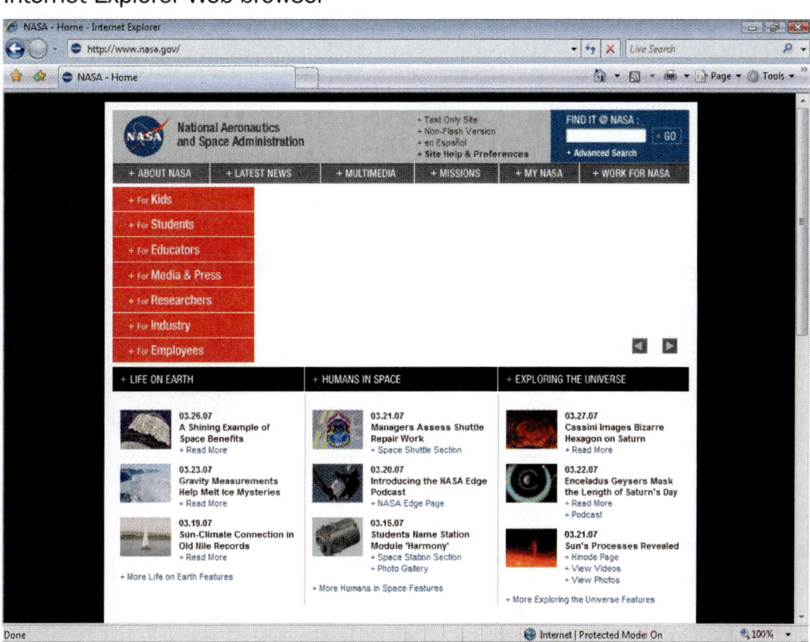

To go to a specific Web page, you click the Address bar in your browser, type the URL, and then click the Go button or press the Enter key. You can jump to other pages by clicking links on the page you are viewing. Click the Back button to move back to previous pages you viewed, and click the Forward button to move to subsequent pages you viewed. Click the Home Page button to load your **home page** (or *start page*), which is the first page that opens when you start your browser.

Careers

You can use the Internet to research different careers in business. Find out about careers in business by typing the following URL in the Address bar in your browser: *www.careers-in-business.com*.

STEP-BY-STEP 1.8

1. On the taskbar, click the **Start** button, and then click **Internet Explorer**. The home page begins loading. 

2. Click the Address bar, type **www.nasa.gov**, and then press the **Enter** key. The NASA home page appears in the browser, as shown in Figure 1-22.

3. Click a link to see more information.

4. Click the **Back** button to return to the previous page. 

5. Click another link to display a different page.

6. Click the **Home** button to return to the home page for your computer. 

7. On the title bar, click the **Close** button. Internet Explorer closes. 

Net Tip

The length of time it takes to load a page depends upon the speed of your connection as well as the file size of the page you are viewing. If you want to go to a different address or click a link you can see on the page, you do not have to wait for the page to finish loading. Even when you cannot see the entire page, you can type a different URL in the Address bar or click a link on the partially loaded page.

Important

Because Web pages are updated frequently, the page you see might not look exactly like the one shown in Figure 1-22 even if you entered the same URL.

SUMMARY

In this lesson, you learned:

- Microsoft Office 2007 is a combination of programs that can include a word-processor program, a spreadsheet program, a database program, a presentation program, a schedule/organizer program, and a desktop publishing program. The files of these programs can be used together.

- Office programs can be started by clicking the Start button, clicking All Programs, clicking Microsoft Office, and then clicking the program name.

- The basic parts of the program window are similar in all of the Office programs.

- The Ribbon is "command central" for all the Office programs. Commands are organized in groups on tabs on the Ribbon. You click a button to choose the command you want. Some buttons open a menu of additional commands or a gallery of options.

- Contextual tabs on the Ribbon, the Mini toolbar, and shortcut menus are tools that appear when you work with a specific object in the program window.

- You can open an existing file from the Office menu. The Open dialog box appears, enabling you to open a file from any available disk or directory.

- No matter which Office program you are using, the files are opened, saved, and closed the same way.

- You can open recently used files quickly by clicking the file name in the Recent Documents list on the right side of the Office menu. You can also click the Start button, and then click Recent Items to list the most recently used files.

- To exit an Office program, click the Office Button and click the Exit button, or click the Close button on the program window title bar.

- The Office Help system provides additional information about the many features of the Office programs. In the Help window, you can use the Table of Contents or the *Type word to search for* box to get information. If your computer is connected to the Internet, you see Help topics and additional information from Microsoft Office Online.

- Internet Explorer is a Web browser. You can use it to view Web pages.

VOCABULARY *Review*

Define the following terms:

Button	Menu	Sizing button
Contextual tab	Microsoft Office 2007	Status bar
Dialog box	(Office)	Tab
File extension	Mini toolbar	Task pane
Gallery	Office Button	Title bar
Group	Program window	Toolbar
Home page	Quick Access Toolbar	Uniform Resource Locator
Icon	Ribbon	(URL)
Insertion point	ScreenTip	Web browser
Internet	Scroll bar	Work area
Link	Shortcut menu	World Wide Web (Web)
Live Preview		

REVIEW *Questions*

WRITTEN QUESTIONS

Write a brief answer to each of the following questions.

1. List four of the programs that are included in Office 2007.

2. How do you start an Office program?

3. What is the location and the function of the following: title bar, Ribbon, and status bar?

4. What is the difference between the Save and Save As commands?

5. Describe two ways to get help in an Office program.

TRUE/FALSE

Circle T if the statement is true or F if the statement is false.

T   F   **1.** Excel is the spreadsheet program in Office.

T   F   **2.** You must type a file extension if you want to include it in the file name.

T   F   **3.** To save a file with a different name and to a different location, click the Save button on the Quick Access Toolbar.

T   F   **4.** Live Preview lets you see how an option affects your file without making the change.

T   F   **5.** When you point to a button on the Ribbon, a gallery appears that shows the button's name and a description of its function.

PROJECTS

PROJECT 1-1

1. Start Word.

2. Start Excel. Use the Open dialog box to locate the **Employees** folder in the Data Files. Open the **Schedule.xlsx** Data File from the **Perez** folder.

3. Use the Save As command to save the workbook in the **Abbott** folder as **June Work Schedule** followed by your initials.

4. Repeat the process to save the file in the **Brown, Garner, Kamnani, Reid, Tam**, and **Wong** folders.

5. Close the **June Work Schedule** workbook and exit Excel. Word remains on the screen.

6. Use the Open dialog box to open the **Memo.docx** Data File from the **Perez** folder.

7. Save the document in the **Garner** folder with the same name followed by your initials.

8. Close the document, and then exit Word.

PROJECT 1-2

1. Start Word and open the Word Help window.

2. Search for how to minimize the Ribbon, and then open the *Minimize the Ribbon* Help topic.

3. Read the information in the Help topic, and then follow the directions to minimize the Ribbon.

4. Click the Insert tab to display the full Ribbon.

5. In the Pages group, click the Blank Page button. A new page is added to the document, and the Ribbon minimizes again.

6. Follow the directions in the Help topic to restore the Ribbon.

7. Close the Word Help window, and then exit Word. If prompted to save changes, click No.

PROJECT 1-3

1. Open your Web browser.

2. Go to the Microsoft Web site at *www.microsoft.com*.

3. Search for information about at least two Microsoft programs.

4. Return to your home page.

5. Close your Web browser.

CRITICAL *Thinking*

ACTIVITY 1-1

The Office program can include Word, Excel, Access, PowerPoint, Outlook, and Publisher. Describe how you could use each of these Office programs in your personal life. Imagine you are a business owner. Describe how each of these Office programs would help you increase productivity. When you run a business, you need to correspond with clients, vendors, and employees; you need to track income and spending; you need to keep track of items, such as inventory, documents, and so on; and you need to market and advertise your business.

ACTIVITY 1-2

Use the Office Help system to find out more about keyboard shortcuts. If you are connected to the Internet, you can click the Training Keyboard shortcuts in the 2007 Office system. Write a description of the different types of shortcuts. List one advantage of using shortcuts. Then list the three shortcuts you think you would use most frequently.

ACTIVITY 1-3

Start your Web browser. Describe the function of all the buttons you see. Remember to point to each button to see its ScreenTip. Then describe the steps to print a Web page. Use the Help system as needed.

MICROSOFT EXCEL

Unit

Estimated Time for Unit: 16.5 hours

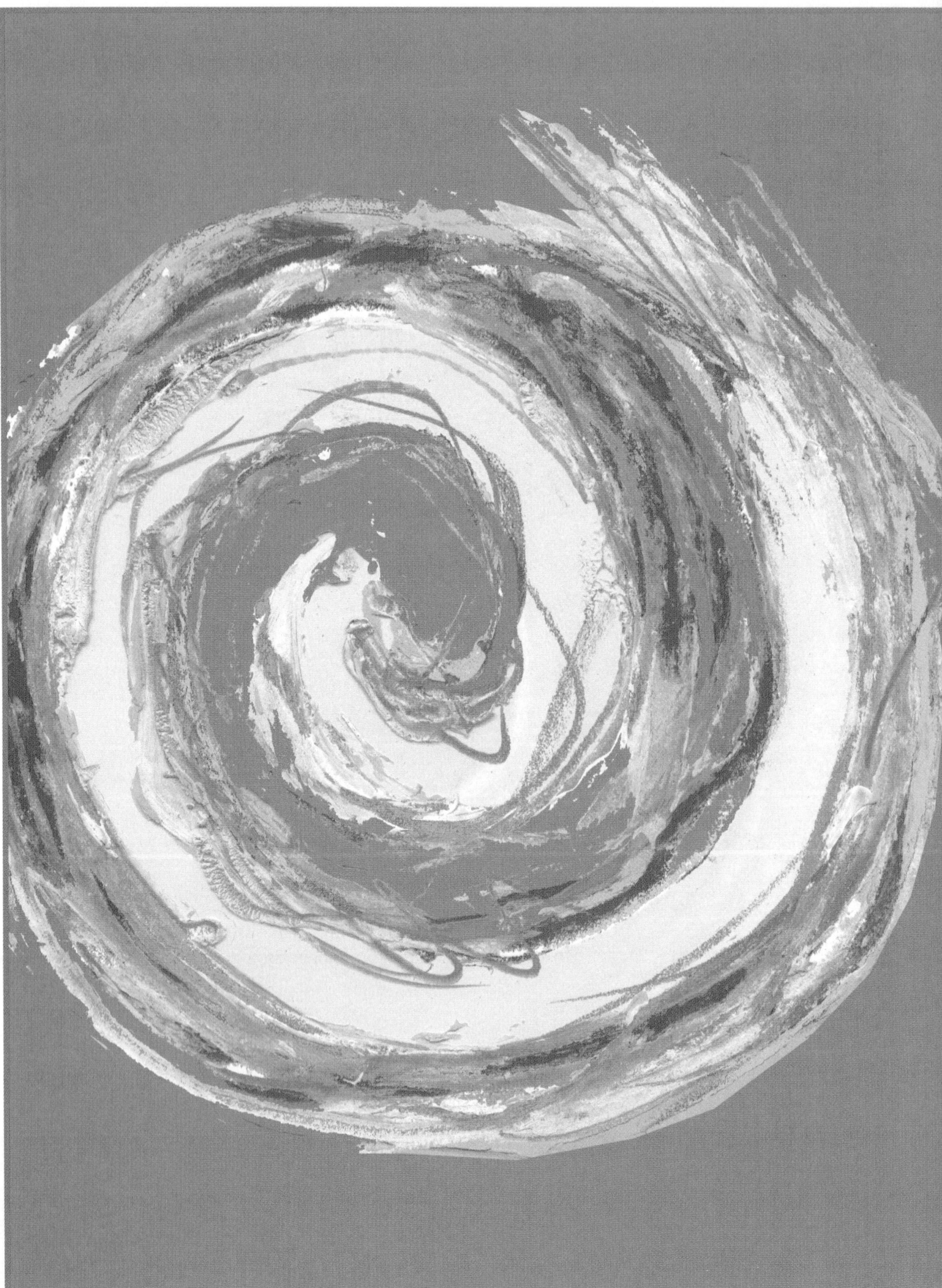

EXCEL BASICS

Introduction to Spreadsheets

Microsoft Office Excel 2007 (or Excel) is the spreadsheet program in Microsoft Office 2007. A spreadsheet is a grid of rows and columns in which you enter text, numbers, and the results of calculations. The purpose of a spreadsheet is to solve problems that involve numbers. Without a computer, you could try to solve these types of problems by creating rows and columns on paper and using a calculator to determine the results (see Figure 1-1). Spreadsheets have many uses. For example, you can use a spreadsheet to calculate grades for students in a class, to prepare a budget for the next few months, or to determine payments for repaying a loan.

FIGURE 1-1
Spreadsheet prepared on paper

Microteers Software Inc.
Salary Expense 2007

Employee	Jan.	Feb.	March	April	May
Ean N.	5156	2254	2050	3518	2285
Gerald R.	2500	2345	2514	245	
Mitch G.	2100	2728	2261	155	
Pamela A.	1425	1544	1297	15	
Rosa E.	1755	1688	1736	1	
Beverly P.	3697	2564	3719	3	
Ira S.	2785	2811	2719		
Total	19418	15934	16301		

Computer spreadsheets also contain rows and columns with text, numbers, and the results of calculations. But, computer spreadsheets perform calculations faster and more accurately than you can do with spreadsheets you create on paper, using a pencil and a calculator. The primary advantage of computer spreadsheets is their ability to complete complex and repetitious calculations quickly and accurately.

Computer spreadsheets are also flexible. Making changes to an existing computer spreadsheet is usually as easy as pointing and clicking with the mouse. Suppose, for example, you use a computer spreadsheet to calculate your budget (your monthly income and expenses) and overestimate the amount of money you need to pay for electricity. You can change a single entry in the computer spreadsheet, and the entire spreadsheet will be recalculated to determine the new budgeted amount. Think about the work this change would require if you were calculating the budget by hand on paper with a pencil and calculator.

In Excel, a computerized spreadsheet is called a worksheet. The file used to store worksheets is called a workbook. Usually, workbooks contain a collection of related worksheets.

Starting Excel

You start Excel from the Start menu in Windows. Click the Start button, click All Programs, click Microsoft Office, and then click Microsoft Office Excel 2007. When Excel starts, the program window displays a blank workbook titled *Book1*, which includes three blank worksheets titled *Sheet1*, *Sheet2*, and *Sheet3*. The Excel program window has the same basic parts as all Office programs: the title bar, the Quick Access Toolbar, the Office Button, the Ribbon, and the status bar. However, as shown in Figure 1-2, Excel also has additional buttons and parts.

FIGURE 1-2
Excel program window

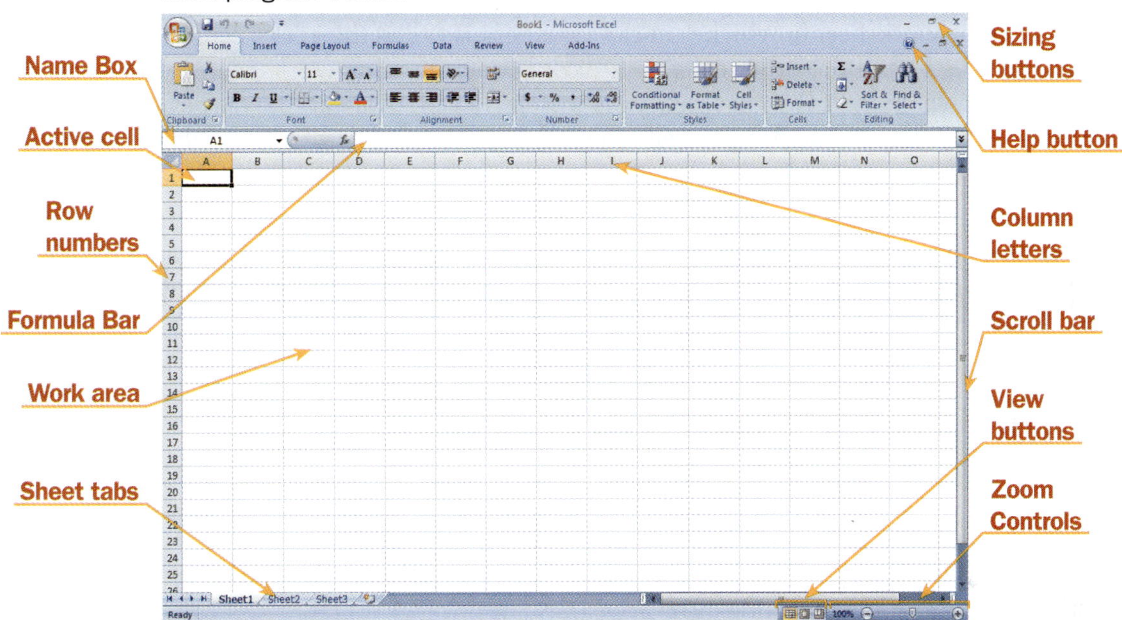

STEP-BY-STEP 1.1

1. With Windows running, click the **Start** button, click **All Programs**, click **Microsoft Office**, and then click **Microsoft Office Excel 2007**. Excel starts and a blank workbook titled *Book1* appears, as shown in Figure 1-2.

2. If the Excel program window does not fill your screen, click the **Maximize** button in the title bar. 

3. Leave the workbook open for the next Step-by-Step.

Exploring the Parts of the Worksheet

Each new workbook contains three worksheets by default. The name of each worksheet appears in the **sheet tab** at the bottom of the worksheet window. **Columns** of the worksheet appear vertically and are identified by letters at the top of the worksheet window. **Rows** appear horizontally and are identified by numbers on the left side of the worksheet window. A **cell** is the intersection of a row and a column. Each cell is identified by a unique **cell reference**, which is formed by combining the cell's column letter and row number. For example, the cell that intersects at column C and row 4 has the cell reference C4.

The pointer becomes a thick white plus sign when it is in the worksheet. If you move the pointer up to the Ribbon, the pointer changes to a white arrow.

The cell in the worksheet in which you can type data is called the **active cell**. The active cell is distinguished from the other cells by a dark border. In your worksheet, cell A1 has the dark border, which indicates that cell A1 is the active cell. You can move the active cell from one cell to another. The **Name Box**, or cell reference area located below the Ribbon, displays the cell reference of the active cell.

The **Formula Bar** appears to the right of the Name Box and displays a formula when the cell of a worksheet contains a calculated value (or the results of the formula). A **formula** is an equation that calculates a new value from values currently in a worksheet, such as adding the numbers in cell A1 and A2.

Opening an Existing Workbook

Opening a workbook means loading an existing workbook file from a disk into the  program window. You can open a workbook stored on any available disk or folder. To open an existing workbook, you click the Office Button to display the Office menu, and then click Open. The Open dialog box appears. The Open dialog box shows all the workbooks in the displayed folder that were created with Excel.

You need to display the location where the workbook you want to open is stored. In the Open dialog box, use the Address bar, Navigation pane, and Folders list to display the drive and folder containing the workbook you want to open. After you have located the file you want to open, double-click the file. When you start Excel, the program displays a new workbook titled *Book1*. This blank workbook disappears when you open another workbook.

Did You Know?

You can quickly open one of the most recent workbooks you have worked on. Click the Office Button. The right side of the Office menu contains the Recent Documents list. Just click the file name of the workbook you want to open. The selected workbook opens in Excel.

STEP-BY-STEP 1.2

1. Click the **Office Button**, and then click **Open**. The Open dialog box appears.

2. Use the Address bar, Navigation pane, and Folders list to display the location of the Data Files for this lesson.

3. Open the **Frogs.xlsx** Data File. Depending on how Windows is set up on your computer, you might not see the file extension after the file name; in that case, open **Frogs**. The workbook appears in the program window, as shown in Figure 1-3.

FIGURE 1-3
Open workbook

Current workbook name (you may not see the file extension)

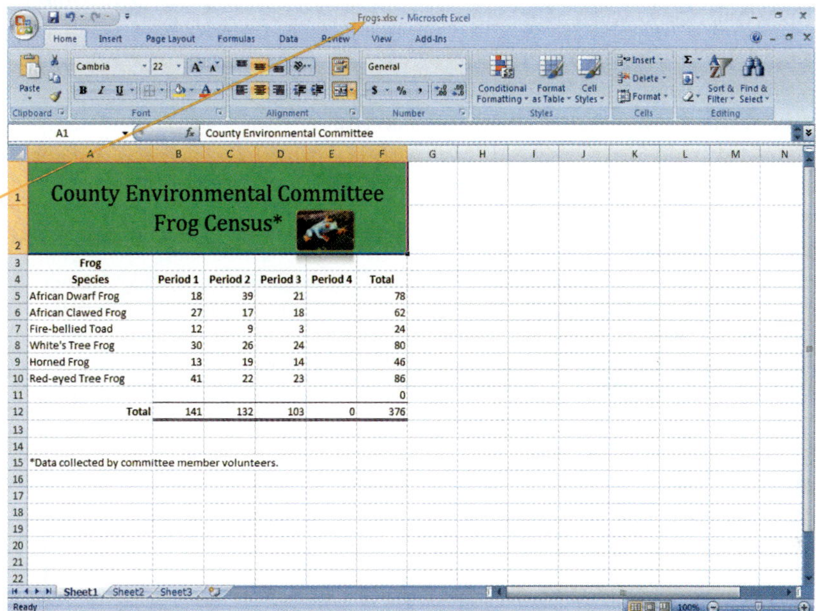

4. Leave the workbook open for the next Step-by-Step.

Saving a Workbook

Saving is done two ways. The Save command saves an existing workbook on a disk, using its current name and save location. The Save As command lets you save a workbook with a new name or to a new location.

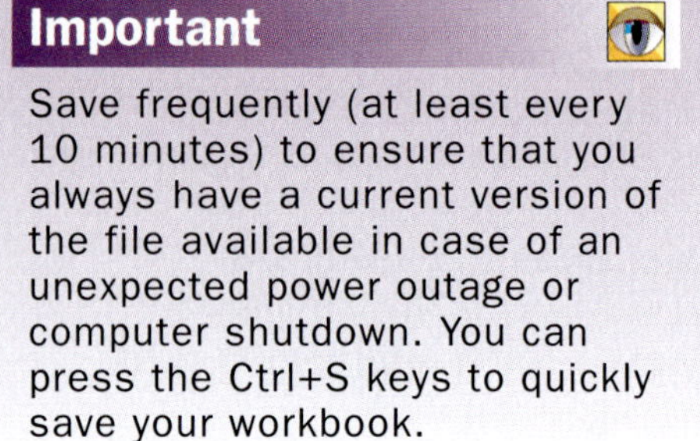

The first time you save a new workbook, the Save As dialog box appears, as shown in Figure 1-4, so you can give the workbook a descriptive name and choose a save location. After you have saved the workbook, you can use the Save command on the Office menu or the Save button on the Quick Access Toolbar to periodically save the latest version of the workbook with the same name in the same location. To save a copy of the workbook with a new name or save location, you need to use the Save As dialog box. You'll use this method to save the Data File you opened with a new name, leaving the original workbook intact.

> **Important**
>
> Save frequently (at least every 10 minutes) to ensure that you always have a current version of the file available in case of an unexpected power outage or computer shutdown. You can press the Ctrl+S keys to quickly save your workbook.

FIGURE 1-4
Save As dialog box

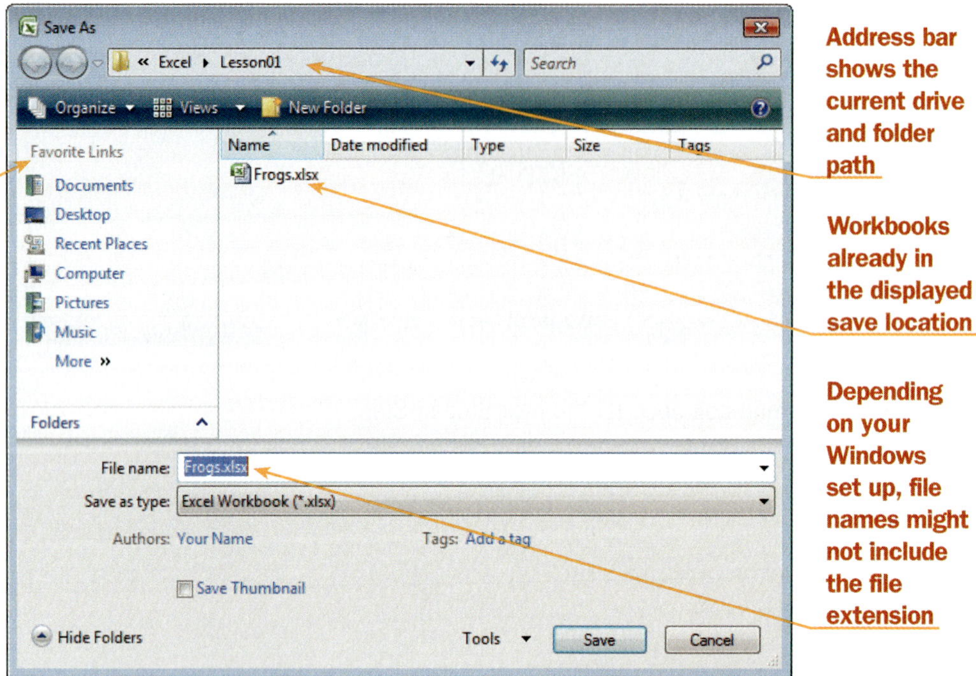

Use the Navigation pane to change the current save location

Address bar shows the current drive and folder path

Workbooks already in the displayed save location

Depending on your Windows set up, file names might not include the file extension

> **Did You Know?**
>
> You can create a new folder in which to save a file by clicking the New Folder button in the Save As dialog box. Type a name for the new folder, and then press the Enter key.

S TEP-BY-STEP 1.3

1. Click the **Office Button**, and then click **Save As**. The Save As dialog box appears.

2. Change the save location to the drive and folder where you store the Data Files for this lesson.

3. In the File name box, type **Frog Census** followed by your initials.

4. Click **Save**.

5. Leave the workbook open for the next Step-by-Step.

Moving the Active Cell in a Worksheet

The easiest way to change the active cell in a worksheet is to move the pointer to the cell you want to make active and click. The dark border surrounds the cell you clicked, and the Name Box shows its cell reference. When working with a large worksheet, you might not be able to see the entire worksheet in the program window. You can display different parts of the worksheet by using the mouse to drag the scroll box in the scroll bar to another position. You can also move the active cell to different parts of the worksheet using the keyboard or the Go To command.

> **Did You Know?**
>
> The column letter and row number of the active cell are shaded in orange for easy identification.

Using the Keyboard to Change the Active Cell

You can change the active cell by pressing the keys or keyboard shortcuts shown in Table 1-1. When you press an arrow key, the active cell moves one cell in that direction. When you press and hold down an arrow key, the active cell shifts in that direction repeatedly and quickly.

TABLE 1-1
Keys for moving the active cell in a worksheet

TO MOVE	PRESS
Left one column	Left arrow key
Right one column	Right arrow key
Up one row	Up arrow key
Down one row	Down arrow key
To the first cell of a row	Home key
To cell A1	Ctrl+Home keys
To the last cell of the column and row that contain data	Ctrl+End keys
Up one window	Page Up key
Down one window	Page Down key

Using the Go To Command to Move the Active Cell

You might want to change the active cell to a cell in a part of the worksheet that you cannot see in the work area. The fastest way to move to that cell is with the Go To dialog box. On the Home tab of the Ribbon, in the Editing group, click the Find & Select button, and then click Go To. The Go To dialog box appears, as shown in Figure 1-5. Type the cell reference in the Reference box, and then click OK. The cell you specified becomes the active cell.

FIGURE 1-5
Go To dialog box

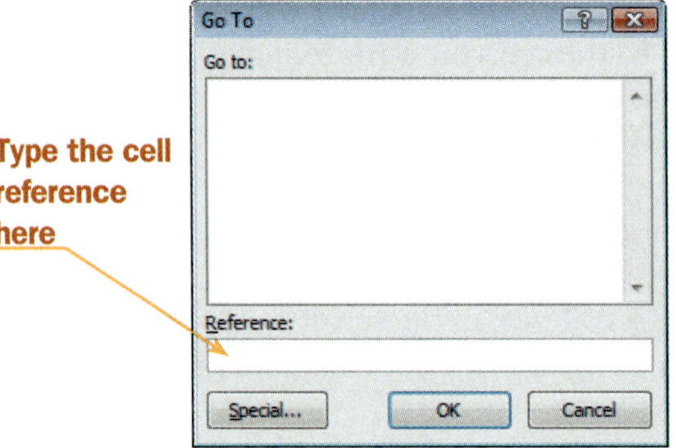

S TEP-BY-STEP 1.4

1. Press the **Ctrl+End** keys. The active cell moves from cell A1 to cell F15, which is the cell that intersects the last column and row that contain data in the worksheet.

2. Press the **Home** key. The active cell moves to the first cell of row 15—cell A15, which contains the words *Data collected by committee member volunteers.*

3. Press the **Up arrow** key six times to move the active cell up six rows. The active cell is cell A9, which contains the words *Horned Frog.*

4. On the Ribbon, click the **Home** tab, if the tab is not already active.

5. In the Editing group, click the **Find & Select** button to open a menu of commands, and then click **Go To**. The Go To dialog box appears, as shown in Figure 1-5. 

STEP-BY-STEP 1.4 Continued

6. In the Reference box, type **B4**.

7. Click **OK**. The active cell moves to cell B4.

8. On the Quick Access Toolbar, click the **Save** button to save the workbook. 

9. Leave the workbook open for the next Step-by-Step.

Selecting a Group of Cells

Often, you will perform operations on more than one cell at a time. A group of selected cells is called a range. In an adjacent range, all cells touch each other and form a rectangle. The range is identified by its range reference, which is the cell in its upper-left corner and the cell in its lower-right corner, separated by a colon (for example, A3:C5). To select an adjacent range, click the cell in one corner of the range, drag the pointer to the cell in the opposite corner of the range, and then release the mouse button. As you drag, the range of selected cells becomes shaded (except for the first cell you selected), and the dark border expands to surround all the selected cells. In addition, the column letters and row numbers of the range you select change to orange. The active cell in a range is white; the other cells are shaded.

You can also select a range that is non-adjacent. A non-adjacent range includes two or more adjacent ranges and selected cells. The range reference for a non-adjacent range separates each range or cell with a semi-colon (for example, A3:C5;E3:G5). To select a non-adjacent range, select the first adjacent range or cell, press the Ctrl key as you select the other cells or ranges you want to include, and then release the Ctrl key and the mouse button.

> **Teamwork**
>
> Have a classmate call out cell references so you can practice moving the active cell in a worksheet using the methods you have learned.

STEP-BY-STEP 1.5

1. Click cell **B4**.

2. Press and hold the left mouse button as you drag the pointer to the right until cell **F4** is selected.

STEP-BY-STEP 1.5 Continued

3. Release the mouse button. The range B4:F4 is selected, as you can see from the shaded cells and the dark border. Also, the column letters B through F and the row number 4 are orange. See Figure 1-6.

FIGURE 1-6
Selected range

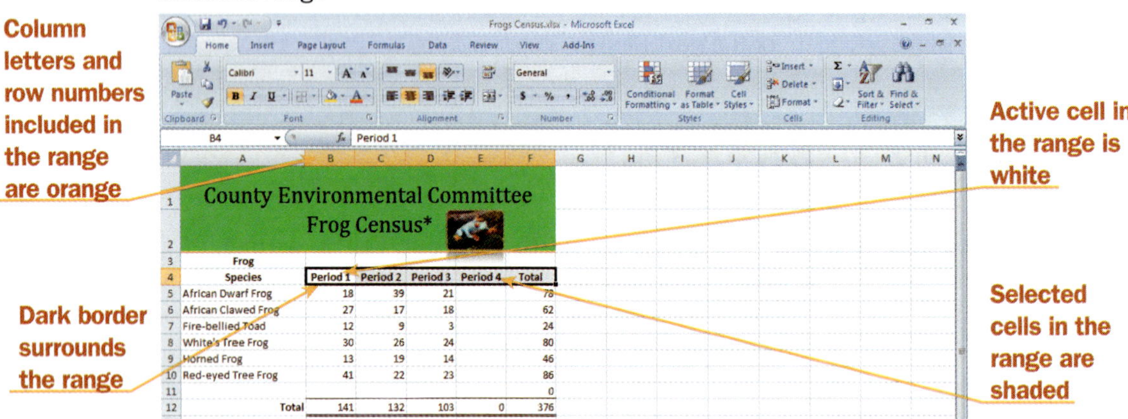

4. Click cell **B5**.

5. Press and hold the left mouse button as you drag down and to the right until cell **F12** is selected.

6. Release the mouse button. The range B5:F12 is selected.

7. Leave the workbook open for the next Step-by-Step.

Entering Data in a Cell

Worksheet cells can contain text, numbers, or formulas. Text is any combination of letters and numbers and symbols, such as headings, labels, or explanatory notes. Numbers are values, dates, or times. Formulas are equations that calculate a value.

You enter data in the active cell. First, type the text, numbers, or formula in the active cell. Then, click the Enter button on the Formula Bar or press the Enter or Tab key on the keyboard. The data you typed is entered in the cell. If you decide not to enter the data you typed, you can click the Cancel button on the Formula Bar or press the Esc key to delete the data without making any changes to the cell.

If you have already entered the data in the cell, you can undo, or reverse, the entry. On the

Did You Know?

If a cell is not long enough to display all the cell's contents, extra text extends into the next cells, if they are blank. If not, only the characters that fit in the cell appear, and the rest are hidden from view, but they are still stored. Numbers that extend beyond a cell's width appear as #### in the cell.

Did You Know?

After you type data in a cell, the active cell changes, depending on how you enter the data. If you click the Enter button on the Formula Bar, the cell you typed in remains active. If you press the Enter key, the cell below the cell you typed in becomes active. If you press the Tab key, the cell to the right of the cell you typed in becomes active.

Quick Access Toolbar, click the Undo button to reverse your most recent change. To undo multiple actions, click the arrow next to the Undo button. A list of your previous actions appears, and you can choose how many actions you want to undo. 

S TEP-BY-STEP 1.6

1. Click cell **E5** to make it active.

2. Type **15**. As you type, the numbers appear in the cell and in the Formula Bar.

3. Press the **Enter** key. The number is entered in cell E5, and the active cell moves to cell E6. The totals in cells F5, E12, and F12 change as you enter the data.

4. Type **22**.

5. On the Formula Bar, click the **Enter** button. The totals in cells F6, E12, and F12 change as you enter the data. 

6. On the Quick Access Toolbar, next to the Undo button, click the **arrow**. A menu appears listing the actions you have just performed. 

7. Click **Typing '22' in E6**, as shown in Figure 1-7. The data is removed from cell E6, and the data in cells F6, E12, and F12 return to their previous totals.

FIGURE 1-7
Undo menu

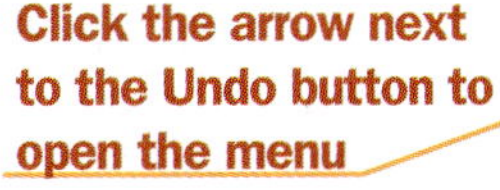
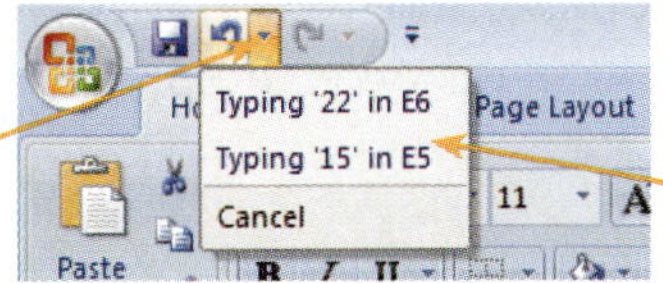

8. Click cell **A11**, and then enter **Pac Frog**. The Pac Frog species is added to the Frog Census.

> **Important**
>
> The instruction to click a cell and then enter data means you should click the specified cell, type the data indicated, and then enter that data in the cell by pressing the Enter key, pressing the Tab key, or clicking the Enter button on the Formula Bar.

STEP-BY-STEP 1.6 Continued

9. In the range **E6:E11**, enter the data, as shown in Figure 1-8, to include the number of frogs sighted for each species in Period 4.

FIGURE 1-8
Data entered in the Frog Census

Frog Species	Period 1	Period 2	Period 3	Period 4	Total
African Dwarf Frog	18	39	21	15	93
African Clawed Frog	27	17	18	20	82
Fire-bellied Toad	12	9	3	8	32
White's Tree Frog	30	26	24	29	109
Horned Frog	13	19	14	12	58
Red-eyed Tree Frog	41	22	23	6	92
Pac Frog				3	3
Total	141	132	103	93	466

10. Save the workbook, and leave it open for the next Step-by-Step.

Changing Data in a Cell

After you enter data in cells in the worksheet, you might change your mind or discover a mistake. If so, you can edit, replace, or clear the data.

Editing Data

When you need to make a minor change to data in a cell, you can edit it in the Formula Bar or in the cell. The contents of the active cell always appear in the Formula Bar. To edit the data in the Formula Bar, click in the Formula Bar and then drag to select the text you want to edit. You can also use the arrow keys to position the insertion point. Then, press the Backspace or Delete key to remove data, or type the new data. To edit the data directly in a cell, make the cell active and then press the F2 key or double-click the cell. A blinking insertion point appears in the cell, and you can make changes to the data. When you are done, click the Enter button in the Formula Bar or press the Enter or Tab key.

Replacing Data

When you need to make significant changes to cell data, you can replace the entire cell contents. To replace cell contents, select the cell, type the new data, and then enter the data by clicking the Enter button on the Formula Bar or by pressing the Enter or Tab key. This is the same method used to enter data in a blank cell. The only difference is that you overwrite the existing cell contents.

Clearing Data

Clearing a cell removes all the data in the cell. To clear the active cell, you can use the Ribbon, the keyboard, or the mouse. On the Ribbon, on the Home tab, in the Editing group, click the Clear button to display a menu with options to clear the cell's format, contents, comments, or all of these. To use the keyboard, press the Delete or Backspace key. To use your mouse, right-click the active cell and then click Clear Contents on the shortcut menu.

S TEP-BY-STEP 1.7

1. Click cell **A11** to make it the active cell.

2. Press the **F2** key. A blinking insertion point appears in cell A11.

3. Press the **left arrow** key five times to move the insertion point after *Pac*.

4. Type **Man**, and then press the **Enter** key. The contents of cell A11 are edited to *PacMan Frog*.

5. Click cell **D10**, and then type **18**.

6. On the Formula Bar, click the **Enter** button. The number 18 is entered in cell D10, replacing the previous contents.

7. Click cell **A3**, and then press the **Delete** key. The contents are cleared from cell A3. Your screen should look similar to Figure 1-9.

8. Save the workbook, and leave it open for the next Step-by-Step.

FIGURE 1-9
Data in cells changed and cleared

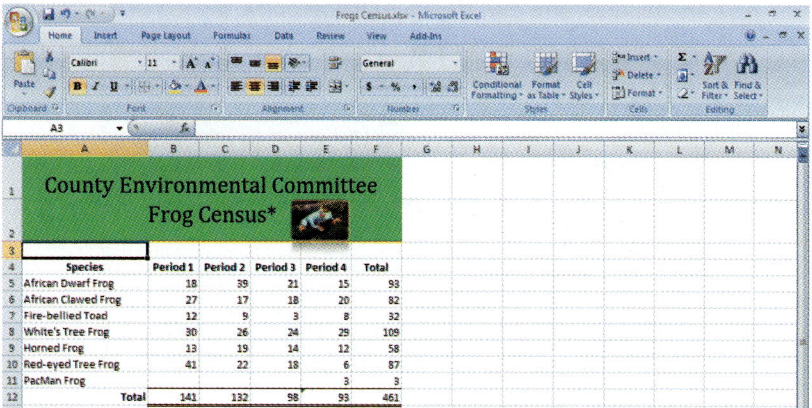

Searching for Data

The Find and Replace dialog box enables you to locate specific words or numbers in a worksheet. If you like, you can then change data you find.

Finding Data

The Find command locates data in a worksheet, which is particularly helpful when a worksheet contains a large amount of data. You can use Find to locate words or parts of words. For example, searching for *emp* finds the words *employee* and *temporary*. Likewise, searching for *85* finds the numbers *85*, *850*, and *385*. On the Home tab of the Ribbon, in the Editing group, click the Find & Select button, and then click Find. The Find and Replace dialog box appears, with the Find tab active. 

> 
> **Did You Know?**
>
> You can use wildcard characters in the Find what box to search for data that matches a particular pattern. Use ? (a question mark) for a single character. Use * (an asterisk) for two or more characters. For example, Br?an finds Brian and Bryan, whereas Sam* finds Samuel, Samantha, Sammy, and Sammi.

Replacing Data

The Replace command is an extension of the Find command. Replacing data substitutes new data for the data found. In the Editing group on the Home tab of the Ribbon, click the Find & Select button, and then click Replace. The Find and Replace dialog box appears, with the Replace tab active. If the Find and Replace dialog box is already open, click the Replace tab in the dialog box.

You can perform more specific searches by clicking the Options button in the dialog box. Figure 1-10 shows the Replace tab in the expanded Find and Replace dialog box. Table 1-2 lists the options you can specify in the Find and Replace dialog box.

FIGURE 1-10
Expanded Find and Replace dialog box

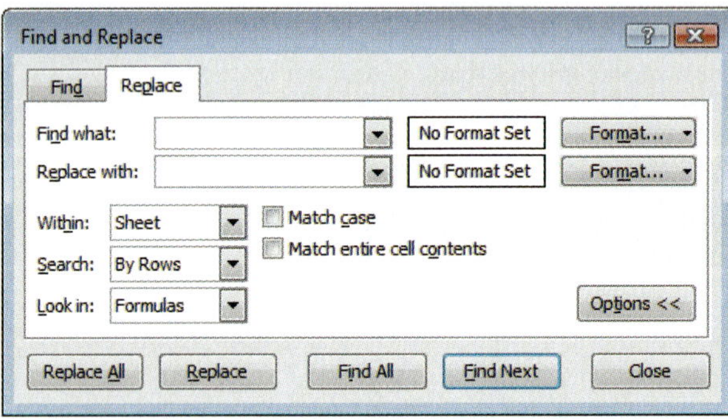

TABLE 1-2
Find and Replace options

SEARCH OPTION	SPECIFIES
Find what	The data to locate
Replace with	The data to insert in place of the located data
Format	The format of the data you want to find or replace
Within	Whether to search the worksheet or the entire workbook
Search	The direction to search: across rows or down columns
Look in	Whether to search cell contents (values) or formulas
Match case	Whether the search must match the capitalization you used for the find or search data
Match entire cell contents	Whether the search should locate cells whose contents exactly match the find data

STEP-BY-STEP 1.8

1. Click cell **A1**.

2. On the Home tab of the Ribbon, locate the **Editing** group.

3. Click the **Find & Select** button, and then click **Find**. 

4. In the Find what box, type **Period**.

5. Click **Find Next**. The active cell moves to cell B4, the first cell with the search data.

6. In the Find and Replace dialog box, click the **Replace** tab. A Replace with box appears.

7. In the Replace with box, type **Month**.

8. Click **Replace**. The word *Period* is replaced by *Month* in cell B4, and the active cell moves to cell C4, which is the next cell that contains the search data.

9. Click **Replace All**. A dialog box appears, indicating that Excel has completed the search and made three additional replacements of the word *Period* with the word *Month*.

10. Click **OK**.

11. In the Find and Replace dialog box, click **Close**.

12. Save the workbook, and leave it open for the next Step-by-Step.

Zooming Worksheets

You can magnify or reduce the view of a worksheet with the Zoom controls on the status bar. The default magnification for the workbooks is 100%, which you can see in the Zoom level button. For a closer view of a worksheet, click the Zoom In button or drag the Zoom slider to the right to increase the zoom percentage. The entire worksheet looks larger, and you see fewer cells in the work area. If you want to see more cells in the work area, click the Zoom Out button or drag the Zoom slider to the left to decrease the zoom percentage. The entire worksheet looks smaller. To select a specific magnification, click the Zoom level button to open the Zoom dialog box, type the zoom percentage you want in the Custom box, and then click OK. Figure 1-11 shows the Zoom dialog box and the zoom controls.

FIGURE 1-11
Zoom dialog box and controls

STEP-BY-STEP 1.9

1. On the status bar, click the **Zoom In** button three times. The worksheet zooms to 130%, and you see a close-up view of fewer cells.

2. On the status bar, drag the **Zoom slider** right to approximately 200%. The view of the worksheet is magnified even more.

3. On the status bar, click the **Zoom level** button. The Zoom dialog box appears, as shown in Figure 1-11.

4. Click **50%**, and then click **OK**. The view of the worksheet is reduced to half of its default size, and you see a long-distance view of more cells.

5. On the status bar, click the **Zoom In** button five times. The worksheet returns to its original zoom level of 100%.

> **Did You Know?**
>
> Zoom controls are also available on the Ribbon. On the View tab, in the Zoom group, click the Zoom button to open the Zoom dialog box. Click the 100% button to zoom the worksheet to 100% magnification. Click the Zoom to Selection button to zoom the worksheet so the selected range fills the worksheet window.

STEP-BY-STEP 1.9 Continued

6. Click cell **A16**, and then enter your name.

7. Save the workbook, and leave it open for the next Step-by-Step.

Previewing and Printing a Worksheet

Sometimes you need a printed copy of a worksheet to give to another person or for your own files. You can print a worksheet by clicking the Office Button, and then clicking Print to open the Print dialog box (see Figure 1-12). The Print dialog box enables you to select a printer, the number of copies to print, the parts of the worksheet to print, and the way the printed worksheet will look. For now, you will print the entire worksheet using the default settings.

Did You Know?

You can print a worksheet without opening the Print dialog box. Click the Office Button, point to Print, and then click Quick Print. The workbook is printed using the default settings in the Print dialog box. Use this method only if you have previously verified that the default printer and settings are the ones you want to use.

FIGURE 1-12
Print dialog box

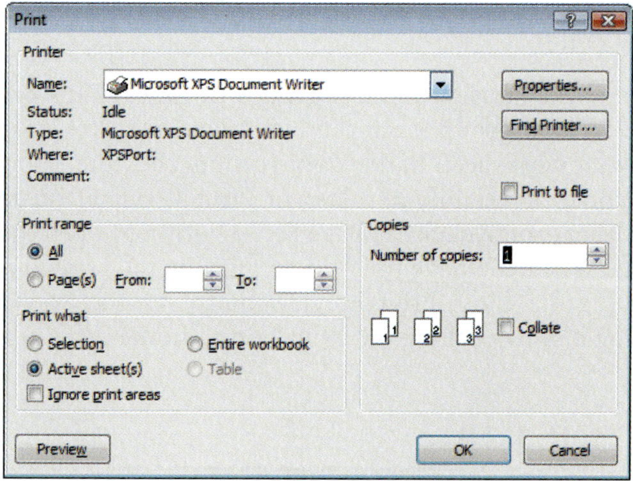

Before you use the resources to print a worksheet, you should use Print Preview to see how the printed pages will look. To switch to Print Preview (see Figure 1-13), click Preview in the Print dialog box. You can also click the Office Button, point to Print to open a menu with options to preview and print the document, and then click Print Preview.

FIGURE 1-13
Worksheet in Print Preview

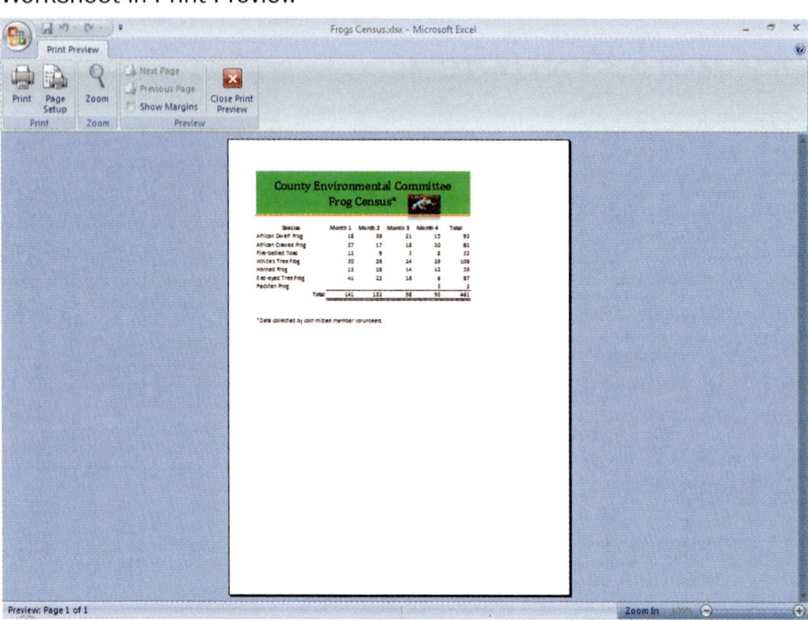

On the Ribbon, the Print Preview tab has groups of buttons for printing, zooming, and previewing. In the Preview group, click the Next Page and Previous Page buttons to display other pages of your worksheet. In the Zoom group, click the Zoom button or click the pointer (which becomes a magnifying glass in Print Preview) on the page to magnify or reduce the view. In the Print group, click the Page Setup button to open the Page Setup dialog box and select other options. When you have finished previewing the printed pages, you can return to the worksheet by clicking the Close Print Preview button in the Preview group. Or, you can return to the Print dialog box by clicking the Print button in the Print group.

S TEP-BY-STEP 1.10

1. Click the **Office Button**, and then click **Print**. The Print dialog box appears, as shown in Figure 1-12. 

2. Click **Preview**. The worksheet appears in Print Preview, as shown in Figure 1-13.

3. Move the pointer over the page in Print Preview, and then click. The previewed page becomes larger so you can examine it in more detail.

4. On the Print Preview tab of the Ribbon, locate the **Print** group. Click the **Print** button. The active worksheet is printed. 

5. Leave the workbook open for the next Step-by-Step.

Closing a Workbook

You can close a workbook by clicking the Office Button to display the Office menu and clicking Close. If you use the Close command on the Office menu to close a workbook, Excel remains open and ready for you to open or create another workbook.

If you try to close a workbook that contains changes you haven't saved, a dialog box opens, asking whether you want to save the file. Click Yes to save and close the workbook. Click No to close the workbook without saving. Click Cancel to return to the Excel program window without saving or closing the workbook.

> **Did You Know?** 
>
> You can also close the workbook and leave Excel open by clicking the Close Window button located below the sizing buttons in the title bar. To close the workbook and exit Excel, you can click the Close button in the title bar.

STEP-BY-STEP 1.11

1. Click the **Office Button**, and then click **Close**.

2. If you are asked to save changes, click **Yes**. The workbook closes.

SUMMARY

In this lesson, you learned:

- The purpose of a spreadsheet is to solve problems involving numbers. The advantage of using a computer spreadsheet is that you can complete complex and repetitious calculations quickly and accurately.

- A worksheet consists of columns and rows that intersect to form cells. Each cell is identified by a cell reference, which combines the letter of the column and the number of the row.

- The first time you save a workbook, the Save As dialog box opens so you can enter a descriptive name and select a save location. After that, you can use the Save command on the Office menu or the Save button on the Quick Access Toolbar to periodically save the latest version of the workbook.

- You can change the active cell in the worksheet by clicking the cell with the pointer, pressing keys, or using the scroll bars. The Go To dialog box lets you quickly move the active cell anywhere in the worksheet.

- A group of selected cells is called a range. A range is identified by the cells in the upper-left and lower-right corners of the range, separated by a colon. To select an adjacent range, drag the pointer across the rectangle of cells you want to include. To select a nonadjacent range, select the first adjacent range, hold down the Ctrl key, select each additional cell or range, and then release the Ctrl key.

- Worksheet cells can contain text, numbers, and formulas. After you enter data or a formula in a cell, you can change the cell contents by editing, replacing, or deleting it.

- You can search for specific characters in a worksheet. You can also replace data you have searched for with specific characters.

- Zoom enables you to enlarge or reduce the view of the worksheet in the worksheet window.

- You can print a worksheet to create a hard copy. Before you print, you should use Print Preview to see how the printed pages will look.

- When you finish your work session, you should save your final changes and close the workbook.

VOCABULARY *Review*

Define the following terms:

Active cell	Formula Bar	Row
Active worksheet	Microsoft Office Excel 2007	Sheet tab
Cell	(Excel)	Spreadsheet
Cell reference	Name Box	Workbook
Column	Range	Worksheet
Formula	Range reference	

REVIEW *Questions*

TRUE/FALSE

Circle T if the statement is true or F if the statement is false.

T   F   **1.** The primary advantage of the worksheet is the ability to solve numerical problems quickly and accurately.

T   F   **2.** A range is the intersection of a row and a column.

T   F   **3.** You use the Go To command to preview a worksheet before you print it.

T   F   **4.** You can use the Replace command to substitute *Week* for all instances of *Period* in a worksheet.

T   F   **5.** Each time you save a worksheet, you must open the Save As dialog box.

WRITTEN QUESTIONS

Write a brief answer to the following questions.

1. What term describes a cell that is ready for data entry?

2. How are columns identified in a worksheet?

3. What term describes a group of cells?

4. What key(s) do you press to move the active cell to the first cell of the row?

5. If you decide not to enter data you just typed in the active cell, how do you delete the data without making any changes to the cell?

PROJECTS

PROJECT 1-1

In the blank space, write the letter of the key or keys from Column 2 that correspond to the movement of the active cell in Column 1.

Column 1	Column 2
___ 1. Left one column	A. Ctrl+Home keys
___ 2. Right one column	B. Page Up key
___ 3. Up one row	C. Left arrow key
___ 4. Down one row	D. Home key
___ 5. To the first cell of a row	E. Down arrow key
___ 6. To cell A1	F. Right arrow key
___ 7. To the last cell containing data	G. Ctrl+End keys
___ 8. Up one window	H. Up arrow key
___ 9. Down one window	I. Page Down key

PROJECT 1-2

1. Open the **Homes.xlsx** Data File.

2. Save the workbook as **Homeownership** followed by your initials.

3. In cell A15, enter **Colorado**.

4. In cell B15, enter **67.3**.

5. In cell C15, enter **62.2**.

6. In cell A16, edit the data to **Connecticut**.

7. In cell B16, edit the data to **66.8**.

8. In cell A5, delete the data.

9. In cell H1, enter your name.

10. Save, preview, print, and then close the workbook.

PROJECT 1-3

1. Open the **Neighborhood.xlsx** Data File.

2. Save the workbook as **Neighborhood Estimates** followed by your initials.

3. Enter the square footages in the following cells to estimate the home costs. The estimated home cost in each neighborhood will change as you enter the data.

Cell	Enter
C6	1250
C7	1500
C8	2200
C9	1500

4. After selling several houses in the Lake Side neighborhood, Neighborhood Properties has determined that the cost per square foot is $71, rather than $68.75. Edit cell B7 to **$71**.

5. In cell B1, enter your name.

6. Save, preview, print, and then close the workbook.

PROJECT 1-4

1. Open the **Names.xlsx** Data File.

2. Save the workbook as **Last Names** followed by your initials.

3. Use the Find command to locate the name *CHAVEZ*. The active cell should be cell A199.

4. Click in the worksheet outside the dialog box, and then press the Ctrl+Home keys to return to cell A1.

5. Click in the Find and Replace dialog box, and then locate the name *YORK*. The active cell should be cell A618. (*Hint*: The Find and Replace dialog box remains on-screen from Steps 3 and 4. You can simply enter the new search in the Find what box.)

6. Click in the worksheet, and then press the Ctrl+Home keys to return to cell A1.

7. Click in the Find and Replace dialog box, click the Replace tab, and then replace the name *FORBES* with **FABERGE**. The active cell should be cell A988.

8. Undo the last change you made to the workbook.

9. Save and close the workbook.

Extra Challenge

Try to find your last name, or the last names of three of your friends, in the LastNames.xlxs workbook you just worked on.

CRITICAL *Thinking*

 ACTIVITY 1-1

The purpose of a spreadsheet is to solve problems that involve numbers. Identify two numerical problems in each of the following categories that might be solved by using a spreadsheet.

1. Business

2. Career

3. Personal

4. School

 ACTIVITY 1-2

You have selected a large range of adjacent cells that extends over several screens. You realize that you incorrectly included one additional column of cells in the range.

To reselect the range of cells, you must page up to the active cell (the first cell of the range) and drag through several screens to the last cell in the range. Is there a better way to remove the column from the range, without having to reselect the entire range? Also, is there a faster way to select such a large range—one that doesn't include dragging through several screens?

Click the Microsoft Office Excel Help button to open the Excel Help window. Research how to select fewer cells without canceling your original selection. Then research how to select a large range without dragging. In your word processor, write a brief explanation of the steps you would take to change the selected range and to select a large range without dragging. (*Hint*: The answer appears in the topic "Select cells and their contents on a worksheet.")

Changing the Appearance of a Worksheet

Changing the Size of a Cell

Worksheets are most valuable when the information they present is simple for the user to understand. Data in a worksheet must be accurate, but it is also important that the data be presented in a way that is visually appealing.

Changing Column Width

Sometimes the data you enter in a cell does not fit in the column. When you enter information that is wider than the column, one of the following happens:

- Text that fits in the cell is displayed. The rest is stored but hidden if the next cell contains data.

- Text that does not fit in the cell extends into the next cell, if that cell is empty.

- Numbers are converted to a different numerical form (for example, long numbers change to exponential form).

- Numbers that do not fit in the cell are shown as a series of number signs (######).

You can resize the column to fit a certain number of characters. Place the pointer on the right edge of the **column heading** (the column letter) until the pointer changes to a double-headed arrow. Click and drag to the right until the column expands to the width you want. Drag to the left to make the column width smaller. As you drag, a ScreenTip appears near the pointer, displaying the new column width measurement.

If you want to specify a precise column width, use the Column Width dialog box shown in Figure 2-1. To access the dialog box, click any cell in the column you want to change. On the Home tab of the Ribbon, in the Cells group, click the Format button, and then click Column Width. In the Column width box, type the width you want, and then click OK. The column resizes to fit the number of characters you specified.

> **Did You Know?**
>
> You can also open the Column Width dialog box with the mouse. Right-click the column heading of the column you want to resize, and then click Column Width on the shortcut menu.

FIGURE 2-1
Column Width dialog box

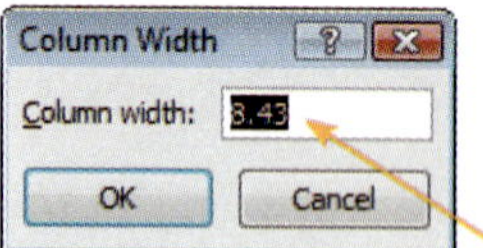

Changing Row Height

The process for changing row height is similar. Place the pointer below the **row heading** (the row number) until the pointer changes to a double-headed arrow. Click and drag down until the row has the number of lines you want. You can also use the Row Height dialog box to specify an exact row height. Click a cell in the row you want to resize. In the Cells group on the Home tab of the Ribbon, click the Format button, and then click Row Height to open the Row Height dialog box. In the Row height box, type the height you want, and then click OK.

Using AutoFit to Change Column Width or Row Height

Columns often contain data of varying widths. To make the worksheet easier to read, a column should be wide enough to display the longest entry, but no wider

> **Did You Know?**
>
> You can change the width of several columns at one time. Select the columns you want to resize. Then, use the pointer to click and drag the right edge of one of the selected column headings. You can use the same process to change the height of several rows. Select the rows you want to resize. Then, use the pointer to click and drag the bottom edge of one of the selected row headings.

than necessary. **AutoFit** determines the best width for a column or the best height for a row, based on its contents. Place the pointer on the right edge of the column heading (or below the row heading) until the pointer changes to a double-headed arrow. Then, double-click to resize the column or row to the best fit.

S TEP-BY-STEP 2.1

1. Open the **Budget.xlsx** Data File.

2. Save the workbook as **Nigel Budget** followed by your initials. Notice that the text in some cells extends into the empty cells in the next column; for example, the month name in cell D3 extends into column E. Some text is hidden because the adjacent cell contains data, such as the month name in cell C3.

3. Place the pointer on the right edge of the column D heading. The pointer changes to a double-headed arrow.

4. Click and drag to the right until the ScreenTip reads *Width: 10.00 (75 pixels)*, as shown in Figure 2-2. Release the mouse button. The entire word *December* now fits within column D.

FIGURE 2-2
Column width ScreenTip

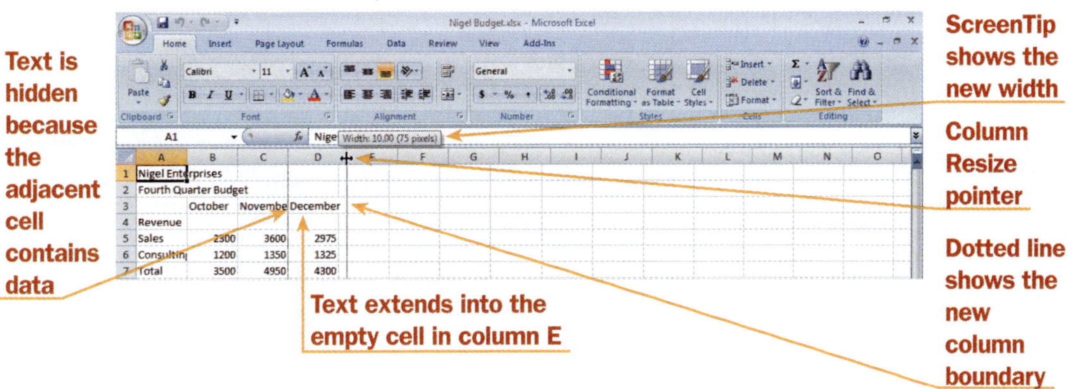

5. Select columns **B** and **C**. You want these two columns to be the same width as column D.

6. On the Ribbon, click the **Home** tab, and then locate the **Cells** group.

7. Click the **Format** button, and then click **Column Width**. The Column Width dialog box appears, as shown in Figure 2-1. 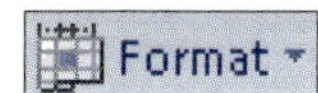

8. In the Column width box, type **10**.

9. Click **OK**. The widths of the selected columns change to 10.

10. Place the pointer on the bottom edge of the row 18 heading. The pointer changes to a double-headed arrow. 

11. Click and drag down until the ScreenTip reads *Height: 18.00 (24 pixels)*.

12. Look at the data in column A. Some cells are not wide enough to display all the contents.

13. Click cell **A20**. You see only a portion of the words *Cumulative Profit* in the cell. The Formula Bar shows the complete contents of the cell.

STEP-BY-STEP 2.1 Continued

14. Double-click the right edge of the column A heading. Column A widens so you can see all of its data.

15. Save the workbook, and leave it open for the next Step-by-Step.

Positioning Data Within a Cell

Unless you specify otherwise, text you enter in a cell is lined up along the bottom-left side of the cell, and numbers you enter in a cell are lined up along the bottom-right side of the cell. However, you can position data within a cell in a variety of ways, as described in Table 2-1. All of these positions are available on the Home tab of the Ribbon, in the Alignment group.

TABLE 2-1
Positioning data within a cell

Position	Description	Example
Alignment	Specifies where data is lined up within the cell	Align Text Left is the default for text Align Text Right is the default for numbers Center is used for column headings
Indent	Changes the space between the cell border and its content	Increase Indent adds space; used for subheadings Decrease Indent removes space
Orientation	Rotates cell contents to an angle or vertically	Labels in a narrow column
Wrap Text	Moves data to a new line when the cell is not wide enough to display all the contents	Long descriptions
Merge	Combines multiple cells into one cell	Title across the top of a worksheet Merge & Center centers contents in the merged cell

Aligning Text

You can align the contents of a cell horizontally and vertically within the cell. Horizontal alignments are left, centered, or right. Vertical alignments are top, middle, or bottom, as shown in Figure 2-3. Excel left-aligns all text and right-aligns all numbers. All data is bottom-aligned. You can select a different horizontal and/or vertical alignment for any cell. 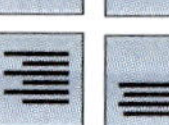

FIGURE 2-3
Horizontal and vertical alignments

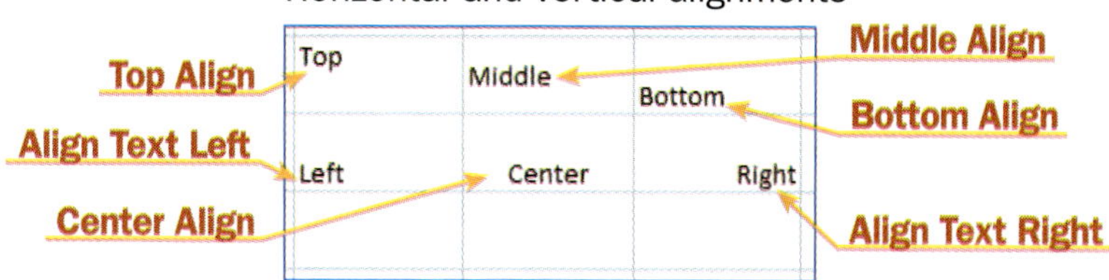

To change the **alignment** of a cell, select the cell and then click an alignment button in the Alignment group on the Home tab of the Ribbon. For other alignment options, click the Format Cells: Alignment Dialog Box Launcher to display the Alignment tab in the Format Cells dialog box. In the Text alignment section, click the alignment you want in the Horizontal or Vertical boxes, and then click OK.

Merging and Centering Data

You can also center cell contents across several columns. Select the cells, and then click the Merge & Center button in the Alignment group on the Home tab of the Ribbon. The selected cells **merge**, or combine into one cell, and the contents from the upper-left cell are centered in the newly merged cell.

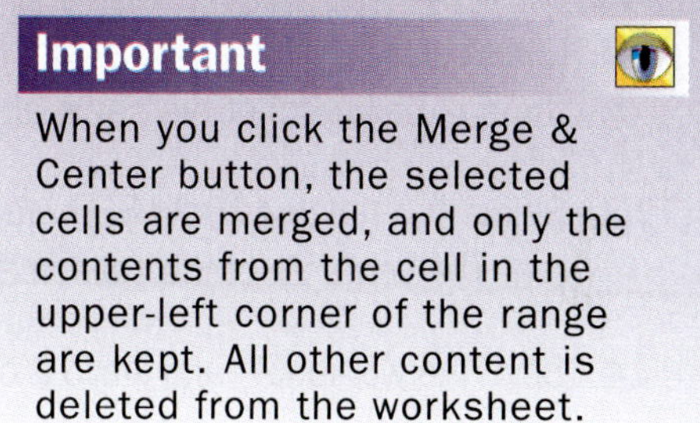

> **Important**
>
> When you click the Merge & Center button, the selected cells are merged, and only the contents from the cell in the upper-left corner of the range are kept. All other content is deleted from the worksheet.

Indenting Data

Data can be **indented** (or shifted to the right) within cells to help distinguish categories or set data apart. Instead of trying to indent data with spaces, you should use the Increase Indent button in the Alignment group on the Home tab of the Ribbon. This way, all cells' contents are indented evenly. To move the indent in the other direction, click the Decrease Indent button.

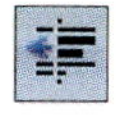
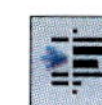

S TEP-BY-STEP 2.2

1. Select the range **B3:D3**.

2. On the Home tab of the Ribbon, locate the **Alignment** group. All the positioning buttons are located in this group.

3. Click the **Center** button. The headings are centered.

4. Click cell **A7**.

5. On the Home tab, in the Alignment group, click the **Align Text Right** button. *Total Revenue* is aligned at the right of the cell.

6. Click cell **A17**, press and hold the **Ctrl** key, click cells **A19** and **A20**, and then release the **Ctrl** key. The nonadjacent range is selected.

STEP-BY-STEP 2.2 Continued

7. On the Home tab, in the Alignment group, click the **Align Text Right** button. The contents of the three cells are right-aligned.

8. Select the range **A1:D1**.

9. On the Home tab, in the Alignment group, click the **Merge & Center** button. Cells A1 through D1 are combined into one cell, and the title *Nigel Enterprises* is centered in the merged cell. 

10. Select the range **A2:D2**. On the Home tab, in the Alignment group, click the **Merge & Center** button. Cells A2 through D2 are merged, and the subtitle *Fourth Quarter Budget* is centered in the merged cell.

11. Click cell **A5**. On the Home tab, in the Alignment group, click the **Increase Indent** button. The content of cell A5 shifts to the right.

12. Click cell **A6**. On the Home tab, in the Alignment group, click the **Increase Indent** button. The contents of cell A6 shift the same distance to the right and line up with the contents of cell A5.

13. Select the range **A10:A16**. On the Home tab, in the Alignment group, click the **Increase Indent** button. The contents of the cells in the range shift right.

14. Save the workbook, and leave it open for the next Step-by-Step.

Changing Text Orientation

Sometimes labels that describe the column data, or the data itself, are longer than the column widths. To save space in the worksheet, you can change each cell's text orientation to rotate its data to any angle. Changing the text orientation of some cells can also help give your worksheet a more professional look.

To change text orientation, select the cells whose contents you want to rotate. Click the Orientation button in the Alignment group on the Home tab of the Ribbon. A menu of orientation options appears, with commands for angling the text at 45-degree angles clockwise or counterclockwise, stacking the text vertically, or rotating the text up or down.

If you want to use a different angle, you need to use the Alignment tab in the Format Cells dialog box, as shown in Figure 2-4. Click the Format Cells: Alignment Dialog Box Launcher to display the Alignment tab in the Format Cells dialog box. In the Orientation box, click a degree point, drag the angle indicator, or type the angle you want in the Degrees box. Click OK. 

Computer Concepts

Rotated text is often used for labels on charts. Angled or vertical text fits more data in a label, while remaining readable.

FIGURE 2-4
Alignment tab in the Format Cells dialog box

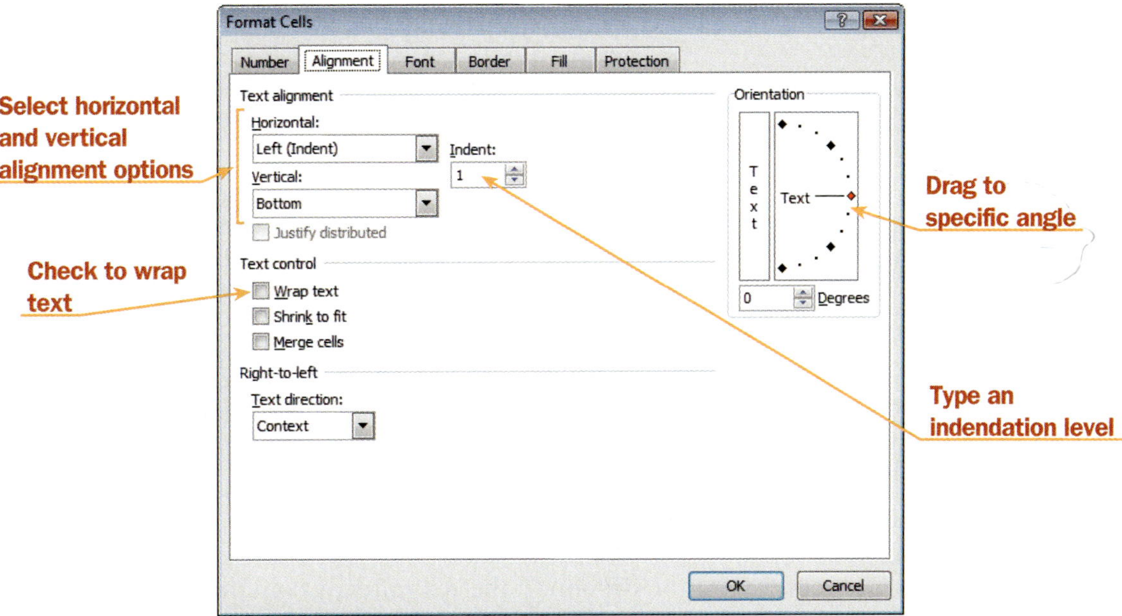

S TEP-BY-STEP 2.3

1. Select the range **B3:D3**.

2. On the Home tab, in the Alignment group, click the **Orientation** button. A menu appears with the most common orientations. 

3. Click **Angle Counterclockwise**. The text in cells B3 through D3 shifts to a 45-degree angle, and the height of row 3 increases to accommodate the angled text, as shown in Figure 2-5.

FIGURE 2-5
Alignments modified

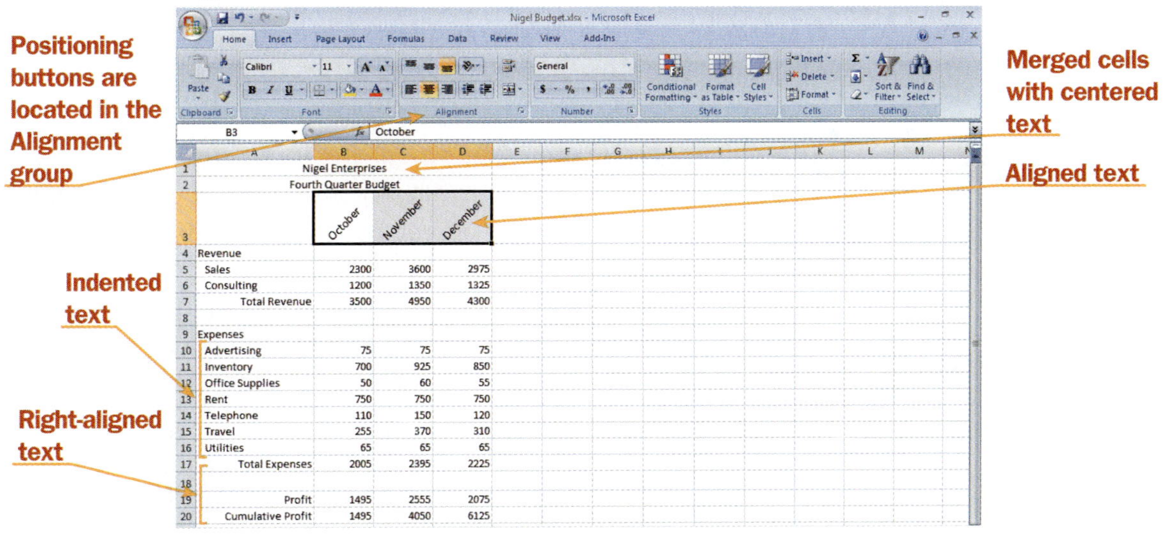

STEP-BY-STEP 2.3 Continued

4. If the width of columns B through D changed, set their widths to **10**.

5. Save the workbook, and leave it open for the next Step-by-Step.

Wrapping Text

Text that is too long to fit within a cell is dis-  played in the next cell, if it is empty. If the next cell already contains data, any text that does not fit in the cell is truncated, or hidden from view. One way to see all the text stored in a cell is to wrap text. The row height adjusts automatically to include additional lines until all the text is visible. When you wrap text, the column width is not changed.

To wrap text, select the cells in which you want to wrap text. Then, click the Wrap Text button in the Alignment group on the Home tab of the Ribbon. If the cells already contain text, the row height increases as needed to display all the content. If you enter text after you turn on Wrap Text, the row height expands to fit the text as you type.

> **Did You Know?**
>
> If you expand or reduce the column width for a cell in which text is wrapped, the contents readjust to fit the new size. Be aware that row height does not automatically adjust, and you might need to AutoFit the row height to eliminate extra blank lines within the cell.

STEP-BY-STEP 2.4

1. Click cell **A22**. Type **Budget submitted for approval**. Click the **Enter** button on the Formula Bar.

2. On the Home tab, in the Alignment group, click the **Wrap Text** button. The text wraps in the  cell, and the row height adjusts to fit all the lines of text. The Wrap Text button remains selected.

3. Save the workbook, and leave it open for the next Step-by-Step.

> **Extra for Experts**
>
> You can choose where a new line begins in a cell. Double-click in the cell to position the insertion point in the cell. Use the arrow keys to move the insertion point to where you want the new line to begin. Press the Alt+Enter keys to insert a line break. Press the Enter key to accept the change.

Changing the Appearance of Cells

You can change the appearance of cells to make them easier to read, to differentiate sections in a worksheet, or to create a specific look and feel for the worksheet. To do this, you can modify the cell's default font, font size, font style, font and fill colors, and borders.

The fonts and colors used in each workbook are part of a theme. A theme is a preset collection of design

> **Extra for Experts**
>
> You can select a different theme for your workbook. Click the Page Layout tab on the Ribbon. In the Themes group, click the Themes button to display a gallery of themes. Point to different themes to see how your workbook changes. When you find a theme you like, click that theme to make the change.

elements, including fonts, colors, and other effects. By default, the Office theme is applied to each workbook. To change a workbook's appearance, you can select a different theme, or you can format cells with other fonts and colors. If you select another theme font or theme color, it will change when you apply a different theme. Or, you can choose non-theme or standard fonts and colors that stay the same no matter which theme is applied to the workbook.

As you format cells, Live Preview shows the results of the different formatting options you can choose. Select the cell or range you want to format, and then point to the formatting option you are considering. The cell or range changes to reflect that option. To accept that format, click the option.

Changing Fonts and Font Sizes

A font is the design of text. The default font for cells is Calibri. Font size determines the height of characters, as measured in points. The default font size for cells is 11 points. You can choose different fonts and font sizes in a worksheet to emphasize part of a worksheet or to distinguish worksheet titles and column headings from other data. The fonts and font sizes you use can significantly affect the readability of the worksheet. Office 2007 comes with a variety of fonts and sizes. However, the available fonts and sizes can change from one computer to another, depending largely on what fonts are installed on that computer.

To change fonts and sizes, you must first select the cells you want to change. Then, on the Home tab of the Ribbon, in the Font group, click the arrow next to the Font box to display a gallery of available fonts, or click the arrow next to the Font Size box to display a menu of available font sizes. When you point to a font or a size, Live Preview changes the cell contents to reflect that selection. Click the font or size you want to use.

> **Did You Know?** 
>
> You can also use the Mini toolbar to change the font, font size, font style, and font color. Double-click the cell to enter **editing mode**, which places the insertion point within the cell contents, and then select the text you want to format. The transparent Mini toolbar appears above the selected text. Move the pointer to the Mini toolbar to bring it into full view, and then click the appropriate buttons to apply the formatting.

Applying Font Styles

Bold, *italic*, and underlining can add emphasis to the contents of a cell. These features are referred to as font styles. You can also combine font styles to change the emphasis, such as ***bolditalic***. To apply a font style, select the cell or range you want to change. Click the appropriate style button in the Font group on the Home tab of the Ribbon. To remove a font style from the cell contents, simply click the button again.

> **Did You Know?** 
>
> You can quickly apply a font style to a selected cell or range. Press the Ctrl+B keys to apply bold. Press the Ctrl+I keys to apply italics. Press the Ctrl+U keys to apply underlining. Use the shortcut keys again to remove that font style from the selected cell or range.

Careers

Excel workbooks are helpful to people and businesses in sales. Salespeople use worksheets to determine what items are available in inventories, analyze sales performance, and track customer orders.

S TEP-BY-STEP 2.5

1. Select the range **B3:D3**.

2. On the Home tab, in the Font group, next to the Font box, click the **arrow**. A menu appears, listing the fonts available on your computer, as shown in Figure 2-6.

FIGURE 2-6
Font menu

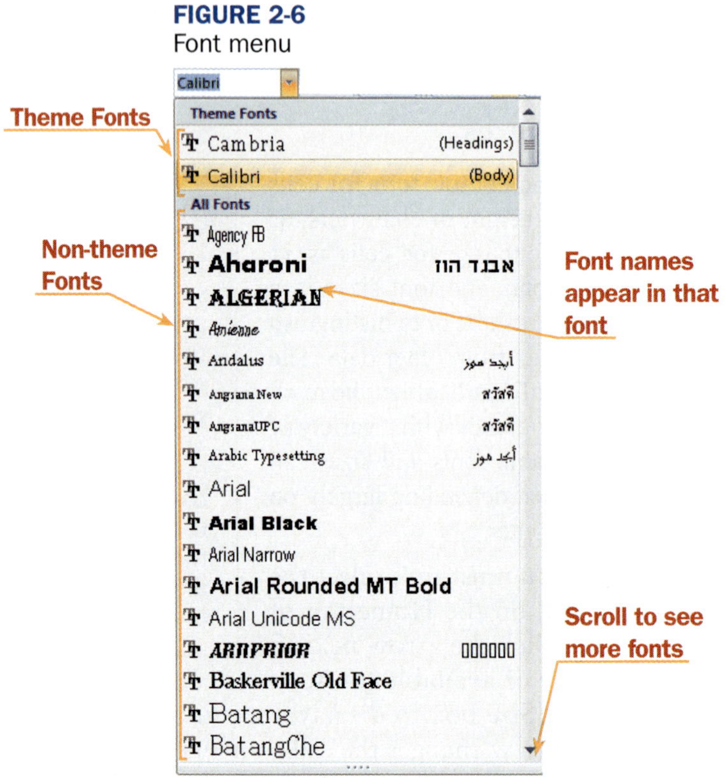

3. Scroll down the list and click **Times New Roman** (or a similar font). The font of the month names in cells B3, C3, and D3 changes from Calibri to Times New Roman.

4. On the Home tab, in the Font group, next to the Font Size box, click the **arrow**. A menu appears, listing the available font sizes.

5. Click **8**. The font of the month names in cells B3, C3, and D3 is reduced in size from 11 points to 8 points.

6. Click cell **A1** (which is the cell you merged from the range A1:D1). On the Home tab, in the Font group, next to the Font box, click the **arrow**. Click **Times New Roman**. The font of the company name in cell A1 changes to Times New Roman. Cell A1 remains active.

7. On the Home tab, in the Font group, next to the Font Size box, click the **arrow**. Click **14**. The font size of the company name in cell A1 increases to 14 points. Cell A1 remains active.

8. On the Home tab, in the Font group, click the **Bold** button. The text in cell A1 changes to bold, and the button remains selected to show it is toggled on. 

STEP-BY-STEP 2.5 Continued

9. Click cell **A2**. On the Home tab, in the Font group, click the **Bold** button. The text in cell A2 changes to bold.

10. Apply bold to cells A4, A7, A9, A17, A19, and A20.

11. Reduce the width of column A to **18**.

12. Select the range **A5:A6**. In the Font group, click the **Italic** button. The revenue items are italicized. 

13. Apply italic to the range A10:A16.

14. Select cell **A4**. In the Font group, click the **Underline** button. *Revenue* is underlined. 

15. Click the **Underline** button. The underlining is removed from the text.

16. Save the workbook, and leave it open for the next Step-by-Step.

Choosing Font and Fill Colors

You can use color to emphasize cells or distinguish them from one another. The default font color is black, but you can select a different color to make the cell contents stand out. The default **fill** (or background) color of cells is white, but you can change this background color to help accentuate certain cells, such as descriptive labels or totals.

To change the color of text in a cell, select the cell you want to change. In the Font group on the Home tab of the Ribbon, click the arrow next to the Font Color button. A gallery appears showing a palette of colors, as shown in Figure 2-7. Click the color you want. The cell contents change to that color.

Extra Challenge

Experiment by changing the font, font size, and font style of data in the worksheet. When you are done, use the Undo button on the Quick Access Toolbar to undo changes you made.

Did You Know?

You can also change font and fill colors with the Format Cells dialog box. Press the Ctrl+1 keys to open the dialog box. On the Font tab, click the Color arrow, and then click the font color you want to use. On the Fill tab, click a color in the Background Color section to select a solid color. You can also select a pattern: click the Pattern Style arrow, and then click the pattern you want. To select a color for the pattern, click the Pattern Color arrow, and then click the color you want the pattern to appear in.

FIGURE 2-7
Font colors

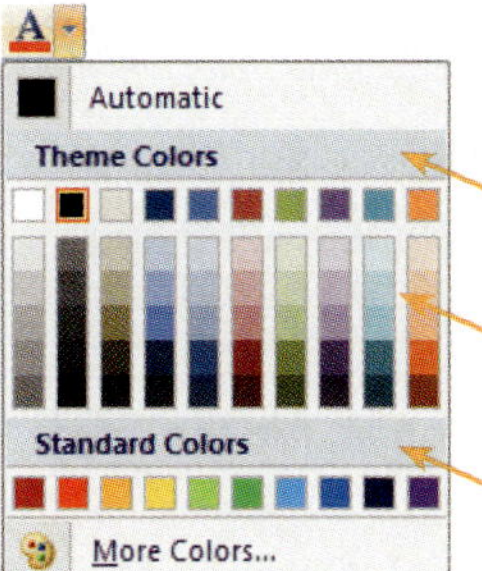

Theme colors change when you select a new theme

Theme colors are available in different shades

Standard colors are available in all themes

To change the background color of a cell, select the cell you want to change. In the Font group on the Home tab of the Ribbon, click the arrow next to the Fill Color button. A gallery appears with a palette of colors, as shown in Figure 2-8. Click the color you want. The cell is filled with that color.

Extra for Experts

You can create dynamic headings by using a light font color with a dark fill color. For example, format cell text in white or yellow and format the cell background in green or blue.

FIGURE 2-8
Fill colors

Theme colors change when you select a new theme

Theme colors are available in different shades

Click to remove a fill color from the selected cell range

Standard colors are available in all themes

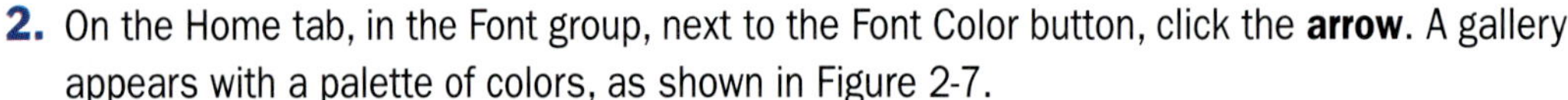

STEP-BY-STEP 2.6

1. Click cell **A1**.

2. On the Home tab, in the Font group, next to the Font Color button, click the **arrow**. A gallery appears with a palette of colors, as shown in Figure 2-7. 

3. Point to the **Orange** color (the third color in the Standard Colors section). A ScreenTip displays the name of the color, and *Nigel Enterprises*, the text in cell A1, changes to orange, showing you a Live Preview of that selection.

4. Point to the **Aqua, Accent 5** color (the ninth color in the first row of the Theme Colors section). A ScreenTip displays the name of the color, and Live Preview shows the company name in aqua.

5. Click the **Aqua, Accent 5** color. The gallery closes and the company name remains aqua. Cell A1 is still the active cell.

6. On the Home tab, in the Font group, next to the Fill Color button, click the **arrow**. A gallery appears with a palette of colors, as shown in Figure 2-8. 

7. Click the **Aqua, Accent 5, Lighter 80%** color (the ninth color in the second row of the Theme Colors section). The cell background becomes light aqua. Cell A1 is still the active cell.

8. Save the workbook, and leave it open for the next Step-by-Step.

Extra Challenge

Change the font and fill colors of all the headings to appropriate colors.

Inserting Cell Borders

You can add emphasis to a cell by placing a border (or line) around its edges. You can place the border around the entire cell or only on certain sides of the cell. You can also select different border styles, such as a thick border or a double border.

To insert a border, select a cell or range, and then, in the Font group on the Home tab of the Ribbon, click the arrow next to the Borders button. A menu appears with border styles, as shown in Figure 2-9. Click the border style you want to add. You can remove the borders from a selected cell by clicking No Border in the border style menu.

Did You Know?

The Borders button (instead of the arrow) shows the most recently selected border style. Select a cell or range and then click the Borders button to apply that style.

FIGURE 2-9
Borders menu

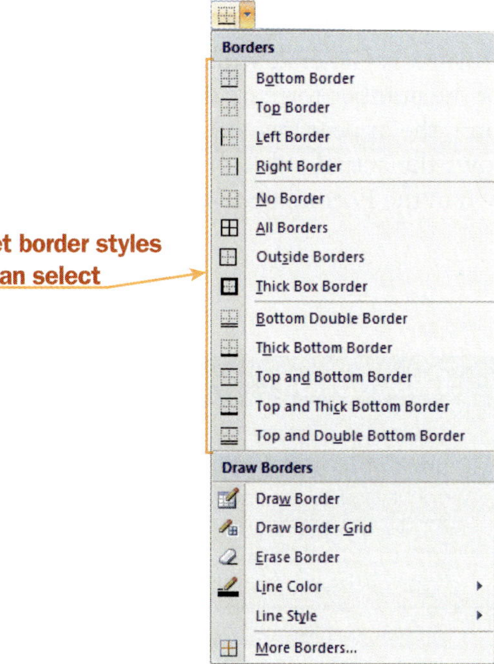

Preset border styles you can select

S TEP-BY-STEP 2.7

1. Select the range **B7:D7**.

2. On the Home tab, in the Font group, next to the Borders button, click the **arrow**. A menu of border styles appears, as shown in Figure 2-9.

3. Click **Top and Double Bottom Border**. A single border appears above the range, and a double border appears below the range. The Borders button changes to Top and Double Bottom Border.

4. Select the range **B17:D17**.

STEP-BY-STEP 2.7 Continued

5. On the Home tab, in the Font group, click the **Top and Double Bottom Border** button. A single border appears above the range, and a double border appears below the range. 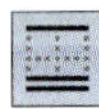

6. Save the workbook, and leave it open for the next Step-by-Step.

Careers

Standard accounting format uses a single border below a column of numbers and a double border below the total.

Selecting Number Formats

Number formats change the way data looks in a cell. The actual content you entered is not changed. The default number format is General, which displays numbers the way you type them. However, you can select any of the number formats described in Table 2-2. Be aware that changing a number format affects only the appearance of the data in the cell. The actual value is not affected. The Formula Bar shows the actual value of the contents you see in the active cell. For example, the actual value shown in the Formula Bar might be 1000, whereas the number you see in the active cell is $1,000.00.

TABLE 2-2
Number formats

Format	Example	Description
General	1000	The default format; displays numbers as typed. If the number doesn't fit in the cell, decimals are rounded, or the number is converted to scientific notation.
Number	1000.00	Displays numbers with a fixed number of places to the right of the decimal point; the default is two decimal places
Currency	$1,000.00	Displays numbers preceded by a dollar sign with a thousands separator and two decimal places
Accounting	$1,000.00 $ 9.00	Displays numbers in the Currency format but lines up the dollar signs and the decimal points vertically within a column
Date	6/8/02	Displays text and numbers as dates
Time	7:38 PM	Displays text and numbers as times
Percentage	35.2%	Displays numbers with two decimal places followed by a percent sign
Fraction	35 7/8	Displays decimal numbers as fractions
Scientific	1.00E+03	Displays numbers in exponential (or scientific) notation
Text	45-875-33	Displays text and numbers exactly as you type them

TABLE 2-2 CONTINUED
Number formats

Format	Example	Description
Special	79410-1234 (503) 555-4567	Displays numbers with a specific format: zip codes, zip+4 codes, phone numbers, and Social Security numbers
Custom	000.00.0	Displays data in the format you create, such as with commas or leading zeros

To change the number format, select the cell or range. Then, click the appropriate buttons in the Number group on the Home tab of the Ribbon. You can also click the arrow next to the Number Format box to open a menu of number formats. The accounting and percentage number formats also have buttons you can click to quickly apply these common number formats. The other buttons let you choose whether the number includes a thousands separator (a comma) and how many decimal places to show.

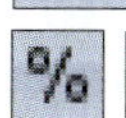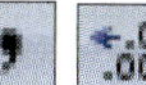

Copying Cell Formatting

Format Painter enables you to copy formatting from one worksheet cell to another without copying the cell's contents. This is especially helpful when the cell formatting you want to copy includes several formats. For example, after formatting a cell as a percentage with a white font, a green fill, and a double bottom border, you can use the Format Painter to quickly format other cells the same way.

To copy a cell's formatting, select the cell that has the format you want to copy. Click the  Format Painter button in the Clipboard group on the Home tab of the Ribbon. Then, click another cell or drag to select the range of cells you want to format in the same way.

> **Did You Know?**
>
> You can use the Format Painter to copy the same formatting to non-adjacent cells or ranges. Double-click the Format Painter button in the Clipboard group on the Home tab of the Ribbon. Select the cells or ranges you want to format. When you are done, click the Format Painter button again.

S TEP-BY-STEP 2.8

1. Select the range **B5:D5**, press and hold the **Ctrl** key, select the range **B7:D7**, and then release the **Ctrl** key. The non-adjacent range is selected.

2. On the Home tab, in the Number group, next to the Number Format box, click the **arrow**. A menu of number formats appears.

3. Click **Accounting**. The numbers in the selected ranges include a dollar sign, a thousands separator, and two decimal places, which is the standard Accounting number format.

4. Click cell **B5**. Compare the value in the Formula Bar with the value in the active cell. The Formula Bar shows *2300*, which is the actual value stored in cell B5. Cell B5 shows *$2,300.00*, which is the stored value formatted for display.

STEP-BY-STEP 2.8 Continued

5. On the Home tab, in the Clipboard group, click the **Format Painter** button. The pointer changes to a paintbrush next to the white plus pointer. A flashing dashed border surrounds cell B5 to remind you that the formatting from this cell is being copied. 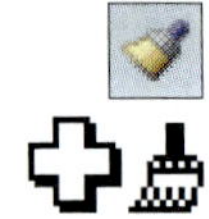

6. Click and drag from cell **B10** to cell **D10**. The format of the range B10:D10 changes to the Accounting number format.

7. Select the range **B11:D16**.

8. On the Home tab, in the Number group, next to the Number Format box, click the **arrow**, and then click **Number**. The cells in the range are formatted with two decimal places.

9. On the Home tab, in the Number group, click the **Comma Style** button. A thousands separator is added to numbers with four digits and the decimals points align with the values in the Accounting number format that appear in the cells above them.

10. On the Home tab, in the Clipboard group, click the **Format Painter** button. The range B11:D16 is surrounded by a blinking border.

11. Click and drag from cell **B6** to cell **D6**. The format of the range B6:D6 is formatted with both the Number and Comma Style number formats.

12. Apply the **Accounting** number format to the ranges B17:D17 and B19:D20.

13. Click cell **A1** to deselect the range. Your screen should look similar to Figure 2-10.

FIGURE 2-10
Formatted worksheet

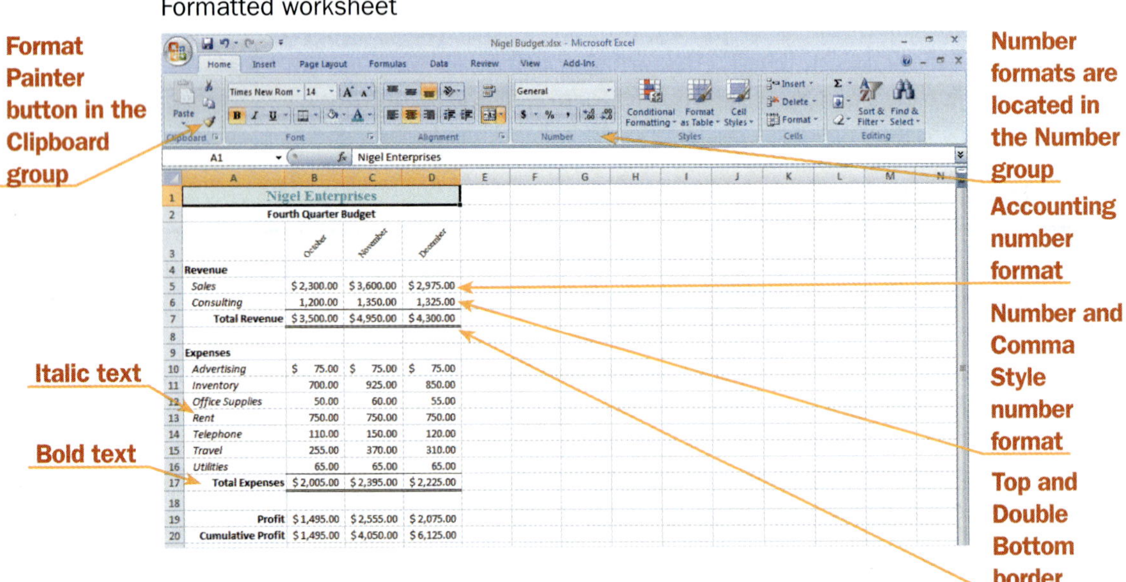

14. Save the workbook, and leave it open for the next Step-by-Step.

Using the Format Cells Dialog Box

The Format Cells dialog box provides access to all the formatting options available on the Ribbon, as well as some additional formatting options. To open the Format Cells dialog box, you can click the Dialog Box Launcher in the Font, Alignment, or Number group on the Home tab of the Ribbon, or you can press the Ctrl+1 keys. As shown in Figure 2-11, the Format Cells dialog box has Number, Alignment, Font, Border, and Fill tabs. You can use these tabs to change the number format, position of data, font options, borders, and cell background color as you have done so far.

FIGURE 2-11
Format Cells dialog box

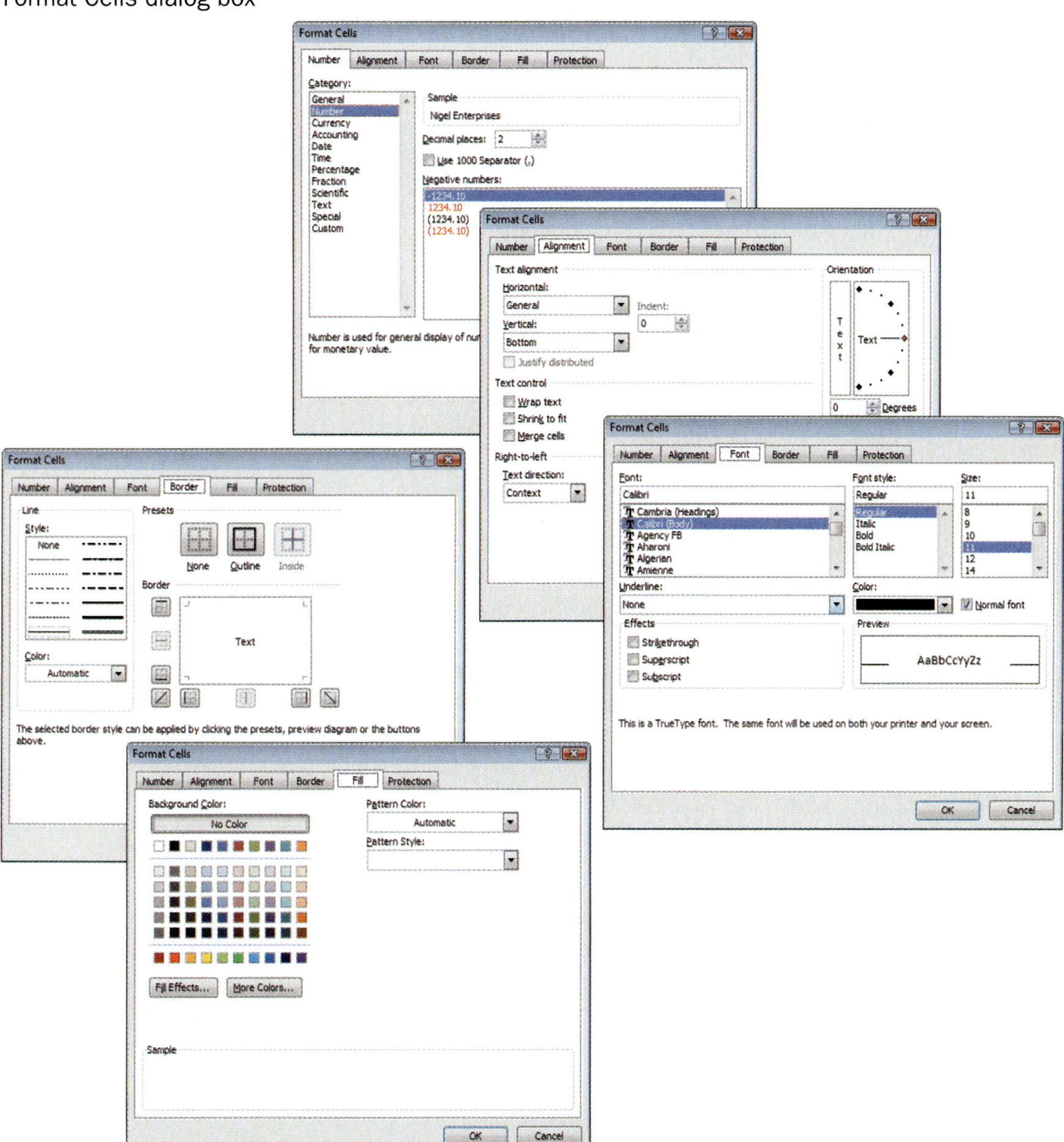

Using Styles

A **style** is a combination of formatting characteristics such as alignment, font, font size, font color, fill color, and borders. When you apply a style to a cell, you apply all the formatting characteristics simultaneously, saving you the time of applying the formats individually. Styles also help you format a worksheet consistently. When you use a style, you know that each cell with that style is formatted the same way.

Applying Cell Styles

A **cell style** is a collection of formatting characteristics you apply to a cell or range of data. To apply a cell style, select the cells you want to format. In the Styles group on the Home tab of the Ribbon, click the Cell Styles button. The Cell Style gallery appears, as shown in Figure 2-12. Point to a cell style in the gallery to see a Live Preview of that style on the selected cell or range in the worksheet. When you find a style you like, click the style to apply it. To remove a style from the selected cell, simply click Normal in the Good, Bad and Neutral section of the Cell Styles gallery.

FIGURE 2-12
Cell Styles gallery

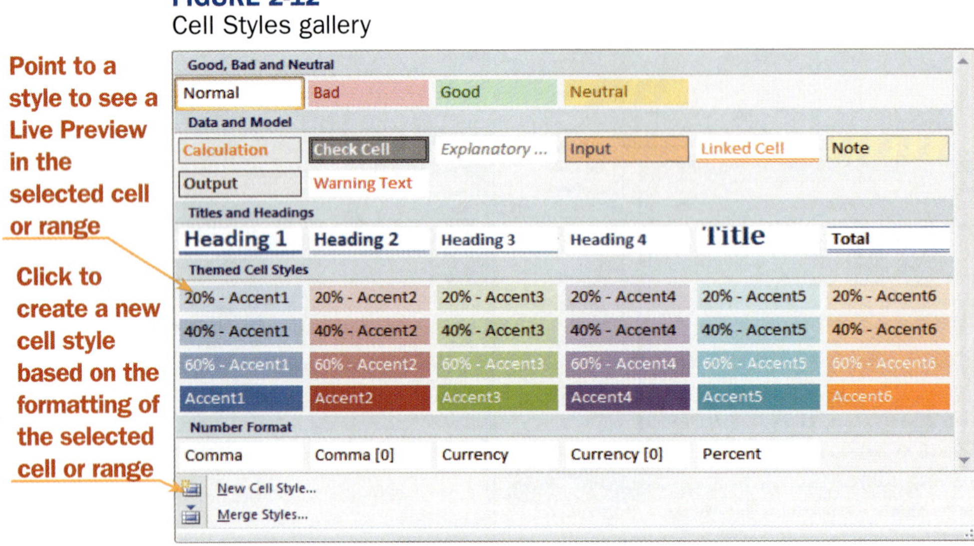

The Cell Styles gallery includes many predefined styles. However, if none of these styles meets your needs, you can define styles of your own. First, format a cell with the exact combination of formats you want. Then, select the formatted cell, and click New Cell Style at the bottom of the Cell Styles gallery. In the Style dialog box that opens, shown in Figure 2-13, type a descriptive name for the style in the Style name box, verify the formatting in the Style Includes section (uncheck any format you don't want to include), and then click OK. The style you created appears at the top of the Cell Styles gallery in the Custom section.

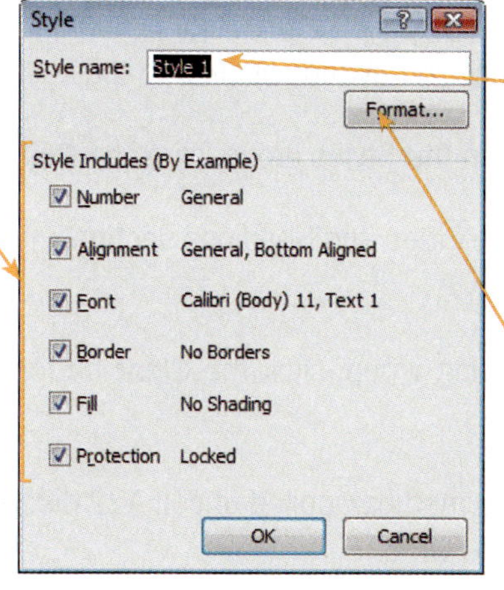

Clearing Cell Formats

You have learned how to change the appearance of cells in a worksheet by applying individual formats as well as cell styles. At times, you might need to remove, or *clear*, all the formatting applied to a cell or range of cells. Select the cell or range, click the Clear button in the Editing group on the Home tab of the Ribbon, and then click Clear Format. Only the cell formatting is removed; the cell content remains unchanged. 

$\mathcal{S}$ TEP-BY-STEP 2.9

1. Select the range **A4:D4**.

2. On the Home tab, in the Styles group, click the **Cell Styles** button. The Cell Styles gallery appears, as shown in Figure 2-12. 

3. In the Titles and Headings section, point to **Heading 2**. Live Preview shows the selected range with the font, font size, color, and border in that style.

4. In the Titles and Headings section, point to **Accent5** to see the Live Preview, and then click **Accent5**. Aqua fill and white font colors are applied to the cells in the selected range.

5. Select the range **A9:D9**.

6. On the Home tab, in the Styles group, click the **Cell Styles** button.

7. In the Cell Styles gallery, in the Titles and Headings section, click **Accent5**. Aqua fill and white font are applied to the cells in the selected range.

8. Click **A1**. On the Home tab, in the Styles group, click the **Cell Styles** button.

9. In the Cell Styles gallery, in the Titles and Headings section, click **Heading 1**. The formatting for this style is added to the formatting you already applied to the cell.

10. Click **A22**. On the Home tab, in the Styles group, click the **Cell Styles** button.

11. In the Cell Styles gallery, in the Titles and Headings section, click **Accent2**. The cell is formatted with the selected style.

12. On the Home tab, in the Editing group, click the **Clear** button. A menu appears with the Clear commands. 

13. Click **Clear Formats**. All the formatting applied to cell A22 disappears. The cell returns to the default font color and fill color and text wrap.

14. Click cell **A23**, and then enter your name.

15. Save, print, and close the workbook.

Finding and Replacing Cell Formatting

You have already learned to find and replace data in a workbook. You can also find and replace specific formatting in a workbook. For example, you might want to replace all italicized text with bolded text, or you might want to change all cells with a yellow fill color to another color.

S TEP-BY-STEP 2.10

1. Open the **Basketball.xlsx** Data File.

2. Save the workbook as **Basketball Standings** followed by your initials.

3. On the Home tab, in the Editing group, click the **Find & Select** button, and then click **Replace**. The Find and Replace dialog box appears, with the Replace tab displayed. 

4. Click the **Options** button to expand the Find and Replace dialog box, if it is not already expanded.

5. Delete any entries that appear in the Find what or Replace with boxes.

6. Click the top **Format** button. The Find Format dialog box appears. This dialog box has all the same tabs and options as the Format Cells dialog box.

7. Click the **Font** tab if it is not the active tab. In the Font style list, click **Italic**. This is the formatting you want to find.

8. Click **OK**. The Find Format dialog box disappears, and the Find and Replace dialog box reappears. The Find what Preview box shows the italic formatting you want to find.

STEP-BY-STEP 2.10 Continued

9. Click the lower **Format** button. The Replace Format dialog box appears. This dialog box has all the same tabs and options as the Format Cells dialog box.

10. On the Font tab, in the Font style list, click **Bold**.

11. Click **OK**. The Replace Format dialog box disappears, and the Find and Replace dialog box reappears. The Replace with Preview box shows the bold formatting you want to use instead of the italics.

12. Click **Replace All**. A dialog box appears, stating that Excel has completed the search and 5 replacements were made.

13. Click **OK**. The dialog box closes.

14. Click **Close**. The Find and Replace dialog box closes. Your screen should look similar to Figure 2-14.

FIGURE 2-14
Worksheet with formatting replaced

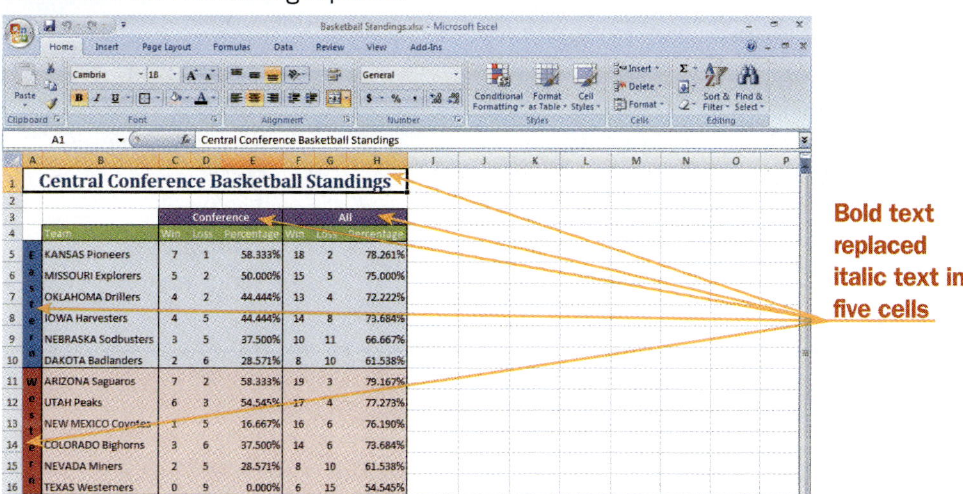

15. Click cell B2, and then enter your name.

16. Save, print, and close the workbook.

SUMMARY

In this lesson, you learned:

■ If data does not fit in a cell, you can resize the columns and rows to make the data easier to read.

■ You can align, indent, rotate, wrap text, and merge cells to reposition data in worksheet cells.

■ You can change the appearance of cells to make the worksheet easier to read or to create a specific look and feel. Choose the appropriate fonts, font sizes, font styles, font and fill colors, and borders.

- A variety of number formats enable you to change how a number is displayed in the cell. No matter which number format you select, the actual value stored in the cell does not change. You can see this by comparing the formatted value in the active cell with the stored value in the Formula Bar.

- Format Painter copies all the formatting from one cell to another cell or range without copying the contents of the cell.

- The Format Cells dialog box provides all the number, alignment, font, border, and fill formatting options available on the Ribbon, as well as some additional ones.

- A style is a combination of formatting characteristics, such as alignment, font, font size, font color, fill color, and borders, that you can apply simultaneously. The Cell Styles gallery lets you quickly apply a style to selected cells.

- The Find and Replace dialog box can be used to change cell formatting.

VOCABULARY *Review*

Define the following terms:

Alignment	Font	Orientation
AutoFit	Font size	Points
Border	Font style	Row heading
Cell style	Format Painter	Style
Clear	Indent	Theme
Column heading	Live Preview	Truncate
Editing mode	Merge	Wrap text
Fill	Number format	

REVIEW QUESTIONS

TRUE/FALSE

Circle T if the statement is true or F if the statement is false.

T   F   1. A series of number signs (######) in a cell indicates that the data entered in the cell is longer than the width of the cell.

T   F   2. Wrapped text is truncated within the cell when the data exceeds the width of a column.

T   F   3. The Merge & Center button combines several cells into one cell and places the data in the center of the merged cell.

T   F   4. You can place a border around the entire cell or only on certain sides of the cell.

T   F   5. The default number format for data in a cell is Text.

WRITTEN QUESTIONS

Write a brief answer to the following questions.

1. Which cell formats display numerical data preceded by a dollar sign?

2. How can you have Excel determine the best width of a column?

3. What is one reason for changing the orientation of text in a cell?

4. What is the difference between fill color and font color?

5. What is an advantage of using cell styles?

PROJECTS

PROJECT 2-1

Write the letter of the cell format option in Column 2 that matches the worksheet format described in Column 1.

Column 1

____ 1. Displays data as typed

____ 2. Displays numbers with a fixed number of decimal places

____ 3. Displays numbers preceded by a dollar sign with a thousands separator and two decimal places; however, dollar signs and decimal points do not necessarily line up vertically within a column

____ 4. Displays numbers preceded by a dollar sign with a thousands separator and two decimal places; dollar signs and decimal points are lined up vertically within a column

____ 5. Displays text and numbers as dates

____ 6. Displays text and numbers as times

____ 7. Displays numbers with two decimal places followed by a percent sign

____ 8. Displays the value of 0.5 as 1/2

____ 9. Displays numbers in exponential notation

____ 10. Displays numbers with a specific format, such as zip codes, phone numbers, and Social Security numbers

____ 11. Displays data in the format you design

Column 2

A. Accounting

B. Time

C. Scientific

D. Fraction

E. Special

F. General

G. Date

H. Number

I. Percentage

J. Custom

K. Currency

 PROJECT 2-2

1. Open the **Bird.xlsx** Data File.

2. Save the workbook as **Bird Census** followed by your initials.

3. Change the width of column A to 24.

4. Merge and center the range A1:F1 and the range A2:F2.

5. Format cell A1 with the Title cell style. Change the fill color of the range A1:A2 to Orange, Accent 6.

6. Bold the range A4:F4.

7. Angle the data in the range B4:F4 counterclockwise.

8. Change the width of column B through column E to 6.

9. Bold the range A12:F12.

10. Indent and italicize the range A5:A11.

11. Right-align the data in cell A12.

12. Format the range B12:F12 with a top and double bottom border.

13. Change the font color of the range F4:F12 to Orange, Accent 6.

14. In cell A3, type **Prepared by:** followed by your name.

15. Save, print, and close the workbook.

 PROJECT 2-3

1. Open the **Phone.xlsx** Data File.

2. Save the workbook as **Phone Shop** followed by your initials.

3. AutoFit column A.

4. Change the width of columns B, C, and D to 10.

5. Bold and center the text in the range B4:D5.

6. Bold the text in cell A5.

7. Indent the range A6:A9.

8. Change the text in cell A1 to 14-point Cambria. Merge and center the range A1:D1.

9. Change the fill color of cell A1 to the Standard Color Green.

10. Change the fill color of the range A2:D2 to the Standard Color Yellow.

11. Format the range C6:D9 and cell D10 as Currency with two decimal places.

12. Format cell D10 with the Total cell style. Change the fill color of cell D10 to Standard Color Yellow.

13. Add a thick bottom border to the range A5:D5.

14. In cell C2, enter your name.

15. Save, print, and close the workbook.

PROJECT 2-4

1. Open the **Cell.xlsx** Data File.

2. Save the workbook as **Cell Bill** followed by your initials.

3. In cell A1, type **Cell Phone Bill Estimate**.

4. Bold the text in cell A1.

5. In cell A1, change the font size of the text to 14.

6. Merge and center the range A1:D1.

7. Change the fill color of cell A1 to Blue, Accent 1.

8. Change the font color of cell A1 to White, Background 1.

9. Underline the contents of cell A1.

10. Center the contents of the range B3:C3.

11. Format the range C4:D7 in the Currency number format with two decimal places.

12. Add a bottom border to cell D6.

13. Widen column A to 17. In cell A4, wrap text.

14. Middle-align the range B4:D4.

15. Apply the 20% - Accent 1 cell style to the range D4:D7.

16. In cell A2, enter your name.

17. Save, print, and close the workbook.

PROJECT 2-5

1. Open the **Balance.xlsx** Data File.

2. Save the workbook as **TechSoft Balance** followed by your initials. This workbook contains a *balance sheet*, which is a financial statement that lists a corporation's assets (resources available), liabilities (amounts owed), and equity (ownership in the company).

3. Change the column width of column C to 5.

4. Format cell A1 with the Heading 1 cell style.

5. Format the range A2:A3 with the 20% - Accent 1 cell style.

6. Merge and center the ranges A1:E1, A2:E2, and A3:E3.

7. Bold cells A5, A6, A20, D5, D6, D17, and D21.

8. Apply a bottom border to cells B8, B13, E11, and E19. Apply a top and double bottom border to cells B20 and E21.

9. Format cells B7, E7, B20, and E21 in the Accounting number format with no decimal places.

10. Format the ranges B8:B19, E8:E15, and E18:E20 in the Number format with a thousands separator and no decimal places.

11. In cell A4, enter your name. Italicize the text in cell A4.

12. Save, print, and close the workbook.

PROJECT 2-6

1. Open the **Mileage.xlsx** Data File.

2. Save the workbook as **Mileage Chart** followed by your initials.

3. Change the font size of the range A1:O15 to 8 points.

4. Format the range B2:O15 in the Number format with a thousands separator and no decimal places.

5. Bold the ranges B1:O1 and A2:A15.

6. Change the width of column A to 10.

7. Right-align the content of the range A2:A15.

8. Change the orientation of the range B1:O1 to Angle Clockwise.

9. Change the width of columns B through O to 5.

10. In cell A1, enter your name, and then change the font size to 12 points and wrap text.

11. Save, print, and close the workbook.

CRITICAL *Thinking*

ACTIVITY 2-1

To be useful, worksheets must convey information clearly, both on-screen and on the printed page. Identify ways to accomplish the following:

1. Emphasize certain portions of a worksheet.

2. Make data in a worksheet easier to read.

3. Distinguish one part of a worksheet from another.

4. Format similar elements in a worksheet consistently.

ACTIVITY 2-2

You have been spending a lot of time formatting worksheets. A friend tells you that you could save some time by using the Mini toolbar to apply formatting. Use Excel Help to research the following:

1. How do you access the Mini toolbar?

2. What formatting can you apply from the Mini toolbar?

3. How do you use the Mini toolbar to apply formatting to text in a cell?

4. Why might the Mini toolbar save you time formatting?

ORGANIZING THE WORKSHEET

OBJECTIVES

Upon completion of this lesson, you will be able to:

- Copy and move data to other cells.
- Use the drag-and-drop method and Auto Fill options to add data to cells.
- Insert and delete rows, columns, and cells.
- Freeze panes in a worksheet.
- Split a worksheet window.
- Check spelling in a worksheet.
- Prepare a worksheet for printing.
- Insert headers and footers.

Estimated Time: 2 hours

VOCABULARY

Automatic page break

Copy

Cut

Fill

Fill handle

Footer

Freeze pane

Header

Landscape orientation

Manual page break

Margins

Normal view

Office Clipboard (Clipboard)

Page Break Preview

Page Layout view

Paste

Portrait orientation

Print area

Print title

Scale

Split

Data in a worksheet should be arranged so that it is easy to locate, read, and interpret. You can reorganize data by moving it to another part of the worksheet. You can also reduce data entry time by copying data to another part of the worksheet. If you no longer need certain data, you can delete entire rows or columns. If you want to include additional information within existing data, you can insert another row or column.

Copying and Moving Cells

When creating or editing a worksheet, you might want to use the contents of one or more cells in another part of the worksheet. Rather than retype the same content, you can copy or move a cell or range, including its contents and formatting, to another area of the worksheet. Copying duplicates the cell's or range's contents in another location, while also leaving the content in its original location. Moving places the

Important

Data moved or copied to a cell replaces any content already in that cell. Be sure to check the destination cells for existing data before moving or copying.

contents of the cell or range in another location, and removes that content from its original position in the worksheet. In this lesson, you learn to use the Copy, Cut, and Paste buttons, the drag-and-drop method, and AutoFill to copy and move data in a worksheet.

Copying Cell Contents

When you want to copy the contents of a cell or range, you first select the cell or range. 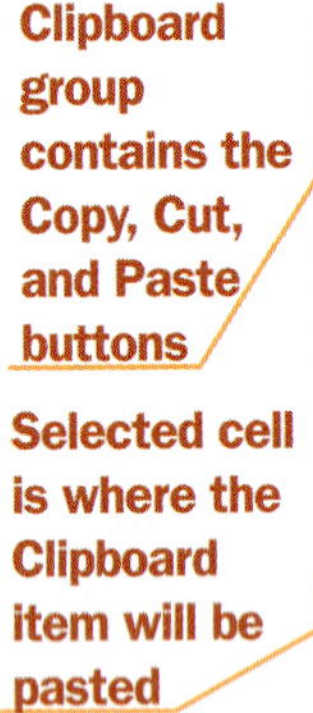 Then, you use buttons in the Clipboard group on the Home tab of the Ribbon. To duplicate the cell's contents without affecting the original cell, you click the **Copy** button. The selected cell contents are placed as an item on the Office Clipboard. The **Office Clipboard** (or **Clipboard**) is a temporary storage area for up to 24 selections you copy or cut. A flashing border appears around the copied selection, as shown in Figure 3-1.

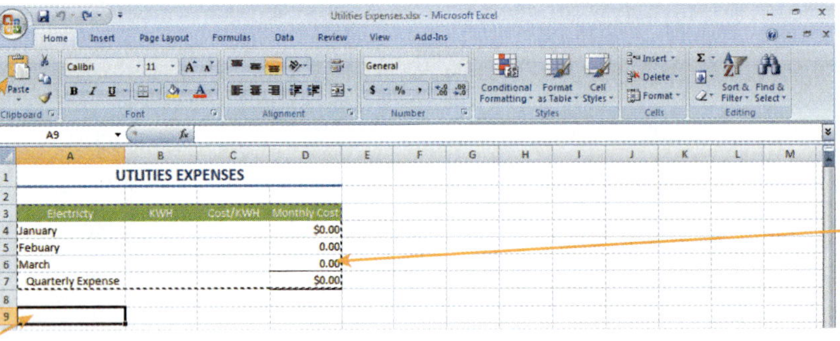

Next, you select the cell or upper-left cell of the 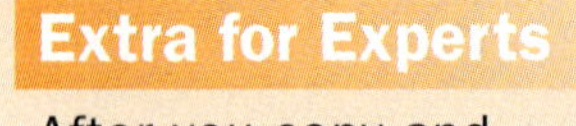 range where you want the copied item to appear in the worksheet. Click the Paste button in the Clipboard group on the Home tab. The Clipboard item is pasted into the selected cell or range. **Pasting** places the last item from the Clipboard into the cell or range selected in the worksheet. You can continue to paste that item in the worksheet, as long as the flashing border appears around the cell. Just select the new destination cell or range, and then click the Paste button again.

Extra for Experts

After you copy and paste, the Paste Options button appears next to the cell or range with the pasted item. Clicking the Paste Options button provides a menu of options, so you can choose how the pasted item is formatted.

Moving Cell Contents

The process for moving cell contents is similar. 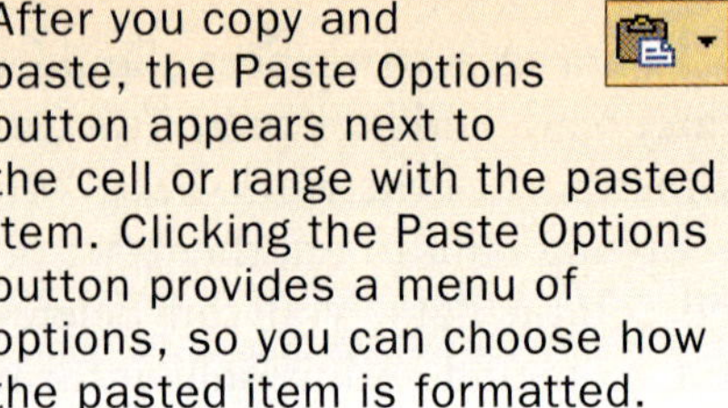 First, select the cell or range whose contents you want to move. Then, click the **Cut** button in the Clipboard group on the Home tab of the Ribbon. A flashing border appears around the selection, and the selected cell contents are placed as an item on the Clipboard. Next, select the cell or upper-left cell of the range where you want to move the cut item. Click the Paste button in the Clipboard group on the Home tab. The cell contents are removed from the original position and placed in the new location. The flashing border disappears from the worksheet.

Computer Concepts

You can use shortcut keys to quickly cut, copy, and paste cells. Click the Ctrl+X keys to cut selected cells. Click the Ctrl+C keys to copy selected cells. Click the Ctrl+V keys to paste the selected cells.

S TEP-BY-STEP 3.1

1. Open the **Utilities.xlsx** Data File.

2. Save the workbook as **Utilities Expenses** followed by your initials. Some words in the workbook are misspelled. Ignore them for now.

3. Select the range **A3:D7**.

4. On the Home tab of the Ribbon, locate the **Clipboard** group. This group includes all the buttons for cutting, copying, and pasting.

5. Click the **Copy** button. A flashing border surrounds the selected range to indicate that it has been placed on the Clipboard. 

6. Click cell **A9**. Cell A9 is the upper-left cell of the range in which you want to paste the copied cells, as shown in Figure 3-1.

7. On the Home tab, in the Clipboard group, click the **Paste** button. The range A3:D7 is copied from the Clipboard to the range A9:D13. All the formatting from the range A3:D7 is copied along with the data. The flashing border surrounds the range A3:D7 until you click another button on the Ribbon or type in a cell. 

8. Click cell **A9**, and then enter **Natural Gas**. The flashing border disappears from the range A3:D7.

9. Click cell **B9**, and then enter **100 cf** to indicate the number of cubic feet in hundreds.

10. Click cell **C9**, and then enter **Cost/100 cf** to indicate the cost per hundred cubic feet.

11. Select the range **A9:D13**.

12. On the Home tab, in the Clipboard group, click the **Cut** button. A flashing border surrounds the range you selected. 

13. Click cell **A8**.

14. On the Home tab, in the Clipboard group, click the **Paste** button. The data moves to the range A8:D12.

15. Save the workbook, and leave it open for the next Step-by-Step.

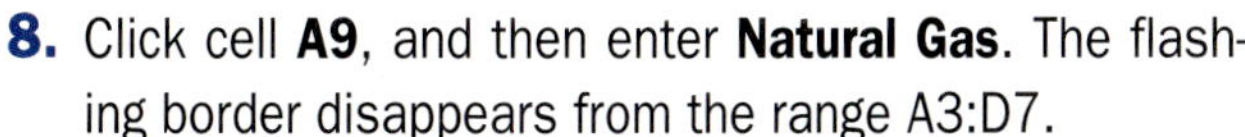

> ### Extra for Experts
>
> You can paste any of the last 24 items you cut or copied to the Clipboard. On the Home tab of the Ribbon, click the Clipboard Dialog Box Launcher. The Clipboard task pane appears in a separate pane along the left side of the worksheet. In the worksheet, click the cell where you want to paste an item. In the Clipboard task pane, click the item you want to paste. When you are done, click the Close button in the task pane title bar.

> ### Did You Know? 
>
> Sometimes you might need to paste only part of the item you copy or cut. On the Home tab, in the Clipboard group, click the arrow below the Paste button. The Paste menu provides additional commands. The Formulas command pastes the actual formulas entered in the cells, whereas the Paste values command pastes the formula results. The Transpose command pastes a row of cells into a column, or a column of cells into a row. For even more options, click the Paste Special command to open the Paste Special dialog box.

Using the Drag-and-Drop Method

You can quickly move or copy data using the drag-and-drop method. First, select the cell or range you want to move or copy. Then, position the pointer on the top border of the selected cells. The pointer changes from a white cross to a four-headed arrow. To move the selected cells, drag them to a new location. A dashed border shows where the selected cells will be positioned after you release the mouse button, and a ScreenTip lists the destination cell or range address, as shown in Figure 3-2. When the destination you want is selected, release the mouse button. To copy the cells, press and hold the Ctrl key to include a plus sign above the pointer as you drag the cells to a new location, and then release the Ctrl key and mouse button.

Computer Concepts

The drag-and-drop method is the fastest way to copy or move data short distances in a worksheet. For longer distances, especially when you want the data in an area of the worksheet not currently visible, copy and paste or cut and paste the data.

FIGURE 3-2
Range ready to drag and drop

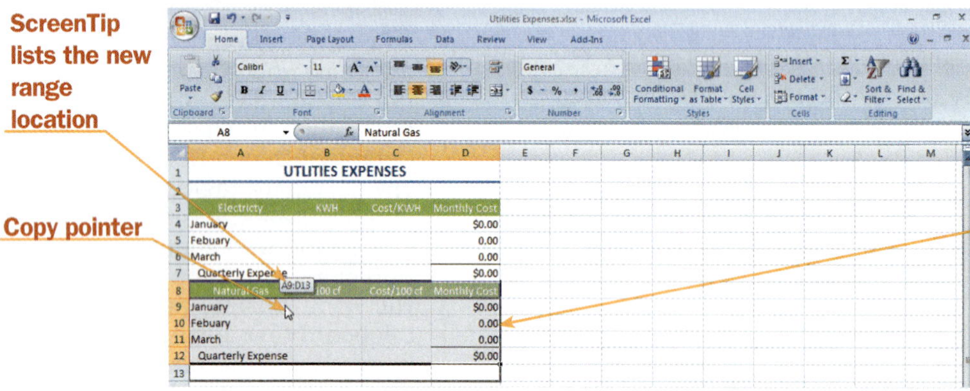

S TEP-BY-STEP 3.2

1. Select the range **A8:D12**.

2. Move the pointer to the top edge of cell A8 until it changes to a four-headed arrow.

3. Click the top border of cell **A8**, press and hold the **left mouse button**, and then drag down to cell **A9** until the ScreenTip reads *A9:D13*, as shown in Figure 3-2.

4. Release the mouse button. The data moves to range A9:D13 and remains selected.

5. Move the pointer to the top edge of cell A9 until it changes to a four-headed arrow.

6. Press and hold the **Ctrl** key. The pointer changes to a white arrow with a plus sign.

7. Click and drag down to cell **A15** until the ScreenTip reads *A15:D19*.

8. Release the mouse button, and then release the **Ctrl** key. The data is copied from range A9:D13 to range A15:D19.

STEP-BY-STEP 3.2 Continued

9. Click cell **A15**, and then enter **Water**.

10. Click cell **B15**, and then enter **1000 gallons**.

11. Click cell **C15**, and then enter **Cost/1000 gal** to indicate the cost per 1000 gallons of water.

12. Save the workbook, and leave it open for the next Step-by-Step.

Using the Fill Handle

Filling copies a cell's contents and/or formatting into an adjacent cell or range. Select the cell or range that contains the content and formatting you want to copy. The **fill handle** appears in the lower-right corner of the active cell or range. When you place the pointer over the fill handle, it changes to a black cross. Click and drag the fill handle over the cells you want to fill. Then, release the left mouse button. The cell contents and formatting are duplicated into the range you selected, and the Auto Fill Options button appears below the filled content. Click the Auto Fill Options button to open the menu shown in Figure 3-3. You choose whether you want to fill both the cell's formatting and the cell's contents, only the cell's contents, or only the cell's formatting. Be aware that you can fill data only when the destination cells are adjacent to the original cell.

Did You Know?

You can also use the fill handle to continue a series of text items, numbers, or dates. For example, you might want to enter column labels of months, such as January, February, March, and so on, or row labels of even numbers, such as 2, 4, 6, and so forth. First, enter data in at least two cells to establish the pattern you want to use. Then, select the cells that contain the series pattern. Finally, drag the fill handle over the range of cells you want to fill. Excel enters appropriate data in the cells to continue the pattern.

FIGURE 3-3
Auto Fill Options menu

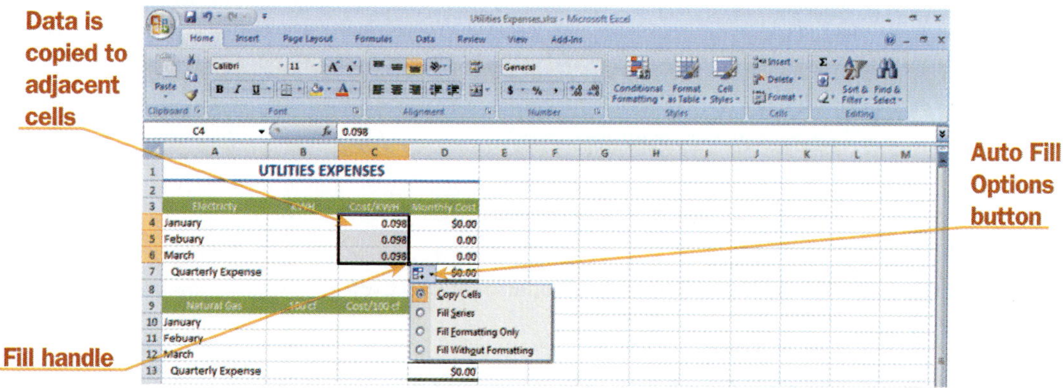

STEP-BY-STEP 3.3

1. Click cell **C4**, and then enter **.098** to record the cost of electricity. The cost of electricity for all three months is $0.098 per kilowatt hour.

2. Click cell **C4**. You want to fill this amount in cells C5 and C6.

3. Point to the **fill handle** in the lower-right corner of cell C4. The pointer changes to a black cross. 

4. Drag the fill handle down to cell **C6**. The contents of C4 are copied to cells C5 and C6.

5. Click cell **C10**, and then enter **1.64** to record the cost per 100 cubic feet of natural gas.

6. Drag the fill handle in the lower-right corner of cell C10 down to cell **C12**. The data from cell C10 is copied to cells C11 and C12.

7. Click cell **C16**, and then enter **1.98** to record the cost per 1000 gallons of water.

8. Drag the fill handle in the lower-right corner of cell C16 down to cell **C18**. The data from cell C16 is copied to cells C17 and C18.

9. In column B, enter the utility usage data shown in Figure 3-4. The monthly costs are calculated based on the data you entered.

FIGURE 3-4
Utility usage data

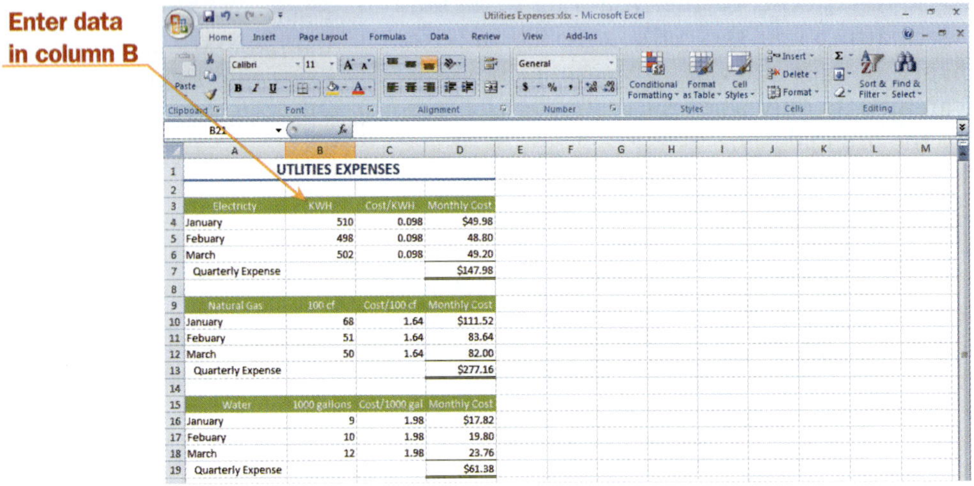

10. Save the workbook, and leave it open for the next Step-by-Step.

Inserting and Deleting Rows, Columns, and Cells

As you build a worksheet, you may discover that you need to add another row or column to store more data. Sometimes, you may find you need to remove a row or column of data that is no longer needed. At other times, you may need to insert or delete specific cells. On the Home tab of the Ribbon, the Cells group includes buttons for inserting and deleting rows, columns, and cells.

Inserting Rows and Columns

To insert a row, click the row number to select the row where you want the new row to appear. Then, click the Insert button in the Cells group on the Home tab. A blank row is added, and the existing rows shift down. To insert a column, click the column letter to select the column where you want the new column to appear. Then, click the Insert button in the Cells group. A blank column is added, and the existing columns shift to the right.

Did You Know?

If you select more than one row or column, the same number of rows or columns you selected is inserted in the worksheet.

Deleting Rows and Columns

The process is similar when you want to delete a row or column. First, click the row number or column letter of the row or column you want to delete. Then, in the Cells group on the Home tab, click the Delete button. The selected row or column disappears, erasing all its data and formatting. The existing rows shift up, or the existing columns shift left.

If you accidentally delete the wrong column or row, you can click the Undo button on the Quick Access Toolbar to restore the data. You can click the Redo button on the Quick Access Toolbar to cancel the Undo action.

Did You Know?

You can select one or more rows or columns, right-click the selected rows or columns, and then click Insert on the shortcut menu to insert an equal number or rows or columns in that location. To remove one or more rows or columns, right-click the selected rows or columns, and then click Delete on the shortcut menu.

Inserting and Deleting Cells

When entering a long column of data, it is not unusual to discover an omitted number near the top of the column. Rather than move the existing data to make room for entering the omitted data, you can insert a new, blank cell. First, select the cell where you want to insert the new cell. Then, in the Cells group on the Home tab, click the arrow next to the Insert button, and then click Insert Cells. The Insert dialog box appears, as shown in Figure 3-5. In this dialog box, you choose whether to shift the existing cells down or to the right.

FIGURE 3-5
Insert dialog box

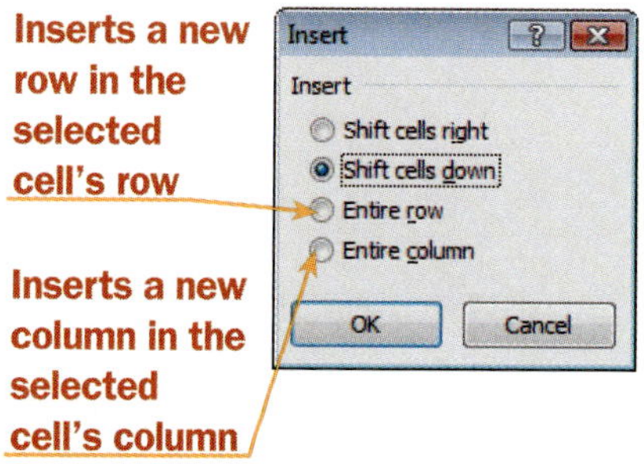

Did You Know?

You can also right-click a cell or selected range, and then, on the shortcut menu, click Insert to open the Insert dialog box or click Delete to open the Delete dialog box. In the dialog box, you can decide which way to shift cells. In addition, you can click the Entire row or Entire column option button, to add or remove the row or column that includes the selected cell.

Another common scenario is accidentally entering a number twice in a long column of data. To eliminate the duplicate data and reposition the rest of the data correctly, you can delete the individual cell. Select the cell you want to delete. Then, in the Cells group on the Home tab, click the arrow next to the Delete button, and then click Delete Cells. The Delete dialog box appears so you can choose whether to shift the remaining cells up or to the left.

S TEP-BY-STEP 3.4

1. Click the row **3** heading. The entire row 3 is selected.

2. On the Home tab, in the Cells group, click the **Insert** button. A new, blank row appears as row 3. The original row 3 becomes row 4.

3. Click cell **B3**, and then enter **Units Used**. Click cell **C3**, and then enter **Unit Cost**. Click cell **D3**, and then enter **Billed**.

4. Select the range **B3:D3**, and then apply the **20% - Accent3** cell style to the range.

5. Click the column **B** heading. The entire column B is selected.

6. On the Home tab, in the Cells group, click the **Insert** button. A new, blank column appears as column B. The original column B becomes column C.

7. Click cell **B3**, and then enter **Date Paid**. The active cell is cell B4.

8. On the Home tab, in the Cells group, next to the Delete button, click the **arrow**, and then click **Delete Sheet Columns**. Column B is deleted, and the remaining columns shift left.

9. Click the row **4** heading. The entire row 4 is selected.

10. In the Cells group, click the **Delete** button. Row 4 disappears, and the remaining rows shift up.

11. On the Quick Access Toolbar, click the **Undo** button. Row 4 reappears in the worksheet. 

12. Click cell **B18**.

13. In the Cells group, next to the Insert button, click the **arrow**, and then click **Insert Cells**. The Insert dialog box appears, as shown in Figure 3-5.

Careers

Business managers use Excel worksheets in a variety of ways. For example, human resource managers use spreadsheets to conduct performance reviews and keep track of employee records. Production managers use spreadsheets to track machine production efficiency and to keep machine maintenance records.

STEP-BY-STEP 3.4 Continued

14. Click the **Shift cells down** option button, if it is not selected. Click **OK**. The data in the range B18:B19 shifts to the range B19:B20.

15. Click cell **B18**, if it is not already the active cell.

16. On the Home tab, in the Cells group, next to the Delete button, click the **arrow**, and then click **Delete Cells**. The Delete dialog box appears.

17. Click the **Shift cells up** option button, if it is not selected. Click **OK**. The data in the range B19:B20 shifts back to the range B18:B19.

18. Save the workbook, and leave it open for the next Step-by-Step.

Freezing Panes in a Worksheet

Often a worksheet includes too much data to view on the screen at one time. As you scroll to other parts of the worksheet, titles and labels at the top or side of the worksheet might shift out of view, making it difficult to identify the contents of particular columns. For example, the worksheet title *Utilities Expenses* in the previous Step-by-Step might have scrolled off the screen when you were working in the lower part of the worksheet.

You can view two parts of a worksheet at once by freezing panes. When you freeze panes, you select which rows and/or columns of the worksheet remain visible on the screen as the rest of the worksheet scrolls. For example, you can freeze the row or column titles so they appear on the screen no matter where you scroll in the worksheet. As shown in Figure 3-6, rows 1, 2, and 3 are frozen so they remain on-screen even when you scroll down to row 16 (hiding rows 4 through 15).

FIGURE 3-6
Worksheet with rows 1 through 3 frozen

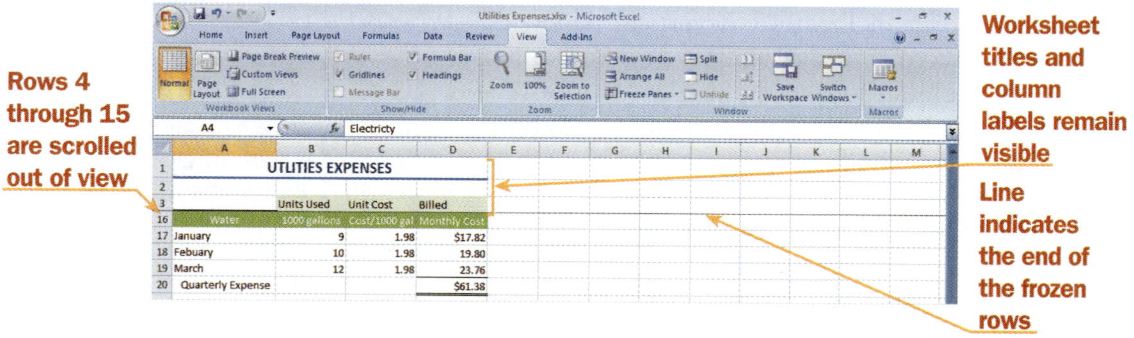

When you freeze panes in a worksheet, the rows and columns that remain locked on-screen depend on the location of the active row, column, or cell. Table 3-1 describes the different selection options. On the View tab of the Ribbon, in the Window group, click the Freeze Panes button, and then click Freeze Panes. A black gridline appears between the frozen and unfrozen panes of the worksheet.

TABLE 3-1
Freeze panes options

TO FREEZE	DO THE FOLLOWING
Rows	Select the first row below the row(s) you want to freeze
Columns	Select the first column to the right of the column(s) you want to freeze
Rows and columns	Select the first cell below and to the right of the row(s) and column(s) you want to freeze

When you want to unlock all the rows and columns to allow them to scroll, you need to unfreeze the panes. On the View tab of the Ribbon, in the Window group, click the Freeze Panes button, and then click Unfreeze Panes. The black gridline disappears, and all rows and columns are unfrozen.

Splitting a Worksheet Window

You might want to view different parts of a large worksheet at the same time. Splitting divides the worksheet window into two or four panes that you can scroll independently. This enables you to see distant parts of a worksheet at the same time. Splitting is particularly useful in a large worksheet when you want to copy data from one area to another. You can click in one pane and scroll the worksheet as needed while the other part of the worksheet remains in view in a different pane.

You can split the worksheet window into horizontal panes, as shown in Figure 3-7, vertical panes, or both. Select a row to split the window into horizontal panes. Select a column to split the worksheet into vertical panes. Select a cell to split the worksheet into both horizontal and vertical panes. Then, on the View tab of the Ribbon, in the Window group, click the Split button. The Split button remains selected, and a split bar separates the panes you created. If you want to resize the panes, drag the split bar. When you want to return to a single pane, click the Split button in the Window group again.

Did You Know? 

You can also use the mouse to add, resize, and remove panes. Drag the split box above the vertical scroll bar down to create horizontal panes. Drag the split box that appears to the right of the horizontal scroll bar to the left to create vertical panes. Drag a split bar to resize the panes. Double-click a split bar to remove it.

FIGURE 3-7
Worksheet window split into horizontal panes

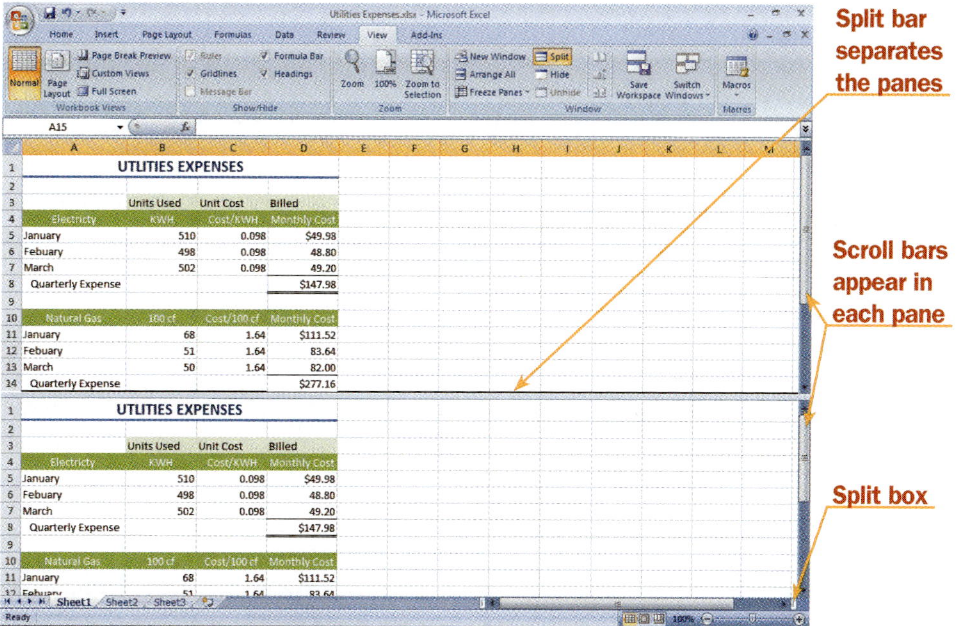

S TEP-BY-STEP 3.5

1. Click cell **A4**.

2. Click the **View** tab on the Ribbon, and then locate the **Window** group. This group contains the buttons for freezing and splitting panes.

3. Click the **Freeze Panes** button, and then click **Freeze Panes**. The title and column headings in rows 1 through 3 are locked. A black gridline appears between rows 3 and 4.

4. Scroll the worksheet down until row 16 is at the top of the worksheet window. The worksheet title and column headings remain locked at the top of the screen, even as other rows scroll out of view, as shown in Figure 3-6.

5. On the View tab, in the Window group, click the **Freeze Panes** button, and then click **Unfreeze Panes**. The title and column headings are no longer frozen.

6. Click the row **15** heading.

7. On the View tab, in the Window group, click the **Split** button. A split bar appears above row 15, dividing the worksheet into two horizontal panes.

8. Click in the lower pane and scroll up to row **1**. The same part of the worksheet appears in both panes, as shown in Figure 3-7.

9. Double-click the **split bar**. The split is removed, and worksheet is again one pane.

10. Save the workbook, and leave it open for the next Step-by-Step.

Checking Spelling in a Worksheet

An important step in creating a professional workbook is to correct any misspelling. Typographical errors can be distracting at best, and can cause others to doubt the accuracy of the rest of the workbook's content at worst. To help track down and correct spelling errors in a worksheet, you can use the Spelling command, which checks the spelling in the entire active worksheet against the dictionary that comes with Microsoft Office. To check the spelling in a worksheet, click the Review tab on the Ribbon, and then, in the Proofing group, click the Spelling button. The Spelling dialog box appears, as shown in Figure 3-8, with the first potential spelling error shown in the Not in Dictionary box.

FIGURE 3-8
Spelling dialog box

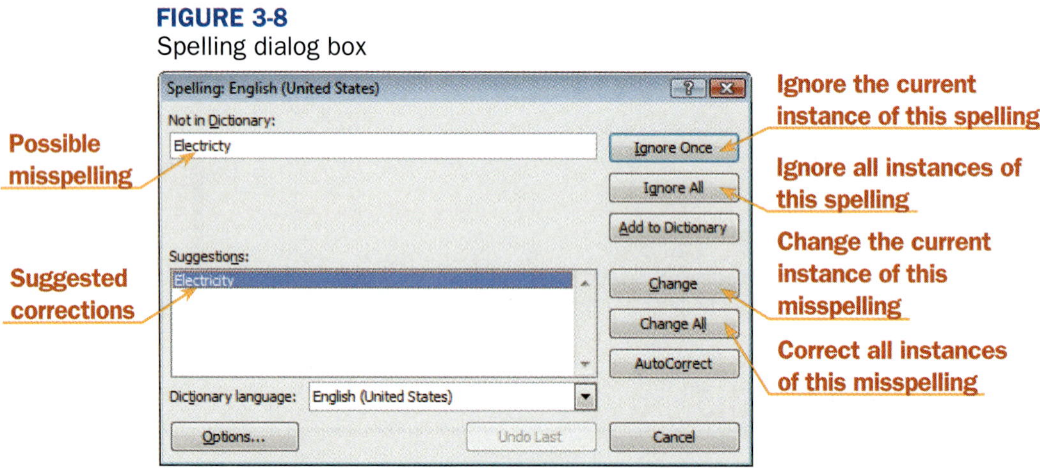

The Spelling dialog box provides many options for dealing with a possible misspelling. If the word is mistyped, you can correct the spelling yourself or click the correct word in the Suggestions box. Then, click Change to replace the current instance of the misspelling with the corrected word, or click Change All to replace every instance of the misspelling. If the word is correct (as often happens with company and product names), you can click Ignore to move to the next potential spelling error without making a change to the word, or click Ignore All to skip every instance of this word in the worksheet. After you have addressed all the possible misspellings in the worksheet, a dialog box appears to let you know that the spelling check is complete for the entire sheet.

Be aware that the spelling checker is not foolproof. As a final check, you should also proofread the worksheet for any misspellings that the spelling checker might have missed. You might find words that are spelled correctly, but used incorrectly (such as *they're*, *their*, and *there*, or *hour* and *our*). In addition, you might discover a missing word or two (*and* or *the*, for instance). This final check helps ensure your worksheet is free from errors.

Extra for Experts

If Excel incorrectly flags a word that you use frequently as a misspelling, you can add the word to a custom dictionary that resides on your computer by clicking the Add to Dictionary button. If the misspelling is a typo you make often, you can select the correct word in the Suggestions box, and then click the AutoCorrect button. Excel will automatically correct this mistake whenever you type it.

S TEP-BY-STEP 3.6

1. Press the **Ctrl+Home** keys. Cell A1 is the active cell in the worksheet.

2. Click the **Review** tab on the Ribbon, and then locate the **Proofing** group. The Spelling button is located here.

3. Click the **Spelling** button. The Spelling dialog box appears, as shown in Figure 3-8. The word *Electricty* is identified as a misspelled word. One correction appears in the Suggestions box.

4. In the Suggestions box, click **Electricity** if it is not selected, and then click **Change**. The spelling of the word in the workbook is corrected, and *Febuary* appears in the dialog box as the next possible misspelled word.

5. In the Suggestions box, click **February**, if it is not selected, and then click **Change All**. All three instances of this misspelling are corrected, and *cf* appears in the Not in Dictionary box as the next possible misspelling. However, *cf* is being used as an abbreviation for cubic feet, so you will ignore all instances of this abbreviation in the worksheet.

6. Click **Ignore All**. A dialog box appears, indicating the spelling check is complete for the entire sheet. (If the spelling checker flags other possible misspellings, change or ignore them as necessary, until the dialog box appears.)

7. Click **OK**.

8. Proofread the worksheet. In cell A1, the word *UTLITIES* is misspelled.

9. Click cell **A1**, and then, in the formula bar, click after *UT* to place the insertion point.

10. Type **I** to insert the missing letter in the word, and then press the **Enter** key.

11. Save the workbook, and leave it open for the next Step-by-Step.

Preparing a Worksheet for Printing

So far, you have used Normal view when entering and formatting data in a worksheet. Excel has other views as well. Page Layout view is helpful when you prepare a worksheet for printing. Excel has many options for changing how a worksheet appears on a printed page.

Setting Margins

Margins are blank spaces around the top, bottom, and sides of a page. The margins determine how many of a worksheet's columns and rows fit on a printed page. You can make the margins wider to leave extra blank space for jotting notes in the printed copy. Or, you can make the margins narrower when you want to print more columns and rows on a page. To change the margins of a worksheet, click the Page Layout tab on the Ribbon, and then, in the Page Setup group, click the Margins button. You can then choose among three preset margins—Normal (the default), Wide, and Narrow, as shown in Figure 3-9.

Extra for Experts

If the preset margins do not fit your needs, you can enter custom measurements for margins. Click the Margins button in the Page Setup group on the Page Layout tab, and then click Custom Margins. In each margin box, type the appropriate measurement, in inches, for the individual margins. Click OK when you are done.

FIGURE 3-9
Margins menu

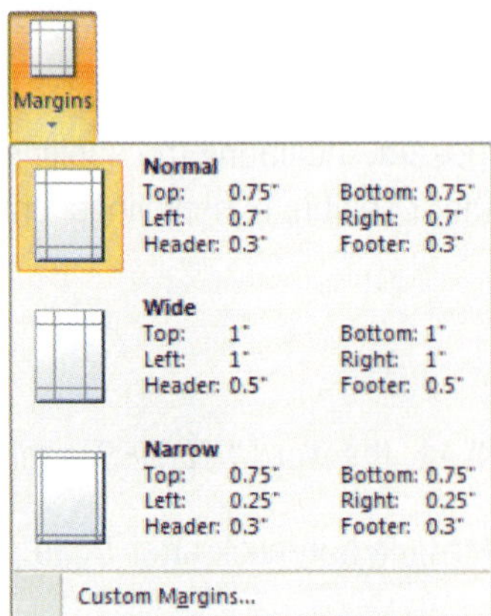

Changing the Page Orientation

Excel has two ways to print on a page. Worksheets printed in **portrait orientation** are longer than they are wide. In contrast, worksheets printed in **landscape orientation** are wider than they are long. By default, Excel is set to print pages in portrait orientation. Many worksheets, however, include more columns of data than fit on pages in portrait orientation. These pages look better and are easier to understand when printed in landscape orientation. You can change the orientation of the worksheet by clicking the Page Layout tab on the Ribbon, and then, in the Page Setup group, clicking the Orientation button. As shown in Figure 3-10, you can then click Portrait or Landscape on the menu.

FIGURE 3-10
Orientation menu

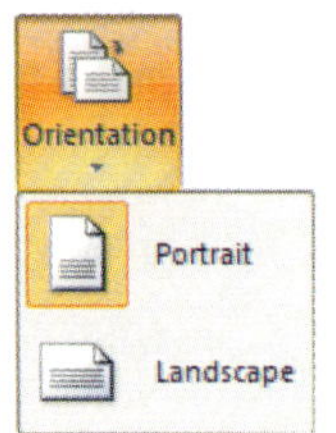

Setting the Print Area

When you print a worksheet, Excel assumes all of the data entered in that worksheet is to be printed. If you want to print only a portion of the data found in a worksheet, you will need to set the print area. The **print area** consists of the cells and ranges designated for printing. For example, you might want to print only the range A1:A19, which shows the utility and month data, and the range D3:D19 (billed amount). To do this, first select the range. Then, click the Page Layout tab on the Ribbon. In the Page Setup group, click the Print Area button, and then click Set Print Area. Each time you print, only the cells in the print area appear on the page. You must clear the print area to print the entire worksheet again. In the Page Setup group on the Page Layout tab, click the Print Area button, and then click Clear Print Area.

Inserting, Adjusting, and Deleting Page Breaks

When a worksheet or the print area doesn't fit on one printed page, page breaks indicate where the next page begins. Excel inserts an **automatic page break** whenever it runs out of room on a page. You can also insert a **manual page break** to start a new page. To insert a manual page break, select the row below where you want to insert a horizontal page break, or select the column to the left of where you want to insert a vertical page break. Then, click the Breaks button in the Page Setup group on the Page Layout tab, and then click Insert Page Break.

The simplest way to adjust page breaks in a worksheet is in **Page Break Preview**, as shown in Figure 3-11. On the status bar, click the Page Break Preview button to switch the worksheet to this view. Dashed lines appear for automatic page breaks, and solid lines appear for manual page breaks. You can drag any page break to a new location.

Did You Know?

You can center the worksheet on the printed page. Click the Page Layout tab on the Ribbon, and then click the Page Setup Dialog Box Launcher. Click the Margins tab in the Page Setup dialog box. In the Center on page section, check the Horizontally box to center the worksheet between the left and right margins. Check the Vertically box to center the worksheet between the top and bottom margins. Check both boxes to center the worksheet in both directions.

Extra for Experts

A print area can include multiple ranges and/or non-adjacent cells. For example, you might want to print the utility and month data as well as the bill amount. Select the cells and ranges you want to print, and then set the print area. The selected cells and ranges will print until you clear the print area.

FIGURE 3-11
Page Break Preview

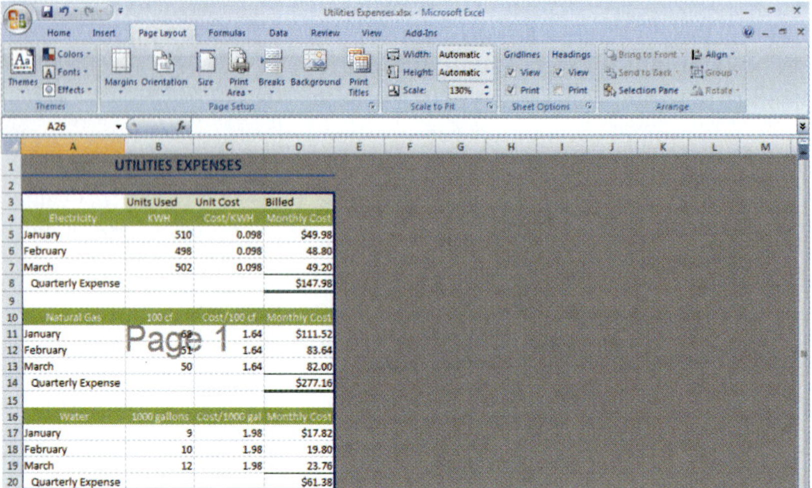

When you no longer want a manual page break, you can delete it. Click below or to the left of the page break you want to remove. Click the Page Layout tab on the Ribbon. In the Page Setup group, click the Breaks button, and then click Remove Page Break.

Scaling to Fit

Scaling enables you to resize a worksheet to print on a specific number of pages. The Scale to Fit group on the Page Layout tab contains three options for resizing a worksheet, as shown in Figure 3-12. You can fit the worksheet on the number of pages you specify for its width or height. Just click the arrow next to the Width or Height box and select the maximum pages for the printed worksheet's width or height. Another option is to set the percentage by which you want to shrink or enlarge the worksheet on the printed page. Click the arrows next to the Scale box to set the percentage.

FIGURE 3-12
Scale to Fit group

Choosing Sheet Options

By default, gridlines, row numbers, and column letters appear in the worksheet—but not on the printed page—to help you as you enter and format data. You can choose to show or hide gridlines and headings in a worksheet, as well as on the printed page. The Sheet Options group, shown in Figure 3-13, contains check boxes for viewing and printing gridlines and headings. Check and uncheck the boxes as needed.

FIGURE 3-13
Sheet Options group

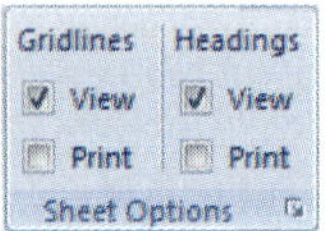

Specifying Print Titles

Print titles are designated rows and/or columns in a worksheet that print on each page. Specified rows print at the top of each page. Specified columns print on the left of each page. To set print titles, click the Page Layout tab on the Ribbon, and then, in the Page Setup group, click the Print Titles button. The Page Setup dialog box appears with the Sheet tab displayed, as shown in Figure 3-14 (left). Click the Collapse button next to the Rows to repeat at top box to shrink the dialog box, as shown in Figure 3-14 (right). Click the row or rows to use as the print title. Then, click the Expand button to restore the dialog box to its full size. You use the same process to select columns to repeat at left. Click OK to add the print titles to the worksheet.

Extra for Experts

The Page Setup dialog box also provides tabs for the Page, Margins, and Header/Footer options available on the Ribbon, as well as a few additional options. To open the Page Setup dialog box, click the Dialog Box Launcher in the Page Setup, Scale to Fit, or Sheet Options group on the Page Layout tab of the Ribbon.

FIGURE 3-14
Sheet tab in the Page Setup dialog box

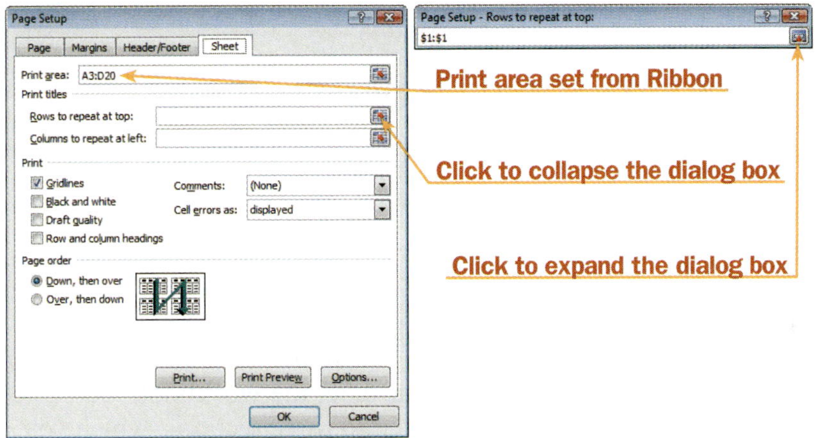

STEP-BY-STEP 3.7

1. Click the **Page Layout** tab on the Ribbon. This tab contains many commands for preparing a worksheet for printing.

2. In the Page Setup group, click the **Margins** tab to open the menu shown in Figure 3-9, and then click **Wide**. The margins are set for 1 inch on all sides. A dashed line, indicating an automatic page break, appears after column F.

3. On the Page Layout tab, in the Page Setup group, click the **Orientation** button to open the menu shown in Figure 3-10, and then click **Landscape**. The automatic page break moves after column J, indicating that the printed workbook will be wider than it is tall.

4. Select the range **A3:D20**.

5. On the Page Layout tab, in the Page Setup group, click the **Print Area** button, and then click **Set Print Area**. Only the selected range will print on the page.

STEP-BY-STEP 3.7 Continued

6. On the Page Layout tab, in the Scale to Fit group, click the **up arrow** next to the Scale box, shown in Figure 3-12, until **130** appears in the box. The printed data will enlarge to take up more of the page.

7. On the Page Layout tab, in the Sheet Options group, click the **Gridlines Print** check box to insert a check mark. The gridlines will print on the page.

8. On the Page Layout tab, in the Page Setup group, click the **Print Titles** button. The Page Setup dialog box appears, as shown in Figure 3-14 (left).

9. On the Sheet tab, in the Print titles section, click the **Collapse** button after the Rows to repeat at the top box. 

10. In the worksheet, click row **1** as the row to repeat at the top of each printed page. The row reference is added to the dialog box, as shown in Figure 3-14 (right). 

11. In the collapsed Page Setup dialog box, click the **Expand** button. 

12. Click **OK**.

13. Save the workbook, and leave it open for the next Step-by-Step.

Inserting Headers and Footers

Headers and footers are useful for adding identifying text to a printed page. A header is text that prints in the top margin of each page, as shown in Figure 3-15. A footer is text that prints in the bottom margin of each page. Text that is commonly included in a header or footer is your name, the page number, the current date, the workbook file name, and the worksheet name. Headers and footers are each divided into three sections, which you can use to organize the text.

FIGURE 3-15
Completed Header section

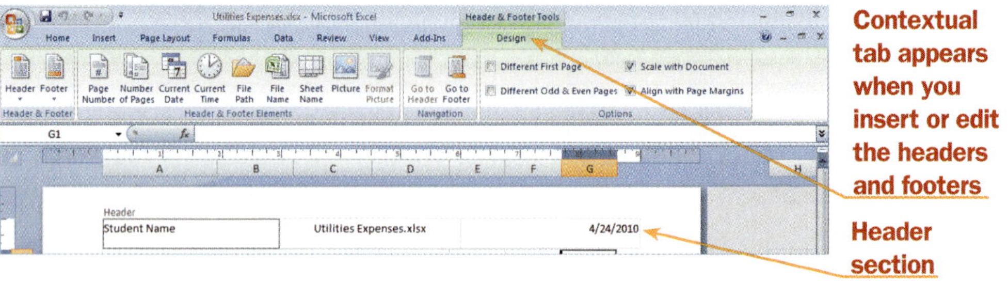

To create a header or footer for a printed worksheet, click the Insert tab on the Ribbon, and then in
the Text group, click the Header & Footer button. The
worksheet switches to Page Layout view, and the
Header & Footer Tools appear on the Ribbon with one
contextual tab—the Design tab. The insertion point is
in the center header box, but you can easily move to

Did You Know?

You can enter, edit, delete, and
format the text in each header
and footer section the same way
you do for text in worksheet cells.

the left or right section by clicking a different box. Type the text you want to enter, or click a
button in the Header & Footer Elements group on the Design tab under Header & Footer Tools
on the Ribbon. To enter a preset header or footer, in the Header & Footer group on the Design
tab, click the Header or Footer button, and then click the header or footer you want to use.
Click anywhere on the worksheet to close the headers and footers.

S TEP-BY-STEP 3.8

1. Click the **Insert** tab on the Ribbon, and then locate the **Text** group.

2. Click the **Header & Footer** button. The Header & Footer Tools appear on the Ribbon with the Design
   contextual tab. The worksheet changes to Page Layout view. The insertion point is in the center
   header box.

3. On the Design contextual tab, in the Header & Footer Elements group, click the **File Name** button.
   The code *&[File]* appears in the center header box.

4. Press the **Tab** key to move to the right header box. The code *&[File]* in the center header box is
   replaced with *Utilities Expenses.xlsx*, which is the current file name of the workbook. Remember, if
   your computer is not set to show file extensions, you see *Utilities Expenses* without the file extension in the center header box.

5. On the Design contextual tab, in the Header & Footer Elements group, click the **Current Date** button.
   The code *&[Date]* appears in the right header box.

6. Press the **Tab** key to move the insertion point to the left header box. The code *&[Date]* in the right
   header box is replaced with the current date.

7. In the left header box, type your name. The header is complete, as shown in Figure 3-15.

8. On the Design contextual tab, in the Navigation group, click the **Go to Footer** button. The insertion
   point moves to the left footer box.

9. Click the center footer box.

10. On the Design contextual tab, in the Header & Footer Elements group, click the **Page Number** button.
    The code *&[Page]* appears in the center footer box. After you move the insertion point out of the cen-
    ter footer box, the actual page number will appear.

STEP-BY-STEP 3.8 Continued

11. Click the worksheet to close the headers and footers. The worksheet appears in Page Layout view, as shown in Figure 3-16, giving a good sense of how it will print on the page.

FIGURE 3-16
Worksheet in Print Layout view

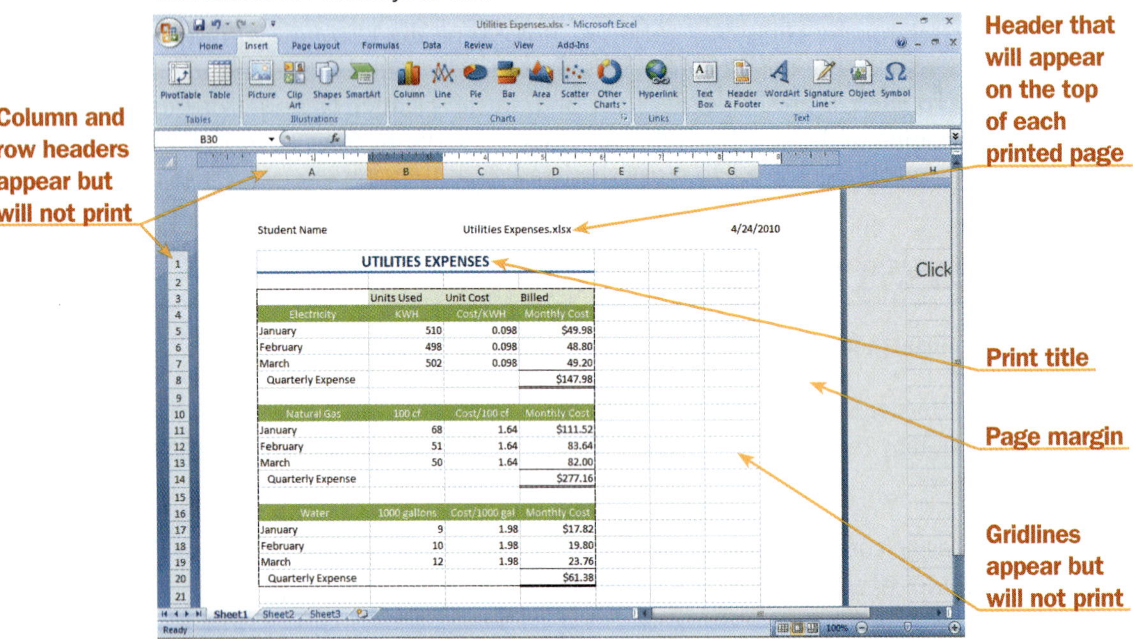

12. Save the workbook.

13. Click the **Office Button**, point to **Print**, and then click **Print Preview**. The worksheet appears in Print Preview, as shown in Figure 3-17. 

FIGURE 3-17
Worksheet in Print Preview

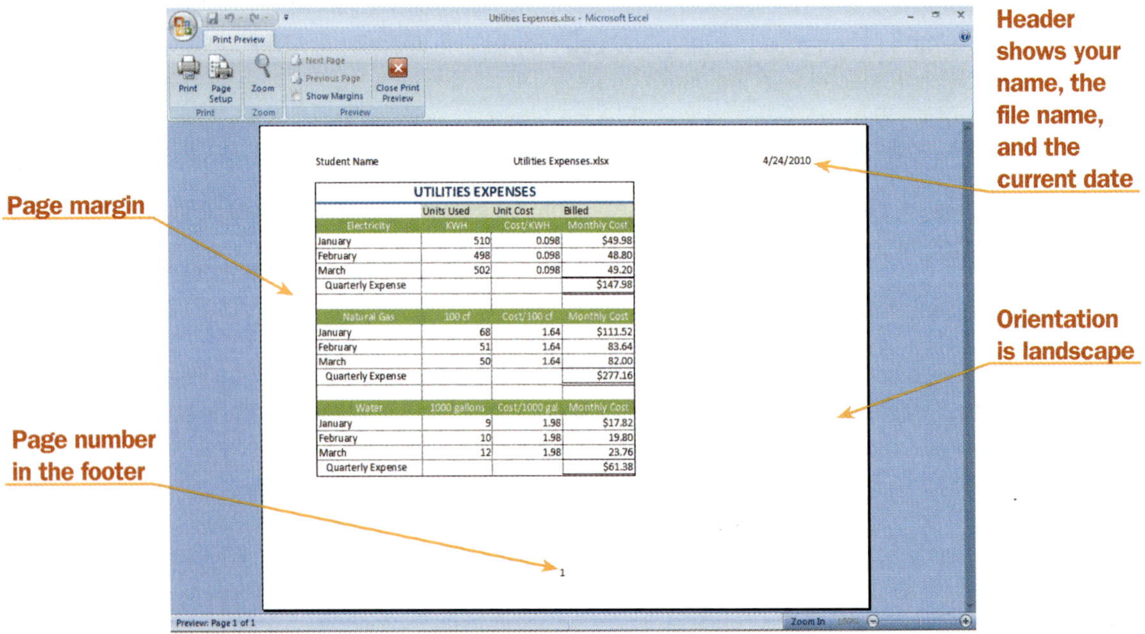

14. On the Print Preview tab, click the **Print** button. The Print dialog box opens. 

15. Click **OK** to print the worksheet, and then close the workbook.

Extra Challenge

Use the formatting skills you learned in earlier lessons to make the worksheet more attractive.

SUMMARY

In this lesson, you learned:

- Worksheet data can be moved or copied to another part of the worksheet. You can use the Copy, Cut, and Paste buttons, the drag-and-drop method, and the fill handle to copy and move data in a worksheet. These tools save time by eliminating the need to retype data.

- As you build a worksheet, you may need to insert a row or column to enter more data, or delete a row or column of unneeded data. You can also insert or delete specific cells within a worksheet.

- When a worksheet becomes large, the column or row labels can scroll out of view as you work on other parts of the worksheet. To keep select rows and columns on the screen as the rest of the worksheet scrolls, you can freeze panes.

- Splitting a large worksheet enables you to view and work in different parts of a worksheet at once, in two or four panes that you can scroll independently.

- You can check a worksheet for possible misspellings and correct them using the Spelling dialog box.

- When you are ready to print a worksheet, switching from Normal view to Page Layout view can be helpful. You can modify how a worksheet appears on the printed page by increasing or decreasing the margins, changing the page orientation, designating a print area, inserting page breaks, scaling, showing or hiding gridlines and headings, and specifying print titles.

- Headers and footers are useful for adding identifying text at the top and bottom of the printed page. Common elements include your name, the page number, the current date, the workbook file name, and the worksheet name.

VOCABULARY *Review*

Define the following terms:

Automatic page break	Header	Page Layout view
Copy	Landscape orientation	Paste
Cut	Manual page break	Portrait orientation
Fill	Margins	Print area
Fill handle	Normal view	Print title
Footer	Office Clipboard (Clipboard)	Scale
Freeze pane	Page Break Preview	Split

REVIEW *Questions*

TRUE/FALSE

Circle T if the statement is true or F if the statement is false.

T   F   **1.** If you paste data into cells with existing data, the pasted data appears after the existing data.

T   F   **2.** The Fill commands are available only if you are copying data to cells adjacent to the original cell.

T   F   **3.** Deleting a row or column erases the data in that row or column.

T   F   **4.** Splitting creates two, three, or four panes in the worksheet.

T   F   **5.** The spelling checker might not find all the misspellings or incorrectly used words in a worksheet.

WRITTEN QUESTIONS

Write a brief answer to the following questions.

1. What key do you press to copy data using the drag-and-drop method?

2. How do you make multiple copies of data that has been copied to the Clipboard?

3. What should you do if you accidentally delete a column or row?

4. How do you keep the titles and column labels of a worksheet on the screen, no matter where the worksheet is scrolled?

5. What is the difference between a header and a footer?

PROJECTS

PROJECT 3-1

Match the correct command in Column 2 to the action indicated in Column 1.

<table>
<tr><td colspan="2" align="center">Column 1</td><td align="center">Column 2</td></tr>
<tr><td>____</td><td>1. You are tired of typing repetitive data.</td><td>A. Print</td></tr>
<tr><td>____</td><td>2. A portion of the worksheet would be more useful in another area of the worksheet.</td><td>B. Cut, Paste</td></tr>
<tr><td>____</td><td>3. You forgot to type a row of data in the middle of the worksheet.</td><td>C. Insert Sheet Rows</td></tr>
<tr><td>____</td><td>4. You no longer need a certain column in the worksheet.</td><td>D. Delete Sheet Columns</td></tr>
<tr><td></td><td></td><td>E. Fill or Copy</td></tr>
<tr><td>____</td><td>5. Column headings scroll out of view when you are working in the lower part of the worksheet.</td><td>F. Print Area</td></tr>
<tr><td></td><td></td><td>G. Spelling</td></tr>
<tr><td>____</td><td>6. You want to be sure that all words are spelled correctly in the worksheet.</td><td>H. Freeze Panes</td></tr>
<tr><td>____</td><td>7. Your boss would rather not view your worksheet on the screen and has requested a copy on paper.</td><td></td></tr>
<tr><td>____</td><td>8. You want to print only a selected area of the worksheet.</td><td></td></tr>
</table>

PROJECT 3-2

1. Open the **Store.xlsx** Data File.

2. Save the workbook as **Store Assets** followed by your initials.

3. Insert a column to the left of column B.

4. Change the width of column A to 45.

5. Move the contents of the range D3:D16 to the range B3:B16.

6. Change the width of columns B and C to 10.

7. Indent the contents of A9, A13, and A16.

8. Underline the contents of B3:C3.

9. Insert a footer that includes your name in the left footer box and the current date in the right footer box.

10. Save, preview, and print the worksheet, and then close the workbook.

 **PROJECT 3-3**

1. Open the **Imports.xlsx** Data File.

2. Save the workbook as **Trade Imports** followed by your initials.

3. Freeze rows 1 through 6.

4. Check the spelling of the countries listed in the worksheet. (*Hint*: You will need to make four corrections.)

5. Change the orientation of the worksheet to portrait.

6. Scale the worksheet to 80% of its original size.

7. Change the margins to Wide.

8. In cell A5, enter your name.

9. Save, preview, and print the worksheet, and then close the workbook.

 **PROJECT 3-4**

1. Open the **Inventory.xlsx** Data File.

2. Save the workbook as **Supply Inventory** followed by your initials.

3. Organize the worksheet so inventory items are grouped by supplier, as shown below. Be sure to insert suitable headings and format them appropriately. Some of the data is out of order and needs to be moved.

Item	Ordering Code	Quantity
Mega Computer Manufacturers		
Mega X-39 Computers	X-39-25879	20
Mega X-40 Computers	X-40-25880	24
Mega X-41 Computers	X-41-25881	28
Xenon Paper Source		
Xenon Letter Size White Paper	LT-W-45822	70
Xenon Letter Size Color Paper	LT-C-45823	10
Xenon Legal Size White Paper	LG-W-45824	40
Xenon Legal Size Color Paper	LG-C-45825	5
MarkMaker Pen Company		
MarkMaker Blue Ball Point Pens	MM-Bl-43677	120
MarkMaker Black Ball Point Pens	MM-Bk-43678	100
MarkMaker Red Ball Point Pens	MM-R-43679	30

4. The following inventory item has been accidentally excluded from the worksheet. Add the item by using the Fill command and then editing the copied data.

Item	Ordering Code	Quantity
MarkMaker Green Ball Point Pens	MM-G-43680	30

5. Delete the following item.

Item	Ordering Code	Quantity
Mega X-39 Computers	X-39-25879	20

6. Change the page orientation to landscape.

7. Hide the gridlines from view.

8. Insert a header that includes your name in the center header box and the current date in the right header box.

9. Save, preview, and print the worksheet, and then close the workbook.

PROJECT 3-5

1. Open the **Time.xlsx** Data File.

2. Save the workbook as **Time Record** followed by your initials.

3. Delete rows 4 and 5.

4. Enter the following data in the time record.

Date	From	To	Admin. Meetings	Phone	Work Description
9-Dec	8:15 AM	12:00 PM	1.00	2.75	Staff meeting and called clients
10-Dec	7:45 AM	11:30 AM	2.00	1.75	Paperwork and called clients
11-Dec	7:45 AM	11:30 AM		3.75	Called clients
13-Dec	8:00 AM	12:00 PM	2.00	2.00	Mailed flyers and met w/KF

5. Freeze headings above row 8.

6. Insert a blank row above row 16. Enter the following information:

Date	From	To	Admin. Meetings	Phone	Work Description
12-Dec	7:45 AM	11:30 AM	2.00	1.75	Paperwork and called clients

7. Change the orientation of the worksheet to landscape.

8. In the range B1:D1, enter your name. Save the workbook.

9. Preview the worksheet and zoom in to see the total hours worked.

10. Print the worksheet, and then close the workbook.

 PROJECT 3-6

1. Open the **Biology.xlsx** Data File.

2. Save the workbook as **Biology Grades** followed by your initials.

3. Merge and center the range A1:H1. Merge and center the range A2:H2.

4. Insert a column between the current columns A and B.

5. In the range B3:B9, enter the following data:

Cell	Data
B3	First Name
B4	Mike
B5	Owen
B6	Cindy
B7	Raul
B8	Alice
B9	Cameron

6. Change the worksheet to landscape orientation.

7. Switch to Page Layout view. Click in the left header box and type your name.

8. Go to the footer, and insert *Page 1* in the center footer box. (*Hint*: Under the Header & Footer tools, on the Design contextual tab, in the Header & Footer group, click the Footer button, and then click Page 1.)

9. Save, preview, and print the worksheet, and then close the workbook.

> **Did You Know?** 
>
> As you type, the AutoComplete function displays the full text entered in other cells that begins with the same letters you have typed. To make a different entry, keep typing the new data. To accept the entry, press the Enter key.

 PROJECT 3-7

1. Open the **Booster.xlsx** Data File.

2. Save the workbook as **Booster Club** followed by your initials.

3. Bold and center the column headings in row 2.

4. Insert a row above row 3.

5. Freeze the column headings in row 2.

6. Insert a row above row 8, and then, in cell A8, enter **Bats**.

7. Copy cell E4 to the range E5:E11.

8. Format the Cost (D4:D11) and Total (E4:E12) columns as currency with two decimal places.

9. In the Sport and Cost columns, enter the following data, and then widen the columns as needed to display all of the data:

Item	Sport	Cost
Basketballs	Basketball	28
Hoops	Basketball	40
Backboards	Basketball	115
Softballs	Softball	5
Bats	Softball	30
Masks	Softball	35
Volleyballs	Volleyball	25
Nets	Volleyball	125

10. In the Quantity column, enter the following data.

Basketballs	5	Bats	5
Hoops	2	Masks	1
Backboards	2	Volleyballs	7
Softballs	20	Nets	1

11. You have $1210 to spend on equipment. Use any remaining cash to purchase as many basketballs as possible. Increase the number of basketballs and watch the dollar amount in the total. You should use $1203.00 and have $7.00 left over.

12. In cell A16, enter **Prepared by:** followed by your name.

13. Save, preview, and print the worksheet, and then close the workbook.

PROJECT 3-8

1. Open the **Pool.xlsx** Data File. The workbook contains attendance data for a neighborhood swimming pool.

2. Save the workbook as **Pool Attendance** followed by your initials.

3. Move data as needed to better organize the worksheet.

4. Format the worksheet in an appropriate and appealing way.

5. Insert your name, the workbook file name, and the current date in the appropriate header and footer boxes.

6. Save, preview, and print the worksheet, and then close the workbook.

CRITICAL *Thinking*

 **ACTIVITY 3-1**

As a zoo employee, you have been asked to observe the behavior of a chimpanzee during a three-day period. You need to record the number of minutes the animal displays certain behaviors during the time that the zoo is open to visitors. Set up a worksheet to record the number of minutes that the chimpanzee participates in the following behaviors during each of the three days.

- Sleeping
- Eating
- Walking
- Sitting
- Playing

Format the worksheet to make it attractive and easy to read. Change margins, orientation, and other page setup options to prepare the worksheet for printing. Include appropriate headers and footers, including at least your name in one of the boxes. Save the workbook with the file name **Chimpanzee Behavior** followed by your initials.

ENTERING WORKSHEET FORMULAS

OBJECTIVES

Upon completion of this lesson, you will be able to:

- Enter and edit formulas.
- Distinguish between relative, absolute, and mixed cell references.
- Use the point-and-click method to enter formulas.
- Use the Sum button to view summary calculations.
- Preview a calculation.
- Display formulas instead of results in the worksheet.
- Manually calculate formulas.

Estimated Time: 2.5 hours

VOCABULARY

Absolute cell reference

Formula

Manual calculation

Mixed cell reference

Operand

Operator

Order of evaluation

Point-and-click method

Relative cell reference

Sum button

What Are Formulas?

One of the main advantages of Excel is that you can use numbers entered in cells to make calculations in other cells. The equation used to calculate values in a cell is called a formula. Each formula begins with an equal sign (=). The results of the calculation appear in the cell in which the formula is entered. The formula itself appears in the formula bar. For example, if you enter the formula =8+6 in cell B3, the value 14 appears in the cell, and the formula =8+6 appears in the formula bar when cell B3 is the active cell, as shown in Figure 4-1.

FIGURE 4-1
Formula and formula results

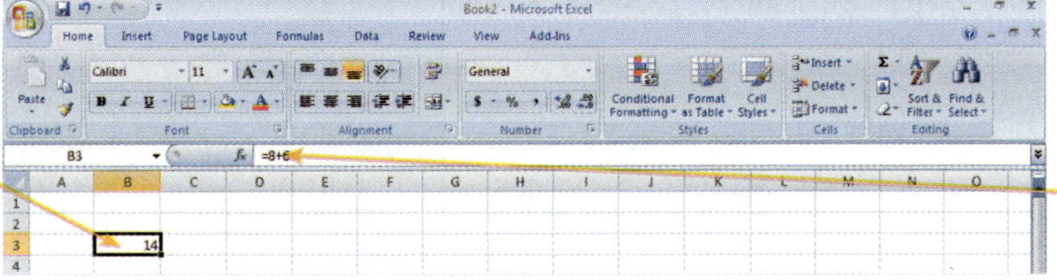

Entering a Formula

Worksheet formulas consist of two components: operands and operators. An **operand** is a constant (text or number) or cell reference used in a formula. You can type cell references in uppercase (A1) or lowercase (a1). An **operator** is a symbol that indicates the type of calculation to perform on the operands, such as a plus sign (+) for addition. Table 4-1 shows the different mathematical operators you can use in formulas. Consider the formula =B3+5. In this formula, the cell reference B3 and the constant 5 are operands, and the plus sign (+) is an operator. This formula tells Excel to add the value in cell B3 to the value 5. After you finish typing a formula in a cell, you must enter it by pressing the Enter or Tab key or by clicking the Enter button on the formula bar.

TABLE 4-1
Mathematical operators

OPERATOR	OPERATION	EXAMPLE	MEANING
+	Addition	B5+C5	Adds the values in cells B5 and C5
−	Subtraction	C8–232	Subtracts 232 from the value in cell C8
*	Multiplication	D4*D5	Multiplies the value in cell D4 by the value in cell D5
/	Division	E6/4	Divides the value in cell E6 by 4
^	Exponentiation	B3^3	Raises the value in cell B3 to the third power

STEP-BY-STEP 4.1

1. Open the **Formula.xlsx** Data File.

2. Save the worksheet as **Formula Practice** followed by your initials.

3. Click cell **C3**. You'll enter a formula in this cell.

4. Type **=A3+B3**, and then press the **Enter** key. The formula result 380 appears in the cell. Cell C4 is the active cell.

5. Click cell **C4**, type **=A4–B4**, and then press the **Enter** key. The formula result –246 appears in the cell. Cell C5 is the active cell.

6. Click cell **C5**, type **=A5*B5**, and then press the **Enter** key. The formula result 18850 appears in the cell. Cell C6 is the active cell.

7. Click cell **C6**, type **=A6/B6**, and then press the **Enter** key. The formula result 2 appears in the cell. Compare your results to Figure 4-2.

> **Computer Concepts** 
>
> The cell references you use in formulas are color-coded. Each cell reference in the formula appears in a specific color. The cell itself in the worksheet is outlined in the same color. You can change a cell reference in a formula by dragging the outlined cell to another location in the worksheet. You can also change which cells are included in a reference by dragging any corner of the colored outline to resize the selected range.

STEP-BY-STEP 4.1 Continued

FIGURE 4-2
Formulas entered in worksheet

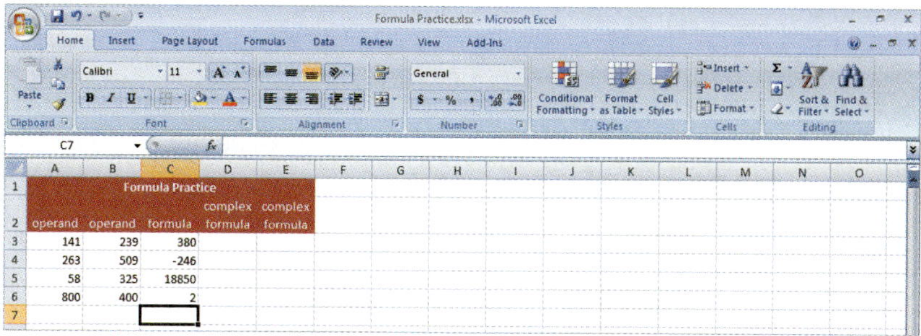

8. Save the workbook, and leave it open for the next Step-by-Step.

Order of Evaluation

Formulas can include more than one operator. For example, the formula =C3*C4+5 includes two operators and performs both multiplication and addition to calculate the value in the cell. The sequence used to calculate the value of a formula is called the order of evaluation.

Formulas are evaluated as follows:

1. Contents within parentheses are evaluated first. You can use as many pairs of parentheses as you want. The innermost set of parentheses is evaluated first.

2. Mathematical operators are evaluated in the order of priority shown in Table 4-2.

3. If two or more operators have the same order of evaluation, the equation is evaluated from left to right. For example, in the formula =20–15–2, first the number 15 is subtracted from 20, then 2 is subtracted from the difference (5).

TABLE 4-2
Order of evaluation priority

ORDER OF EVALUATION	OPERATOR	SYMBOL
First	Exponentiation	^
Second	Positive or negative	+ or −
Third	Multiplication or division	* or /
Fourth	Addition or subtraction	+ or −

STEP-BY-STEP 4.2

1. Click cell **D3**, and then type **=(A3+B3)*20**. This complex formula adds the values in cells A3 and B3, and then multiplies the result by 20.

2. Press the **Enter** key. The formula results in the value 7600, which appears in cell D3.

STEP-BY-STEP 4.2 Continued

3. Click cell **E3**, and then type **=A3+B3*20**. This formula is the same as the one you entered in cell D3, but without the parentheses. The lack of parentheses changes the order of evaluation and the resulting value.

4. Press the **Enter** key. As you see in cell E3, the formula results in the value 4921. This differs from the formula results in cell D3 because Excel multiplied the value in cell B3 by 20 before adding the value in cell A3. In cell D3, Excel added the values in cells A3 and B3, and then multiplied the sum by 20.

5. Save the workbook, and leave it open for the next Step-by-Step.

Editing Formulas

You cannot enter a formula with an incorrect structure in Excel. If you attempt to do so, a dialog box appears, explaining the error and providing a possible correction. You can accept that correction or choose to correct the formula yourself. For example, if you enter a formula with an opening parenthesis but no closing parenthesis, a dialog box appears, as shown in Figure 4-3, indicating that Excel found an error and proposing a correction that adds a closing parenthesis to the formula. Click Yes to accept the proposed correction. Click No to see a description of the error in another dialog box, and then click OK to return to the formula. You can correct the formula by editing it directly in the worksheet cell or by clicking in the formula bar.

FIGURE 4-3
Formula error message

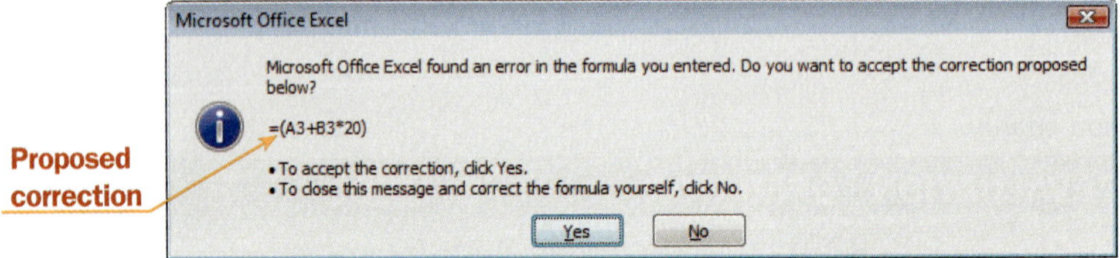

Proposed correction

Although Excel checks that the formula has the correct structure, it does not check that the formula contains the correct values or cell references. If you discover that you need to make a correction, you can edit the formula. Click the cell with the formula you want to edit. Press the F2 key or double-click the cell to enter editing mode. Move the insertion point as needed to edit the entry. Then, press the Enter key or click the Enter button on the formula bar to enter the formula.

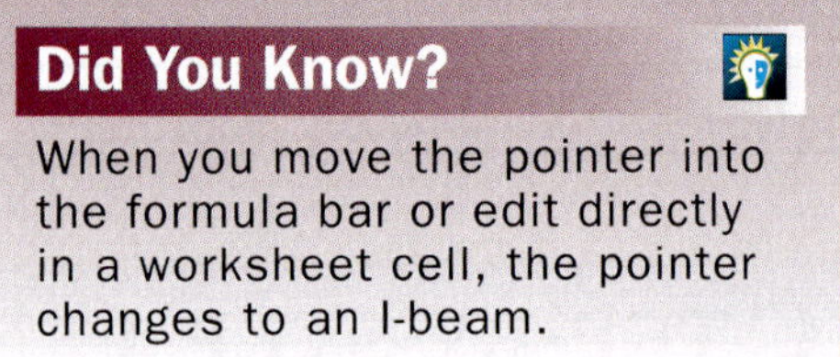
Did You Know?

When you move the pointer into the formula bar or edit directly in a worksheet cell, the pointer changes to an I-beam.

STEP-BY-STEP 4.3

1. Click cell **E3**. The formula is shown in the formula bar.

2. In the formula bar, click after = (the equal sign).

3. Type **(** (an opening parenthesis). You will intentionally leave out the closing parenthesis.

4. Press the **Enter** key. The dialog box shown in Figure 4-3 indicates that Excel found an error and offers a possible correction.

5. Read the message, and then click **No**. You will correct the error yourself. A dialog box appears, describing the specific error Excel found, as shown in Figure 4-4.

FIGURE 4-4
Formula error description message

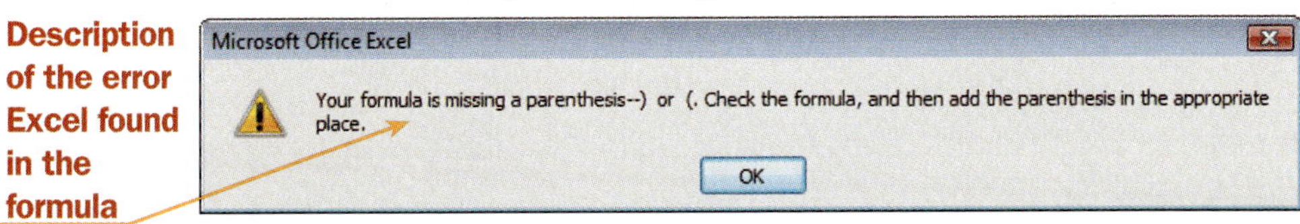

6. Read the message, and then click **OK**.

7. Move the insertion point in the formula bar between the 3 and the *.

8. Type **)** (a closing parenthesis).

9. Press the **Enter** key. The value changes to 7600.

10. Save the workbook, and leave it open for the next Step-by-Step.

Comparing Relative, Absolute, and Mixed Cell References

Three types of cell references are used in formulas: relative, absolute, and mixed. A **relative cell reference** adjusts to its new location when copied or moved. For example, when the formula =A3+A4 is copied from cell A5 to cell B5, the formula changes to =B3+B4, as shown in Figure 4-5. How does Excel know how to change a relative cell reference? It creates the same relationship between the cells in the new location. In other words, the formula =A3+A4 in cell A5 instructs Excel to add the two cells directly above it. When you move this formula to another cell, such as cell B5, Excel uses that same instruction: to add the two cells directly above the cell with the formula. Notice that only the cell references change; the operators remain the same.

FIGURE 4-5
Relative cell references

Original formula with relative references

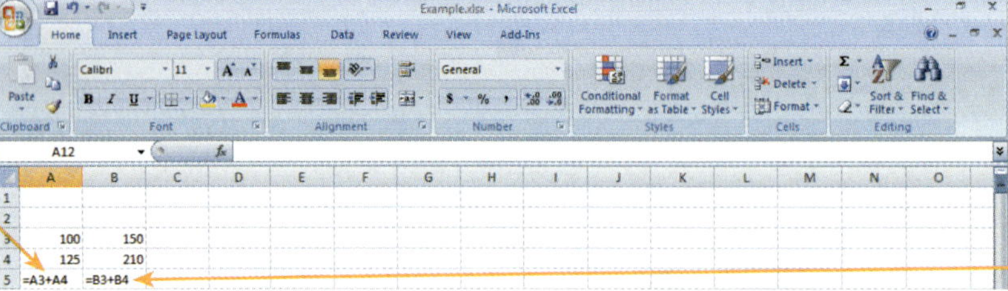

Relative references shift based on new location of copied formula

Absolute cell references do not change when copied or moved to a new cell. To create an absolute cell reference, you insert a dollar sign ($) before the column letter and before the row number. For example, when the formula =$A$3+$A$4 in cell A5 is copied to cell B7, the formula remains unchanged, as shown in Figure 4-6.

FIGURE 4-6
Absolute cell references

Original formula with absolute references

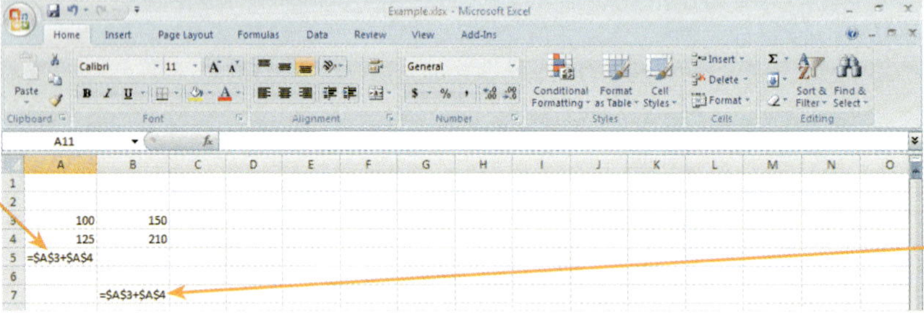

Absolute references remain unchanged in new location of copied formula

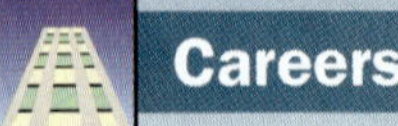

Careers

Engineers use Excel worksheets to perform complex calculations in areas such as construction, transportation, and manufacturing. For example, Excel worksheets are used to fit equations to data, interpolate between data points, solve simultaneous equations, evaluate integrals, convert units, and compare economic alternatives.

Cell references that contain both relative and absolute references are called **mixed cell references**. When formulas with mixed cell references are copied or moved, the row or column references preceded by a dollar sign do not change; the row or column references not preceded by a dollar sign adjust to match the cell to which they are moved. As shown in Figure 4-7, when the formula =A$3+A$4 is copied from cell A5 to cell B7, the formula changes to =B$3+B$4.

FIGURE 4-7
Mixed cell references

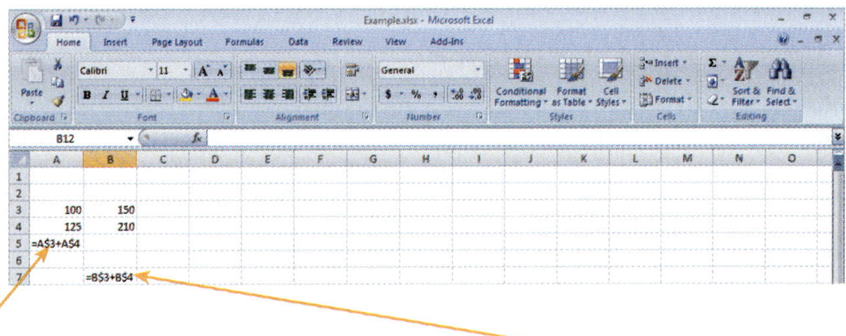

STEP-BY-STEP 4.4

1. Click cell **D3**. The formula =(A3+B3)*20 (shown in the formula bar) contains only relative cell references.

2. Drag the fill handle to cell **D4** to copy the formula from cell D3 to cell D4.

3. Click cell **D4**. The value in cell D4 is 15440, and the formula in the formula bar is =(A4+B4)*20. The operators in the formula remain the same, but the relative cell references change to reflect the new location of the formula.

4. Click cell **D5**, type **=$A$3*($B$3–200)**, and then press the **Enter** key. The value in cell D5 is 5499. The formula contains absolute cell references, which are indicated by the dollar signs that precede the row and column references.

5. Copy the formula in cell **D5** to cell **D6**. The value in cell D6 is 5499, the same as in cell D5.

6. Click cell **D5** and look at the formula in the formula bar.

> ### Extra for Experts 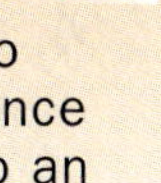
>
> You can press the F4 key to cycle a selected cell reference from a relative reference to an absolute reference to a mixed reference with an absolute row to a mixed reference with an absolute column and back to a relative reference.

7. Click cell **D6** and look at the formula in the formula bar. The formula in cell D5 is exactly the same as the formula in cell D6, because the formula you copied from cell D5 contains absolute cell references.

8. Click cell **E4**, type **=$A$4+B4**, and then press the **Enter** key. This formula contains mixed cell references (relative and absolute). The value in cell E4 is 772.

9. Copy the formula in cell **E4** to cell **E5**, and then click cell **E5**. The relative cell reference B4 changes to B5, but the absolute reference $A$4 stays the same. The value in cell E5 is 588.

10. Copy the formula in cell **E5** to cell **F5**, and then click cell **F5**. The relative cell reference B5 changes to C5, but the absolute reference $A$4 stays the same. The value in cell F5 is 19113.

11. Click cell **A8**, and then enter your name. Save, print, and close the workbook.

Creating Formulas Quickly

So far, you have created formulas by typing the formula or editing an existing formula. You can also create formulas quickly by using the point-and-click method and the Sum button.

Using the Point-and-Click Method

Earlier, you constructed formulas by typing the entire formula directly in a worksheet cell. You can include cell references in a formula more quickly by using the **point-and-click method** to click each cell, rather than typing cell references. The point-and-click method is particularly helpful when you need to enter long formulas that contain multiple cell references.

To use the point-and-click method, simply click the cell instead of typing the cell reference. For example, to use the point-and-click method to enter the formula =A3+B3, click the cell in which you want to enter the formula, press =, click cell A3, press +, click cell B3, and then press the Enter key.

STEP-BY-STEP 4.5

1. Open the **Drink.xlsx** Data File.

2. Save the workbook as **Drink Sales** followed by your initials.

3. Click cell **F6**, type **=(** to begin the formula, and then click cell **B6**. A flashing blue border surrounds cell B6 to indicate it is selected, and its cell reference in the formula is also blue.

4. Type *. The flashing border disappears, but the cell border and reference remain blue.

5. Click cell **C6**. A flashing green border appears around cell C6, and its cell reference in the formula is the same color.

6. Type **)+(** and then click cell **D6**. The cell and formula reference are purple.

7. Type * and then click cell **E6**. The cell border and reference are red. Figure 4-8 shows the color-coded formula and cell references.

Did You Know?

A flashing colored border indicates that you can replace the current reference in the formula by clicking another cell or selecting a range. When the border is no longer flashing, the cell reference is "locked," and you must select the reference in the formula to replace it.

STEP-BY-STEP 4.5 Continued

FIGURE 4-8
Color-coded formula

Each cell reference in the formula is color-coded to match the selected cell border

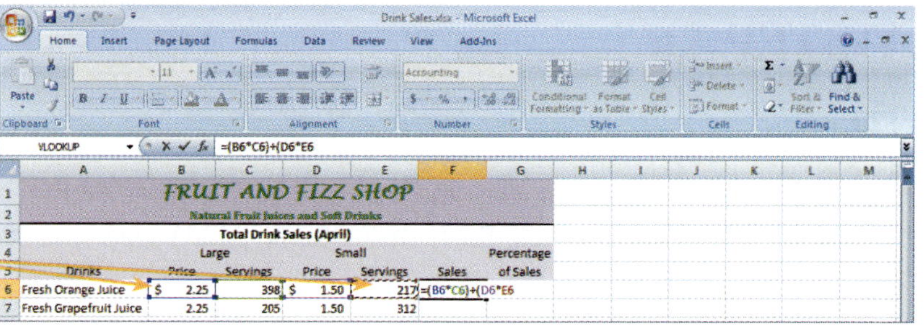

8. Type **)** and then press the **Enter** key. The amount $1,221.00 appears in cell F6.

9. Use the fill handle to copy the formula in cell **F6** to the range **F7:F11**. All the monthly sales are calculated for each type of drink, as shown in Figure 4-9.

FIGURE 4-9
Monthly drink sales

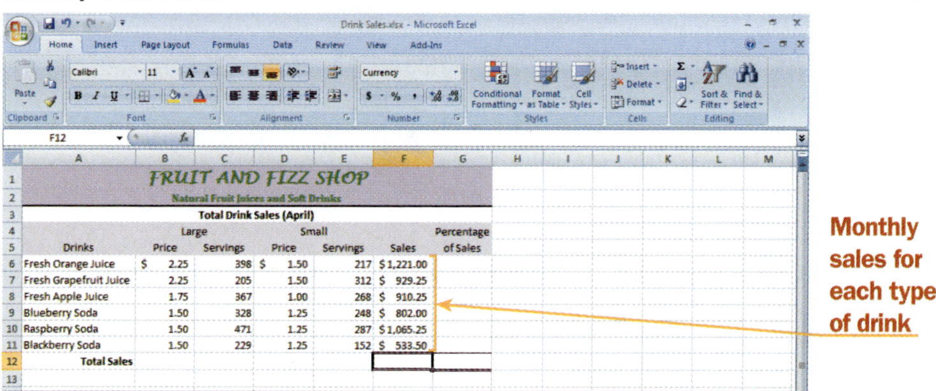

Monthly sales for each type of drink

10. Save the workbook, and leave it open for the next Step-by-Step.

Using the Sum Button

 Worksheet users frequently need to add long columns or rows of numbers. The **Sum button**, located in the Editing group on the Home tab of the Ribbon, makes this operation simple.  To use the Sum button, click the cell where you want the total to appear, and then click the Sum button. Excel scans the worksheet to determine the most logical adjacent column or row of cells with numbers to add. An outline appears around the range it selects, and the range reference appears in the active cell. If you want to add the numbers in a different range, drag to select those cells. Press the Enter key to complete the formula. The active cell displays the sum.

Extra for Experts

Other commonly used functions find the AVERAGE, MAX (maximum), and MIN (minimum) of a range, as well as COUNT NUMBERS, to determine how many entries are included in the range. You can enter these from the Sum button menu. Click the cell in which you want to enter the function. On the Home tab, in the Editing group, click the arrow next to the Sum button. A menu lists these common functions. Click the function you want to use. Verify the range, and then press the Enter key.

The Sum button enters a formula with the SUM function, which is a shorthand way to specify adding numbers in a range. The SUM function that adds the numbers in the range D5:D17, for example, is =SUM(D5:D17). Functions are discussed in greater detail in the next lesson.

STEP-BY-STEP 4.6

1. Click cell **F12**.

2. On the Home tab, in the Editing group, click the **Sum** button. The range F6:F11 is outlined, which is the range of cells you want to add. The formula =SUM(F6:F11) appears in the formula bar. See Figure 4-10.

FIGURE 4-10
Sum function in the formula

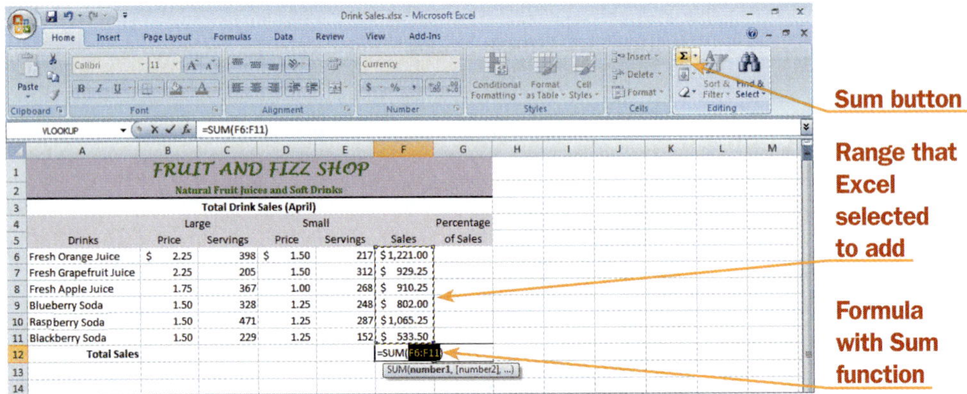

3. Press the **Enter** key. Cell F12 displays $5,461.25, the sum of the numbers in column F.

4. Click cell **G6**, and then type **=**.

5. Click cell **F6**, and then type **/**.

6. Click cell **F12**, press the **F4** key, and then press the **Enter** key. You used an absolute reference to cell F12 because you want the cell reference to remain unchanged when you copy it to the rest of the range.

7. Copy the formula in cell **G6** to the range **G7:G11**. The Percentage of Sales is entered for all of the drinks.

8. Click cell **G12**. On the Home tab, in the Editing group, click the **Sum** button. Press the **Enter** key. The total percentage of sales is 100%. See Figure 4-11.

STEP-BY-STEP 4.6 Continued

FIGURE 4-11
Percentage of Sales calculated

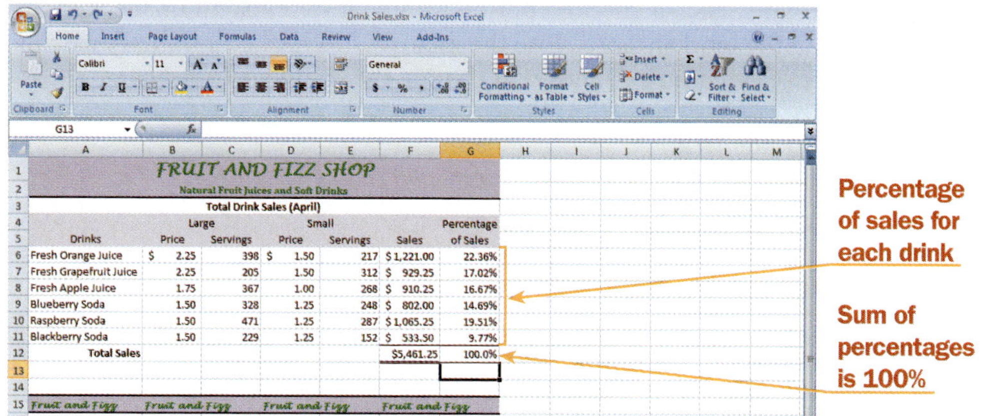

9. Save the workbook, and leave it open for the next Step-by-Step.

Previewing Calculations

Whenever you select a range, the status bar shows the results of common calculations for the selected cells. These summary calculations appear without your having to enter a formula. By default, Average, Count, and Sum appear in the status bar. You can also display Numerical Count, Minimum, and Maximum. Table 4-3 describes each of these options.

TABLE 4-3
Summary calculation options for the status bar

CALCULATION	DESCRIPTION
Average	Averages all the numbers in the selected cells
Count	Lists how many cells are selected
Numerical Count	Lists how many of the selected cells contain numbers
Minimum	Shows the smallest number in the selected cells
Maximum	Shows the largest number in the selected cells
Sum	Adds all the numbers in the selected cells

To display the default calculations in the status bar, just select a range. You can change which summary calculations appear in the status bar. Right-click the status bar to open the Customize Status Bar menu shown in Figure 4-12. Options that are preceded by a check mark appear in the status bar. Options without a check mark are hidden. You can choose which calculations you want to show or hide. Click a checked option to hide it, or click an unchecked option to show it. Click anywhere in the worksheet to close the menu. The checked summary calculations appear in the status bar for selected ranges until you change the displayed options.

FIGURE 4-12
Customize Status Bar menu

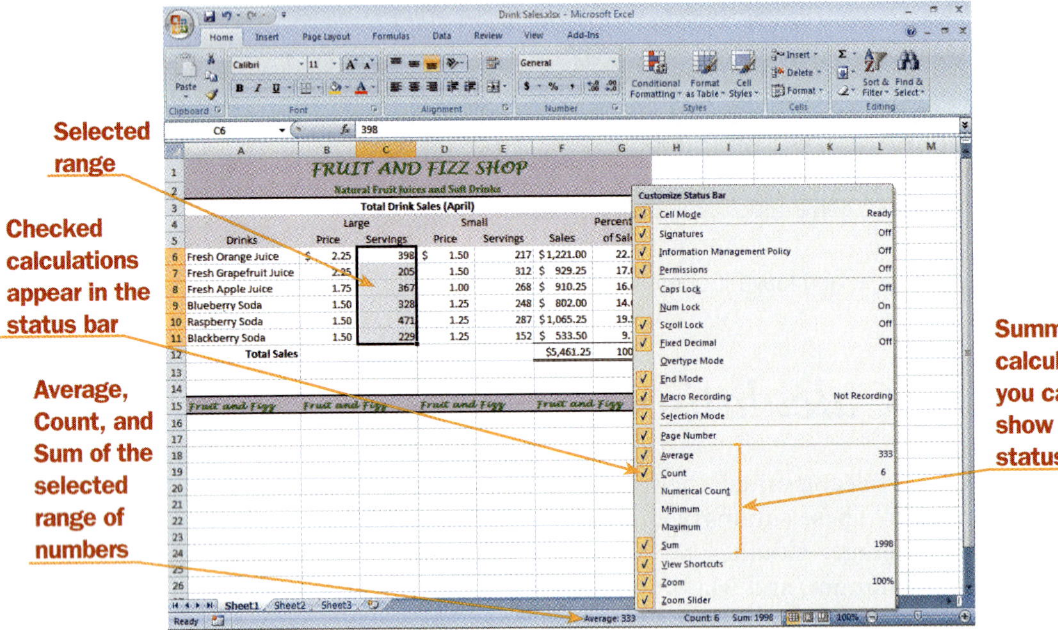

STEP-BY-STEP 4.7

1. Select the range **C6:C11**. Summary calculations for the large servings appear in the status bar, showing an Average of 333, a Count of 6, and the Sum of 1998.

2. Right-click the **status bar**. The Customize Status Bar menu appears, as shown in Figure 4-12.

3. Click **Minimum**. A check mark precedes Minimum on the menu, and the menu remains open so you can click additional options. The smallest number of large drinks served, 205, appears in the status bar.

4. Click **Minimum** to hide the calculation from the status bar, and then press the **Esc** key to close the menu.

5. Select the range **E6:E11**. Summary calculations for the small servings appear in the status bar, showing an Average of 247.333, a Count of 6, and the Sum of 1484.

Extra Challenge 

You can use the summary calculations in the status bar to check formula results. Cell F12 contains the SUM function formula that adds the values in the range F6:F11. To confirm these results, select the range F6:F11, then compare the Sum value in the status bar with the value in cell F12. The sum in the status bar should equal the value in cell F12.

STEP-BY-STEP 4.7 Continued

6. Click cell **A13** to deselect the range.

7. Save the workbook, and leave it open for the next Step-by-Step.

Showing Formulas in the Worksheet

In previous Step-by-Steps, you viewed formulas in the formula bar or directly in worksheet cells as you typed or edited the formulas. After you enter the formulas, the cells show the formula results rather than the formulas themselves. Typically, this is what you want to view. However, when creating a worksheet with many formulas, you may find it simpler to organize formulas and detect formula errors when all formulas are visible. To do this, click the Formulas tab on the Ribbon, and then click the Show Formulas button in the Formula Auditing group. The formulas replace the formula results in the worksheet. If a cell does not contain a formula, the data entered in the cell remains displayed. The Show Formulas button remains selected until you click it again to redisplay the formula results. It can be helpful to print the worksheet showing formulas for reference.

> **Did You Know?**
>
> 
>
> You can use also switch between showing formulas and showing formula results in a worksheet by pressing the Ctrl+` keys (the grave accent is located in the upper-left area of most standard keyboards).

Calculating Formulas Manually

Excel calculates formula results when you enter the formula and recalculates the results whenever the cells used in that formula change. However, the calculation and recalculation process can take a long time when a worksheet contains many formulas. When you need to edit a worksheet with many formulas, you can specify manual calculation, which lets you determine when Excel calculates the formulas.

The Formulas tab on the Ribbon contains all the buttons you need when working with manual calculations. To switch to manual calculation, click the Calculation Options button in the Calculation group on the Formulas tab, and then click Manual. When you want to calculate the formula results for the entire workbook, click the Calculate Now button. To calculate the formula results for only the active worksheet, click the Calculate Sheet button. To return to automatic calculation, click the Calculation Options button in the Calculation group on the Formulas tab, and then click Automatic.

STEP-BY-STEP 4.8

1. Click the **Formulas** tab on the Ribbon. In the Formula Auditing group, click the **Show Formulas** button. All formulas appear in the worksheet cells instead of the formula results.

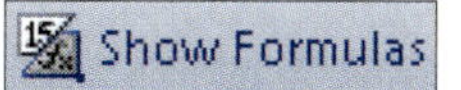

2. Scroll to the right as needed so that columns F and G appear on the screen.

3. On the Formulas tab, in the Calculation group, click the **Calculation Options** button. A menu of options appears, as shown in Figure 4-13. 

FIGURE 4-13
Worksheet with formulas showing

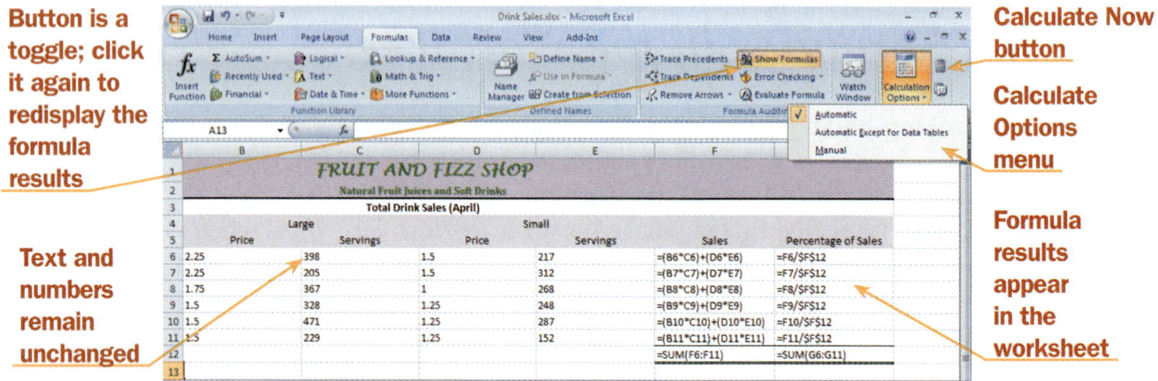

4. Click **Manual**. Automatic calculation is turned off.

5. Press the **Ctrl+`** keys. The formula results reappear.

6. Click cell **C6**, and then enter **402**. Click cell **C7**, and then enter **220**. Click cell **E10**, and then enter **305**. The worksheet values change, but Excel does not recalculate the formula results.

7. On the Formulas tab, in the Calculation group, click the **Calculate Now** button while watching the worksheet. Excel recalculates the formulas when you click the button. The total sales amount in cell F12 is $5,526.50. 

8. On the Formulas tab, in the Calculation group, click the **Calculation Options** button, and then click **Automatic**.

9. Insert a header with your name in the left section and the current date in the right section.

10. Save, print, and close the workbook.

Extra Challenge

In the *Drink Sales.xlsx* workbook, the current sales amount for large and small orange juices sold is $1230. Determine how many large orange juices must sell to achieve more than $1700 in sales. Do this by entering larger amounts in cell C6. When you have determined the amount, close the workbook without saving.

SUMMARY

In this lesson, you learned:

- Formulas are equations used to calculate values in a cell, based on values referenced in other cells of the worksheet. Each formula begins with an equal sign and contains at least two operands and one operator.

- Formulas can include more than one operator. The order of evaluation determines the sequence used to calculate the value of a formula.

- You cannot enter a formula with an incorrect structure. Excel can correct the error for you, or you can choose to edit it yourself. To edit a formula, click the cell with the formula and then make changes in the formula bar. You can also double-click a formula and then edit the formula directly in the cell.

- Relative references adjust to a new location when copied or moved. Absolute references do not change, regardless of where they are copied or moved. Mixed references contain both relative and absolute references.

- Formulas can be created quickly using the point-and-click method. With this method, you insert a cell reference in a formula by clicking the cell rather than typing its column letter and row number.

- The Sum button in the Editing group on the Home tab inserts a formula with the SUM function, which adds the value of cells in the specified range.

- The status bar shows a preview of common formulas, including Average, Count, and Sum, when you select a range of cells. You can choose which formula previews to show or hide.

- You can view the formulas in a worksheet, instead of the formula results, by clicking the Show Formulas button in the Formula Auditing group on the Formulas tab.

- Excel calculates formula results in a worksheet when you enter the formula, and recalculates the results whenever the cells used in that formula change. When you need to edit a worksheet with many formulas, you can click the Calculations Options button in the Calculation group on the Formulas tab, and then click Manual. When you want to calculate the formula results, click the Calculate Now button.

VOCABULARY *Review*

Define the following terms:

Absolute cell reference	Operand	Point-and-click method
Formula	Operator	Relative cell reference
Manual calculation	Order of evaluation	Sum button
Mixed cell reference		

REVIEW *Questions*

TRUE/FALSE

Circle T if the statement is true or F if the statement is false.

T   F   **1.** An operand is a constant or cell reference used in formulas.

T   F   **2.** In a formula, subtraction is performed before multiplication.

T   F   **3.** In a formula, operations within parentheses are performed after operations outside parentheses.

T   F   **4.** An absolute reference does not change if the formula is copied or moved.

T   F   **5.** Manual calculation lets you determine when Excel calculates formula results.

WRITTEN QUESTIONS

Write a brief answer to the following questions.

1. Which operator has the highest priority in the order of evaluation in a worksheet formula?

2. What type of cell reference adjusts to its new location when it is copied or moved?

3. Write an example of a formula with a mixed cell reference.

4. Explain how to enter the formula =C4+B5+D2 using the point-and-click method.

5. How do you display formulas in the worksheet cells rather than the formula results?

PROJECTS

PROJECT 4-1

Match the letter of the worksheet formula in Column 2 to the description of the worksheet operation performed by the formula in Column 1.

<table>
<tr><td align="center">**Column 1**</td><td align="center">**Column 2**</td></tr>
</table>

Column 1	Column 2
____ 1. Adds the values in cells A3 and A4	**A.** =A3/(27+A4)
____ 2. Subtracts the value in cell A4 from the value in cell A3	**B.** =A3/27+A4
____ 3. Multiplies the value in cell A3 times 27	**C.** =A3^27/A4
____ 4. Divides the value in cell A3 by 27	**D.** =A3–A4
____ 5. Raises the value in cell A3 to the 27th power	**E.** =A3/27
____ 6. Divides the value in cell A3 by 27, and then adds the value in cell A4	**F.** =A3^27
____ 7. Divides the value in cell A3 by the result of 27 plus the value in cell A4	**G.** =(A3*27)/A4
____ 8. Multiplies the value in cell A3 times 27, and then divides the product by the value in cell A4	**H.** =A3+A4
____ 9. Divides 27 by the value in cell A4, and then multiplies the result by the value in cell A3	**I.** =A3*(27/A4)
____ 10. Raises the value in A3 to the 27th power, and then divides the result by the value in A4	**J.** =A3*27

 ## PROJECT 4-2

1. Open the **Results.xlsx** Data File.

2. Save the workbook as **Results of Formulas** followed by your initials.

3. Enter formulas in the specified cells that perform the operations listed below. After you enter each formula, write the resulting value in the space provided.

Resulting Value	Cell	Operation
__________ a.	C3	Add the values in cells A3 and B3.
__________ b.	C4	Subtract the value in cell B4 from the value in cell A4.
__________ c.	C5	Multiply the value in cell A5 by the value in cell B5.
__________ d.	C6	Divide the value in cell A6 by the value in cell B6.
__________ e.	B7	Sum the values in the range B3:B6.
__________ f.	D3	Add the values in cells A3 and B3, and then multiply by 3.
__________ g.	D4	Add the values in cells A3 and A4, and then multiply by cell B3.
__________ h.	D5	Copy the formula in cell D4 to cell D5.
__________ i.	D6	Subtract the value in cell B6 from the value in cell A6, and then divide by 2.
__________ j.	D7	Divide the value in cell A6 by 2, and then subtract the value in cell B6.

4. In cell A1, enter your name. Save, print, and close the workbook.

 **PROJECT 4-3**

1. Open the **Zoo.xlsx** Data File.

2. Save the workbook as **Zoo Fundraiser** followed by your initials.

3. In cells D6, D7, D8, and D9, enter formulas that multiply the values in column B by the values in column C.

4. In cell D10, enter a formula to sum the totals in the range D6:D9.

5. In cell D11, enter a formula to calculate a 7% sales tax of the subtotal in cell D10.

6. In cell D12, enter a formula to add the subtotal and sales tax.

7. Change the worksheet to manual calculation.

8. Format the range D6:D12 in the Accounting number format. The worksheet is ready to accept customer data.

9. A customer purchases two tiger T-shirts, three dolphin T-shirts, one sweatshirt, and four coffee mugs. Enter these quantities in column C and press the F9 key to calculate.

10. Verify the formulas to ensure you have entered them correctly. If any of the formulas are incorrect, edit them and recalculate the worksheet. Repeat this process until you are confident that the worksheet is calculating results as intended.

11. Insert a footer with your name in the left section and the current date in the right section.

12. Save the workbook, print the customer's invoice, and then close the workbook.

 **PROJECT 4-4**

1. Open the **Investment.xlsx** Data File.

2. Save the workbook as **Investment Record** followed by your initials.

3. In cells D6 through D8, enter formulas to calculate the values of the stocks. The formulas should multiply the number of shares in column B by the price of the shares in column C.

4. In cells D10 and D11, enter formulas to calculate the values of the mutual funds. As with the stocks, the formulas should multiply the number of shares in column B by the price of the shares in column C.

5. In cell D12, enter a formula that sums the values in cells D4 through D11. Format cell D12 by adding a Top and Double Bottom Border.

6. In cell E4, enter the formula =D4/$D$12. This formula determines the percentage of each investment value with respect to the total investment value.

7. Copy the formula in cell E4 to the ranges E6:E8 and E10:E11. Notice that the absolute reference to cell D12 in the formula remains unchanged as you copy the formula.

8. In cell E12, enter a formula that sums the percentages in cells E4 through E11. Format cell E12 by adding a Top and Double Bottom Border.

9. Save the workbook.

10. Change the worksheet to manual calculation in preparation for updating the investment values.

11. Enter the following updated share price amounts in the appropriate cells:

Investment	Price
MicroCrunch Corp.	$16.25
Ocean Electronics, Inc.	$21.25
Photex, Inc.	$13.50
Prosperity Growth Fund	$ 6.50
Lucrative Mutual Fund	$18.00

12. Perform the manual calculation.

13. Insert a footer with your name in the left section and the current date in the right section.

14. Save, print, and close the workbook.

 **PROJECT 4-5**

1. Open the **Prairie.xlsx** Data File.

2. Save the workbook as **Prairie Development** followed by your initials.

3. Before considering other factors, the cost of a home is approximately $105 per square foot. In cell D5, enter a formula that multiplies the amount of square footage in cell B5 by the value per square foot in cell C5.

4. The cost of a home is increased by $3,500 for each bathroom in the house. In cell D6, enter a formula that multiplies the number of bathrooms in cell B6 by the value per bathroom in cell C6.

5. The cost of a home is increased by $3,250 for each car garage. In cell D7, enter a formula that multiplies the number of car garages in cell B7 by the value per car garage in cell C7.

6. The cost of a home is increased by $3,000 if the house is located on a cul-de-sac. In cell D8, enter a formula that calculates the increase in value in cell C8 if 1 is entered in cell B8.

7. The cost of a home is increased by $6,000 if the house has a swimming pool. In cell D9, enter a formula that calculates the increase in value in cell C9 if 1 is entered in cell B9.

8. In cell D10, use the Sum button to calculate the sum of the numbers in the range D5:D9.

9. A potential buyer inquires about the price of a home with the following qualities:

Square feet:	2000
Number of bathrooms:	3
Number of car garages:	2
On a cul-de-sac?	No
With a swimming pool?	Yes

In the range B5:B9, enter this data to determine the estimated price of the house.

10. Insert a footer with your name in the left section and the current date in the right section.

11. Save, print, and close the workbook.

CRITICAL*Thinking*

ACTIVITY 4-1

You have been offered three jobs, each with a different salary. You know the gross pay (the amount before taxes), but not your net pay (the amount after taxes have been taken out). Assume you will have to pay 10% income tax and 7% Social Security tax. Develop a worksheet with formulas to determine your net pay. The format should be similar to that shown in Figure 4-14.

FIGURE 4-14
Format for net worksheet

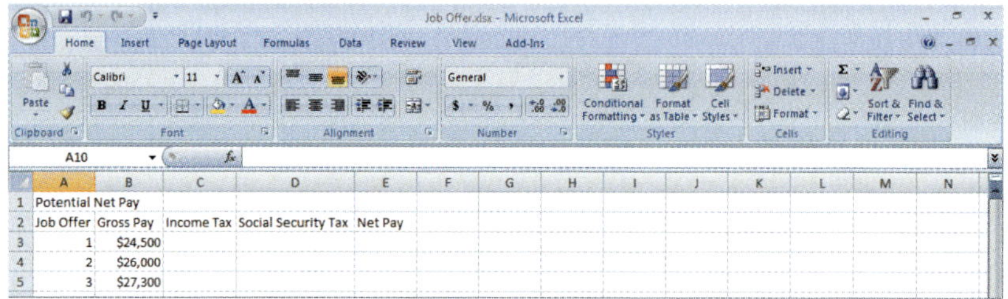

Your worksheet should include the following:

- In the range C3:C5, formulas that multiply the gross pay in column B by .10.

- In the range D3:D5, formulas that multiply the gross pay in column B by .07.

- In the range E3:E5, formulas that subtract the amounts in columns C and D from the amount in column B.

Format the worksheet appropriately and attractively. Insert a header with your name and the current date. Save the workbook as **Job Offer** followed by your initials. Then print and close the workbook.

ACTIVITY 4-2

One of the most difficult aspects of working with formulas in a worksheet is getting them to calculate the proper value after they are copied or moved. This requires an understanding of the differences between relative and absolute cell references. Research the differences between absolute and relative cell references in the Excel Help system. Write a brief explanation of the differences in your own words, and give an example of a situation in which you would use each type of cell reference. List the name(s) of the Help topics you used for reference.

USING FUNCTIONS

What Are Functions?

In the previous lesson, you created formulas that used cell references and constants. A formula can also contain a function. A **function** is a shorthand way to write an equation that performs a calculation. For example, the SUM function adds values in a range of cells. Functions often simplify formulas that are long or complex. Excel includes functions to perform complex calculations in specialized areas of mathematics, including statistics, logic, trigonometry, accounting, and finance. Function formulas are also used to display and determine dates and times.

A formula with a function has three parts: an equal sign, a function name, and at least one argument. The equal sign identifies the cell contents as a formula. The function name identifies the operation to be performed. The **argument** is the value the function uses to perform a calculation, including a number, text, or a cell reference that acts as an operand. The argument follows the function name and is enclosed in parentheses. If a function contains more than one argument, commas separate the arguments.

=SUM(F6:F11)

Equal sign

Function name

Argument

In the previous lesson, you used the Sum button to enter a formula with the SUM function, =SUM(F6:F11). The equal sign specifies that the cell entry is a formula. The function name SUM identifies the operation. Parentheses enclose the argument, which is the range of cells to add—in this case, cells F6 through F11. The function provides a simpler and faster way to enter the formula =F6+F7+F8+F9+F10+F11.

Entering Formulas with Functions

To enter a formula with a function, you need to do the following. First, start the formula with an equal sign. Second, select the function you want to use. Third, enter the arguments. Finally, enter the completed formula. The results appear in the cell.

Because Excel includes so many functions, the best way to select a function is from the Insert Function dialog box. Click the Insert Function button on the Formula Bar to open the Insert Function dialog box. From this dialog box, you can browse all of the available functions to select the one you want. First, click a category in the Or select a category box, and then click the function you want in the Select a function box. A brief description of the selected function appears near the bottom of the dialog box, as shown in Figure 5-1. Click OK. The Function Arguments dialog box then appears.

> **Did You Know?**
>
> If you know the function you want to enter, you can click the appropriate category button in the Function Library group on the Formulas tab of the Ribbon. Then, click the function you want in the menu that appears. The Function Arguments dialog box appears.

FIGURE 5-1
Insert Function dialog box

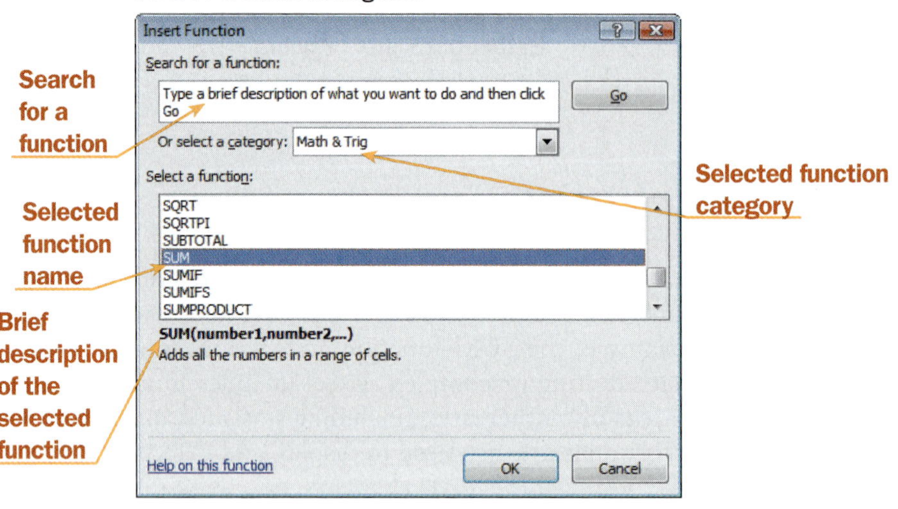

The Function Arguments dialog box, shown in Figure 5-2, provides a description of each argument you need to enter for the selected function. When an argument requires a cell or range, you can choose one of two ways to enter the reference. You can type the range directly in the appropriate argument box of the Function Arguments dialog box. Or, you can click in the appropriate argument box and then select the cell or range directly in the worksheet. When you select a range in the worksheet, the dialog box shrinks to show only the title bar and the argument box, so you can see more of the worksheet. It expands to the full size when you release the mouse button. You can also click the Collapse Dialog Box button at the end of an argument box to shrink the dialog box so only its title bar and the argument box are displayed, and then click the Expand Dialog Box button to return the Function Arguments dialog box to its full size. After all the arguments are complete, click OK. The function is entered in the active cell.

> ### Did You Know?
>
> You can also use the Insert Function dialog box to find a specific function. In the Search for a function box, type a brief description of what you want to do. Then, click Go. A list of functions that match the description you provided appears in the Select a function box. Double-click the appropriate function to open the Function Arguments dialog box.

FIGURE 5-2
Function Arguments dialog box

Entering a Function Directly in a Cell Using Formula AutoComplete

You can also enter a formula with a function directly in a cell by typing an equal sign, the function name, and the argument. **Formula AutoComplete** helps you enter a formula with a valid function name and arguments, as shown in Figure 5-3. As you begin to type the function name, a list of function names appears below the active cell. The functions listed match the letters you have typed. For example, when you type =s, all functions that begin with the letter s appear in the list box, such as SEARCH, SECON, and SERISSUM. When you type =su, the list narrows to show only functions that begin with the letters *su*, such as SUBSTITUTE, SUBTOTAL, and SUM. Continue typing until you see the function you want. Then, double-click the name of the function you want to use. The function and its arguments appear in a ScreenTip below the cell. You can use the ScreenTip as a guide to enter the necessary arguments.

> **Did You Know?**
>
> You can also use the arrow keys to select a function in the list, and then press the Tab key to enter the function.

FIGURE 5-3
Formula AutoComplete

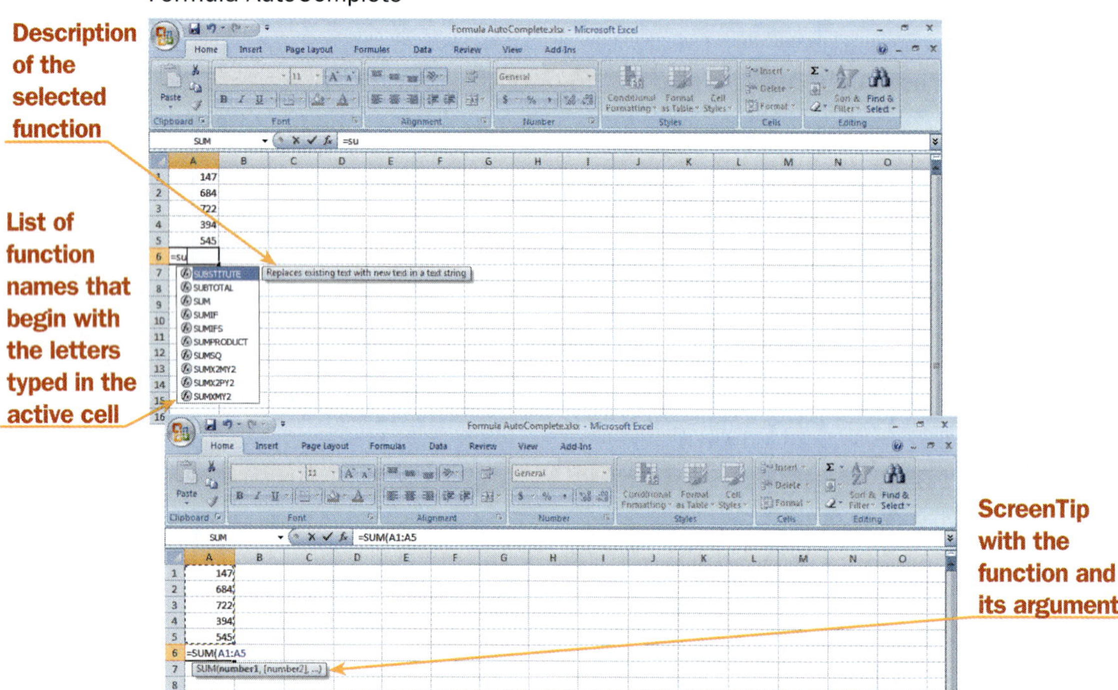

STEP-BY-STEP 5.1

1. Open the **Functions.xlsx** Data File.

2. Save the workbook as **Functions Worksheet** followed by your initials.

3. Click cell **B10**.

STEP-BY-STEP 5.1 Continued

4. On the Formula Bar, click the **Insert Function** button. The Insert Function dialog box appears. 

5. Next to the Or select a category box, click the **arrow**, and then click **Math & Trig**.

6. Scroll down the **Select a function** list, and then click **SUM**. The SUM function and a description of its purpose appear below the Select a function box, as shown in Figure 5-1.

7. Click **OK**. The Function Arguments dialog box appears with a range reference selected in the Number1 box. The Number1 argument is the range of cells whose values you want to add. Excel tried to "guess" which cells you want to add. You want to add a different range.

8. In the worksheet, select the range **B3:B7**. The Function Arguments dialog box collapses when you click a cell in the worksheet and expands when you release the mouse button. The value that will appear in cell B10, 2492, appears below the SUM function section and at the bottom of the dialog box, as shown in Figure 5-2.

9. Click **OK**. The formula in cell B10 is =SUM(B3:B7).

10. Save the workbook, and leave it open for the next Step-by-Step.

Extra for Experts

You can also use the SUM function to total the values stored in up to 255 non-adjacent cells or ranges. You enter additional ranges in the Number2 through Number255 boxes.

Did You Know?

You can also enter the formula with the SUM function in cell B10 by typing *=SUM(B3:B7)* or clicking the Sum button in the Editing group on the Home tab.

Types of Functions

Excel provides many functions you can use in formulas. Each function has a different purpose. The functions are organized by category, such as Math & Trig, Statistical, Financial, Logical, Date & Time, and Text. The next sections introduce some of the most common functions in each of these categories.

Mathematical and Trigonometric Functions

Mathematical functions and trigonometric functions manipulate quantitative data in a worksheet. Some mathematical operations, such as addition, subtraction, multiplication, and division, do not require functions. However, mathematical and trigonometric functions are particularly useful when you need to determine values such as logarithms, factorials, sines, cosines, tangents, and absolute values.

You already used a mathematical and trigonometric function when you created a formula with the SUM function. Table 5-1 describes two other mathematical functions, the square root and rounding functions, as well as a trigonometric function, the natural logarithm. Notice that the rounding operation requires two arguments, which are separated by a comma.

TABLE 5-1
Mathematical and trigonometric functions

FUNCTION	RETURNS
SQRT(number)	The square root of the number in the argument. For example, =SQRT(C4) returns the square root of the value in cell C4.
ROUND(number,num_digits)	The number in the first argument rounded to the number of decimal places designated in the second argument. For example, =ROUND(14.23433,2) returns 14.23, which rounds the number in the first argument to two decimal places. If the second argument is a negative number, the first argument is rounded to the left of the decimal point. For example, =ROUND(142.3433,–2) returns 100.
LN(number)	The natural logarithm of a number. For example, =LN(50) returns 1.69897.

S TEP-BY-STEP 5.2

1. Click cell **B11**. On the Formula Bar, click the **Insert Function** button. The Insert Function dialog box appears. 

2. Next to the Or select a category box, click the **arrow**, and then click **Math & Trig**, if it is not already selected.

3. Click the **Select a function** box, and then press the **S** key five times until *SQRT* is selected. Read the description of the function.

4. Click **OK**. The Function Arguments dialog box appears. Read the description of the argument.

5. In the Number box, type **B10**. You want to calculate the square root of the value in cell B10, which is 2492, as shown to the right of the Number box. The number that will appear in cell B11, 49.9199359, appears under the function and at the bottom of the dialog box next to Formula result =, as shown in Figure 5-4.

FIGURE 5-4
SQRT funtction arguments

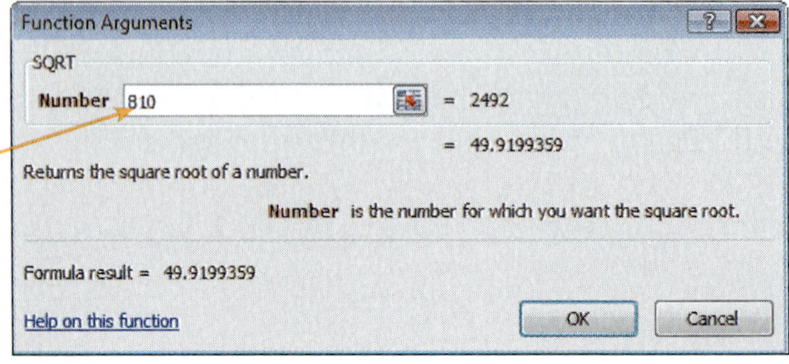

STEP-BY-STEP 5.2 Continued

6. Click **OK**. The formula entered in cell B11 is =SQRT(B10).

7. Click cell **B12**. On the Formula Bar, click the **Insert Function** button. The Insert Function dialog box appears with Math & Trig selected in the Or select a category box.

8. Click the **Select a function** box, and then press the **R** key five times to select *ROUND*.

9. Read the function's description. Click **OK**. The Function Arguments dialog box appears.

10. Read the description of the first argument. In the Number box, type **B11**.

11. Press the **Tab** key to place the insertion point in the Num_digits box. Read the description of the second argument.

12. Type **2**. The formula results appear below the function and at the bottom of the dialog box, as shown in Figure 5-5.

FIGURE 5-5
ROUND function arguments

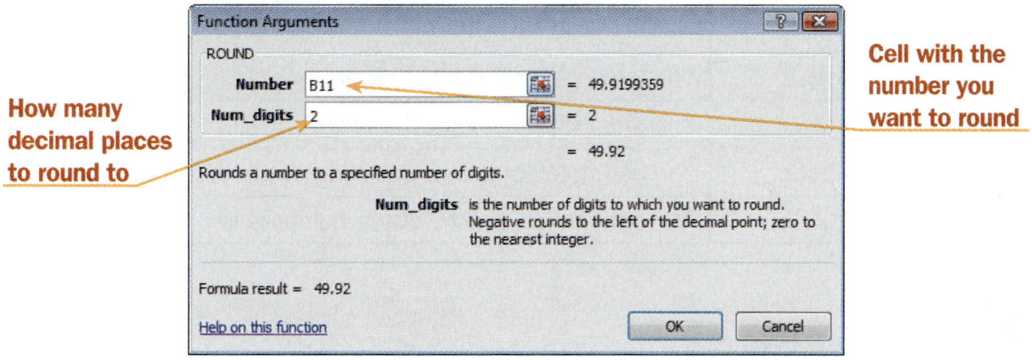

13. Click **OK**. The formula in cell B12 is =ROUND(B11,2), which displays the results of 49.92.

14. Save the workbook, and leave it open for the next Step-by-Step.

Statistical Functions

Statistical functions are used to describe large quantities of data. For example, statistical functions can determine the average, standard deviation, or variance of a range of data. Statistical functions can also determine the number of values in a range, the largest value in a range, and the smallest value in a range. Table 5-2 describes some of the statistical functions available in Excel. All the statistical functions contain a range for the argument. You can include multiple ranges by entering additional arguments. The range is the body of numbers the statistics will describe.

TABLE 5-2
Statistical functions

FUNCTION	RETURNS
AVERAGE(number1,number2...)	The average (or mean) of the range; for example, =AVERAGE(E4:E9) returns the average of the numbers in the range E4:E9
COUNT(value1,value2...)	The number of cells in the range that contain numbers; for example, =COUNT(D6:D21) returns 16 if all the cells in the range contain numbers
COUNTA(value1,value2...)	The number of cells in the range that contain data; for example, =COUNT(B4:B15) returns 11 if all the cells in the range contain data
MAX(number1,number2...)	The largest number in the range
MIN(number1,number2...)	The smallest number in the range
STDEV(number1,number2...)	The estimated standard deviation of the numbers in the range
VAR(number1,number2...)	The estimated variance of the numbers in the range

S TEP-BY-STEP 5.3

1. Click cell **B15**. On the Formula Bar, click the **Insert Function** button. The Insert Function dialog box appears. You want to find the average of values in the range B3:B7. 

2. Next to the Or select a category box, click the **arrow**, and then click **Statistical**. The Statistical functions appear in the Select a function box.

3. In the Select a function box, click **AVERAGE**, and then click **OK**. The Function Arguments dialog box appears.

4. Next to the Number1 box, click the **Collapse Dialog Box** button. The Function Arguments dialog box shrinks to its title bar and Number1 box. 

5. In the worksheet, drag to select the range **B3:B7**. The range reference appears in the Number1 box, as shown in Figure 5-6.

Did You Know?

You can also enter a formula with the AVERAGE, COUNT, MAX, or MIN function in a selected cell by clicking the arrow next to the Sum button in the Editing group on the Home tab, clicking the function name in the list of functions, selecting the appropriate range, and then pressing the Enter key.

STEP-BY-STEP 5.3 Continued

FIGURE 5-6
Collapsed Function Arguments dialog box

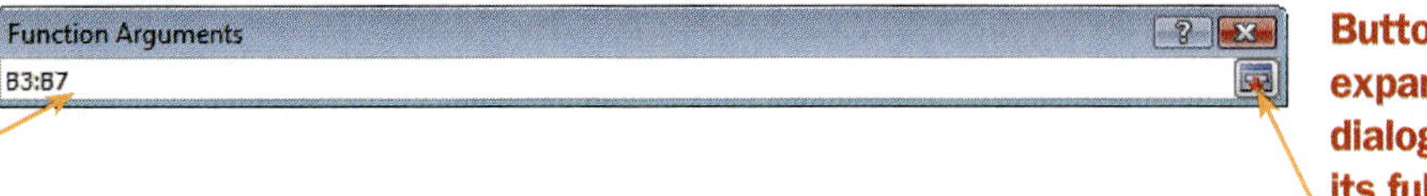

6. Click the **Expand Dialog Box** button. The Function Arguments dialog box expands to its full  size, as shown in Figure 5-7.

FIGURE 5-7
Expanded Function Arguments dialog box

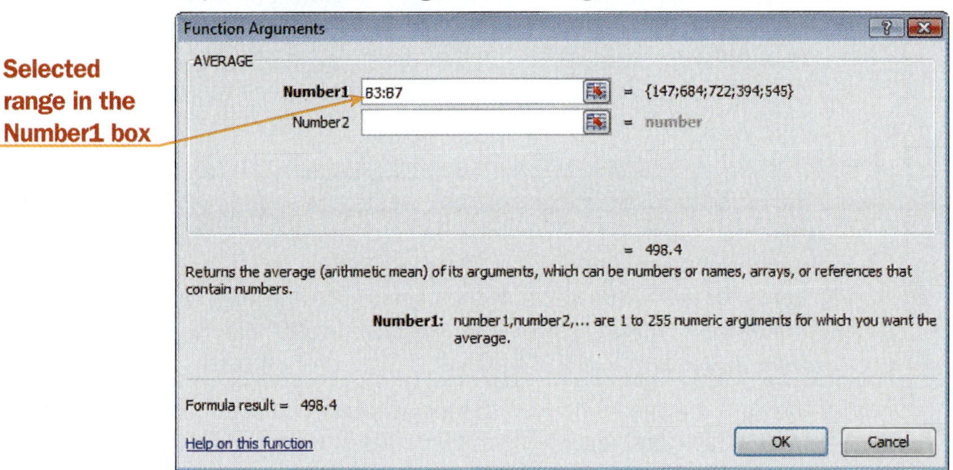

7. Click **OK**. The average of the values in the range B3:B7, which is 498.4, appears in cell B15.

8. Click cell **B16**. On the Formula Bar, click the **Insert Function** button. You want to find how many cells in the range B3:B7 contain numbers.

9. In the Or select a category box, click **Statistical**, if it is not already selected. In the Select a function box, double-click **COUNT**. The Function Arguments dialog box appears.

10. In the Value1 box, enter **B3:B7**, and then click **OK**. The number of cells in the range B3:B7 that contain numbers is 5.

11. Click cell **B17**, and then enter **=MAX(B3:B7)**. The largest number in the range B3:B7 is 722.

12. Click cell **B18**, and then enter **=MIN(B3:B7)**. The smallest number in the range B3:B7 is 147.

13. Click cell **B19**, and then enter **=STDEV(B3:B7)**. The standard deviation of the range B3:B7 is 235.0517.

14. Click cell **B20**, and then enter **=VAR(B3:B7)**. The variance of the range B3:B7 is 55249.3.

15. Save the workbook, and leave it open for the next Step-by-Step.

Financial Functions

Financial functions are used to analyze loans and investments. The primary financial functions are future value, present value, and payment, which are described in Table 5-3. Note that for these functions to return the correct value, the payment and the interest rate must have the same time period. For example, the payment period is usually expressed in months, whereas interest rates are commonly expressed in years. So, if the payment period is monthly, you must divide the annual interest rate by 12 to determine the monthly rate.

TABLE 5-3
Financial functions

FUNCTION	RETURNS
FV(rate,nper,pmt,pv,type)	The future value of an investment based on equal payments (third argument), at a fixed interest rate (first argument), for a specified number of periods (second argument). (The fourth and fifth arguments for the present value of the investment and the timing of the payments are optional.) For example, =FV(.08,5,100) determines the future value of five $100 payments earning an 8% interest rate at the end of five years.
PV(rate,nper,pmt,fv,type)	The present value of a loan or an investment based on equal payments (third argument), at a fixed interest rate (first argument), for a specified number of payments (second argument). (The fourth and fifth arguments for the future value of the investment and the timing of the payments are optional.) For example, =PV(.1,5,500) displays the current value of five payments of $500 at a 10% interest rate.
PMT(rate,nper,pv,fv,type)	The equal payments needed to repay a loan (third argument), at a fixed interest rate (first argument), in a specified number of periods (second argument). (The fourth and fifth arguments for the future value of the loan and the timing of the payments are optional.) For example, =PMT(.01,36,10000) displays the monthly payment needed to repay a $10,000 loan at a 1% monthly interest rate (12% annual interest rate divided by 12 months) for 36 months (three years divided by 12 months).

Careers

Scientists use Excel workbooks to help them as they conduct research. They record collected data in worksheets. Then they use statistical function formulas to analyze experimental results.

STEP-BY-STEP 5.4

1. Click cell **B24**, and then enter **.035**. The annual interest rate of 3.5% appears in the cell.

2. Click cell **B25**, and then enter **6**, which is the number of payment periods—one payment each year for six years.

3. Click cell **B26**, and then enter **–150**. The annual payment of $(150.00) appears in the cell. (A negative number indicates a payment, whereas a positive number indicates income. In this case, you use a negative number because you are making a payment to the bank.)

4. Click cell **B27**. On the Formula Bar, click the **Insert Function** button. The Insert Function dialog box appears. 

5. Next to the Or select a category box, click the **arrow**, and then click **Financial**. In the Select a function box, click **FV**. Click **OK**.

6. In the Rate box, type **B24**, the cell with the annual interest rate. In the Nper box, type **B25**, the cell with the number of payment periods. In the Pmt box, type **B26**, the cell with the annual payment you plan to make (see Figure 5-8).

FIGURE 5-8
FV function arguments

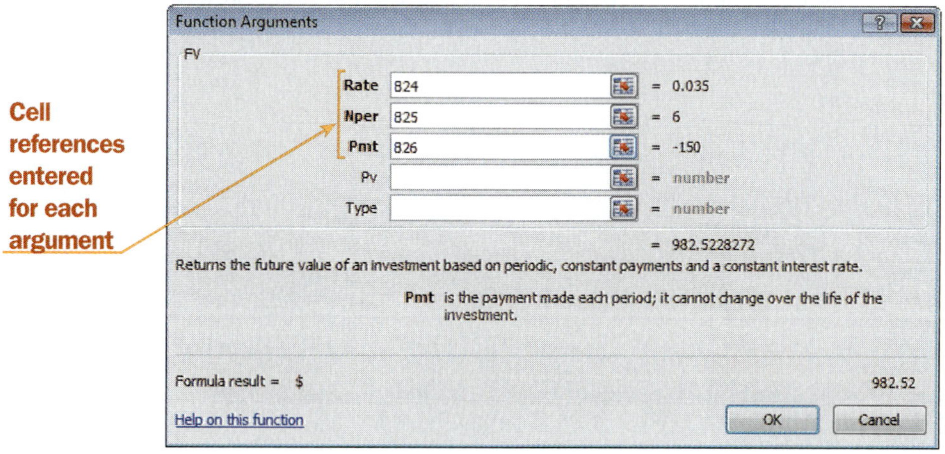

Cell references entered for each argument

7. Click **OK**. As you can see in cell B27, the amount in the savings account will have grown to $982.52 after six years.

8. Click cell **B29**, and then enter **3**. The annual interest rate of 3.0% appears in the cell.

9. Click cell **B30**, and then enter **8**, which is the number of payment periods—one payment each year for eight years.

10. Click cell **B31**, and then enter **–210**. The annual payment of $(210) appears in the cell. (Remember, a negative number indicates a payment, whereas a positive number indicates income. In this case, you use a negative number because you are making a payment.)

STEP-BY-STEP 5.4 Continued

11. Click cell **B32**, and then enter **=PV(B29,B30,B31)**, using Formula AutoComplete to help you enter the function accurately. The delayed payments are more profitable because the present value, $1,474.14, is greater than the immediate lump sum of $1,200.

12. Click cell **B34**, and then enter **1**. The monthly interest rate of 1.0% appears in the cell. The monthly interest rate is determined by dividing the annual interest rate of 12% by 12 months.

13. Click cell **B35**, and then enter **=5*12** to determine the number of monthly payment periods (the number of years, 5, multiplied by 12 months). The number of monthly payment periods, 60, appears in the cell.

14. Click cell **B36**, and then enter **5000**, which is the amount of the loan.

15. Click cell **B37**, and then enter **=PMT(B34,B35,B36)**, using Formula AutoComplete to help you enter the function accurately. The monthly payment ($111.22) appears in the cell in red. The number is negative to indicate that it is a payment.

16. Click cell **B38**, and then enter **=(B37*B35)+B36** to determine the interest you will pay over the life of the loan. The formula multiples the monthly payment returned by the PMT function in cell B37 by the number of monthly payments calculated in cell B35, and then adds the loan amount in cell B36. Because the payments are negative, you need to add the loan amount to calculate the difference between the total payments and the total principal. Under the conditions of this loan, you will pay a total of $1,673.33 in interest over the life of the loan, as shown in Figure 5-9.

FIGURE 5-9
Financial functions

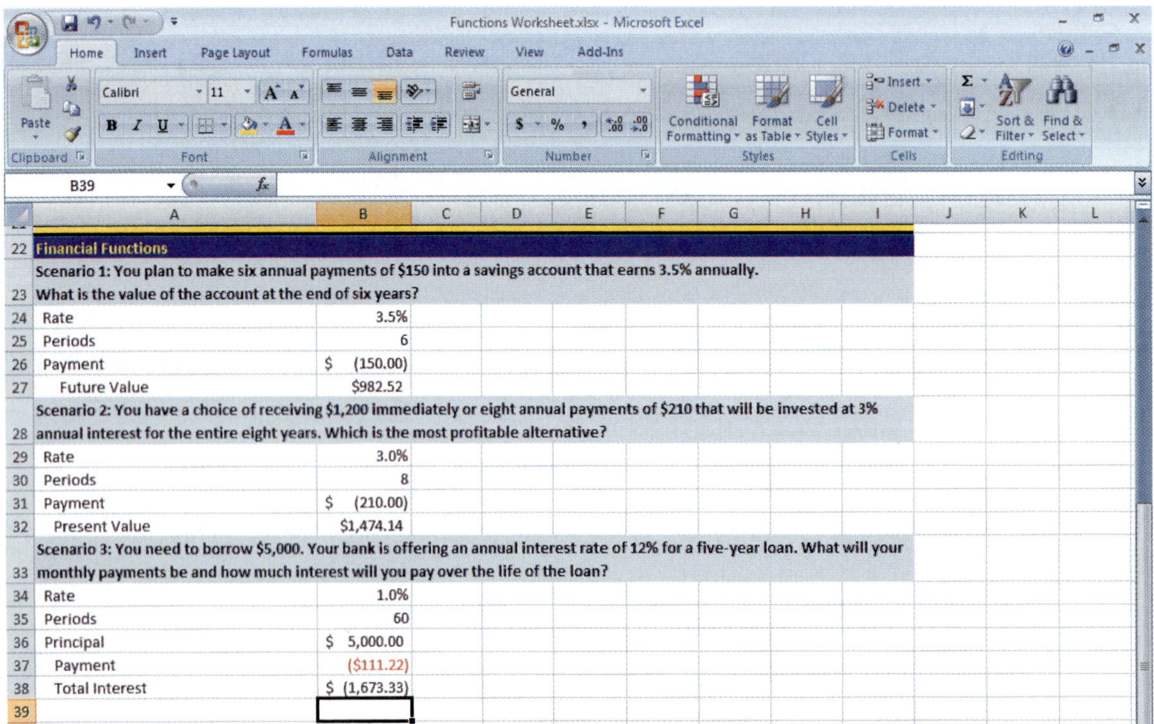

17. Insert a header with your name and the current date. Save, print, and close the workbook.

Logical Functions

 **Logical functions**, such as the IF function, display text or values if certain conditions exist. In the IF function, the first argument sets a condition for comparison, called a *logical test*. The second argument determines the value that appears in the cell if the logical test is true. The third argument determines the value that appears in the cell if the logical test is false.

> **Did You Know?**
>
> You must use quotation marks to enclose the text you want the IF function to return in the second and third arguments. For example, =IF(B10<100,"Low Result","High Result").

For example, a teacher might use the IF function to determine whether a student has passed or failed a course. The formula =IF(C4>60,"PASS","FAIL") returns *PASS* if the value in cell C4 is greater than 60. The formula returns *FAIL* if the value in cell C4 is not greater than 60.

Table 5-4 describes the IF, AND, NOT, OR, and IFERROR functions.

TABLE 5-4
Logical functions

FUNCTION	RETURNS
IF(logical_test,value_if_true,value_if_false)	One value if the condition in the logical test is true, and another value if the condition in the logical test is false; for example, =IF(2+2=4, Over, Under) returns *Over*
AND(logical1,logical2,…)	TRUE if all of the arguments are true, and FALSE if any or all of the arguments are false; for example, =AND(1+1=2,1+2=3) returns *TRUE*, but =AND(1+1=2,1+2=4) returns *FALSE*
OR(logical1,logical2,…)	TRUE if any of the arguments are true, and FALSE if none of the arguments is true; for example, =OR(1+1=2,1+2=3) returns *TRUE*, and =OR(1+1=2,1+2=4) returns *TRUE*, but =OR(1+1=3,1+2=4) returns *FALSE*
NOT(logical)	TRUE if the argument is false, and FALSE if the argument is true; for example, =NOT(2+2=1) returns *TRUE*, but =NOT(2+2=4) returns *FALSE*
IFERROR(value,value_if_error)	The formula results if the first argument contains no error, and the specified value if the argument is incorrect; for example, =IFERROR(2+2=1, "Error in calculation") returns *Error in calculation*

S TEP-BY-STEP 5.5

1. Open the **Occidental.xlsx** Data File.

2. Save the workbook as **Occidental Optical** followed by your initials.

3. Click cell **D6**, and then type **=IF(B6<5,25,0)**. This formula returns 25 (the shipping fee) if the quantity in cell B6 is less than 5. If the quantity in cell B6 is not less than 5, then the formula returns 0.

STEP-BY-STEP 5.5 Continued

4. Press the **Enter** key. This order has no shipping fee because the order quantity is 6, more than the 5 cartons needed for free shipping.

5. Copy the formula in cell **D6** to the range **D7:D15**, and then click cell **A18**. The shipping fee is calculated for all the orders, as shown in Figure 5-10.

FIGURE 5-10
Shipping fee calculated with the IF function

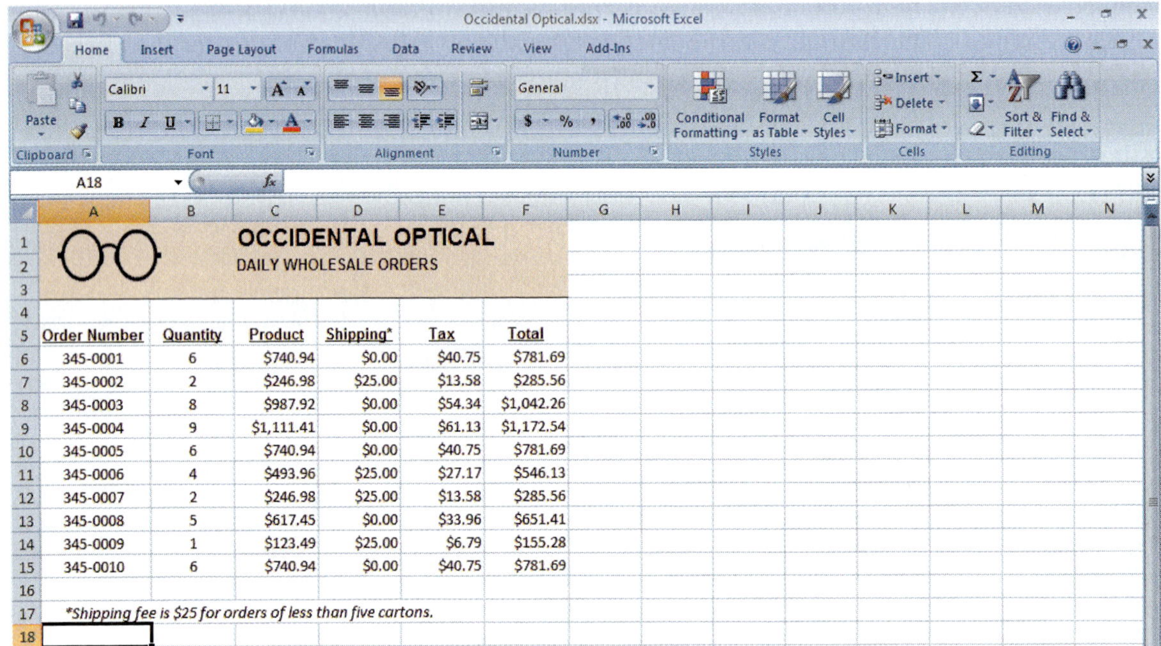

6. Insert a footer that includes your name and the current date. Save, print, and close the workbook.

Date and Time Functions

Functions can also be used to insert dates and times in a worksheet. For example, **date and time functions** can be used to convert serial numbers to a month, a day, or a year. A date function can also be used to insert the current date or the current date and time. Table 5-5 describes the DATE, NOW, and TODAY functions.

TABLE 5-5
Date and time functions

FUNCTION	RETURNS
DATE(year,month,day)	The date specified in the year, month, and day arguments, which are entered as numbers. For example, =DATE(2010,5,23) returns 5/23/2010.
NOW()	The current date and time based on the computer's date and time settings. For example, =NOW() returns the current date and time, such as 5/23/2010 22:05. This function has no arguments.
TODAY()	The current date based on the computer's date setting and formatted as a date. For example, =TODAY() returns the current date, such as 5/23/2010. This function has no arguments.

Text Functions

Text functions are used to format and work with cell contents. A text function can be used to convert text in a cell to all uppercase or lowercase letters. Text functions can also be used to repeat data contained in another cell. These functions are described in Table 5-6.

TABLE 5-6
Text functions

FUNCTION	OPERATION
PROPER(text)	Converts the first letter of each word in the specified cell to uppercase and the rest to lowercase.
LOWER(text)	Converts all letters in the specified cell to lowercase.
UPPER(text)	Converts all letters in the specified cell to uppercase.
SUBSTITUTE(text,old_text,new_text,instance_num)	Replaces existing text (the second argument) in a specified cell (the first argument) with new text (the third argument). If you omit the optional fourth argument, instance_num, every occurrence of the text is replaced. For example, =SUBSTITUTE(C2,"Income","Revenue") replaces every instance of the word Income in cell C2 with the word *Revenue*.
REPT(text,number_times)	Repeats the text (first argument) in the specified cell a specified number of times (second argument). For example, =REPT(B6,3) repeats the text in cell B6 three times.

STEP-BY-STEP 5.6

1. Open the **Finances.xlsx** Data File.

2. Click cell **A1**, and then replace the word *NAME* with your name.

3. Click cell **B13**, and then enter **=NOW()**. The current date and time appear in the cell.

4. Click cell **B13**. Click the **Home** tab on the Ribbon. In the Number group, next to the Number Format box, click the **arrow**, and then click **General**. The date changes to the serial number Excel uses to express the current date and time.

5. On the Home tab, in the Number group, next to the Number Format box, click the **arrow**, and then click **Short Date**. The date changes to the form 5/23/2010.

6. On the Quick Access Toolbar, click the **Undo** button twice. The current date and time reappear in cell B13. 

7. Click cell **B14**. You want to repeat the text in cell A1 in cell B14.

8. Click the **Formulas** tab on the Ribbon. In the Function Library group, click the **Text** button, and then click **REPT**. The Function Arguments dialog box appears.

9. In the Text box, enter **A1**. In the Number_times box, enter **1**. The contents of cell A1 will be repeated one time in cell B14.

10. Click **OK**. The title in cell A1 is repeated in cell B14.

> ### Extra Challenge 
>
> Edit the contents of cell A1 by replacing your name with a friend's name. The REPT function in cell B14 updates the contents in that cell. On the Quick Access Toolbar, click the Undo button to return to your name.

11. Save the workbook using the contents of cell B14 as the file name. Your screen should look similar to Figure 5-11.

FIGURE 5-11
Date & Time and Text functions

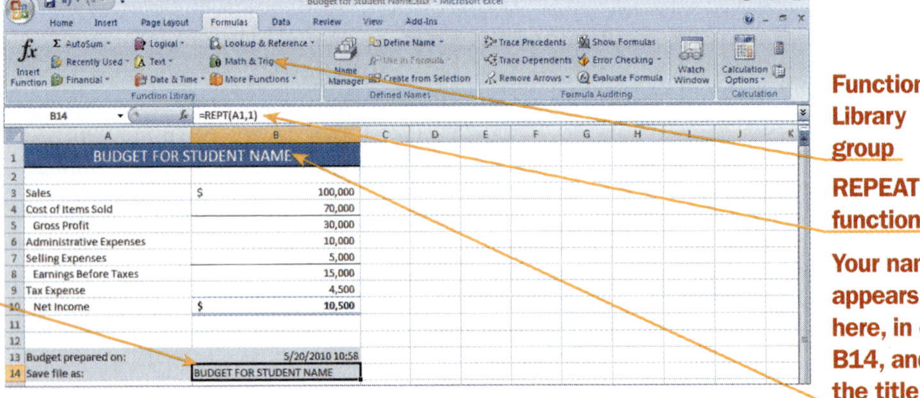

12. Print and close the workbook.

SUMMARY

In this lesson, you learned:

- A function is a shorthand way to write an equation that performs a calculation. A formula with a function has three parts: an equal sign, a function name, and at least one argument, which acts as an operand.

- The best way to select a function is from the Insert Function dialog box. The Function Arguments dialog box provides a description of each argument you enter for the function.

- When you type a formula with a function directly in a worksheet cell, Formula AutoComplete helps you enter a formula with a valid function name and arguments.

- Functions can be used to perform mathematical, statistical, financial, and logical operations. They can also be used to insert and calculate dates and times and to format text.

VOCABULARY *Review*

Define the following terms:

Argument	Function	Statistical functions
Date and time functions	Logical functions	Text functions
Financial functions	Mathematical functions	Trigonometric functions
Formula AutoComplete		

REVIEW *Questions*

TRUE/FALSE

Circle T if the statement is true or F if the statement is false.

T   F   **1.** Formulas with functions have three parts: an equal sign, a function name, and an argument.

T   F   **2.** The argument identifies the function to be performed.

T   F   **3.** You select the function you want to use in the Insert Function dialog box.

T   F   **4.** The NUMBER function returns the number of cells in the range identified in the argument that contain data.

T   F   **5.** The IF function displays one value if the specified condition is true and a different value if the condition is false.

FILL IN THE BLANK

Complete the following sentences by writing the correct word or words in the blanks provided.

1. The _________ is enclosed in parentheses in a formula with a function.

2. The _________ dialog box specifies elements to be included in the function.

3. _________ functions manipulate quantitative data in a worksheet.

4. _________ functions describe large quantities of data, such as by determining the average, standard deviation, or variance of a range of data.

5. _________ functions are used to analyze loans and investments.

PROJECTS

PROJECT 5-1

Write the appropriate formula to perform each of the described operations. Refer to Tables 5-1 through 5-6 to help you determine the function and its arguments.

_______ 1. Determine the average of the values in the range B9:B45.

_______ 2. Determine the smallest value in the range S14:S90.

_______ 3. Determine the standard deviation of the values in the range K4:K27.

_______ 4. Determine the yearly payments on a $4,500 loan at 10% for 8 years.

_______ 5. Determine the value of a savings account at the end of 5 years, after making $450 yearly payments; the account earns 9%.

_______ 6. Round the value in cell D3 to the tenths place.

_______ 7. Determine the present value of a pension plan that will pay you 20 yearly payments of $5,000; the current rate of return is 7.5%.

_______ 8. Determine the square root of 275.

_______ 9. Determine the variance of the values in the range F9:F35.

_______ 10. Add all the values in the range F4:F19.

_______ 11. Determine how many cells in the range H7:H21 are filled with data.

_______ 12. Determine the largest value in the range E45:E92.

PROJECT 5-2

1. Open the **Test.xlsx** Data File.

2. Save the workbook as **Test Grades** followed by your initials.

3. In cell B25, enter a formula with a function to determine the number of students taking the examination.

4. In cell B26, enter a formula with a function to determine the average exam grade.

5. In cell B27, enter a formula with a function to determine the highest exam grade.

6. In cell B28, enter a formula with a function to determine the lowest exam grade.

7. In cell B29, enter a formula with a function to determine the standard deviation of the exam grades.

8. Format cells B26 and B29 to display one digit to the right of the decimal.

9. Insert a header with your name and the current date. Save, print, and close the workbook.

 ## PROJECT 5-3

1. Open the **National.xlsx** Data File.

2. Save the workbook as **National Bank** followed by your initials.

3. In cell B11, enter the PMT function to calculate the yearly payment for borrowers. The lending rate will be entered in cell B7, the term of the loan will be entered in cell B9, and the loan principal (or present value) will be entered in cell B5. (The formula results are *#DIV/0!*, indicating an error due to division by zero, because no data is entered in the argument's cell references.)

4. A potential borrower inquires about the payments on a $5,500 loan for four years. The current lending rate is 8%. Determine the yearly payment on the loan. (The number in cell B11 appears as a negative, because this amount must be paid.)

5. Insert a header with your name and the current date.

6. Print the portion of the worksheet that pertains to the loan (the range A1:C14) to give to the potential borrower.

7. In cell B24, enter the FV function to calculate the future value of periodic payments for depositors. The interest rate will be entered in cell B22, the term of the payments will be entered in cell B20, and the yearly payments will be entered in cell B18. (The formula results show *$0.00*, because no data is entered in the argument's cell references.)

8. A potential depositor is starting a college fund for her child. She inquires about the value of yearly deposits of $2,550 at the end of 15 years. The current interest rate is 4.5%. Determine the future value of the deposits. (Remember to enter the deposit as a negative because the depositor must pay this amount.)

9. Print the portion of the worksheet that pertains to the investment (the range A14:C26) to give to the potential depositor.

10. Save and close the workbook.

PROJECT 5-4

The Tucson Coyotes have just completed seven preseason professional basketball games. Coach Patterson will soon be entering a press conference in which he is expected to talk about the team's performance for the upcoming season. Coach Patterson wants to be well informed about player performance before entering the press conference.

Part 1

1. Open the **Team.xlsx** Data File.

2. Save the workbook as **Team Stats** followed by your initials.

3. In cell J6, enter a function that adds the values in the range B6:I6.

4. Copy the formula in cell J6 to the range J7:J12.

5. In cell J19, enter a function that adds the values in the range B19:I19.

6. Copy the formula in cell J19 to the range J20:J25.

7. In cell B13, enter a function that averages the game points in the range B6:B12.

8. In cell B14, enter a function that determines the standard deviation of the game points in the range B6:B12.

9. In cell B15, enter a function that counts the number of entries in the range B6:B12.

10. Copy the formulas in the range B13:B15 to the range C13:I15.

11. In cell B26, enter a function that averages the rebounds in the range B19:B25.

12. In cell B27, enter a function that determines the standard deviation of the rebounds in the range B19:B25.

13. In cell B28, enter a function that counts the number of entries made in the range B19:B25.

14. Copy the formulas in the range B26:B28 to the range C26:I28.

15. Insert a footer with your name and the current date. Save and print the workbook, and leave it open.

Part 2

Based on the Basketball Stats workbook you prepared, indicate in the blanks the names of the players who are likely to be mentioned in the following interview. When you have finished filling in the blanks, close the workbook.

Reporter: You have had a very successful preseason. Three players seem to be providing the leadership needed for a winning record.

Patterson: Basketball teams win by scoring points. It's no secret that we rely on (1) __________, (2) __________, and (3) __________ to get those points. All three average at least 10 points per game.

Reporter: One player seems to have a problem with consistency.

Patterson: (4) __________ has his good games and his bad games. He is a young player and we have been working with him. As the season progresses, I think you will find him to be a more reliable offensive talent.

(*Hint*: One indication of consistent scoring is the standard deviation. A high standard deviation might indicate high fluctuation of points from game to game. A low standard deviation might indicate that the scoring level is relatively consistent.)

Reporter: What explains the fact that (5) __________ is both an effective scorer and your leading rebounder?

Patterson: He is a perceptive player. When playing defense, he is constantly planning how to get the ball back to the other side of the court.

Reporter: Preseason injuries can be heartbreaking. How has this affected the team?

Patterson: (6) __________ has not played since being injured in the game against Kansas City. He is an asset to the team. We are still waiting to hear from the doctors whether he will be back soon.

Reporter: It is the end of the preseason. That is usually a time when teams make cuts. Of your healthy players, (7) __________ is the lowest scorer. Will you let him go before the beginning of the regular season?

Patterson: I don't like to speculate on cuts or trades before they are made. We'll just have to wait and see.

PROJECT 5-5

1. Open the **Golf.xlsx** Data File.

2. Save the workbook as **Golf Tryouts** followed by your initials. A player must average a score of less than 76 to qualify for the team.

3. In cell I5, enter a function that displays *Made* if the average score in cell H5 is less than 76 and *Cut* if the score is not less than 76. (*Hint*: The IF function has three arguments. The first argument is the logical test that determines whether the value in cell H5 is less than 76. The second argument is the text that appears if the statement is true. The third argument is the text that appears if the statement is false. Because the items to be displayed are words rather than numbers, they must be entered within quotation marks.)

4. Copy the formula from cell I5 to the range I6:I16.

5. In cell B21, enter a function that displays today's date.

6. Format cell B21 so that the date appears as the month followed by the day and year, such as March 14, 2010.

7. Click cell B22, and then enter your name. Save, print, and close the workbook.

PROJECT 5-6

You have worked for Xanthan Gum Corp. for several years and are now eligible for promotion. Promotions at Xanthan are determined by supervisor ratings and a written examination. To be promoted, employees must score an average of 80 or above in the following four categories:

- Supervisor rating of leadership potential

- Supervisor rating of understanding of duties

- Supervisor rating of willingness to work hard

- Written test score

After receiving your supervisor ratings, you prepare a worksheet to determine the minimum written test score you need to be promoted.

1. Open the **Xanthan.xlsx** Data File.

2. Save the workbook as **Xanthan Promotion** followed by your initials.

3. In cell B7, enter **70** as the supervisor rating of leadership potential. In cell B8, enter **85** as the supervisor rating of understanding of duties. In cell B9, enter **80** as the supervisor rating of willingness to work hard.

4. In cell B12, enter a function that determines the average of the values in the range B7:B10.

5. Format cell B12 as a Number with no decimal places.

6. In cell B13, enter an IF function that displays *PROMOTION* if the average score in cell B12 is greater than 80 and *NO PROMOTION* if the average score is less than 80.

7. Format the contents of cell B13 as bold and centered.

8. In cell B10, enter each of the following test scores: **75, 80, 85, 90,** and **95.** Which scores will result in a promotion?

9. Insert a footer with your name and the current date. Save, print, and close the workbook.

CRITICAL*Thinking*

 ACTIVITY 5-1

 You are considering purchasing a car and want to compare prices offered by different dealerships. Some dealerships have cars that include the accessories you want; others need to add the accessories for an additional price. Prepare a worksheet similar to that shown in Figure 5-12.

FIGURE 5-12

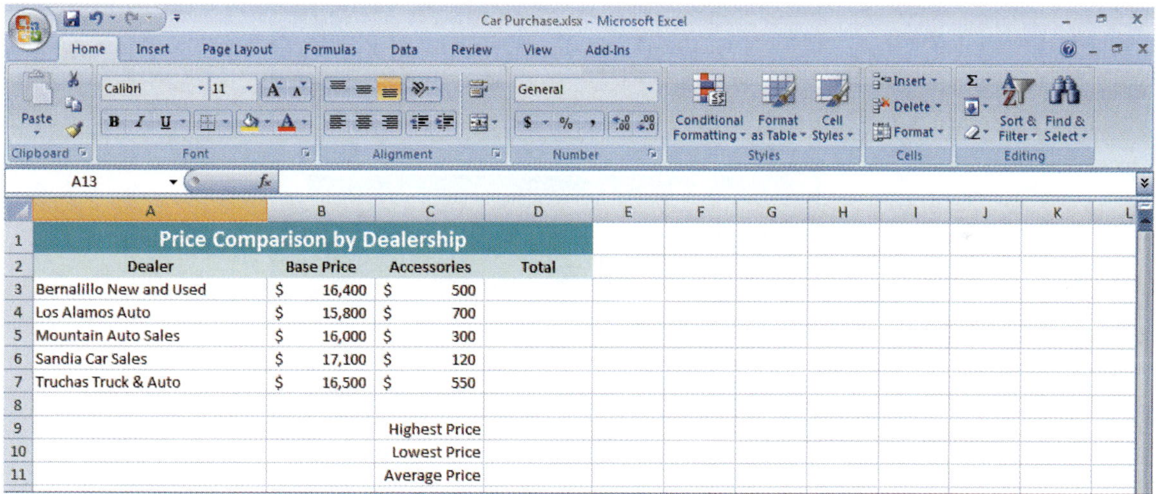

Perform the following operations to provide information that will be useful to making the car purchase decision.

- In the range D3:D7, enter formulas that add the values in column B to the values in column C.

- In cell D9, enter a function that determines the highest price in the range D3:D7.

- In cell D10, enter a function that determines the lowest price in the range D3:D7.

- In cell D11, enter a function that determines the average price in the range D3:D7.

Create a footer with your name and the current date. Save the workbook as **Car Purchase** followed by your initials. Print and close the workbook.

ACTIVITY 5-2

The Insert Function dialog box contains a Search for a function box. When you enter a brief description of what you want to do and click Go, Excel will list functions best suited for the task you want to perform.

FIGURE 5-13
Insert Function dialog box

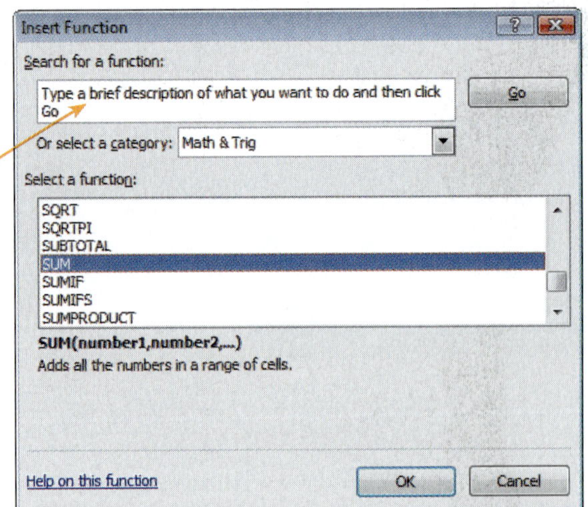

Suppose you are preparing a large worksheet in which all cells in a range should contain data. You want to enter a function near the end of a range that displays the number of cells in the range that are blank. If a number other than zero appears as the function result, you will know that you must search for the cell or cells that are empty and enter the appropriate data.

Open a new workbook, and then click the Insert Function button on the Formula Bar to open the Insert Function dialog box. Enter a description in the Search for a function box that will find a function to count the number of empty cells in a range. If more than one function is suggested, click each function in the Select a function box and read the description of the function that appears below the box. Which function is most appropriate to complete this task?

 **ACTIVITY 5-3**

 A manufacturing company prepares a budget each month. At the end of the month, the Accounting Department prepares a report similar to the one shown in Figure 5-13, which compares the actual amount spent to the budgeted amount.

FIGURE 5-14

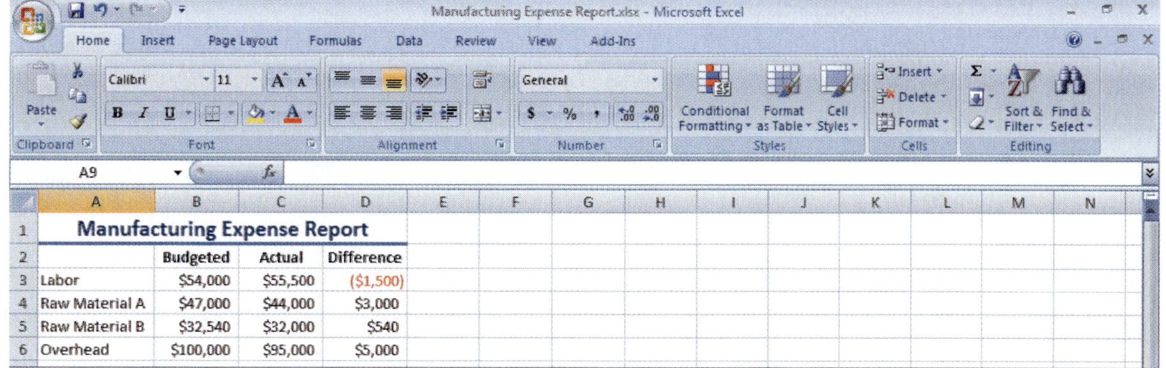

Write an IF function you can use to draw attention to an item that exceeded its budget.

Enhancing A Worksheet

OBJECTIVES

Upon completion of this lesson, you will be able to:

- Sort data in a worksheet.
- Use AutoFilter to display only specified data in a worksheet.
- Apply conditional formatting to highlight data.
- Hide worksheet columns and rows.
- Insert a shape in a worksheet.
- Insert a SmartArt graphic in a worksheet.
- Insert a picture in a worksheet.
- Use a template to create a new workbook.
- Insert a hyperlink in a worksheet.
- Save a workbook in a different file format.
- Insert, edit, and delete comments.
- Use the Research task pane.

Estimated Time: 2.5 hours

VOCABULARY

Ascending sort

AutoFilter

Comment

Conditional formatting

Descending sort

Filter

Filter arrows

Hyperlink

Object

Picture

Research task pane

SmartArt graphic

Sort

Template

Sorting Data

Data entry often occurs in an order that is not necessarily best for understanding and analysis. Sorting rearranges data in a more meaningful order. For example, you might want to sort a list of names in alphabetical order. In an ascending sort, data with letters is arranged in alphabetical order (A to Z), data with numbers is arranged from lowest to highest, and data with dates is arranged from earliest to latest. The reverse order occurs in a descending sort, which arranges data with letters from Z to A, data with numbers from highest to lowest, and data with dates from oldest to newest. When you sort data contained in columns of a worksheet, Excel does not include the column headings.

To sort data, you first click a cell in the column by which you want to sort a range of data. Click the Data tab on the Ribbon. In the Sort & Filter group, click the Sort A to Z button for an ascending text sort or click the Sort Z to A button for a descending text sort. The button names change depending on what type of data you selected for sorting. For numerical data, the buttons are Sort Smallest to Largest and Sort Largest to Smallest. For date and time data, the buttons are Sort Oldest to Newest and Sort Newest to Oldest.  

You can sort by more than one column of data. For example, you might want to sort a list of names in alphabetical order by last name and then within last names by first name. You set up a sort with multiple levels in the Sort dialog box, which is shown in Figure 6-1. To open the Sort dialog box, on the Data tab of the Ribbon, in the Sort & Filter group, click the Sort button. You set up the first-level sort in the Sort by row in the Sort dialog box. The Column box indicates the column that will be used for the top-level sort, such as Last Name. The Sort On box indicates the type of data to be sorted, which is usually Values. If data is formatted with different font or fill colors, you can sort the data by color. The Order box specifies whether the sort is ascending or descending. To create an additional sort level, such as for the First Name column, click Add Level. The Then by row appears. You set up the next-level sort by selecting the sort column, the data type, and the sort order, just as you did for the top-level sort. When all sort levels are created, click OK. The data is rearranged in the order you specified.

> ### Did You Know? 
>
> The Sort commands are also available on the Home tab of the Ribbon and on a shortcut menu. On the Home tab, in the Editing group, click the Sort & Filter button to open a menu with the Sort commands. Or, right-click the cell by which you want to sort the data, and then point to Sort in the shortcut menu to open a submenu with the Sort commands. In either case, click the appropriate Sort command.

FIGURE 6-1
Sort dialog box

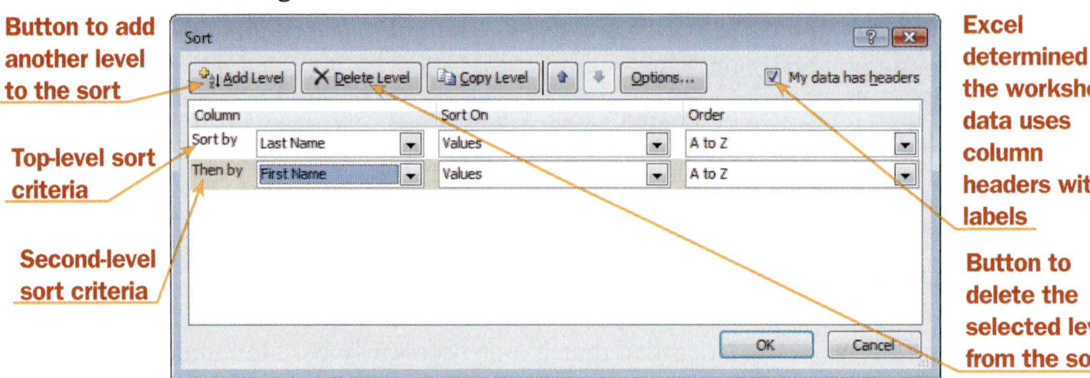

STEP-BY-STEP 6.1

1. Open the **Employee.xlsx** Data File.

2. Save the workbook as **Employee List** followed by your initials.

3. Click cell **D4**. Clicking in the cell indicates that you want to sort by the Salary data in column D.

STEP-BY-STEP 6.1 Continued

4. Click the **Data** tab on the Ribbon, and then locate the **Sort & Filter** group. This group includes the buttons for sorting in ascending or descending order and opening the Sort dialog box.

5. In the Sort & Filter group, click the **Sort Smallest to Largest** button. The data in the range A4:D29 is sorted in ascending order by the numerical values in column D.

6. On the Data tab, in the Sort & Filter group, click the **Sort** button. The Sort dialog box appears. The sort you just created appears as the first-level sort in the Sort by row.

7. Next to the Column box, click the **arrow**, and then click **Last Name**. Values is already selected in the Sort On box.

8. Next to the Order box, click the **arrow**, and then click **A to Z**, if it is not already selected.

9. Click **Add Level**. A Then by row is added so you can specify the second sort level.

10. In the Then by row, next to the Column box, click the **arrow**, and then click **First Name**. Values is already selected in the Sort On box.

11. In the Then by row, next to the Order box, click the **arrow**, and then click **A to Z**, if it is not already selected. Your Sort dialog box should match Figure 6-1.

12. Click **OK**. The data is sorted by last name and then by first name, as shown in Figure 6-2.

FIGURE 6-2
Data sorted by last name and then by first name

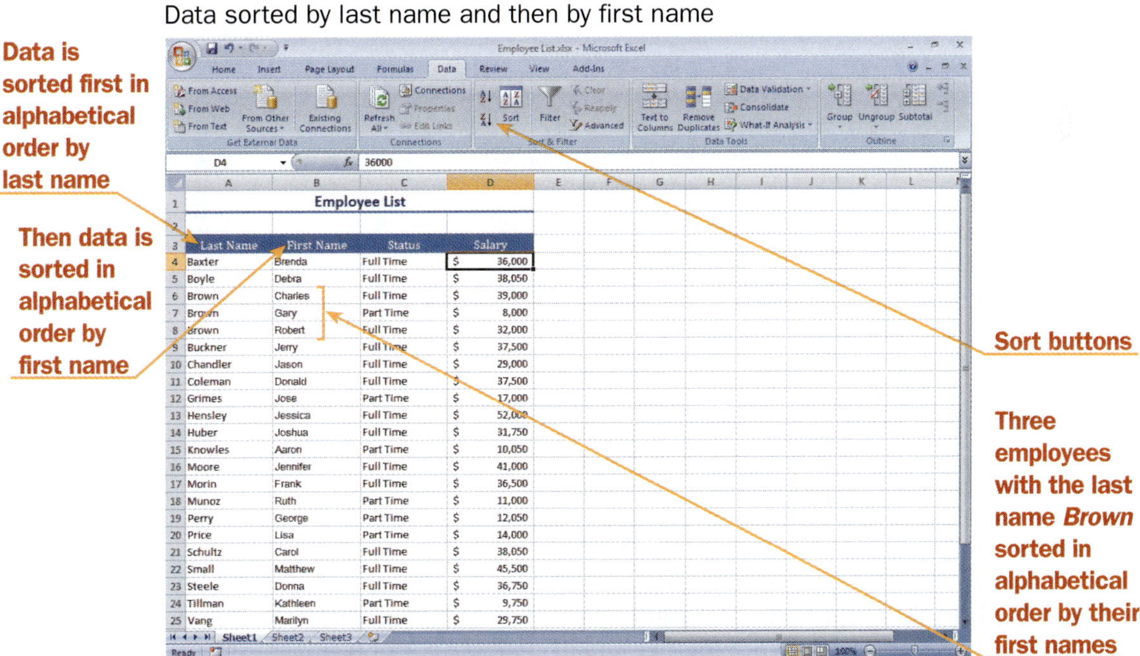

13. Save the workbook, and leave it open for the next Step-by-Step.

Filtering Data

Filtering displays a subset of the data that meets certain criteria and temporarily hides the rows that do not meet the specified criteria. For example, you could filter a list of employees to show only those employees who work full time. The rows that contain part-time employees are then hidden, but not deleted from the worksheet.

You can filter by value, by criteria, or by color. On the Data tab of the Ribbon, in the Sort & Filter group, click the Filter button. **Filter arrows** appear in the lower-right corners of the column heading cells. When you click a filter arrow, the AutoFilter menu for that column appears, as shown in Figure 6-3. The **AutoFilter** menu displays a list of all the values that appear in that column along with additional criteria and color filtering options. Select one of the values to display only those rows in the worksheet in which that value is entered.

Did You Know?

Unlike sorting, filtering does not rearrange the order of the data. But, you can sort, copy, format, and print filtered data.

Did You Know?

The Filter commands are also available on the Home tab of the Ribbon and on a shortcut menu. On the Home tab, in the Editing group, click the Sort & Filter button to open a menu with the Filter commands. Or, right-click the cell by which you want to sort the data, and then point to Filter in the shortcut menu to open a submenu with the Filter commands. In either case, click the appropriate command.

FIGURE 6-3
Auto Filter menu

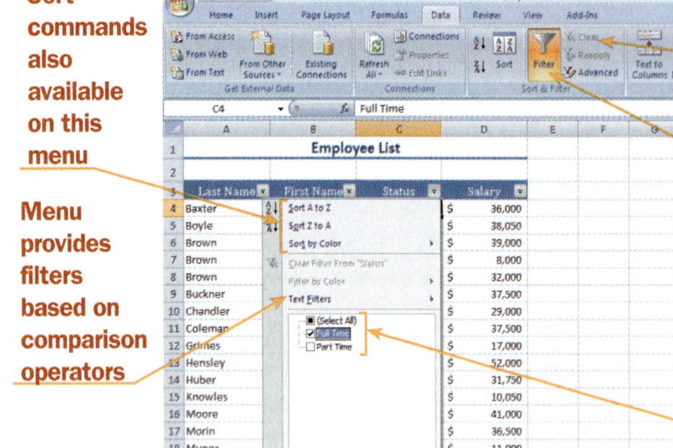

The Number, Text, and Data AutoFilters provide different filtering options. For example, you can use comparison operators, such as equals, between, and begins with, to select data. You can also filter numbers based on their relative values, such as the top 10 and above or below average. If you select the Top 10 number filter, the Top 10 AutoFilter dialog box appears, as shown in Figure 6-4. In the Top 10 AutoFilter dialog box, you can choose to show the highest (top) or lowest (bottom) values in the column. For example, you might show the rows with the 10 largest values in that column of the worksheet. However, you can change the specifications in the dialog box to show a different number of items or a percentage, such as the Bottom 50 Items or the Top 10 Percent.

FIGURE 6-4
Top 10 AutoFilter dialog box

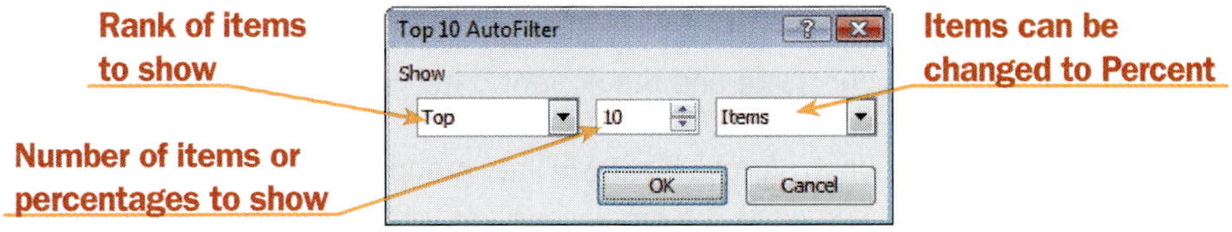

If data is formatted with different font or fill colors, you can filter the data by color. When a column is filtered, the filter arrow icon changes to ▼.

When you want to see all the data in a worksheet again, you can restore all the rows by clearing the filter. Click the filter arrow, and then click the Clear Filter From command or click the Clear button in the Sort & Filter group on the Data tab of the Ribbon. To turn off the filter arrows, click the Filter button in the Sort & Filter group.

> **Extra for Experts**
>
> You can add additional filters to filtered data to limit the subset of data even more. For example, you might filter an employee list to show all part-time employees, and then filter the list of part-time employees to show only those who earn greater than $10,000.

STEP-BY-STEP 6.2

1. Click cell **C4**.

2. On the Data tab, in the Sort & Filter group, click the **Filter** button. Filter arrows appear in cells A3 through D3.

3. In cell C3, click the **filter arrow**. The AutoFilter menu appears.

4. Click the **(Select All)** check box. All of the column values are deselected.

5. Click the **Full Time** check box. The Part Time check box remains deselected on the AutoFilter menu, as shown in Figure 6-3.

6. Click **OK**. The list of employees is filtered to show only the full-time workers. All of the part-time employees are hidden.

7. In cell D3, click the **filter arrow**. You'll add a second filter to show the 10 full-time employees who earn the highest salaries.

STEP-BY-STEP 6.2 Continued

8. On the AutoFilter menu, point to **Number Filters**, and then click **Top 10**. The Top 10 AutoFilter dialog box appears, as shown in Figure 6-4.

9. Click **OK**. The worksheet is filtered to show the 10 employees who work full time and earn the highest salaries.

10. Insert a footer that includes your name and the current date. Save and print the workbook.

11. Click the **Data** tab on the Ribbon. In the Sort & Filter group, click the **Clear** button. The filter is removed from the worksheet, and all of the employees are visible.

12. On the Data tab, in the Sort & Filter group, click the **Filter** button. The filter arrows disappear from the column labels.

13. Save the workbook, and leave it open for the next Step-by-Step.

Applying Conditional Formatting

Conditional formatting highlights worksheet data by changing the look of cells that meet a specified condition. Conditional formatting helps you analyze and understand data by providing answers to questions, such as, "Which employees have worked for the company for more than three years?" The Highlight Cells Rules format cells based on comparison operators such as greater than, less than, between, and equal to. You can also highlight cells that contain specific text, a certain date, or even duplicate values. The Top/Bottom Rules format cells based on their rank, such as the top 10 items, the bottom 15%, or those that are above average. You specify the number of items or the percentage to include.

To add conditional formatting, select the range you want to analyze. In the Styles group on the Home tab, click the Conditional Formatting button, point to Highlight Cells Rules or Top/Bottom Rules, and then click the condition you want. In the dialog box that appears, enter the appropriate criteria, select the formatting you want, and then click OK. The conditional formatting is applied to the selected range. To remove the conditional formatting, click the Conditional Formatting button, point to Clear Rules, and then click Clear Rules from Selected Cells or Clear Rules from Entire Sheet.

Did You Know? 

If you update the data in a range, the conditional formatting changes to reflect the new values. Consider a worksheet that conditionally formats employee salaries to highlight the top 5 salaries. If an employee receives a raise that changes her salary rank from 6 to 5, this employee's salary is conditionally formatted and the salary previously ranked as 5 is cleared of conditional formatting.

STEP-BY-STEP 6.3

1. Select the range **D4:D29**. These cells contain the salaries for each of the 28 employees.

2. Click the **Home** tab on the Ribbon. In the Styles group, click the **Conditional Formatting** button. The Conditional Formatting menu appears, as shown in Figure 6-5.

FIGURE 6-5
Conditional formatting menu

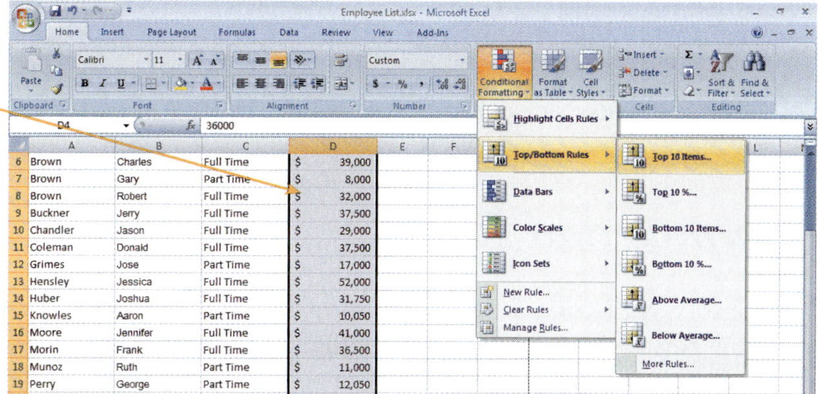

3. Point to **Top/Bottom Rules**, and then click **Top 10 Items**. The Top 10 Items dialog box appears, as shown in Figure 6-6.

FIGURE 6-6
Top 10 Items dialog box

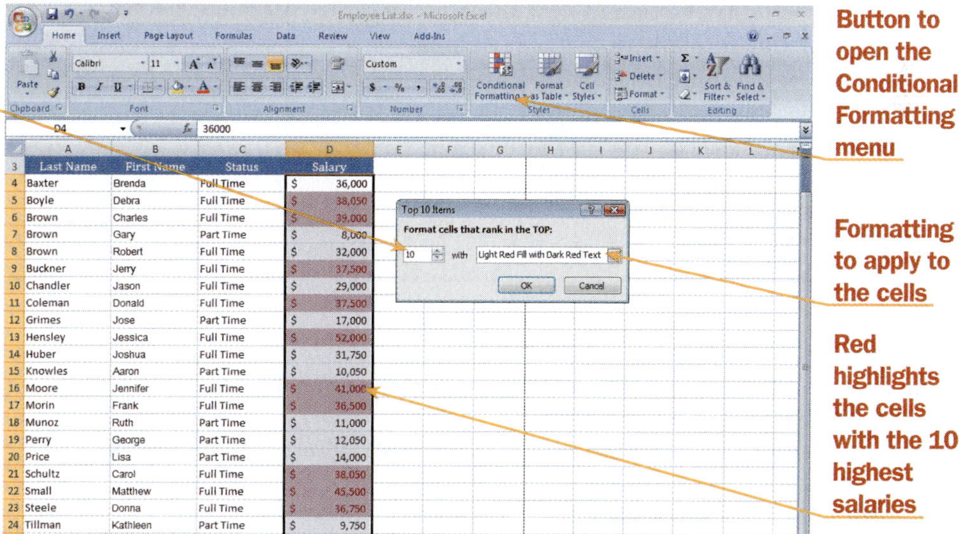

4. Type **5** in the left box to reduce the number of salaries to the top five.

STEP-BY-STEP 6.3 Continued

5. Click **OK**. The five highest salaries appear in red text on a red background.

6. On the Home tab, in the Styles group, click the **Conditional Formatting** button. On the Conditional Formatting menu, point to **Top/Bottom Rules**, and then click **Bottom 10 Items**. The Bottom 10 Items dialog box appears.

7. Type **5** in the left box, click the **arrow**, and then click **Yellow Fill with Dark Yellow Text**.

8. Click **OK**. The five lowest salaries appear in yellow text on a yellow background.

9. Save, print, and close the workbook.

Hiding Columns and Rows

Hiding temporarily removes a row or column from view. Hiding rows and columns enables you to use the same worksheet to emphasize different data. For example, you can hide monthly data to leave only the total values visible. Select how many rows or columns you want to hide, and then right-click the selection. On the shortcut menu that appears, click Hide to remove the selection from view in the worksheet. You can repeat this process to hide as many rows and columns in the worksheet as you like. Hidden rows and columns remain out of sight until you redisplay them. Select the row or column on each side of the hidden rows or columns you want to redisplay. Right-click the selection, and then click Unhide on the shortcut menu.

> **Did You Know?** 
>
> You can also hide and unhide selected rows and columns from the Ribbon. Click the Home tab on the Ribbon. In the Cells group, click the Format button. On the Format menu that appears, in the Visibility section, point to Hide & Unhide. This submenu contains the Hide Columns and Hide Rows commands as well as the Unhide Columns and Unhide Rows commands.

STEP-BY-STEP 6.4

1. Open the **Oil.xlsx** Data File.

2. Save the workbook as **Oil Production** followed by your initials.

3. Select columns **B** through **G**. You'll hide the monthly data for the oil wells.

4. Right-click the selected columns. On the shortcut menu that appears, click **Hide**. Columns B through G are hidden.

5. Click cell **A19** to deselect the range. The worksheet shows the six-month production total for each well in the field, as shown in Figure 6-7.

STEP-BY-STEP 6.4 Continued

FIGURE 6-7
Worksheet with hidden columns

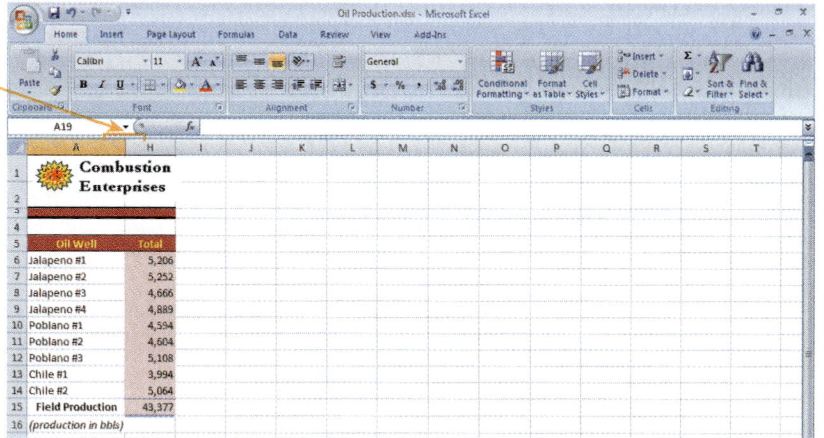

6. Insert a footer with your name and the current date. Save and print the workbook.

7. Select columns **A** and **H**. These columns surround hidden columns.

8. Right-click the selected columns. On the shortcut menu that appears, click **Unhide**. Columns B through G reappear.

9. Select rows **6** through **14**. You'll hide individual oil well data, leaving only the monthly totals.

10. Right-click the selected rows, and then click **Hide** on the shortcut menu. Rows 6 through 14 are hidden.

11. Click cell **A19** to deselect the range. The worksheet shows only the field production totals for each month.

12. Save and print the workbook.

13. Select rows **5** and **15**. These rows surround the hidden rows.

14. Right-click the selected rows, and then click **Unhide** on the shortcut menu. Rows 6 through 14 reappear in the worksheet.

15. Save the workbook, and leave it open for the next Step-by-Step.

Adding Shapes to a Worksheet

Shapes, such as rectangles, circles, arrows, lines, flowchart symbols, and callouts, can help make a worksheet more informative. For example, you might use a rectangle or circle to create a corporate logo. Or, you might use a callout to explain a value in the worksheet. Excel has a gallery of shapes you can use.

Inserting a Shape

To open the Shapes gallery, click the Insert tab on the Ribbon, and then, in the Illustrations group, click the Shapes button. In the Shapes gallery that appears, as shown in Figure 6-8, click the shape you want to insert. The pointer changes to a crosshair, which you click and drag in the worksheet to draw the shape. The shape is inserted in the worksheet.

FIGURE 6-8
Shapes gallery

Modifying Shapes

Shapes are inserted in the worksheet as objects. An **object** is anything that appears on the screen that you can select and work with as a whole, such as a shape, picture, or chart. When the shape is selected, the Drawing Tools appear on the Ribbon and contain the Format contextual tab, as shown in Figure 6-9. You use the tools on the Format tab to modify the shape. For example, you can change the shape's style, fill, and outline as well as add special effects, such as shadows. You can also move and resize the selected shape.

FIGURE 6-9
Formatted shape in the worksheet

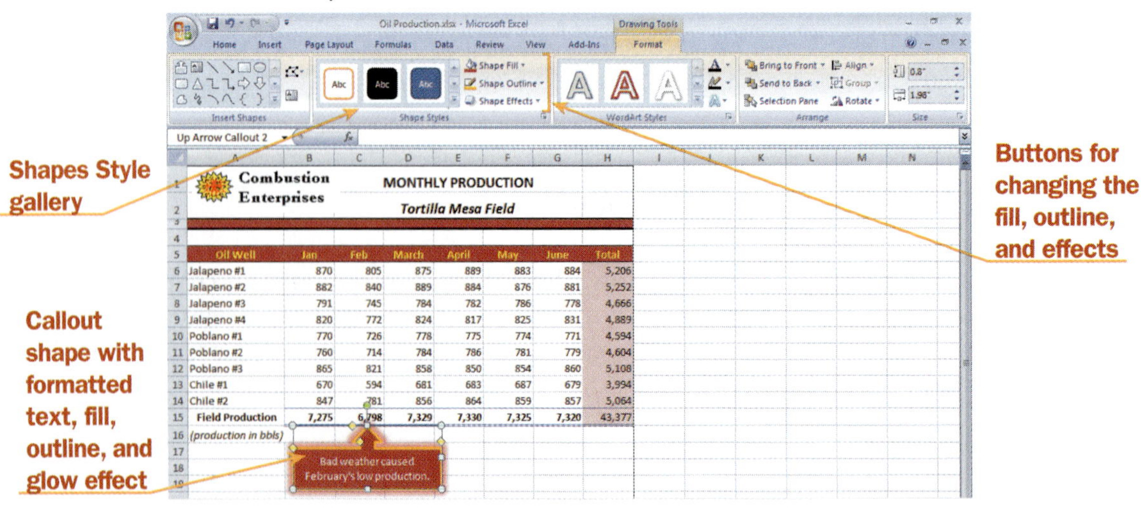

Deleting Objects

When you no longer need a shape or any other object in a worksheet, you can delete it. First click the object to select it. Then press the Delete key. The object is removed from the worksheet.

S TEP-BY-STEP 6.5

1. Click the **Insert** tab on the Ribbon. In the Illustrations group, click the **Shapes** button. The Shapes gallery appears, as shown in Figure 6-8.

2. In the Block Arrows section, click the **Up Arrow Callout** button (the last button in the second row). The pointer changes shape to a crosshair. 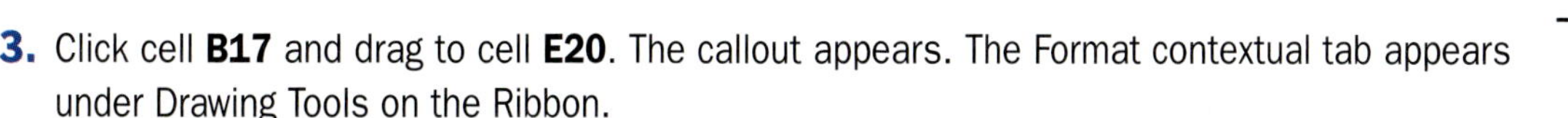

3. Click cell **B17** and drag to cell **E20**. The callout appears. The Format contextual tab appears under Drawing Tools on the Ribbon.

4. Type **Bad weather caused February's low production.** (including the period). The text is inserted in the callout.

5. Point to the middle-right sizing handle until the pointer changes to the Horizontal Resize pointer, and then drag left to column D. The callout is narrower.

6. Point to the callout to display the four-headed move pointer, and then drag the callout until its arrow points to cell **C15**. The callout points to the correct cell and remains selected.

7. Under Drawing Tools, on the Format tab, in the Shape Styles group, next to the Shape Fill button, click the **arrow**. A color palette appears.

8. In the Theme Colors section, click **Red, Accent 2** (the sixth color in the first row). The callout background color changes to red.

9. Under Drawing Tools, on the Format tab, in the Shape Styles group, next to the Shape Outline button, click the **arrow**. A color palette appears.

10. In the Standard Colors section, click **Orange** (the third color). The line around the callout changes to orange.

11. Under Drawing Tools, on the Format tab, in the Shape Styles group, click the **Shape Effects** button.

12. On the Shapes Effects menu, point to **Glow**. In the Glow Variations section, click **Accent color 2, 8 pt glow** (the second effect in the second row). The callout is formatted as shown in Figure 6-9.

13. Click any cell in the worksheet to deselect the shape. The Drawing Tools Format tab disappears from the Ribbon.

14. Save the workbook, and leave it open for the next Step-by-Step.

Extra Challenge

Add other shapes to the workbook, and then format them using the tools on the Format tab under Drawing Tools. When you are done, click the Undo button on the Quick Access Toolbar to undo your changes.

Adding SmartArt Graphics to a Worksheet

SmartArt graphics enhance worksheets by providing a visual representation of information and ideas. SmartArt graphics are often used for organizational charts, flowcharts, and decision trees.

Inserting a SmartArt Graphic

To insert a SmartArt graphic, click the SmartArt button in the Illustrations group on the Insert tab. The Choose a SmartArt Graphic dialog box appears, as shown in Figure 6-10. You can select from a variety of layouts, including list, matrix, and pyramid. Click the SmartArt graphic you want to use in the center pane and read its description in the right pane. Click OK to insert the graphic in the worksheet as an object.

FIGURE 6-10
Choose a SmartArt Graphic dialog box

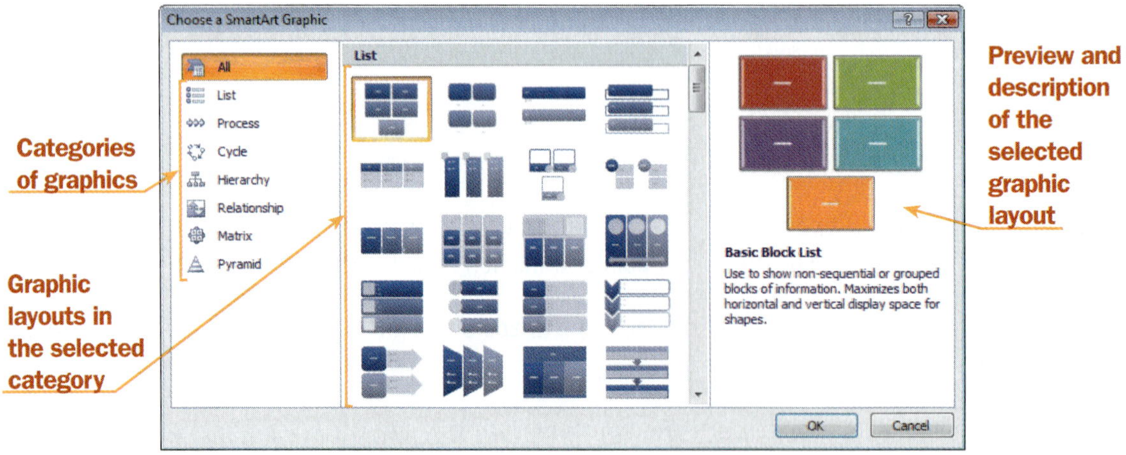

Modifying a SmartArt Graphic

When the SmartArt graphic is selected, SmartArt Tools appear on the Ribbon and contain the Design and Format contextual tabs, as shown in Figure 6-11. You use the tools on the Design tab to select a different layout, apply a style, and change the layout's color. The Format tab has tools to modify the shapes used in the selected layout, by changing shape, size, fill color, and outline color, and tools to apply shape styles and special effects, such as shadows. You can also move and resize the selected shapes.

FIGURE 6-11
Formatted SmartArt graphic

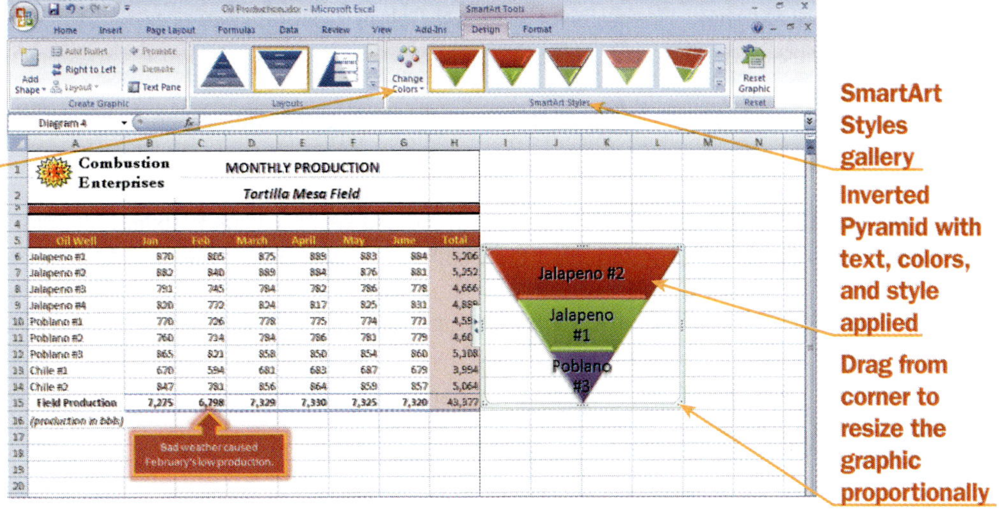

STEP-BY-STEP 6.6

1. Click the **Insert** tab on the Ribbon. In the Illustrations group, click the **SmartArt** button. The Choose a SmartArt Graphic dialog box appears, as shown in Figure 6-10.

2. In the left pane, click **Pyramid**.

3. In the center pane, click **Inverted Pyramid** (the second graphic).

4. Click **OK**. The SmartArt graphic appears in the worksheet. The SmartArt Tools appear on the Ribbon.

5. Click **[Text]** in the top level of the pyramid, if it is not already selected, and then type **Jalapeno #2**.

6. Click **[Text]** in the second level of the pyramid, and then type **Jalapeno #1**.

7. Click **[Text]** in the bottom level of the pyramid, and then type **Poblano #3**.

8. Drag the lower-right sizing handle up until the graphic is about 4 columns wide. Dragging from the corner resizes the graphic proportionally.

9. Drag the picture over the range **I6:L15**.

10. Under SmartArt Tools, on the Design tab, in the SmartArt Styles group, click the **Change Colors** button. The gallery of colors appears.

STEP-BY-STEP 6.6 Continued

11. In the Colorful section, click **Colorful – Accent Colors** (the first color option). Each of the top three oil well producers is a different color in the pyramid.

12. Under SmartArt Tools, on the Design tab, in the SmartArt Styles group, click the **More** button. The gallery of SmartArt Quick Styles appears.

13. Point to each style to see its Live Preview. In the 3-D section, click **Polished** (the first style in the top row). The pyramid changes to reflect the Quick Style, as shown in Figure 6-11.

14. Change the Orientation to **Landscape**. Save, print, and close the workbook.

Adding Pictures to a Worksheet

You might want to use a picture to make the appearance of a worksheet more attractive. A picture is a digital photograph or other image file. Some organizations like to include their corporate logo on their worksheets. Pictures can also be used to illustrate data in a worksheet. For instance, you might want to insert pictures of each product in an inventory list.

Inserting a Picture

You can insert a picture you have stored as a file, or you can use a picture from the Clip Art collection that comes with Excel. If you have access to the Internet, you can also download pictures from Office Online to insert in your worksheets.

To insert a picture from a file, click the Picture button in the Illustrations group on the Insert tab of the Ribbon. The Insert Picture dialog box, which looks and functions like the Open dialog box, appears. Change the location to the folder with the stored picture folder, and then double-click the picture file you want to use.

The Clip Art task pane provides a wide variety of clip art, photographs, movies, and sounds that you can use in a worksheet. To access the Clip Art task pane, click the Clip Art button in the Illustrations group on the Insert tab of the Ribbon. The Clip Art task pane appears on the right side of the program window, as shown in Figure 6-12. In the Search for box, type a brief description of the clip you want to find, and then click Go. Clips that fit the search words appear in the results box. Click an image to insert it in the worksheet.

Did You Know? 

You can place a background pattern or picture in a worksheet. On the Page Layout tab, in the Page Setup group, click the Background button. In the Sheet Background dialog box, select the picture you want in the background of the worksheet, and then click Open.

Important 

All images are protected by copyright law. You cannot download and reuse a picture you find on a Web site without permission. Contact the copyright holder to obtain permission. Some Web sites offer free images for non-commercial use. Others offer images you purchase for a fee.

FIGURE 6-12
Clip Art task pane

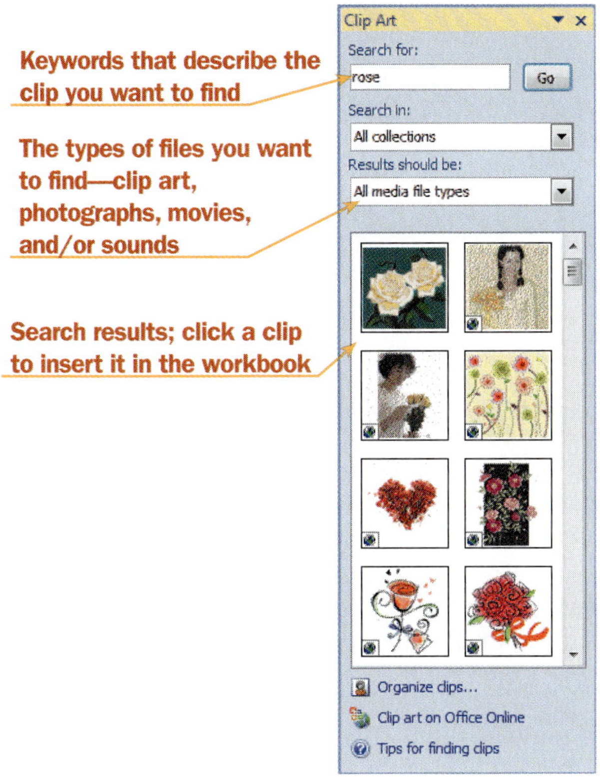

Keywords that describe the clip you want to find

The types of files you want to find—clip art, photographs, movies, and/or sounds

Search results; click a clip to insert it in the workbook

Modifying a Picture

A picture is inserted in the workbook as an object. As with shapes, you can move, resize, or format the picture to fit your needs. Click a picture to select it. The Picture Tools appears on the Ribbon, as shown in Figure 6-13. The Format contextual tab contains tools to edit and format the picture. The tools in the Adjust group enable you to change the look of the picture, including its brightness, contrast, and color. The Picture Styles group includes the Picture Styles gallery as well as tools to change the picture's shape and border, and effects such as shadows and rotation. The Size group includes the Crop button, which you use to cut out parts of the picture you do not want to use.

FIGURE 6-13
Formatted picture

Buttons for changing the brightness, contrast, and color

Picture with increased brightness and style applied

Buttons for changing the shape, border, and effects

Picture Styles gallery

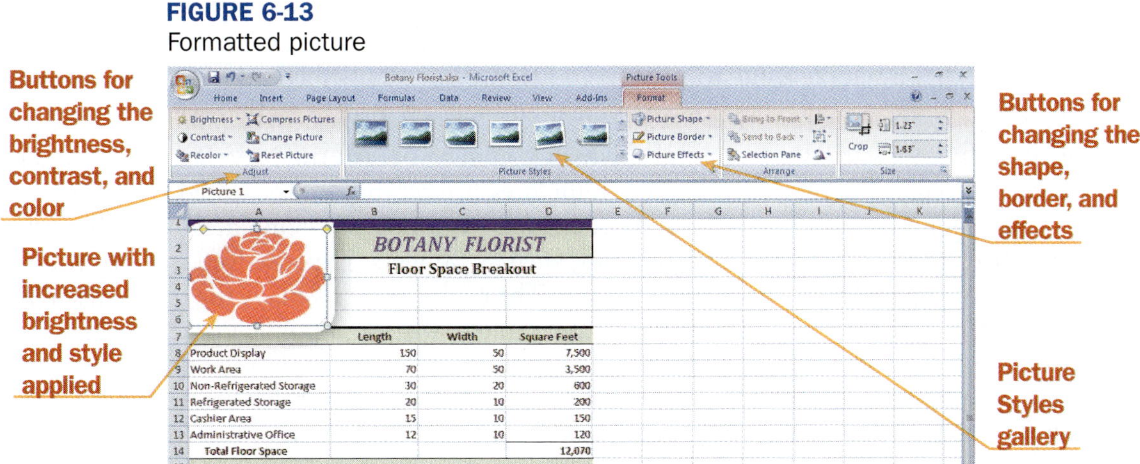

STEP-BY-STEP 6.7

1. Open the **Botany.xlsx** Data File.

2. Save the workbook as **Botany Florist** followed by your initials.

3. Click the **Insert** tab on the Ribbon. In the Illustrations group, click the **Picture** button. The Insert Picture dialog box appears.

4. Click the **Rose.tif** Data File. This is the picture you want to insert.

5. Click the **Insert** button. The picture of a rose is inserted in the worksheet. The Picture Tools appears on the Ribbon.

6. Drag the lower-right sizing handle up until the dark line at the bottom of row 6 is visible.

7. Drag the picture to the range **A2:A6**, if it is not already in that location.

8. Under Picture Tools, on the Format tab, in the Adjust group, click the **Brightness** button, and then click **+40%**. The picture's brightness increases, and the rose color is pinker.

9. Under Picture Tools, on the Format tab, in the Picture Styles group, click the **More** button. The gallery of Picture Styles appears.

10. Point to different picture styles to see the Live Preview, and then click **Rounded Diagonal Corner, White** (the second style in the third row). The picture's overall style changes, as shown in Figure 6-13.

11. Insert a footer with your name and the current date. Save, print, and close the workbook.

Using Templates

Templates are predesigned workbook files that you can use as the basis or model for new workbooks. The template includes all the parts of a workbook that will not change, such as text labels, formulas, and formatting. You save a copy of the template as a workbook and enter the variable data. You can use a template again and again, entering different data each time. For example, suppose your employer requires all employees to submit a weekly time sheet. Each week you use the same worksheet format, but the number of hours you enter in the worksheet changes. You can use a template file to save the portion of the worksheet that is the same every week. Then, each week, you need to add only the data that is pertinent to that week.

Excel comes with a variety of templates, which you access from the New Workbook dialog box, as shown in Figure 6-14. The Installed Templates are template files stored on your computer. If your computer is connected to the Internet, you also see templates available from Microsoft Office Online, organized by categories, such as Budgets, Expense Reports, Forms, and Invoices. Click a template category in the left pane. The center pane displays the templates available for that category. Click a template in the center pane to display a preview and description of the selected template in the right pane. To open a new workbook based on the selected template, click Create. Templates have the file extension .xltx to differentiate them from regular Excel workbook files. After you open a workbook based on a template file, you need to save it with a descriptive name to the appropriate location.

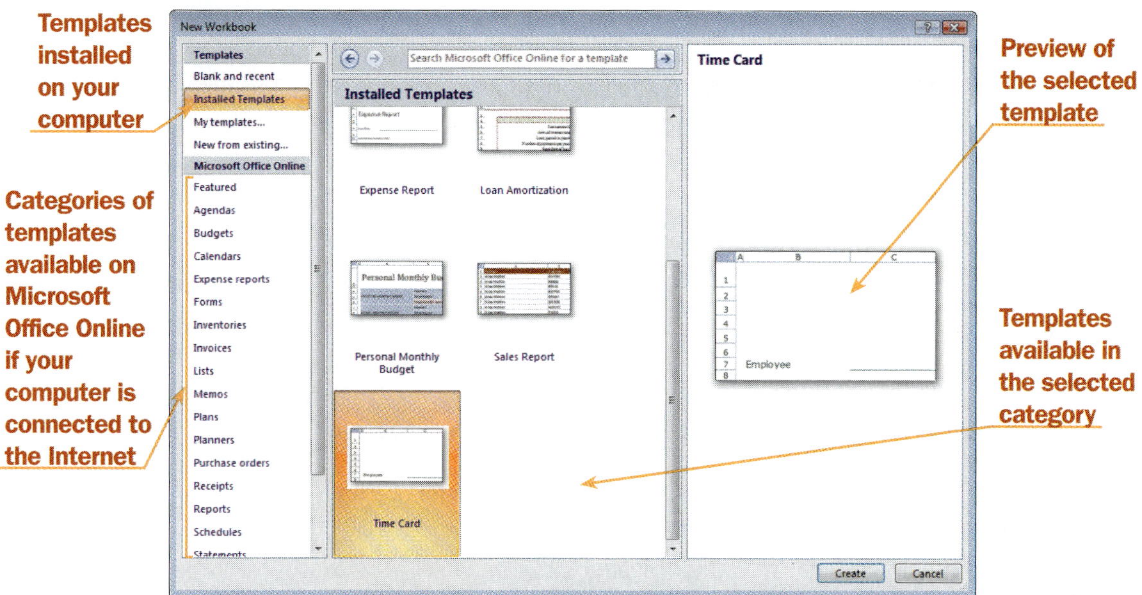

FIGURE 6-14
New Workbook dialog box

Templates installed on your computer

Categories of templates available on Microsoft Office Online if your computer is connected to the Internet

Preview of the selected template

Templates available in the selected category

You can also create a workbook based on an existing file. In the New Workbook dialog box, click the New from existing button in the left pane. The New from Existing Workbook dialog box, which looks and functions like the Open dialog box, appears. Select the workbook you want to use as a model for another workbook, and then click Create New. A copy of the selected workbook appears in the program window. You can modify the file as needed, and then save the file with an appropriate name and location.

> **Important** 
>
> Each time a template from Microsoft Office Online is downloaded to your computer, Microsoft verifies that the version of the Office software on that computer is genuine. Depending on your setup, you might see a message explaining this feature.

STEP-BY-STEP 6.8

1. Click the **Office Button**, and then click **New**. The New Workbook dialog box appears.

2. In the left pane, click **Installed Templates**. A list of templates installed on your computer appears in the center pane.

3. Scroll down the Installed Templates list in the center pane, and then click **Time Card**. A preview of the Time Card template appears in the right pane, as shown in Figure 6-14.

4. Click **Create**. A workbook based on the Time Card template appears in the program window. The workbook is titled *TimeCard1*.

5. Save the workbook as **Time Card** followed by your initials.

6. Zoom the worksheet to **85%** so you can see the entire width of the time card.

STEP-BY-STEP 6.8 Continued

7. Click cell **C7**, if it is not already selected, and then enter your name.

8. Click cell **C16**, and then enter **5/25/2010** as the week ending date. The dates for the specified week appear in the range C21:C27, the Date column in the time card.

9. Click cell **D21**, and then enter **8**. The total hours for the day appear in cell H21, and the total regular hours for the week appear in cell D28.

10. Click cell **D29**, and then enter **10**. The rate of $10 per hour for regular hours is entered. The total regular pay for the day appears in cell D30, and the total pay for the week appears in cell H30.

11. Click cell **E21**, and then enter **1.5**. The total hours for the day in cell H21 are updated to include the overtime hours, and the total overtime hours for the week appear in cell E28.

12. Click cell **E29**, and then enter **15**. The rate of $15 per hour for overtime hours is entered. The total overtime pay for the day appears in cell E30, and the updated total pay for the week appears in cell H30. Your worksheet should look similar to Figure 6-15.

FIGURE 6-15
Worksheet created from a template

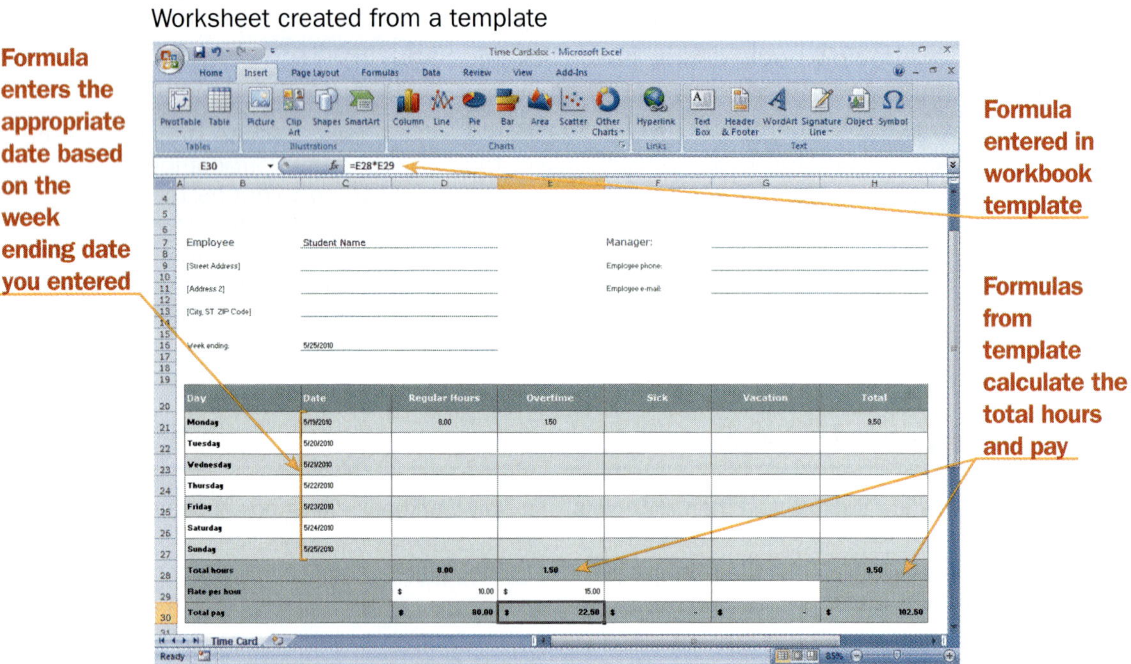

13. Save, print, and close the workbook.

Inserting Hyperlinks

 A hyperlink is a cell in a worksheet that opens another file or page when you click it. You can create hyperlinks to another Web page, another file, a specific location in the current workbook, a new document, and an e-mail address. For example, you might want to create a link to another Excel file that contains the source data for information used in the current worksheet. You might also create a link to a Web page that contains information related to items in the worksheet.

To create a hyperlink, first click the cell you want to use for the hyperlink, or select an object, such as a picture. On the Insert tab of the Ribbon, in the Links group, click the Hyperlink button (or right-click the cell or object, and then click Hyperlink on the shortcut menu). The Insert Hyperlink dialog box appears, as shown in Figure 6-16. Type the filename or Web page address in the Address box, and then click OK. The hyperlink is added to the worksheet, and the pointer appears as a hand when you point to the hyperlink.

> **Did You Know?**
>
> You can enter a custom ScreenTip that appears when a user points to a hyperlink. In the Insert Hyperlink dialog box, click ScreenTip. In the Set Hyperlink ScreenTip dialog box that appears, enter the text you want for the ScreenTip in the ScreenTip text box, and then click OK. Complete the Insert Hyperlink dialog box, and then click OK.

FIGURE 6-16
Insert Hyperlink dialog box

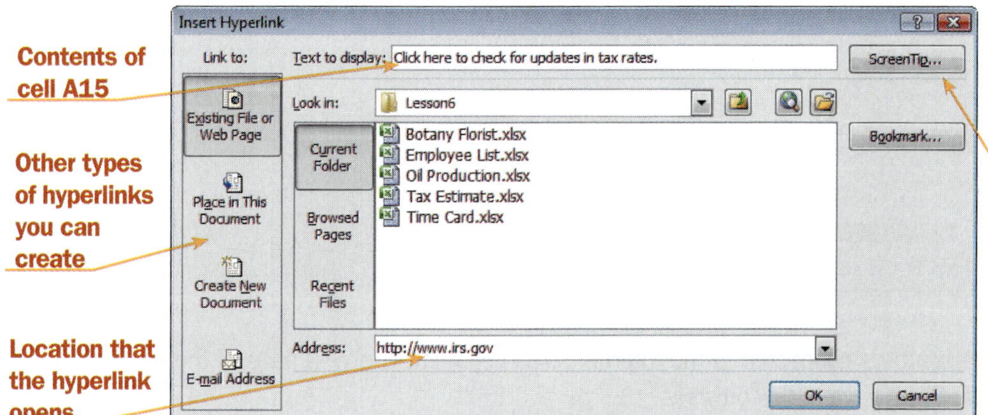

To use the hyperlink, click the cell or object. If you created a hyperlink to a file, that file opens when you click the hyperlink. If you created a hyperlink to a Web page, that page is opened in your Web browser when you click the hyperlink.

You can edit a hyperlink to change its displayed text, ScreenTip, and even link. Click the cell or object with the hyperlink, and then click the Edit Hyperlinks button in the Links group on the Insert tab. The Edit Hyperlink dialog box appears, and looks and functions just like the Insert Hyperlink dialog box. In addition, it contains the Remove Link button, which you can click to delete the hyperlink from the cell but leave its contents unaffected.

> **Important** 
>
> The worksheet cell is the hyperlink, not the contents entered in that cell. If the contents extend beyond the cell's border, the hyperlink will not work if the user clicks the text that extends into the next cell. The actual cell must be clicked.

STEP-BY-STEP 6.9

1. Open the **Tax.xlsx** Data File.

2. Save the workbook as **Tax Estimate** followed by your initials.

3. Click cell **A15**. You want to use this cell as the hyperlink.

4. Click the **Insert** tab on the Ribbon. In the Links group, click the **Hyperlink** button. The Insert Hyperlink dialog box appears.

5. In the Address box, type **www.irs.gov**. This is the Web page you want to open when a user clicks the hyperlink. Excel precedes the Web address with *http://*, as shown in Figure 6-16.

6. Click **OK**, and then click cell **A17**. Cell A15 is a hyperlink with blue and underlined text, which is a common format for indicating a hyperlink, as shown in Figure 6-17.

FIGURE 6-17
Hyperlink added to the worksheet

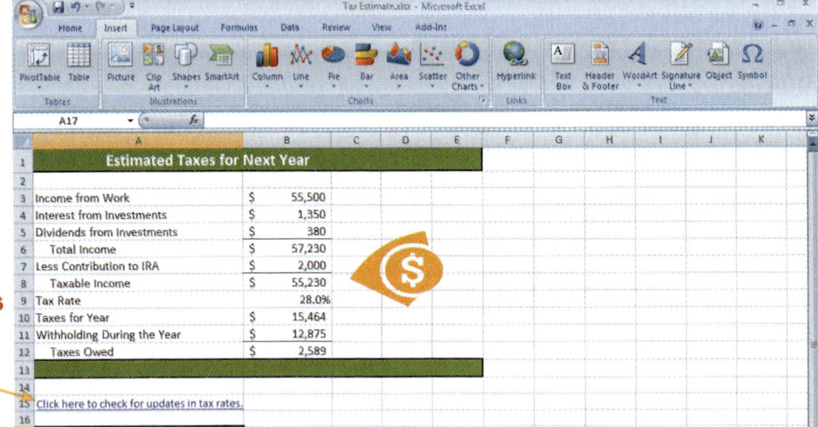

7. If your computer is connected to the Internet, click cell **A15**. The Web page of the Internal Revenue Service appears in your Web browser.

8. Exit your browser and return to the worksheet.

9. Insert a header with your name and the current date. Save, print, and close the workbook.

Saving a Workbook in a Different Format

Excel workbooks can be saved in different file formats so that they can be opened in other programs. For example, if you want to share data with a coworker or friend who uses an earlier version of Excel, you can save your Excel file in a format that is readable by Excel 2003. You can also save the file in a format that can be viewed as a Web page on the Internet. Table 6-1 describes some of the different types of formats in which you can save workbooks.

TABLE 6-1
Common file formats in which to save workbooks

FILE TYPE	DESCRIPTION	FILE EXTENSION
CSV (Comma delimited)	Data separated by commas	.csv
Excel Template	File used to create other similar files	.xltx
Formatted Text (Space delimited)	Data separated by spaces	.prn
Microsoft Excel 97-2003	Data created in an earlier version of Excel	.xls
Text (Tab delimited)	Data separated by tabs	.txt
Single File Web Page	File to be displayed on the Internet	.mhtm, .mhtml
Web Page	File to be displayed on the Internet	.htm, .html
XML Data	Data in Extensible Markup Language	.xml

S TEP-BY-STEP 6.10

1. Open the **Expense.xlsx** Data File.

2. Save the workbook as **Expense Report** followed by your initials.

3. Click the **Office Button**, and then click **Save As**. The Save As dialog box appears.

4. In the File name box, type **Expense Report 2003** followed by your initials.

5. Click the **Save as type** button. A list of file types you can use to save the workbook appears.

6. Click **Excel 97-2003 Workbook (*.xls)**. You want to save the Excel 2007 workbook as an Excel 2003 workbook.

STEP-BY-STEP 6.10 Continued

7. Click **Save**. The Microsoft Office Excel – Compatibility Checker dialog box appears, as shown in Figure 6-18, listing elements of the workbook that are not supported by earlier versions of Excel. In this case, some of the formatting cannot be saved in the earlier file format. These formats will be converted to match the earlier format.

FIGURE 6-18
Microsoft Office Excel – Compatibility Checker dialog box

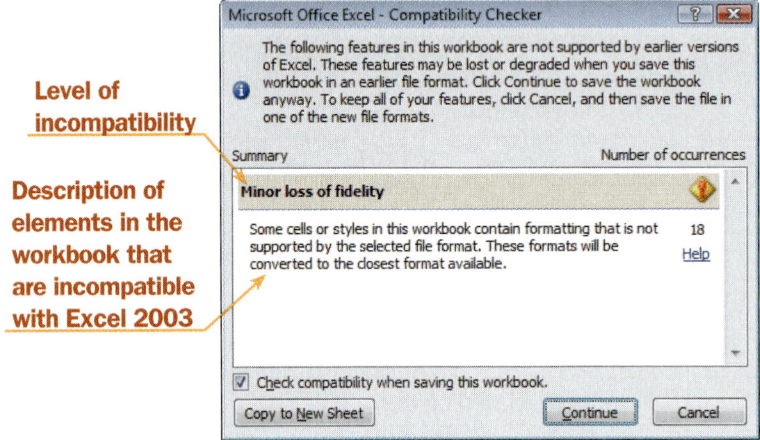

8. Click **Continue**. The workbook is saved as a file that can be opened in Excel 2003.

9. Close the **Expense Report 2003** workbook.

10. Open the workbook **Expense Report** followed by your initials that you created in Step 2.

11. Click the **Office Button**, and then click **Save As**. The Save As dialog box appears.

12. Click the **Save as type** button, and then click **Single File Web Page**. The dialog box expands.

13. Click **Change Title**. The Set Page Title dialog box appears.

14. In the Page title box, type **Expense Report for Sales Staff**, and then click **OK**. The page title will appear in the title bar of the browser.

15. Click **Publish**. The Publish as Web Page dialog box appears.

16. Next to the Choose box, click the **arrow**, and then click **Items on Sheet1**, if it is not already selected.

17. Click **Change**. The Set Title dialog box appears.

18. Press the **Delete** key to delete the text in the Title box, and then click **OK**. You do not want the same text to appear in both the browser title bar and the browser window centered over the worksheet content.

STEP-BY-STEP 6.10 Continued

19. In the File name box, change the file name to **Expense Report Web** followed by your initials. The full path shows the drive and folders in which the file will be saved.

20. Click the **Open published web page in browser** check box, if it is not already checked. The Publish as Web Page dialog box should match Figure 6-19.

FIGURE 6-19
Publish as Web Page dialog box

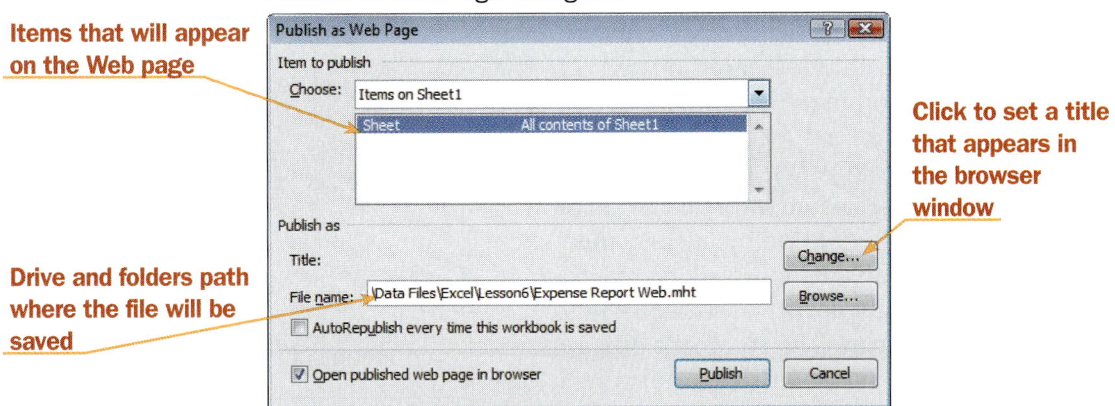

21. Click **Publish**. The Web page appears in your browser, as it would if it were published on the Web. If you use Internet Explorer as your Web browser, your screen should look similar to Figure 6-20.

FIGURE 6-20
Web page in Internet Explorer

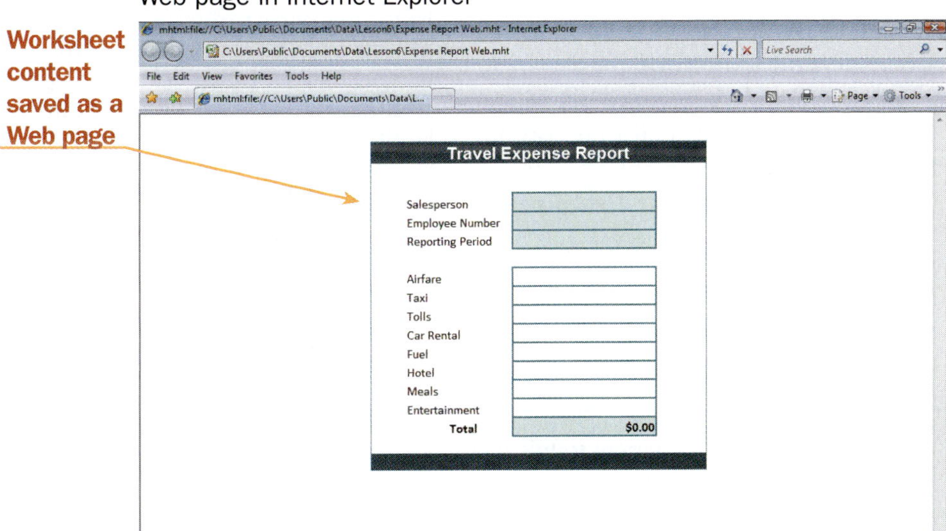

22. Close the browser. Save the workbook, and leave it open for the next Step-by-Step.

Working with Comments

 A **comment** is a note attached to a cell that is usually used to explain or identify information contained in the cell. For example, you might use comments to provide the full text of abbreviations entered in cells. You might also use comments to explain the calculations in cells that contain formulas. Also, you can use comments to provide feedback to others without altering the worksheet structure. For example, a supervisor might use comments to offer suggestions to an employee on how to improve the worksheet format.

Inserting a Comment

All of the comments tools are located on the Review tab of the Ribbon in the Comments group. The New Comment button inserts a comment in the active cell. A comment box appears to the right of the selected cell with the user name followed by a colon at the top of the box. Type the comment, and then click outside the comment box to close it. A red triangle appears in the upper-right corner of the cell to indicate that it contains a comment. The comment box appears whenever you point to the cell that contains it. It disappears when you move the pointer to another cell. You can keep a specific comment onscreen by clicking the Show/Hide Comment button in the Comments group on the Review tab.

Editing and Deleting a Comment

To edit a comment, click the cell that contains the comment. Then click the Edit Comment button in the Comments group on the Review tab. Edit the text as usual. To delete a comment, click the cell that contains the comment. Then click the Delete button in the Comments group on the Review tab. The comment is removed from the cell.

> ### Did You Know?
>
> You can show and hide all the comments in a worksheet by toggling the Show All Comments button in the Comments group on the Review tab. The Comments group also has the Previous and Next buttons for moving between comments in the worksheet.

> ### Computer Concepts
>
> The user name that appears in the comment box matches the user name entered for that copy of Excel. To change the user name, click the Office Button, and then click Excel Options. The Excel Options dialog box appears with the Popular options displayed. In the Personalize your copy of Microsoft Office section, type the name you want to appear in comments in the User name box. Click OK.

STEP-BY-STEP 6.11

1. Click cell **A4**. You want to add a comment to this cell.

2. Click the **Review** tab on the Ribbon. In the Comments group, click the **New Comment** button. The comment box appears to the right of the active cell.

3. In the comment box, type the following comment: **Please change to Employee ID**.

4. Click cell **A13**. The comment box disappears, and a small red triangle appears in the upper-right corner of cell A4 to indicate that the cell contains a comment.

STEP-BY-STEP 6.11 Continued

5. On the Review tab, in the Comments group, click the **New Comment** button.

6. In the comment box, type the following comment: **The per diem maximum is $50**.

7. Click cell **A16**. The comment box disappears, and a small red triangle appears in the upper-right corner of cell A13, indicating that the cell contains a comment.

8. Point to cell **A13**. The cell comment appears, as shown in Figure 6-21.

Comments added to the worksheet

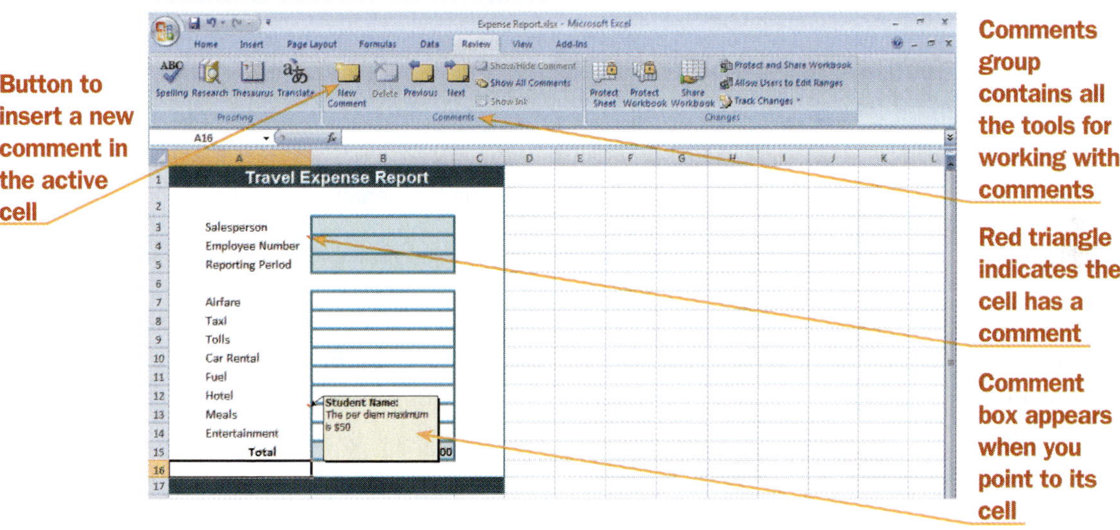

9. Click cell **B3**, and then enter your name. Save, print, and close the workbook.

Using the Research Task Pane

The **Research task pane** provides access to information typically found in references such as dictionaries, thesauruses, and encyclopedias. In Excel, the Research task pane also provides numerical data typically used in a worksheet, such as statistics or corporate financial data.

To open the Research task pane, click the Review tab on the Ribbon, and then, in the Proofing group, click the Research button. The Research task pane appears along the right side of the program window. In the task pane, select a reference book, a research site, or a business and financial site, and then search for a subject or topic. Your computer must be connected to the Internet to use the Research task pane.

STEP-BY-STEP 6.12

1. Open the **Stock.xlsx** Data File.

2. Save the workbook as **Stock Quotes** followed by your initials.

3. Click the **Review** tab on the Ribbon. In the Proofing group, click the **Research** button. The Research task pane appears on the right side of the program window.

4. In the Search for box, type **AMZN**.

5. Click the **arrow** next to the All Reference Books box, and then click **MSN Money Stock Quotes**. The search results appear in the task pane. The Last amount is the most recent price for that stock.

6. Click cell **C5**, and then enter the amount that appears for *Last*. The current price is entered in cell C5. Excel returns the total value in cell E5 by multiplying the value in cell C5 by the value in cell D5.

7. On the Research task pane, in the Search for box, type **HD**. Click the **Start searching** button. The most recent price for The Home Depot stocks appears in the search results box.

8. Click cell **C6**, and then enter the Last amount. The current price is entered in cell C6, and the value amounts are calculated.

9. Repeat the process in Steps 6 and 7 to find the current prices for the ticker symbols INTC, JNJ, and MSFT, and then enter the Last amounts in the range C7:C9. Your worksheet should be similar to Figure 6-22; however, the actual amounts in the Price and Values columns will differ, because they are based on the most recent stock prices.

FIGURE 6-22
Research task pane

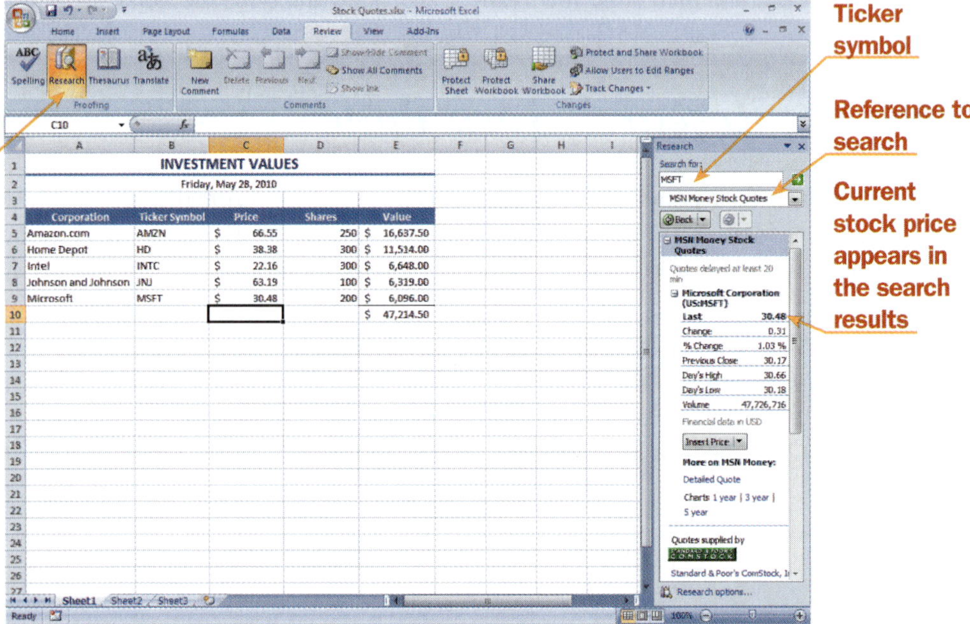

STEP-BY-STEP 6.12 Continued

10. Click the **Review** tab on the Ribbon. In the Proofing group, click the **Research** button. The Research task pane closes.

11. Insert a header with your name and the current date. Save, print, and close the workbook.

SUMMARY

In this lesson, you learned:

- Sorting rearranges worksheet data in ascending or descending alphabetical, numerical, or chronological order.

- Filtering displays a subset of data in a worksheet that meets specific criteria.

- Conditional formatting highlights worksheet data by changing the look of cells that meet a specified condition, such as a comparison or rank.

- Hiding rows and/or columns lets you use the same worksheet to emphasize different data. You can unhide the hidden rows and columns at any time.

- Shapes, such as rectangles, circles, arrows, lines, flowchart symbols, and callouts, can help make a worksheet more informative. Excel has a gallery of shapes you can insert.

- SmartArt graphics enhance worksheets by providing a visual representation of information and ideas. Excel has a variety of layouts you can select.

- Pictures can make a worksheet's appearance more attractive. You can insert a picture you have stored as a file, or one from the Clip Art collection that comes with Excel.

- Templates are predesigned workbook files that can be used as the basis or model when creating a new workbook. A template includes all parts of the workbook that will not change, such as labels, formulas, and formatting.

- A hyperlink in a worksheet open another file or page when clicked. You can create hyperlinks to another Web page, another file, a specific location in the current workbook, a new document, or an e-mail address.

- You can save workbooks in different file formats, so they can be opened in other programs or earlier versions of Excel.

- Comments are notes that can be added to cells to provide additional information or feedback.

- The Research task pane provides access to information typically found in references such as dictionaries, thesauruses, and encyclopedias. In Excel, it also provides numerical data, such as current stock prices.

VOCABULARY *Review*

Define the following terms:

Ascending sort	Filter	Research task pane
AutoFilter	Filter arrows	SmartArt graphic
Comment	Hyperlink	Sort
Conditional formatting	Object	Template
Descending sort	Picture	

REVIEW *Questions*

TRUE/FALSE

Circle T if the statement is true or F if the statement is false.

T   F   **1.** Sorting always arranges data in a worksheet with the smallest values listed first.

T   F   **2.** Filtering reorganizes data so it appears in a different order.

T   F   **3.** Hiding deletes a row or column from a worksheet.

T   F   **4.** Inserting a comment in a cell affects the results of a formula contained in that cell.

T   F   **5.** Excel workbooks can be saved in other file formats.

MATCHING

Match the correct term in Column 2 to its description in Column 1.

Column 1	**Column 2**
___ **1.** Workbook used as a model to create other workbooks	**A.** AutoFilter
___ **2.** Changes the look of cells that meet a specific condition	**B.** Template
___ **3.** Organizes data in a more meaningful order	**C.** Conditional formatting
___ **4.** A cell or graphic that opens another file or Web page when clicked	**D.** Comment
___ **5.** Displays a subset of data that meet certain criteria	**E.** Hyperlink
___ **6.** A message that explains or identifies information in a cell	**F.** Sorting

PROJECTS

 PROJECT 6-1

1. Open the **Impact.xlsx** Data File. Save the workbook as **Impact Salaries** followed by your initials. The worksheet contains the annual salaries and ratings of Level 10 employees.

2. Sort the data in the range A6:E20 by the Performance Rating in descending numerical order (largest to smallest).

3. In cell F5, enter **Salary Category** as the label.

4. In cell F6, enter the following formula to indicate the employee's salary category (low or high) based on his annual salary: **=IF(D6<32001,"Low","High")**.

5. Copy the formula in cell F6 to the range F7:F20.

   The Level 10 management is concerned that employee salaries do not reflect the annual performance ratings. If salaries are allocated based on annual ratings, employees with higher performance ratings should appear near the top of the worksheet and have *High* in the Category column. Employees with lower ratings should appear near the bottom of the worksheet and have *Low* in the Category column. When a salary does not reflect the employee's annual rating, the word in column F might appear to be out of place.

6. Based on the data in the worksheet, which employees do you believe are underpaid? Why?

7. Insert a header with your name and the current date. Save, print, and close the workbook.

 PROJECT 6-2

1. Open the **Top.xlsx** Data File. Save the workbook as **Top Movies** followed by your initials.

2. Conditionally format the data to highlight the top 10 highest grossing films with a light green fill with dark green text. Column D contains the number of dollars that the film grossed.

3. Conditionally format the data to highlight the bottom 10 lowest grossing films with a yellow fill with dark yellow text.

4. Sort the data by Release Date in ascending order (oldest to newest) and then by Movie in ascending order (A to Z).

5. Insert a header with your name and the current date. Save, print, and close the file.

 PROJECT 6-3

1. Open the **City.xlsx** Data File. Save the workbook as **City Facts** followed by your initials.

2. Click cell B2 and turn on the filter arrows.

3. Run the following AutoFilters to answer the following questions. Remember to restore the records after each filter by clearing the filter.

Column	AutoFilter	Criterion
B	Top 10 Items	4 items
C	Bottom 10 Items	4 items
D	Top 10 %	10 percent
G	0	(not needed)

A. What are the four largest cities in the United States?

___________ ___________ ___________ ___________

B. What are the four coldest cities in the United States during January?

___________ ___________ ___________ ___________

C. What cities are in the top 10 percentile of average July temperatures?

___________ ___________ ___________ ___________

D. How many of the 30 largest cities are at sea level (have altitudes of 0)?

4. Save and close the workbook.

PROJECT 6-4

1. Open the **Paper.xlsx** Data File. Save the workbook as **Paper Sales** followed by your initials.

2. Hide columns B through E to remove the quarterly data from view.

3. Unhide columns B through E to restore the quarterly data.

4. Hide rows 7 through 14 to remove the regional data from view.

5. Insert a header with your name and the current date. Print the worksheet.

6. Unhide rows 7 through 14 to restore the regional data.

7. Save and close the workbook.

PROJECT 6-5

1. In the New Workbook dialog box, display the templates installed on your computer, and open the **Billing Statement** template file.

2. Save the workbook as **Roberts Statement** followed by your initials.

3. Zoom the worksheet so you can see the entire statement, if it is not already in view.

4. Enter the following data in the worksheet.

Cell	Data
B1	(your name)
C8	15679
C10	EX6-5
F2	(504) 555-8796
F3	(504) 555-8797

F8	**Anita Roberts**
F9	**4509 Lumpton Road**
F10	**New Orleans, LA, 70135**
F11, F12	(delete cell contents)
B15	**10/8/10**
C15	**Event Planning**
D15	**013**
E15	**Graduation Party**
F15	**350**
G15	**50**

5. Save, print, and close the workbook.

PROJECT 6-6

1. Open the **School.xlsx** Data File. Save the workbook as **School Bus** followed by your initials.

2. On the Insert tab, in the Illustrations group, click the Picture button. The Insert Picture dialog box appears.

3. Insert the **School Bus.bmp** Data File.

4. Under Picture Tools on the Format tab, in the Size group, click the Dialog Box Launcher. The Size and Properties dialog box appears.

5. On the Size tab, in the Scale section, in the Height box, type **41%**. Click Close.

6. Drag the picture so that it fits within the range E1:E3.

7. Under Picture Tools on the Format tab, in the Picture Styles group, click the Picture Effects button, point to Glow, and then click Accent color 6, 18 pt glow.

8. Insert a header with your name and the current date. Save, print, and close the workbook.

PROJECT 6-7

1. Open the **Compact.xlsx** Data File. Save the workbook as **Compact Cubicle** followed by your initials.

2. In cell C8, insert the following comment: **Shut down for two hours for maintenance.**

3. In cell C9, insert the following comment: **Production time increased two hours to make up for maintenance on Machine 102.**

4. In cell G9, insert the following comment: **Shut down for major repairs.**

5. Insert a cube shape in the upper-left corner of the workbook.

6. On the Drawing Tools Format tab, in the Size group, enter 0.5" in the Shape Height box and the Shape Width box.

7. Change the Shape Fill to Orange.

8. Change the Shape Effects so the 3-D Rotation is set to Off Axis 1 Right.

9. Copy and paste the cube shape, and then drag the copy so it overlaps the lower-right corner of the first cube.

10. Insert a header with your name and the current date. Save, print, and close the workbook.

CRITICAL *Thinking*

ACTIVITY 6-1

Additional clip art is available on Microsoft Office Online. You can access the site by clicking *Clip art on Office Online* in the Clip Art task pane. If you have Internet access, use Office Online to locate the following clip art items:

- Lion
- Valentine heart
- Doctor
- Cactus

Copy each clip art item to the worksheet. Resize and format it appropriately. Insert a header with your name and the current date. Save and close the workbook.

ACTIVITY 6-2

SmartArt graphics are a simple way to present hierarchical information or relationships, such as for a team, club, school, family, or organization. For example, your school probably has a principal, teachers, and students. In a worksheet, insert a SmartArt graphic to illustrate at least three levels of that hierarchy. Format the SmartArt graphic appropriately.

WORKING WITH MULTIPLE WORKSHEETS AND WORKBOOKS

<table>
<tr><td valign="top">

OBJECTIVES

Upon completion of this lesson, you will be able to:

- Move between worksheets in a workbook.
- Rename worksheets.
- Change the color of sheet tabs.
- Reposition worksheets.
- Hide and unhide worksheets.
- Insert and delete worksheets.
- Create cell references to other worksheets.
- Create 3-D references.
- Print all or part of workbooks.
- Arrange multiple workbooks in the program window.
- Move and copy worksheets between workbooks.

Estimated Time: 2 hours

</td><td valign="top">

VOCABULARY

3-D reference

Active sheet

Destination

Sheet tab

Source

Worksheet range

</td></tr>
</table>

Moving Between Worksheets

A workbook is a collection of worksheets. The worksheets within the workbook are identified by **sheet tabs** that appear at the bottom of the workbook window. The name of the worksheet appears on the tab. Until the worksheets are named, they are identified as Sheet1, Sheet2, and so on, as shown in Figure 7-1.

FIGURE 7-1
Default sheet tabs in a workbook

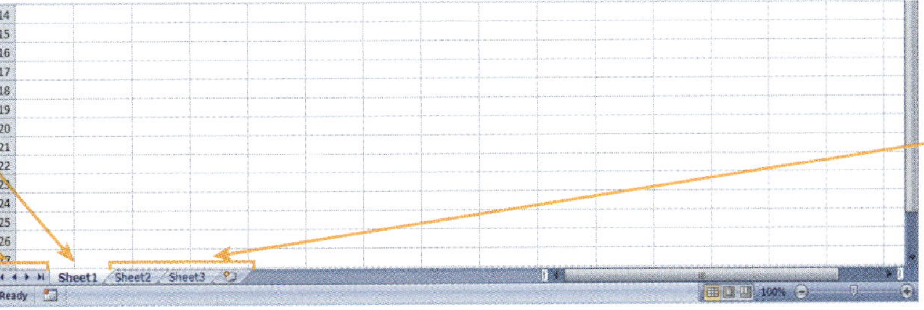

To view a specific worksheet, simply click its sheet tab. The worksheet that appears in the workbook window is called the **active sheet**. The active sheet has a white sheet tab. If you don't see the sheet tab for the worksheet you want to display, use the tab scrolling buttons to display the sheet tab.

Identifying Worksheets

 To better distinguish worksheets, you can give them more descriptive names. You can also change the color of each sheet tab.

Renaming Worksheets

Although you can leave the default worksheet names (Sheet1, Sheet2, and so forth), a good practice is to use descriptive names to help identify the contents of each worksheet. For example, the worksheet name *Quarter 1 Budget* is a better reminder of the worksheet contents than *Sheet1*. To rename a worksheet, double-click its sheet tab, type the new name, and then press the Enter key.

Did You Know?

To rename a worksheet, you can also right-click its sheet tab, and then click Rename on the short-cut menu. The worksheet name in the sheet tab is selected. Type a new name, and then press the Enter key.

Changing the Color of Sheet Tabs

Another way to categorize worksheets is by changing the color of the sheet tabs. For example, a sales manager might use different colors to identify each sales region. To change the tab color of a worksheet, right-click the sheet tab you want to recolor, point to Tab Color on the shortcut menu, and then click the color you want for that tab.

STEP-BY-STEP 7.1

1. Open the **Continental.xlsx** Data File. Save the workbook as **Continental Sales** followed by your initials.

2. Click the **Sheet3** sheet tab. The Sheet3 worksheet appears as the active sheet. It will summarize the sales data stored in other worksheets.

3. Double-click the **Sheet3** sheet tab. The worksheet name is highlighted.

4. Type **Corporate**, and then press the **Enter** key. The name *Corporate* appears on the third sheet tab.

STEP-BY-STEP 7.1 Continued

5. Double-click the **Sheet1** sheet tab, type **Western**, and then press the **Enter** key. The Sheet1 worksheet is renamed as *Western*.

6. Rename the Sheet2 worksheet as **Eastern**.

7. Rename the Sheet4 worksheet as **Northern**.

8. Right-click the **Corporate** sheet tab, and then point to **Tab Color**. A palette of colors appears, as shown in Figure 7-2.

FIGURE 7-2
Shortcut menu for the selected sheet tab

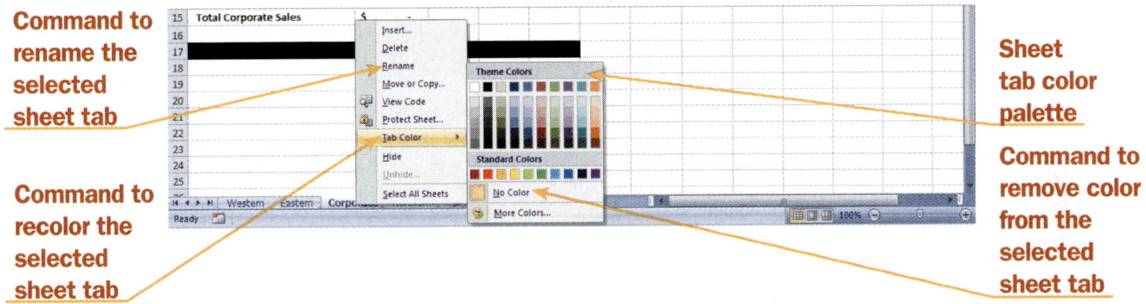

9. In the Theme Colors section, click **Black, Text 1** (the second color in the first row). A black line appears at the bottom of the Corporate sheet tab.

10. Click the **Northern** sheet tab. The Northern worksheet becomes the active sheet, and you can see the black sheet tab for the Corporate worksheet.

11. Right-click the **Northern** sheet tab, point to **Tab Color** to open the color palette, and then, in the Theme Colors section, click **Orange, Accent 6** (the last color in the first row).

12. Right-click the **Western** sheet tab, point to **Tab Color**, and then click **Aqua, Accent 5** (the ninth color in the first row).

13. Right-click the **Eastern** sheet tab, point to **Tab Color**, and then, in the Theme Colors section, click **Purple, Accent 4** (the eighth color in the first row).

STEP-BY-STEP 7.1 Continued

14. Click the **Corporate** sheet tab. The Corporate worksheet is active, and the colored sheet tabs are visible for the regional worksheets, as shown in Figure 7-3.

FIGURE 7-3
Renamed and colored sheet tabs

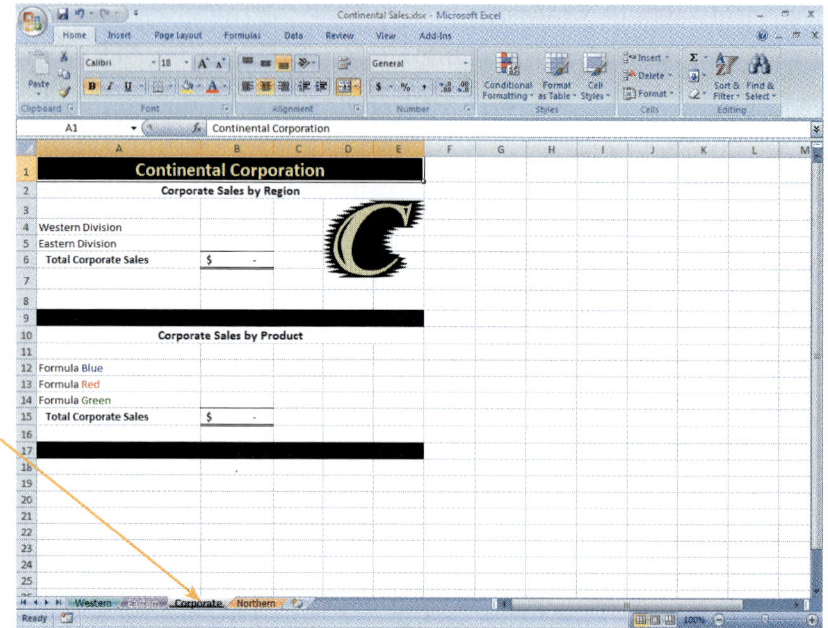

15. Save the workbook, and leave it open for the next Step-by-Step.

Managing Worksheets Within a Workbook

Often, data and analysis are best organized on multiple worksheets. For example, you could enter financial data for each quarter of the year in four different worksheets, and then summarize the annual data in a fifth worksheet. Another common workbook organization is to place sales data for each sales territory or region in its own worksheet, and then summarize the total sales in another worksheet.

Repositioning Worksheets

To make it simpler to find information, you can position worksheets in a logical order, such as placing a summary worksheet first, followed by actual data. You can reposition a worksheet by dragging its sheet tab to a new location. A placement arrow indicates the new location, as shown in Figure 7-4. When you release the mouse button, the worksheet moves to that position.

FIGURE 7-4
Sheet tab being repositioned

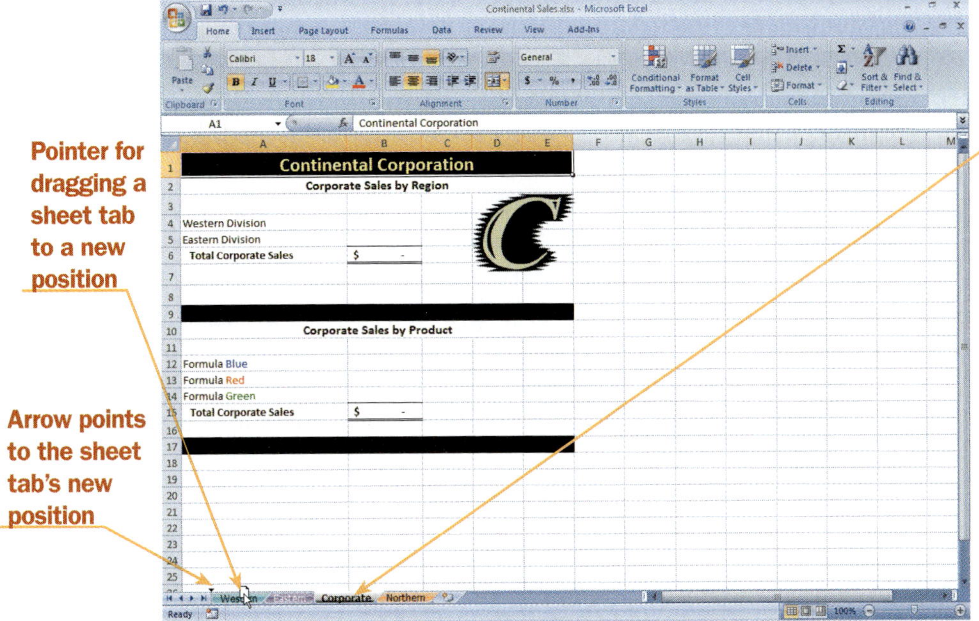

Hiding and Unhiding Worksheets

Some workbooks include many worksheets. Some might contain data you do not need to see, but still want to save, such as a list of employee names or data from past months. You can keep the sheet tabs streamlined by hiding the worksheets to which you do not need immediate access. Right-click the worksheet you want to hide, and then click Hide on the shortcut menu. To unhide a worksheet, right-click any sheet tab, and then click Unhide on the shortcut menu. The Unhide dialog box appears, as shown in Figure 7-5. Click the worksheet you want to unhide, and then click OK.

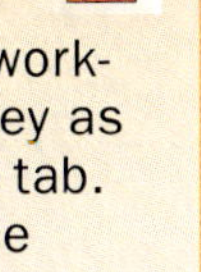

Extra for Experts

You can create a copy of a worksheet by pressing the Ctrl key as you drag and drop its sheet tab. When you release the mouse button, an exact copy of the selected worksheet is added in the location indicated by the arrow and the original worksheet remains in its same location. The sheet tab has the same name as the original worksheet followed by a number in parentheses.

FIGURE 7-5
Unhide dialog box

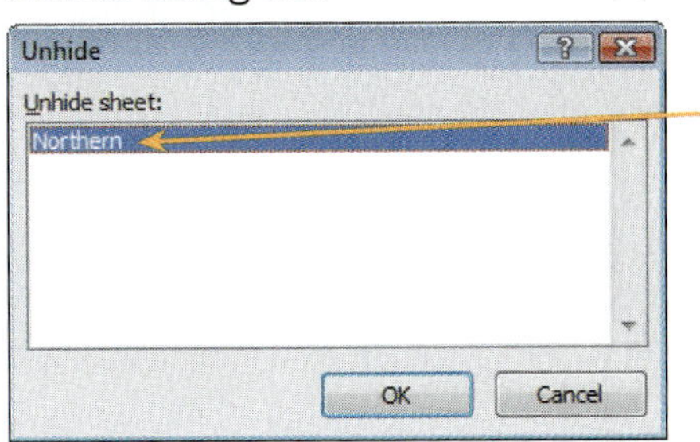

Worksheet hidden in the active workbook

Inserting and Deleting Worksheets

Each workbook opens with three worksheets. But, you can always add or delete worksheets as needed to accommodate your data. To insert a blank worksheet, click the Insert Worksheet tab next to the existing sheet tabs. A new worksheet is added after the other worksheets. You can drag the new worksheet to the position you want. Another option is to click the sheet tab of the worksheet that will *follow* the new sheet. On the Home tab of the Ribbon, in the Cells group, click the arrow to the right of the Insert button, and then click Insert Sheet. A new worksheet is inserted before the sheet you selected.

Deleting permanently removes a worksheet and all its contents from the workbook. You cannot undo the action. To delete a worksheet, click the sheet tab for the worksheet you want to remove. On the Home tab of the Ribbon, in the Cells group, click the arrow to the right of the Delete button, and then click Delete Sheet. A dialog box might appear to confirm that you want to permanently delete the data that might exist in the worksheet. Click Delete to continue the action, or click Cancel to leave the worksheet in the workbook. You can also right-click a sheet tab, and then click Delete on the shortcut menu. The worksheet is permanently removed from the workbook without confirmation.

STEP-BY-STEP 7.2

1. Click and drag the **Corporate** sheet tab to the left until the arrow points to the left of the Western sheet tab, as shown in Figure 7-4.

2. Release the mouse button. The sheet tab for the Corporate worksheet is first.

3. Right-click the **Northern** sheet tab, and then click **Hide** on the shortcut menu. The Northern worksheet and its sheet tab disappear.

4. Right-click any sheet tab, and then click **Unhide** on the shortcut menu. The Unhide dialog box appears, as shown in Figure 7-5, listing the names of the worksheets that are currently hidden.

5. Click **Northern**, if it is not already selected, and then click **OK**. The Northern worksheet and its sheet tab reappear.

6. On the Home tab of the Ribbon, in the Cells group, to the right of the Delete button, click the **arrow**, and then click **Delete Sheet**.

7. If a dialog box appears warning that any data in the worksheet will be permanently deleted, click **Delete**. The Northern worksheet is deleted, and its sheet tab no longer appears at the bottom of the worksheet.

8. Save the workbook, and leave it open for the next Step-by-Step.

Consolidating Workbook Data

In some cases, you might need several worksheets to solve one numerical problem. For example, a business that has several divisions might keep the financial results of each division in a separate worksheet. Then another worksheet might combine those results to show summary results for all divisions.

Creating Cell References to Other Worksheets

Rather than retyping data and formulas, you can create a reference to existing data and formulas in other worksheets. For example, you would use this type of reference to display regional sales totals on a summary sheet. The location the data is being transferred from is the source. The location where the data will appear is the destination.

To display data or formula results from one worksheet in another worksheet of the same workbook, you use a formula. First, click the destination cell where you want to display the data or formula results from another worksheet. Type an equal sign to begin the formula. Click the sheet tab for the worksheet that contains the source cell or range you want to reference, and then click the source cell or select the source range to include it in the formula. Finally, press the Enter key to complete the formula. The contents of the source cell appear in the destination cell. Any change you make to the source cell also changes the value in the destination cell. For example, the reference *Sheet2!B3* refers to the value contained in cell B3 on Sheet 2.

Creating 3-D References

A 3-D reference is a reference to the same cell or range in multiple worksheets that you use in a formula. You can use 3-D references to incorporate data from other worksheets into the active worksheet. You use a 3-D reference with 18 different functions, including SUM, AVERAGE, COUNT, MIN, MAX, and PRODUCT. For example, you might want to enter the SUM function in a summary worksheet to add several numbers contained in other worksheets, such as with quarterly or regional sales data. In general, to use 3-D references, worksheets should have the same organization and structure.

A 3-D reference lists the worksheet range, an exclamation point, and a cell or range. A worksheet range is a group of adjacent worksheets. In a worksheet range, as in a cell range, a colon separates the names of the first worksheet and the last worksheet in the group. An exclamation mark separates the worksheet range from its cell or range reference. For example, the reference *Sheet2:Sheet4!B3* refers to the values contained in cell B3 on Sheet2, Sheet3, and Sheet4.

Because a worksheet range is a group of adjacent worksheets, moving a worksheet into the range or removing a worksheet from the range affects the formula results. In the previous example, if you move Sheet1 between Sheet3 and Sheet4, the value in cell B3 of Sheet1 is also included in the 3-D reference.

Table 7-1 gives other examples of how 3-D references might be used.

<table>
<tr><td>

Important 

Moving a worksheet can affect 3-D references in the workbook. Be cautious when moving or copying worksheets with 3-D references.

</td></tr>
</table>

TABLE 7-1
Formulas that reference other worksheets

FORMULA	DESCRIPTION
=Sheet4!D9	Displays the value from cell D9 in the Sheet4 worksheet
=Sheet1!D10+Sheet2!D11	Adds the value from cell D10 in the Sheet1 worksheet and the value from cell D11 in the Sheet2 worksheet
=SUM(Sheet2!D10:D11)	Adds the values from cells D10 and D11 in the Sheet2 worksheet
=SUM(Sheet2:Sheet4!D12)	Adds the value from cell D12 in the Sheet2, Sheet3, and Sheet4 worksheets

S TEP-BY-STEP 7.3

1. Click the **Corporate** sheet tab. You will enter formulas in this worksheet that reference cells in the Western and Eastern worksheets.

2. Click cell **B4**, and then type **=** to begin the formula.

3. Click the **Western** sheet tab. The worksheet name is added to the formula in the Formula Bar, which is =Western!. The Western worksheet appears in the workbook window so you can select a cell or range.

4. Click cell **B6**. The cell address is added to the reference in the Formula Bar, which is =Western!B6. The Western worksheet remains visible so you can select additional cells.

5. Press the **Enter** key. The formula is entered, and the Corporate worksheet is active again. The formula results $543,367 appear in cell B4.

6. Click cell **B5**, if it is not the active cell in the Corporate worksheet, and then type **=** to begin the formula.

7. Click the **Eastern** sheet tab, and then click cell **B6**. The formula =Eastern!B6 appears in the Formula Bar.

8. Press the **Enter** key. The formula is entered in cell B5 of the Corporate worksheet.

9. In the Corporate worksheet, click cell **B12**, and then type **=** to begin the formula.

10. Click the **Western** sheet tab, and then click cell **B3**. The formula =Western!B3 appears in the Formula Bar.

11. Type **+** to enter the operator, click the **Eastern** sheet tab, and then click cell **B3**. The formula =Western!B3+Eastern!B3 appears in the Formula Bar.

12. Press the **Enter** key. The formula is entered in cell B12 of the Corporate worksheet, which shows the formula results $306,744.

STEP-BY-STEP 7.3 Continued

13. Click cell **B13**, if it is not already selected, and then type **=SUM(** to begin the formula.

14. Click the **Western** sheet tab, press and hold the **Shift** key, and then click the **Eastern** sheet tab. Release the Shift key. The formula with the worksheet range reference *=SUM('Western:Eastern'!* appears in the Formula Bar.

15. Click cell **B4**, and then press the **Enter** key. The cell reference is added to the 3-D reference in the formula, which is *=SUM('Western:Eastern'!B4)*. The formula results $566,399, which add the value from cell B4 in the Eastern and Westerns worksheets, appear in cell B13.

16. Copy the formula in cell B13 to cell B14. The value in cell B15 is the same as the value in cell B6, as shown in Figure 7-6.

FIGURE 7-6
Data summarized on one worksheet

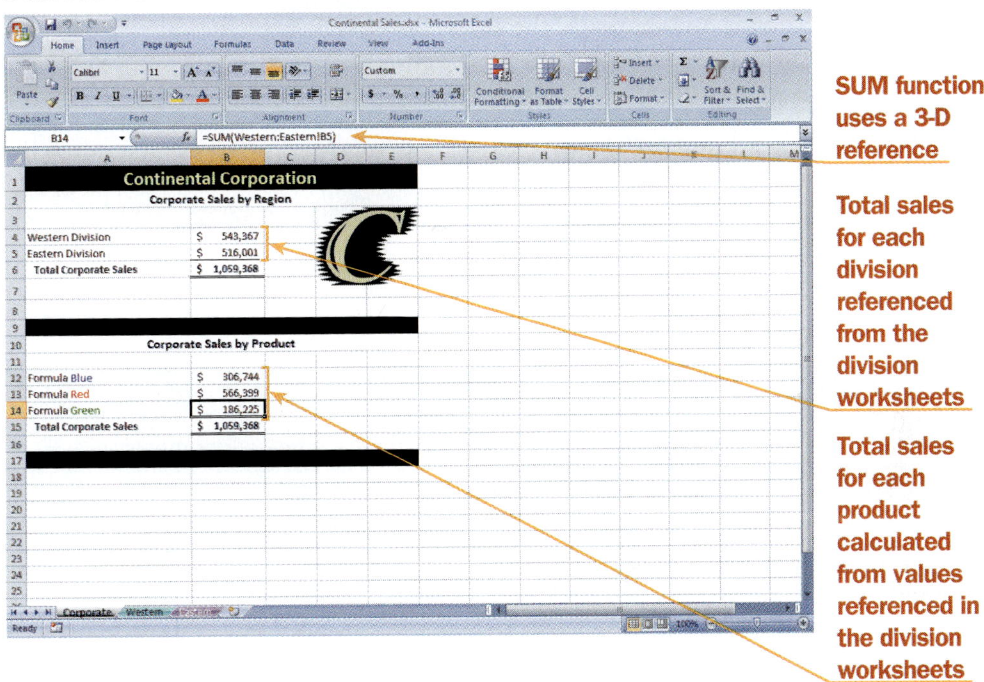

17. Save the workbook, and leave it open for the next Step-by-Step.

Careers

Excel workbooks are extremely useful in areas of business that have a quantitative orientation, such as accounting and finance. In accounting, formulas are used to build financial statements. Financial officers in corporations use spreadsheets to project sales and control costs.

Printing a Workbook

So far, you have printed an active worksheet or selected areas of an active worksheet. You can also print an entire workbook, selected worksheets, or selected areas of a workbook. You designate the portion of the workbook to print in the Print what section of the Print dialog box, as shown in Figure 7-7. The print options are described in Table 7-2.

FIGURE 7-7
Print dialog box

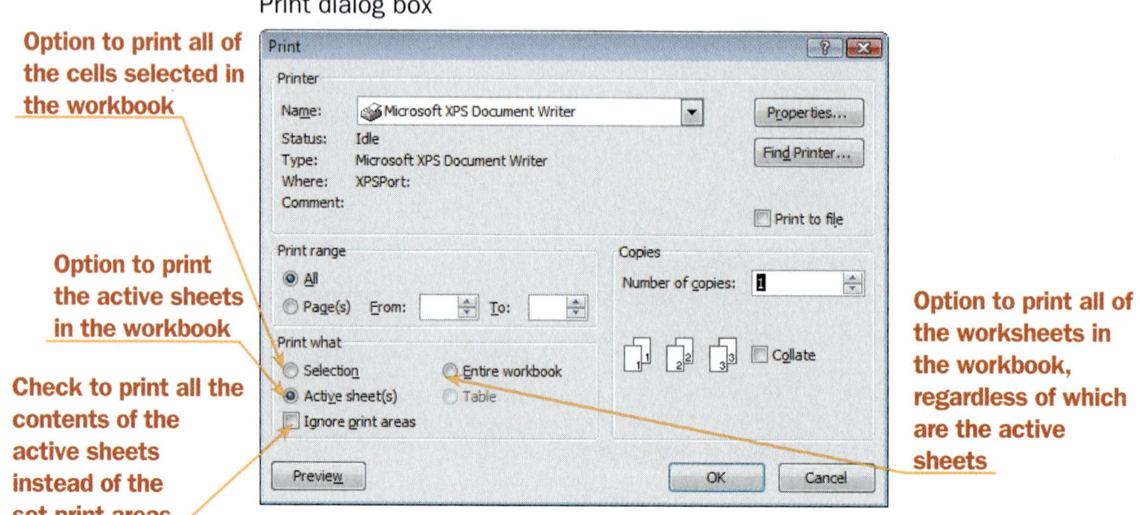

TABLE 7-2
Print what options

OPTION	PRINTS
Selection	The range or ranges selected within a single worksheet
Active sheet(s)	The worksheet that appears on-screen, or a group of selected worksheets (Ctrl+click sheet tabs to select multiple worksheets)
Entire workbook	All of the worksheets in a workbook

Printing Non-adjacent Selections of a Worksheet

You have already learned how to set a print area for a specific range in a worksheet. However, at times you might want to print more than one part of a worksheet on a page. For example, you might want to print the top and bottom sections of a worksheet, but not the middle portion. To do this, you need to select multiple ranges in the worksheet. To select more than one cell or range in a worksheet, select the first cell or range, hold down the Ctrl key, select each additional cell or range, and then release the Ctrl key. You can set the print area to include the non-adjacent range, and then print the active sheet as usual. Another alternative is to click the Selection option in the Print what section of the Print dialog box.

Printing More Than One Worksheet

When a workbook includes multiple worksheets, you will often want to print more than one worksheet at a time. To print all of the worksheets in the workbook, click the Entire workbook option in the Print what section of the Print dialog box. To print specific worksheets in a workbook, you must first select the worksheets. To select multiple worksheets in a workbook, hold down the Ctrl key as you click the sheet tab of each worksheet you want to include in the group, and then release the Ctrl key. In the Print dialog box, select the Active sheet(s) option in the Print what section.

S TEP-BY-STEP 7.4

1. Insert a header with your name and the current date.

2. In the Corporate worksheet, select the range **A4:B6**.

3. Hold down the **Ctrl** key and select the range **A12:B15**. Non-adjacent ranges are selected in the Corporate worksheet.

4. Click the **Office Button**, and then click **Print**. The Print dialog box appears, as shown in Figure 7-7. 

5. In the Print what section, click the **Selection** option button.

6. Click **Preview**. The range A4:B6 will print on page 1 and the range A12:B15 will print on page 2, as shown in Figure 7-8.

FIGURE 7-8
Print Preview of the selected ranges

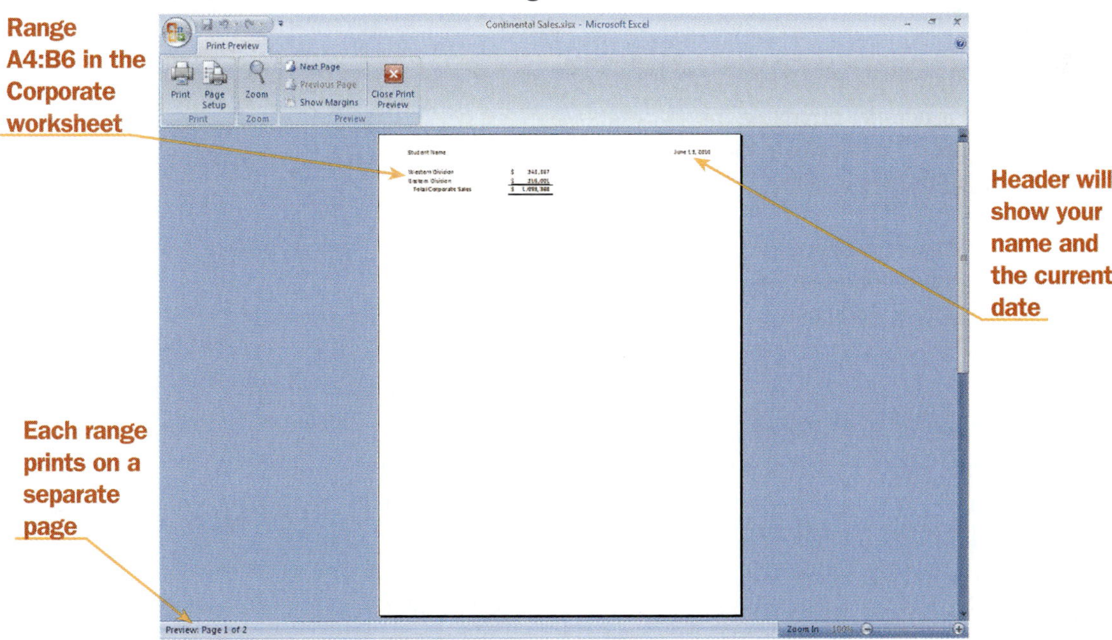

Range A4:B6 in the Corporate worksheet

Header will show your name and the current date

Each range prints on a separate page

7. Click **Print**. The selected areas print.

STEP-BY-STEP 7.4 Continued

8. Click the **Western** tab.

9. Hold down the **Ctrl** key and click the **Eastern** tab. The two sheet tabs are selected.

10. Click the **Office Button**, and then click **Print**. The Print dialog box appears.

11. In the Print what section, click the **Active sheet(s)** option button, if it is not already selected.

12. Click **Print**. The worksheets with the data for each division print on separate pages.

13. Save and close the workbook.

Working with Multiple Workbooks

So far, you have worked with worksheets in the same workbook. Sometimes you might want to use data from worksheets in different workbooks. You can view these worksheets on the screen by arranging the workbooks. If you want to use the data from a worksheet in one workbook in another workbook, you can move or copy the worksheet to the new workbook.

Arranging Workbooks

Arranging lets you view more than one workbook on the screen at the same time. To arrange all the open workbooks, click the Arrange All button in the Window group on the View tab of the Ribbon. The Arrange Windows dialog box appears, as shown in Figure 7-9. Click the arrangement in which you want to view the workbooks: Tiled, Horizontal, Vertical, or Cascade.

FIGURE 7-9
Arrange Windows dialog box

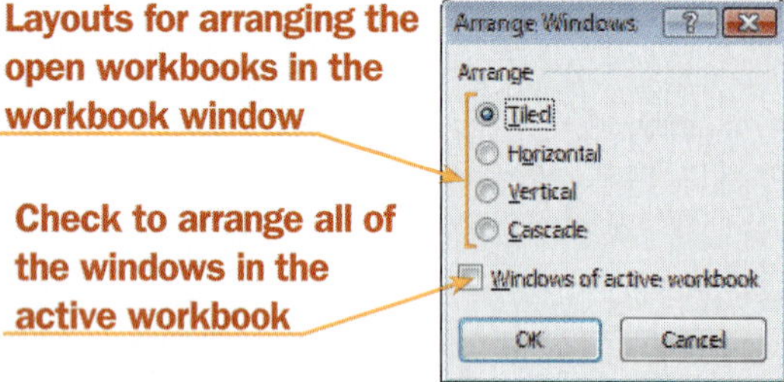

You can tell which workbook is active by looking at its title. The active workbook has a blue title bar with the sizing buttons. Also, the active workbook contains scroll bars. To make a workbook active, just click its title bar or anywhere in the worksheet. All of the buttons and commands are available as usual.

Moving and Copying Worksheets Between Workbooks

When you need to use a worksheet from one workbook in another, you can copy or move the worksheet. Right-click the sheet tab of the worksheet you want to move or copy, and then click Move or Copy on the shortcut menu. The Move or Copy dialog box appears. Click the arrow next to the To book box and click the workbook in which you want the selected worksheet to appear. After you select the destination workbook, the names of all of its worksheets appear in the Before sheet box. Click the worksheet that you want to appear after the copied or moved worksheet. If you want to move the worksheet, click OK. If you want to copy the worksheet, click the Create a copy check box and then click OK.

S TEP-BY-STEP 7.5

1. Open the **Annual.xlsx** Data File. Save the workbook as **Annual Statement** followed by your initials.

2. Open the **February.xlsx** Data File. Save the workbook as **February Statement** followed by your initials.

3. Click the **View** tab on the Ribbon. In the Window group, click the **Arrange All** button. The Arrange Windows dialog box appears, as shown in Figure 7-9.

4. Click the **Horizontal** button, and then click **OK**. Both workbooks appear on the screen, as shown in Figure 7-10.

FIGURE 7-10
Workbooks arranged horizontally

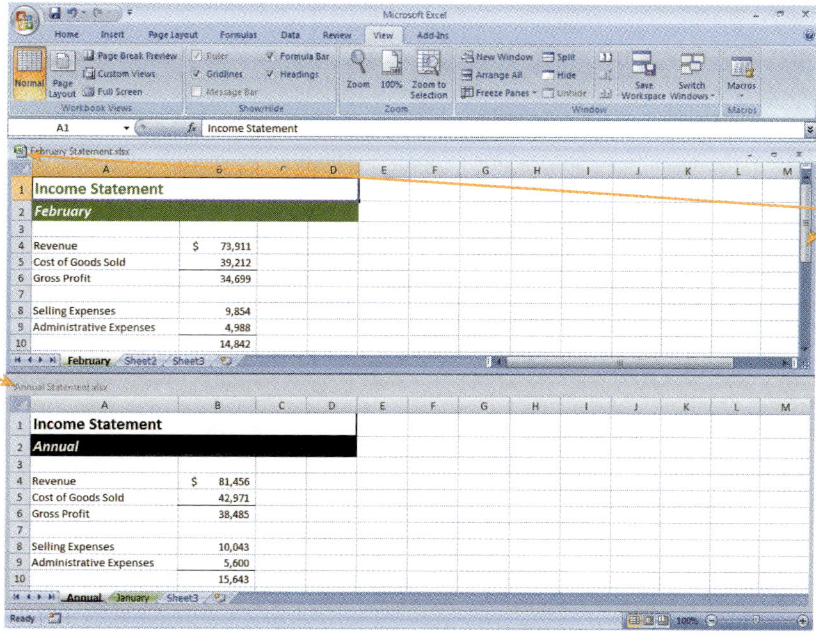

5. In the February Statement workbook, right-click the **February** sheet tab, and then click **Move or Copy** on the shortcut menu. The Move or Copy dialog box appears.

6. Click the **arrow** next to the To book box, and then click **Annual Statement.xlsx**. The worksheets in the Annual Statement workbook appear in the Before sheet box.

7. In the Before sheet box, click **Sheet3** so the February worksheet will follow the January worksheet.

STEP-BY-STEP 7.5 Continued

8. Click the **Create a copy** check box. The dialog box settings should appear similar to those in Figure 7-11.

FIGURE 7-11
Move or Copy dialog box

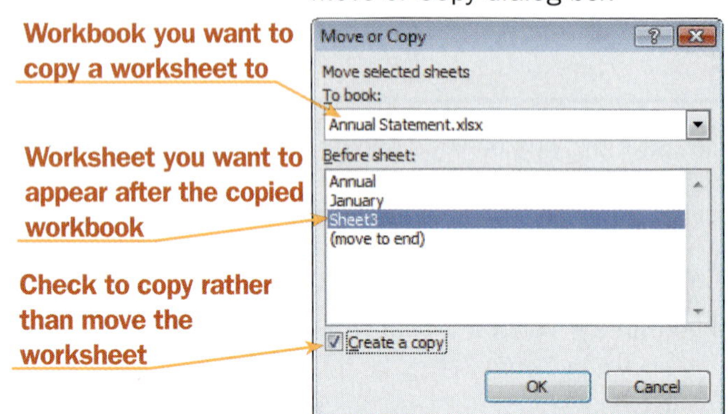

9. Click **OK**. A copy of the February worksheet appears in the Annual Statement workbook.

10. Click in the **February Statement** workbook to make it the active workbook, and then close the workbook.

11. Click the **Maximize** button on the title bar of the Annual Statement workbook. The workbook expands to fill the program window. 

12. Click the **Annual** tab. Notice that the totals include the values from the February worksheet, because of the 3-D references in the formulas.

13. Insert a header with your name and the current date. Print the January and February worksheets.

14. Save and close the workbook.

SUMMARY

In this lesson, you learned:

■ Sheet tabs identify the names of worksheets. You click a sheet tab to make a worksheet the active sheet.

■ You can rename worksheets with more descriptive names to better distinguish them. You can also change the color of the sheet tabs.

■ Data is often best organized in multiple worksheets. You can drag a sheet tab to a new position to organize the worksheets in a more logical order. You can hide worksheets from view and then unhide them when needed. You can also insert and delete worksheets to accommodate the data.

- Rather than retyping data, you can create references to cells in another worksheet. You can also create formulas with 3-D references to the same cell or range in multiple worksheets.

- Entire workbooks, selected worksheets, or selected ranges in a worksheet can be printed.

- Arranging multiple workbooks in the program window lets you view their contents at the same time. Worksheets can be moved or copied from one workbook to the location you specify in the same or another workbook.

VOCABULARY *Review*

Define the following terms:

3-D reference	Destination	Source
Active sheet	Sheet tab	Worksheet range

REVIEW *Questions*

MATCHING

Match the correct formula result in Column 2 to its formula in Column 1.

Column 1

_____ 1. =Sheet2!D10

_____ 2. =Sheet2!D10+Sheet3!D11

_____ 3. =SUM(Sheet2:Sheet4!D10)

_____ 4. =SUM(Sheet2!D10:D11)

_____ 5. =Sheet3!D10+Sheet3!D11

Column 2

A. Adds the values in cells D10 and D11 of the Sheet2 worksheet

B. Adds the values in cells D10 and D11 of the Sheet3 worksheet

C. Adds the values in cell D10 of the Sheet2 worksheet and cell D11 of the Sheet3 worksheet

D. Inserts the value in cell D10 of the Sheet2 worksheet

E. Adds the values in cell D10 in the Sheet2, Sheet3, and Sheet4 worksheets

FILL IN THE BLANK

Complete the following sentences by writing the correct word or words in the blanks provided.

1. A(n) ___________ is a collection of worksheets.

2. The worksheet that appears in the workbook window is the ___________.

3. ___________ identify worksheets within a workbook at the bottom of a workbook window.

4. You can create formulas with ___________ to the same cell or range in multiple worksheets.

5. ___________ multiple workbooks in the program window lets you view their contents at the same time.

PROJECTS

 ## PROJECT 7-1

1. Open the **Rainfall.xlsx** Data File. Save the workbook as **Rainfall Records** followed by your initials.

2. Rename the worksheets and change the sheet tab colors as listed below:

Worksheet	New Name	Tab Color
Sheet1	**Annual**	Blue, Accent 1
Sheet2	**January**	Blue, Accent 1, Lighter 80%
Sheet3	**February**	Blue, Accent 1, Lighter 60%
Sheet4	**March**	Blue, Accent 1, Lighter 40%

3. In the Annual worksheet, in cell B3, display the total rainfall recorded in the January worksheet in cell B34.

4. In the Annual worksheet, in cell B4, display the total rainfall recorded in the February worksheet in cell B31.

5. In the Annual worksheet, in cell B5, display the total rainfall recorded in the March worksheet in cell B34.

6. Insert a header with your name and the current date, and then save the workbook.

7. Print the Annual worksheet, and then close the workbook.

 ## PROJECT 7-2

1. Open the **Voting.xlsx** Data File. Save the workbook as **Voting Tally** followed by your initials.

2. Rename the worksheets and change the sheet tab colors as listed below:

Worksheet	New Name	Tab Color
Sheet1	**District 5**	Red
Sheet2	**P107**	Yellow
Sheet3	**P106**	Purple
Sheet4	**P105**	Green

3. Reposition the worksheets so they appear in the following order: District 5, P105, P106, and P107.

4. In the District 5 worksheet, in cell D7, enter a formula that adds the values in cell C5 of each of the precinct worksheets.

5. In the District 5 worksheet, in cell D9, enter a formula that adds the values in cell C7 of each of the precinct worksheets.

6. In the District 5 worksheet, in cell D11, enter a formula that adds the values in cell C9 of each of the precinct worksheets.

7. In the District 5 worksheet, in cell D13, enter a formula that adds the values in cell C11 of each of the precinct worksheets.

8. Insert a header with your name and the current date, and then save the workbook.

9. Print the District 5 worksheet, and then close the workbook.

 PROJECT 7-3

1. Open the **Alamo.xlsx** Data File. Save the workbook as **Alamo Amalgamated** followed by your initials.

2. Change the sheet tab colors as listed below:

Worksheet	Tab Color
Consolidated	Green
Alamogordo	Light Green
Artesia	Light Blue

3. In the Consolidated worksheet, in cell D6, enter a formula that adds the values in cell B6 of the Alamogordo and Artesia worksheets.

4. In the Consolidated worksheet, in cell D7, enter a formula that adds the values in cell B7 of the Alamogordo and Artesia worksheets.

5. In the Consolidated worksheet, in cell D9, enter a formula that adds the values in cell B9 of the Alamogordo and Artesia worksheets.

6. In the Consolidated worksheet, in cell D10, enter a formula that adds the values in cell B10 of the Alamogordo and Artesia worksheets.

7. Insert a header with your name and the current date, and then save the workbook.

8. Print all of the worksheets in the workbook, and then close the workbook.

 **PROJECT 7-4**

1. Open the **United.xlsx** Data File. Save the workbook as **United Circuitry** followed by your initials.

2. Change the worksheet tab colors as listed below:

Worksheet	Tab Color
Year	Red
January	Purple, Accent 4
February	Orange, Accent 6
March	Blue, Accent 1

3. In the Year worksheet, in cells B5, B6, and B7, display the total January monthly production for Circuits 370, 380, and 390. These values are recorded in the January worksheet in the range F4:F6.

4. In the Year worksheet, in cells C5, C6, and C7, display the total February monthly production for each circuit. These values are recorded in the February worksheet in the range F4:F6.

5. In the Year worksheet, in cells D5, D6, and D7, display the total March monthly production for each circuit. These values are recorded in the March worksheet in the range F4:F6.

6. Insert a header with your name and the current date, and then save the workbook.

7. Print the entire Year worksheet, and then close the workbook.

CRITICAL *Thinking*

SCANS   ACTIVITY 7-1

Suppose you manage a local clothing store chain. Each of the three stores has sent you a workbook in the same format that contains inventory data. You want to use the data you received to create a summary workbook with totals from all three stores. Use Excel Help to find out how you can create an external reference to a cell or range in another workbook. Write a brief description of what you learn.

WORKING WITH CHARTS

OBJECTIVES

OBJECTIVES

Upon completion of this lesson, you will be able to:

- Identify the purpose of charting worksheet data.
- Identify the types of charts you can create in Excel.
- Create a chart embedded in a worksheet.
- Move a chart to a chart sheet.
- Update a data source.
- Select chart elements.
- Choose a chart layout and style.
- Create a 3-D chart.
- Display or hide chart elements.
- Format and modify a chart.
- Edit and format chart text.
- Change the chart type.

Estimated Time: 2.5 hours

VOCABULARY

Axis

Chart

Chart area

Chart layout

Chart sheet

Chart style

Column chart

Data label

Data marker

Data series

Data source

Data table

Embedded chart

Exploded pie chart

Legend

Line chart

Pie chart

Plot area

Scatter chart

Selection box

Sizing handles

What Is a Worksheet Chart?

A **chart** is a graphical representation of data. Charts make the data in a worksheet easier to understand by providing a visual picture of the data. For example, the left side of the worksheet in Figure 8-1 shows the populations of three major American cities for three years. You might be able to detect the population changes by carefully examining the table. However, the population increases and decreases in each city are easier to see when the data is illustrated in a chart, such as the one shown on the right side of the worksheet in Figure 8-1.

FIGURE 8-1
Worksheet data and chart

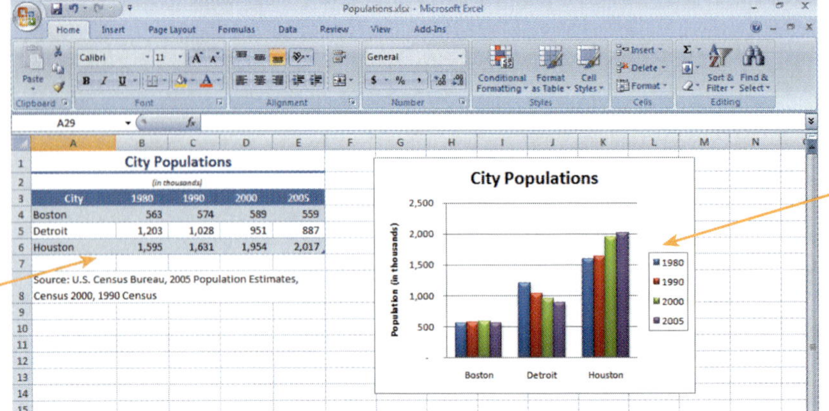

Comparing Chart Types

You can create a variety of charts in Excel. Each type of chart has a different look and works best for certain types of data. In this lesson, you create four of the most commonly used charts: column chart, line chart, pie chart, and scatter chart. These charts and several other types of charts are available from the Insert tab on the Ribbon, in the Charts group, as shown in Figure 8-2.

FIGURE 8-2
Charts group on the Insert tab of the Ribbon

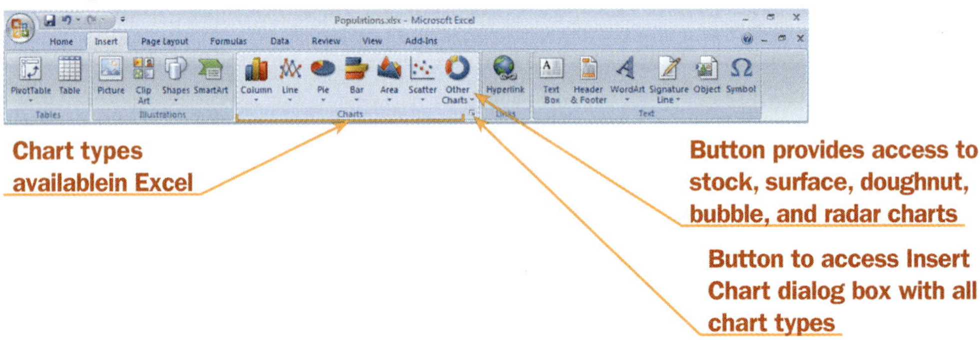

Column Chart

A column chart uses bars of varying heights to illustrate values in a worksheet. It is useful for showing relationships among categories of data. For example, the column chart in Figure 8-1 has one vertical column to show the population of a city for each of four years, and shows how the population of one city compares to populations of other cities.

Did You Know?

Businesses often use column, bar, and line charts to illustrate growth over several periods. For example, the changes in yearly production or income over a 10-year period can be shown easily in a column chart.

Line Chart

A line chart is similar to the column chart, but columns are replaced by points connected by a line. The line chart is ideal for illustrating trends over time. For example, Figure 8-3 is a line chart that shows the growth of the federal budget debt from 1990 to 2006. The vertical axis represents the amount of debt in billions of dollars, and the horizontal axis shows the years. The line chart makes it easy to see how the federal debt has grown over time. You can include multiple lines to compare two or more sets of data. For example, you could use a second line to chart the tax revenue received during the same time period.

FIGURE 8-3
Line chart

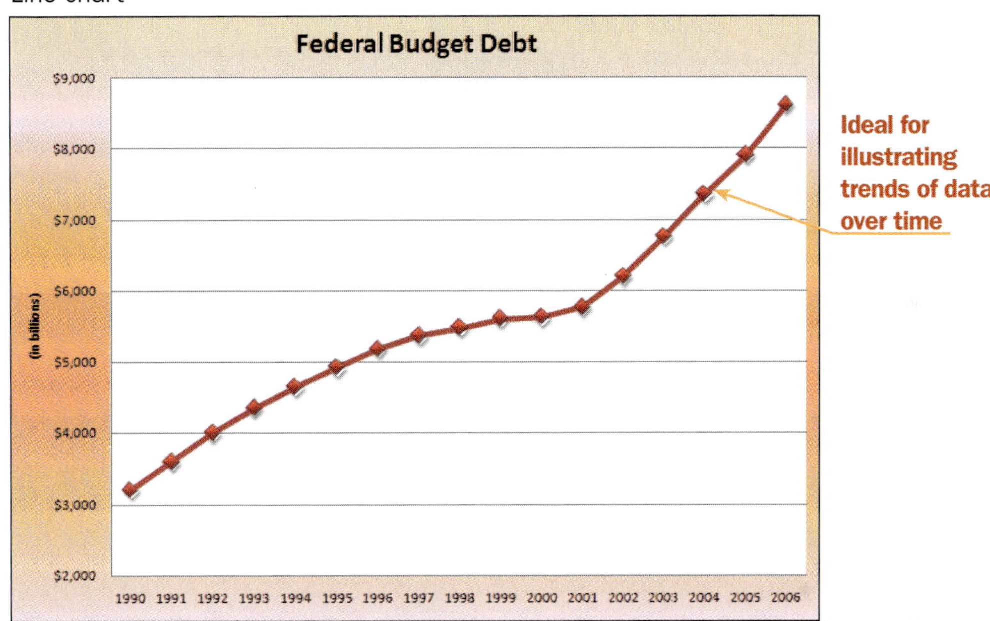

Pie Chart

A pie chart shows the relationship of a part to a whole. Each part is shown as a "slice" of the pie. For example, a teacher could create a pie chart of the distribution of grades in a class, as shown in Figure 8-4. Each slice represents the portion of grades given for each letter grade.

FIGURE 8-4
Pie chart

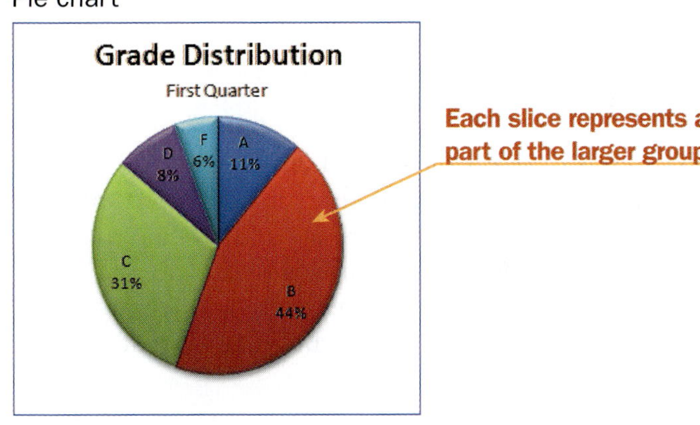

Scatter Chart

A scatter chart, sometimes called an XY chart, shows the relationship between two categories of data. One category is represented on the vertical axis, and the other category is represented on the horizontal axis. It is not practical to connect the data points with a line because points on a scatter chart usually do not relate to each other, as they do in a line chart. For example, the scatter chart in Figure 8-5 shows a data point for each of 12 individuals, based on the person's height and weight. In most cases, a tall person tends to be heavier than a short person. However, because some people are tall and skinny and others are short and stocky, the relationship between height and weight cannot be represented by a line.

FIGURE 8-5
Scatter chart

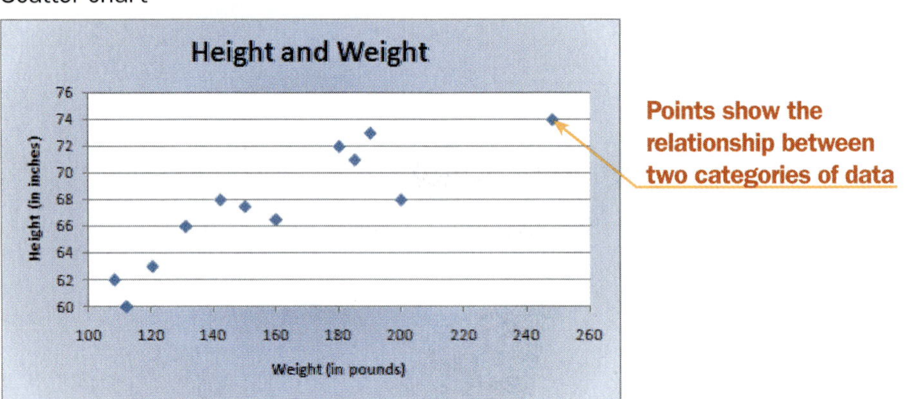

Creating Charts

The process for creating a chart is similar no matter which chart type you want to create. First, you select the data you want to use for the chart. Second, you select a chart type. Finally, you select the chart location. In this section, you will create a column chart.

Selecting Chart Data

Charts are based on data. In Excel, the chart data, called the data source, is stored in a range of cells in the worksheet. When you select the data source for a chart, you should also include the text you want to use as labels in the chart. You can also choose whether to chart more than one series of data. A data series is a group of related information in a column or row of a worksheet that is plotted on the chart.

Selecting a Chart Type

The next step is to select the type of chart you want to create, such as a column chart, a pie chart, or a line chart. Each type of chart has a variety of subtypes you can choose from. The chart types are available on the Insert tab in the Charts group. You can click the button for a specific chart type and then select the style you want. The Insert Chart dialog box, shown in Figure 8-6, provides access to all of the chart subtypes for each chart type. You open the Insert Chart dialog box by clicking the Dialog Box Launcher in the Charts group on the Insert tab.

FIGURE 8-6
Insert Chart dialog box

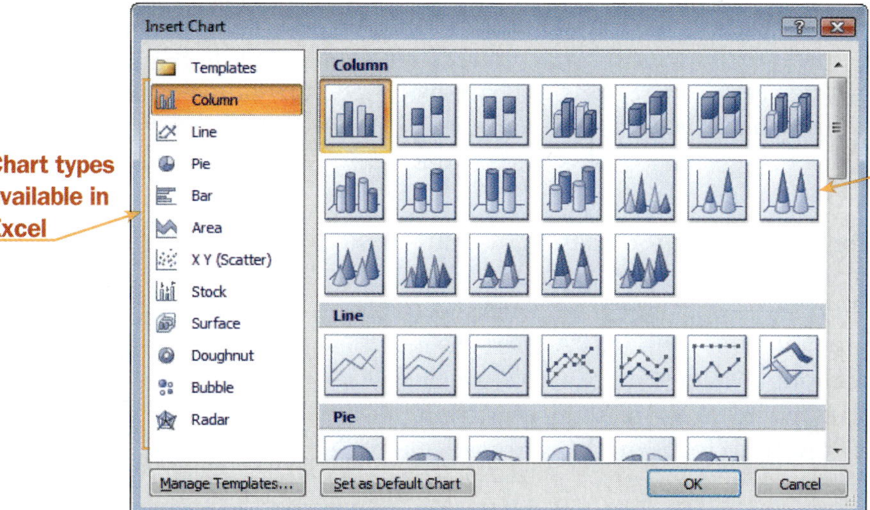

Choosing the Chart Location

After you select a chart type and style, the chart is inserted as an **embedded chart** in the center of the worksheet, as shown in Figure 8-7. The Chart Tools appear on the Ribbon with three contextual tabs: Design, Layout, and Format. The primary advantage of an embedded chart is that it can be viewed at the same time as the data from which it is created. When you print the worksheet, the chart is printed on the same page.

Computer Concepts

Embedded charts are useful when you want to print a chart next to the data the chart illustrates. When a chart will be displayed or printed without the data used to create the chart, a separate chart sheet is usually more appropriate.

FIGURE 8-7
Embedded chart

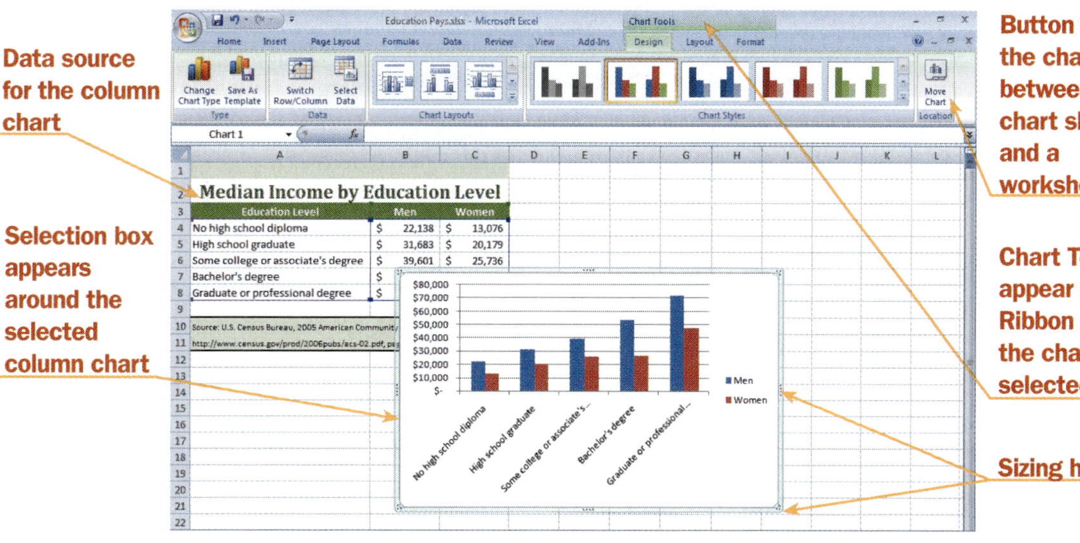

An embedded chart might cover the data source or other information in the worksheet. You can quickly move and resize the embedded chart. You move an embedded chart by dragging the selected chart to a different part of the worksheet. You resize the chart by dragging one of the sizing handles, which are indicated by the black dots at the corners and sides of the selected chart.

You can also choose to move the chart to a chart sheet, which is a separate sheet in the workbook that stores a chart. A chart sheet does not have worksheet cells and cannot contain data or formulas. A chart sheet displays the chart without its data source, and is convenient when you plan to create more than one chart from the same data or want to focus on the chart rather than its underlying data.

To move an embedded chart to a chart sheet, click the Design contextual tab under the Chart Tools on the Ribbon. Then, in the Location group, click the Move Chart button. The Move Chart dialog box appears, as shown in Figure 8-8. You can choose to move the chart to a new sheet that you name or to embed the chart in any worksheet in the workbook. You can use the same process to move a chart from a chart sheet to any worksheet as an embedded object.

Extra for Experts

You can keep a chart's height and width in the same proportion by pressing the Shift key as you drag a corner sizing handle.

Did You Know?

You can rename a chart sheet like any other worksheet. Right-click its sheet tab, and then click Rename on the shortcut menu. Type a descriptive name for the chart sheet, and then press the Enter key.

Did You Know?

A chart, whether embedded in a worksheet or on a chart sheet, is considered part of a workbook. When you save the workbook, you also save the charts you have created.

FIGURE 8-8
Move Chart dialog box

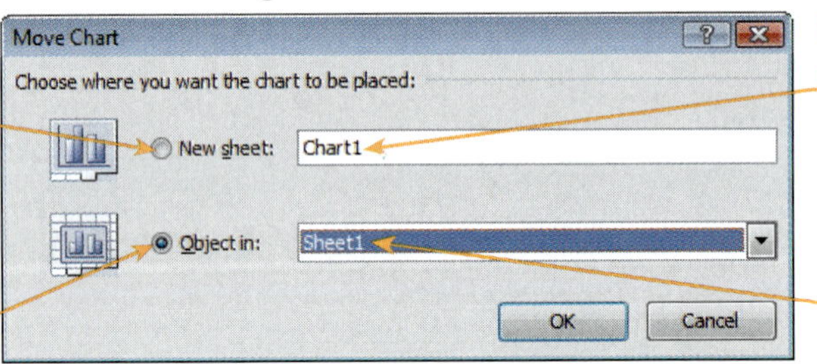

STEP-BY-STEP 8.1

1. Open the **Education.xlsx** Data File. Save the workbook as **Education Pays** followed by your initials. Column A contains educational levels, and columns B and C contain the median incomes of men and women with corresponding levels of education.

2. Select the range **A3:C8**. This is the data you want to chart.

3. Click the **Insert** tab on the Ribbon. In the Charts group, click the **Column** button. A menu of available column chart subtypes appears.

4. In the 2-D Column section, point to **Clustered Column** (the first chart in the first row). A ScreenTip appears with a description of the selected chart: *Clustered Column. Compare values across categories by using vertical rectangles.*

5. Click the **Clustered Column** button. The 2-D clustered column chart is embedded in the worksheet. A selection box with sizing handles appears around the chart, as shown in Figure 8-7.

6. Drag the selected chart so that the upper-left corner of the chart is in cell E1. The chart is repositioned in the worksheet.

7. Drag the lower-right sizing handle to cell **K13**. The chart is sized to cover the range E1:K13.

8. On the Ribbon, under Chart Tools, click the **Design** tab, if it is not already selected.

9. In the Location group, click the **Move Chart** button. The Move Chart dialog box appears, as shown in Figure 8-8.

10. Click the **New sheet** option button. The text in the New sheet box is selected so you can type a descriptive name for the chart sheet.

11. In the New sheet box, type **Column**.

Careers

Excel worksheets are used in education to evaluate and instruct students. Instructors use worksheets to track student grades and to organize the number of hours spent on certain topics. Charts help illustrate numerical relationships for students.

STEP-BY-STEP 8.1 Continued

12. Click **OK**. The chart moves to a chart sheet named *Column*, as shown in Figure 8-9. The chart illustrates the value of education in attaining higher income. The columns get higher on the right side of the chart, indicating that those who stay in school are rewarded with higher incomes.

FIGURE 8-9
Chart sheet

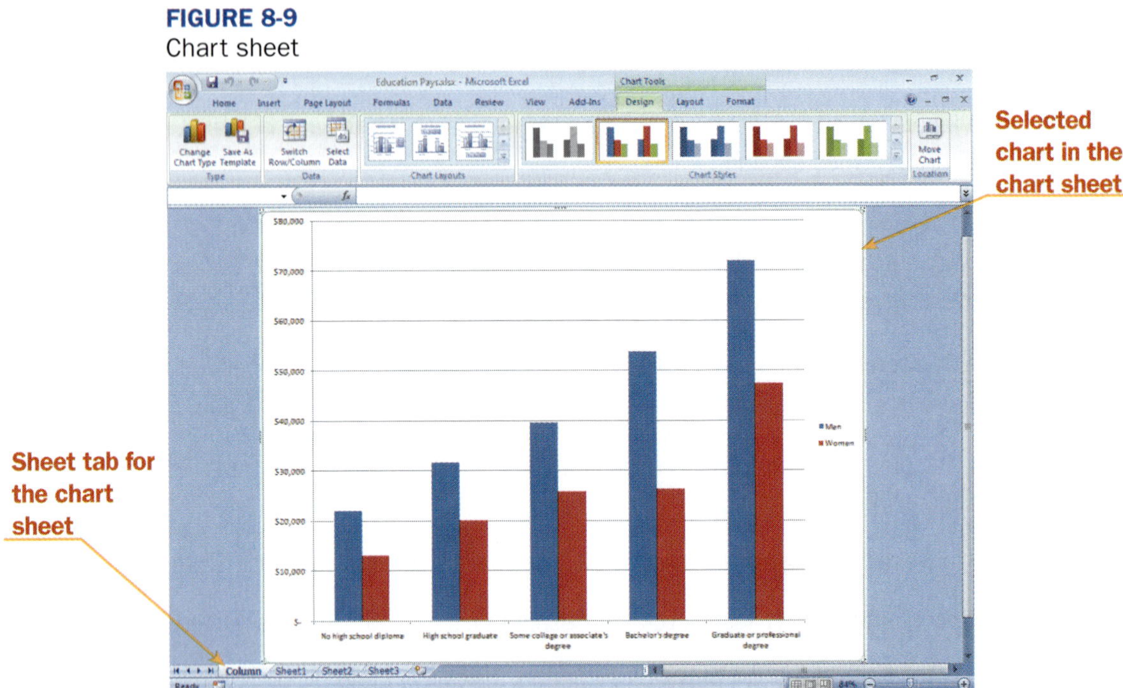

13. Save the workbook, and leave it open for the next Step-by-Step.

Updating the Data Source

Charts are closely related to their underlying data stored in a worksheet. If you need to change the data in the worksheet, the chart is automatically updated to reflect the new data. You switch between a chart sheet and a worksheet by clicking the appropriate sheet tab.

STEP-BY-STEP 8.2

1. Click the **Sheet1** sheet tab. The worksheet with the data source appears.

2. Click cell **A5**, and then enter **High school diploma**. The label is updated.

STEP-BY-STEP 8.2 Continued

3. Click the **Column** sheet tab. The chart sheet appears. The label for the second column reflects the edit you made to the data source.

4. Save the workbook, and leave it open for the next Step-by-Step.

Designing a Chart

Charts have some basic elements, which you can choose to include or hide. You can also choose a chart style and layout to give the chart a cohesive design. Finally, you can add labels and other elements to make the chart easier to understand and interpret and more attractive.

Selecting Chart Elements

Charts are made up of different parts, or elements. The common chart elements are identified in Figure 8-10 and described in Table 8-1. Not all elements appear in every type of chart. For example, a pie chart does not have axes. Also, you can choose which chart elements to use in a chart.

FIGURE 8-10
Chart elements

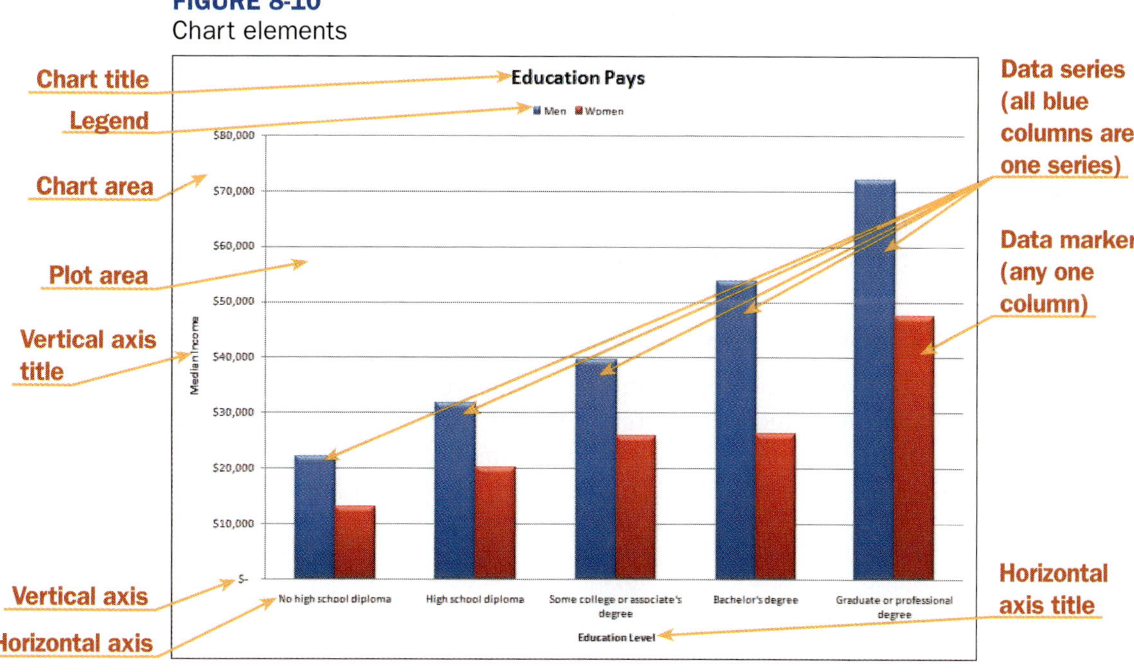

TABLE 8-1
TABLE 8-1
Chart elements

ELEMENT	DESCRIPTION
Chart area	The entire chart and all other chart elements
Plot area	The graphical representation of all of the data series
Data series	Related information in a column or row that is plotted on a chart; many charts can include more than one data series
Data marker	A symbol (such as a bar, line, dot, slice, and so forth) that represents a single data point or value from the corresponding worksheet cell
Data label	Text or numbers that provide additional information about a data marker, such as the value from the worksheet cell (not shown in Figure 8-10)
Axes	Lines that establish a relationship between data in a chart; most charts have a horizontal x-axis and a vertical y-axis
Titles	Descriptive labels that identify the contents of the chart and the axes
Legend	A list that identifies patterns, symbols, or colors used in a chart
Data table	A grid that displays the data plotted in the chart (not shown in Figure 8-10)

The quickest way to select a chart element is to click it with the pointer. You can tell that you are clicking the right element by first pointing to the element to display a ScreenTip with its name. A selected chart element is surrounded by a selection box. You can also use the Ribbon to select chart elements. Click the Format tab under Chart Tools on the Ribbon. In the Current Selection group, click the arrow next to the Chart Elements box. A menu of chart elements for the selected chart appears. Click the name of the element you want to select.

After you select a chart element, you can modify it. For example, you can select the chart title or an axis title, and then enter new text for the title. You can also use the standard text formatting tools to change the font, font size, font color, and so forth of the selected title.

Choosing a Chart Layout and Style

You can quickly change the look of any chart you created by applying a layout and style. A chart layout specifies which elements are included in a chart and where they are placed. Figure 8-11 shows the chart layouts available for column charts. For example, the legend appears above, below, to the right of, or to the left of the chart in different layouts.

FIGURE 8-11
Chart Layouts gallery for column charts

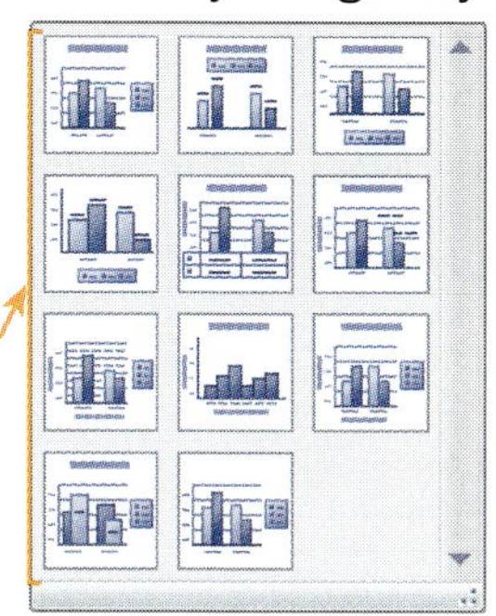

A **chart style** formats the chart based on the colors, fonts, and effects associated with the workbook's theme. Figure 8-12 shows the chart styles available for column charts.

FIGURE 8-12
Chart Styles gallery for column charts

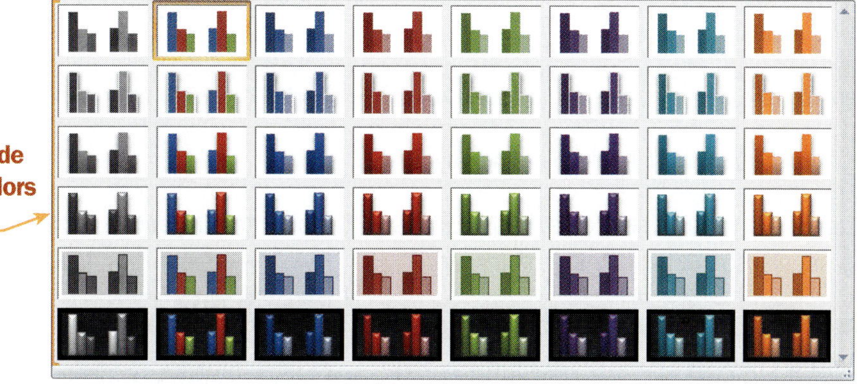

You can quickly choose a layout and styles for a selected chart from the Ribbon. Click the Design tab under Chart Tools on the Ribbon. In the Chart Layouts group, click the chart layout you want to use. In the Chart Styles group, click the chart style you want to use.

Arranging Chart Elements

You can also create a specific look for a chart by specifying which chart elements appear in the chart and where they are located. For example, you can choose when and where to display the chart title, axis titles, legend, data labels, data table, axes, gridlines, and the plot area. Select the chart. Then, click the Layout tab under Chart Tools on the Ribbon. The Labels, Axes, and Background groups contain buttons for each element. Use the commands on the appropriate button to display the element in a particular location in the chart area or to hide the element from the chart.

STEP-BY-STEP 8.3

1. On the Ribbon, under Chart Tools, click the **Design** tab, if it is not already selected.

2. In the Chart Layouts group, click the **More** button. A gallery of chart layouts appears, as shown in Figure 8-11.

3. Click **Layout 9** (the third layout in the third row). Placeholders for the chart title and axes titles are added to the chart.

4. Click the **Chart Title** to select it.

5. Type **EDUCATION PAYS**, and then press the **Enter** key. The chart title is updated.

6. Click the vertical **Axis Title** to select it, type **Median Income**, and then press the **Enter** key.

7. Click the horizontal **Axis Title** to select it, type **Education Level**, and then press the **Enter** key.

8. On the Design tab under Chart Tools, in the Chart Styles group, click the **More** button. A gallery of chart styles appears, as shown in Figure 8-12.

9. Click **Style 26** (the second style in the fourth row). The chart changes to match the selected style.

10. On the Ribbon, under Chart Tools, click the **Layout** tab.

11. On the Layout tab under Chart Tools, in the Labels group, click the **Legend** button. A menu appears with different placement options for the legend.

12. Click **Show Legend at Top**. The legend moves to below the chart title, as shown in Figure 8-10.

13. Insert a header with your name and the current date, and then print the chart sheet.

14. Save and close the workbook.

Did You Know?

You can delete a selected chart by pressing the Delete key. You can delete chart sheets by right-clicking the chart sheet tab, and then clicking Delete on the shortcut menu.

Creating a 3-D Chart

A pie chart shows the relationship of a part to a whole. Each part is shown as a "slice" of the pie. The slices are different colors to distinguish each data marker. Pie charts, as with many chart types, can be either 2-D or 3-D. When you select the chart style, click a 3-D chart subtype to create a 3-D chart.

Computer Concepts

Businesses often use pie charts to indicate the magnitude of certain expenses in comparison to other expenses. Pie charts are also used to illustrate the company's market share in comparison to its competitors'.

S TEP-BY-STEP 8.4

1. Open the **Grains.xlsx** Data File. Save the workbook as **Grains Sales** followed by your initials.

2. Select the range **A7:B10**. This range contains the data that shows the sales for each product segment.

3. Click the **Insert** tab on the Ribbon. In the Charts group, click the **Pie** button.

4. In the 3-D Pie section, click **Pie in 3-D** (the first chart in the first row). The pie chart is embedded in the worksheet.

5. On the Ribbon, under Chart Tools, click the **Design** tab, if the tab is not already selected. In the Chart Layouts group, click the **More** button. A gallery of chart layouts appears.

6. Click **Layout 1** (the first layout in the first row). The legend disappears, and each slice of the pie shows the segment name and the percentage of the whole it comprises.

7. Click the **Chart Title**, type **Annual Sales by Segment**, and then press the **Enter** key. The new chart title is entered above the chart.

8. Move and resize the chart to fit within the range **D1:H15**. The 3-D pie chart, shown in Figure 8-13, illustrates that corn accounts for the largest percentage of sales.

> **Extra for Experts** 
>
> You can pull one or more slices away from the pie to distinguish them, creating what is called an **exploded pie chart**. Click the data markers to select the series. Then, click the individual slice you want to explode to select just that one data marker. Finally, drag the selected slice away from the pie.

FIGURE 8-13
3-D pie chart

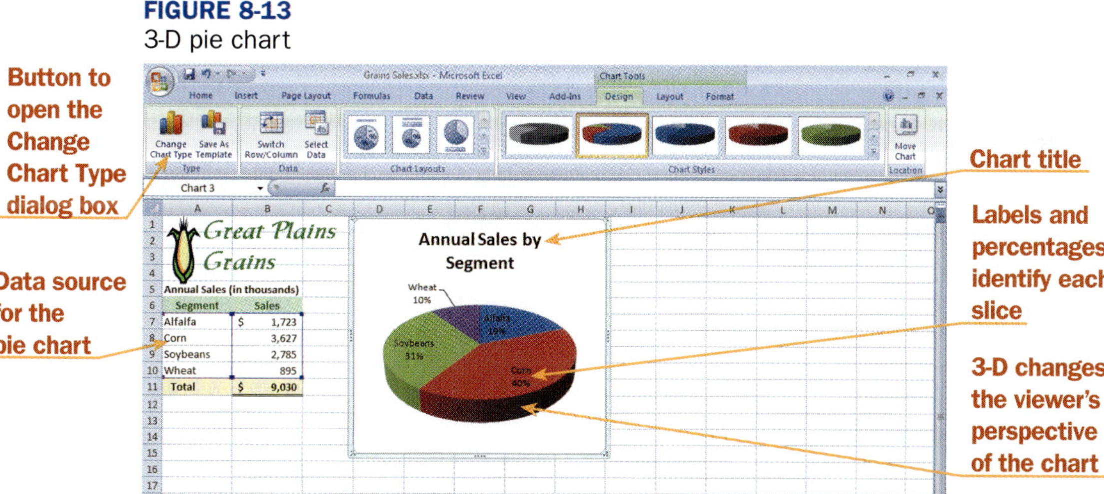

9. Insert a header with your name and the current date, and then print the worksheet.

10. Save and close the workbook.

Formatting and Modifying a Chart

Scatter charts are sometimes referred to as XY charts because they place data points between an x- and y-axis. Scatter charts can be harder to prepare because you must designate which data should be used as a scale on each axis.

STEP-BY-STEP 8.5

1. Open the **Coronado.xlsx** Data File. Save the workbook as **Coronado Foundries** followed by your initials.

2. Select the range **B6:B16**. Press and hold the **Ctrl** key as you select the range **D6:D16**. This nonadjacent range contains the data you want to chart.

3. Click the **Insert** tab on the Ribbon. In the Charts group, click the **Scatter** button. In the Scatter section, click **Scatter with only Markers** (the first chart in the first row). The scatter chart is embedded in the worksheet.

4. On the Ribbon, under Chart Tools, click the **Layout** tab.

5. In the Labels group, click the **Chart Title** button to open the menu of placement options, and then click **Above Chart**. The chart title appears above the scatter chart and is selected.

6. Type **Production and Scrap Report**, and then press the **Enter** key.

7. On the Layout tab under Chart Tools, in the Labels group, click the **Axis Titles** button, point to **Primary Horizontal Axis Title**, and then click **Title Below Axis**. The axis title appears below the horizontal axis and is selected.

8. Type **Units Produced**, and then press the **Enter** key. The horizontal axis title is updated.

9. On the Layout tab under Chart Tools, in the Labels group, click the **Axis Titles** button, point to **Primary Vertical Axis Title**, and then click **Rotated Title**. The axis title appears rotated along the vertical axis and is selected.

10. Type **Units of Scrap**, and then press the **Enter** key. The vertical access title is updated.

11. Click the **Legend** to select it, and then press the **Delete** key. The legend is removed from the chart.

12. Right-click the selected chart, and then click **Move Chart** on the shortcut menu. The Move Chart dialog box appears.

13. Click the **New sheet** option button. In the New sheet box, type **Scatter Chart**.

14. Click **OK**. The scatter chart appears on a chart sheet. The chart illustrates that factories with larger production tend to generate more scrap.

15. Save the workbook, and leave it open for the next Step-by-Step.

Formatting a Chart

The Chart Tools provide a simple way to create professional-looking charts. However, you might want to fine-tune a chart's appearance to better suit your purposes. For example, you might want to change the color of a data marker or the scale used for the axis. To make changes to an element's fill, border color, border style, shadow, 3-D format, alignment, and so forth, you need to open the Format dialog box. The Format dialog box for each element of a chart contains options for editing specific characteristics of that element.

To access the Format dialog box, select the chart you want to edit. Then, on the Format tab under Chart Tools on the Ribbon, in the Current Selection group, click the Format Selection button. The Format dialog box for the selected element appears. You can also right-click the part you want to edit, and then click the Format command on the shortcut menu.

S TEP-BY-STEP 8.6

1. On the Ribbon, under Chart Tools, click the **Format** tab.

2. In the Current Selection group, next to the Chart Elements box, click the **arrow** to open a menu of elements on the selected chart, and then click **Horizontal (Value) Axis**.

3. In the Current Selection group, click the **Format Selection** button. The Format Axis dialog box appears with the Axis Options active, as shown in Figure 8-14.

FIGURE 8-14
Format Axis dialog box

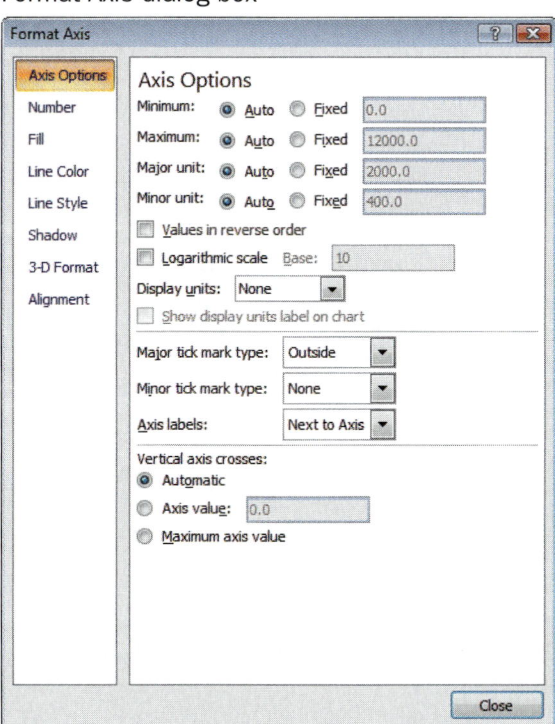

4. Next to Minimum, click the **Fixed** option button. In the Minimum Fixed box, type **4000**.

STEP-BY-STEP 8.6 Continued

5. Click **Close**. The section of the chart to the left of 4,000 on the x-axis, which did not have any data points, disappears.

6. Right-click the **Vertical (Value) Axis** on the chart, and then click **Format Axis** on the shortcut menu. The Format Axis dialog box appears with the Axis Options active.

7. Next to Maximum, click the **Fixed** option button. In the Maximum Fixed box, type **250**.

8. Click **Close**. The section of the chart above 250 on the y-axis, which did not have any data points, disappears.

9. Select the **Chart Area** (see Figure 8-15).

FIGURE 8-15
Scatter chart

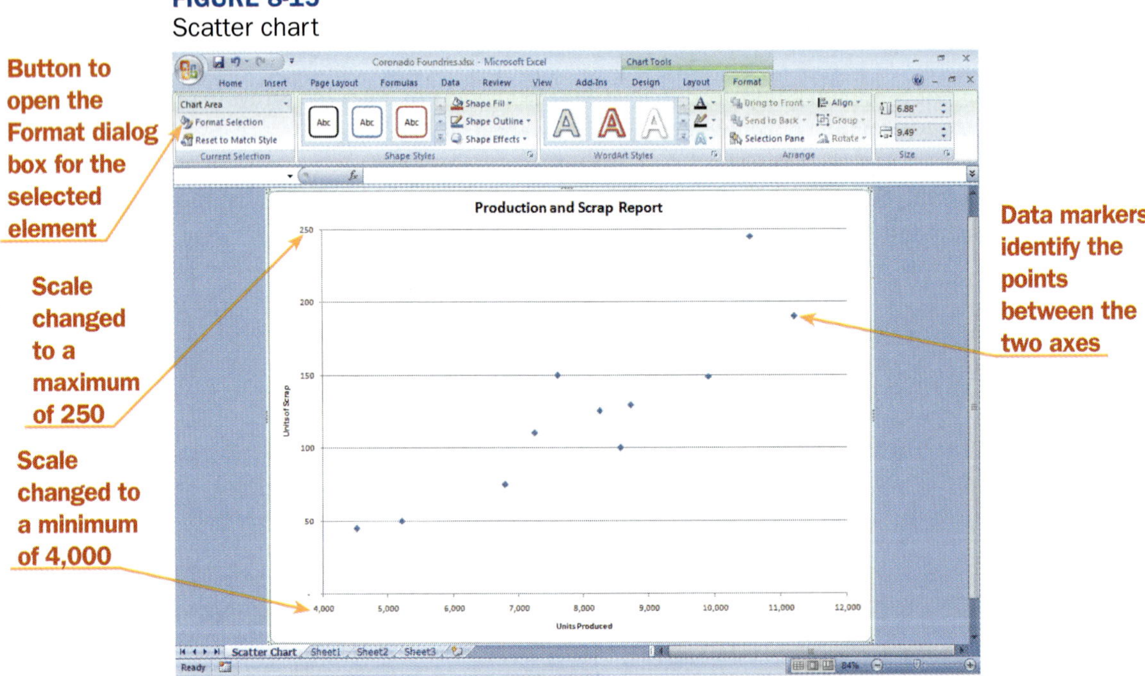

10. Insert a header with your name and the current date, and then print the worksheet.

11. Save and close the workbook.

Editing and Formatting Chart Text

You might want to change a title font or color to make a chart more attractive and interesting. You use the standard text formatting tools to make changes to the fonts used in the chart.

STEP-BY-STEP 8.7

1. Open the **Red** Data File. Save the workbook as **Red Cross** followed by your initials.

2. Click the **Bar Chart** sheet tab. The bar chart illustrates the operating expenses for each year.

3. Click **American Red Cross** to select chart title.

4. Click to the right of the last **s** in the title. An insertion point appears at the end of the title.

5. Press the **Enter** key. The insertion point is centered under the first line of the title.

6. Type **Operating Expenses**, and then click the **Chart Area**. The chart resizes to accommodate the new subtitle.

7. Click the **Horizontal (Value) Axis** to select it.

8. On the Home tab, in the Font group, next to the Font Size box, click the **arrow**, and then click **12**. The horizontal axis labels change to 12 points.

9. Click the **Vertical (Category) Axis** to select it.

10. On the Home tab, in the Font group, next to the Font Size box, click the **arrow**, and then click **12**. The vertical axis labels change to 12 points.

11. Save the workbook, and leave it open for the next Step-by-Step.

Changing the Chart Type

You can change a chart type or subtype at any time. On the Design tab, under Chart Tools on the Ribbon, in the Type group, click the Change Chart Type button. The Change Chart Type dialog box appears, and has the same options as the Insert Chart Type dialog box. The only difference is that the chart type and subtype you select affect the selected chart and do not create a new chart.

> **Computer Concepts**
>
> Not all charts are interchangeable. For example, data suitable for a pie chart is often not logical in a scatter chart. However, most line charts are easily converted into column or bar charts.

STEP-BY-STEP 8.8

1. On the Ribbon, under Chart Tools, click the **Design** tab.

2. In the Type group, click the **Change Chart Type** button. The Change Chart Type dialog box appears with the Bar chart type selected.

3. In the Line section, click the **Line with Markers** (the fourth line chart subtype).

4. Click **OK**. The bar chart changes to a new line chart.

STEP-BY-STEP 8.8 Continued

5. Rename the chart sheet as **Line Chart**. The line chart should appear, as shown in Figure 8-16.

FIGURE 8-16
Line chart

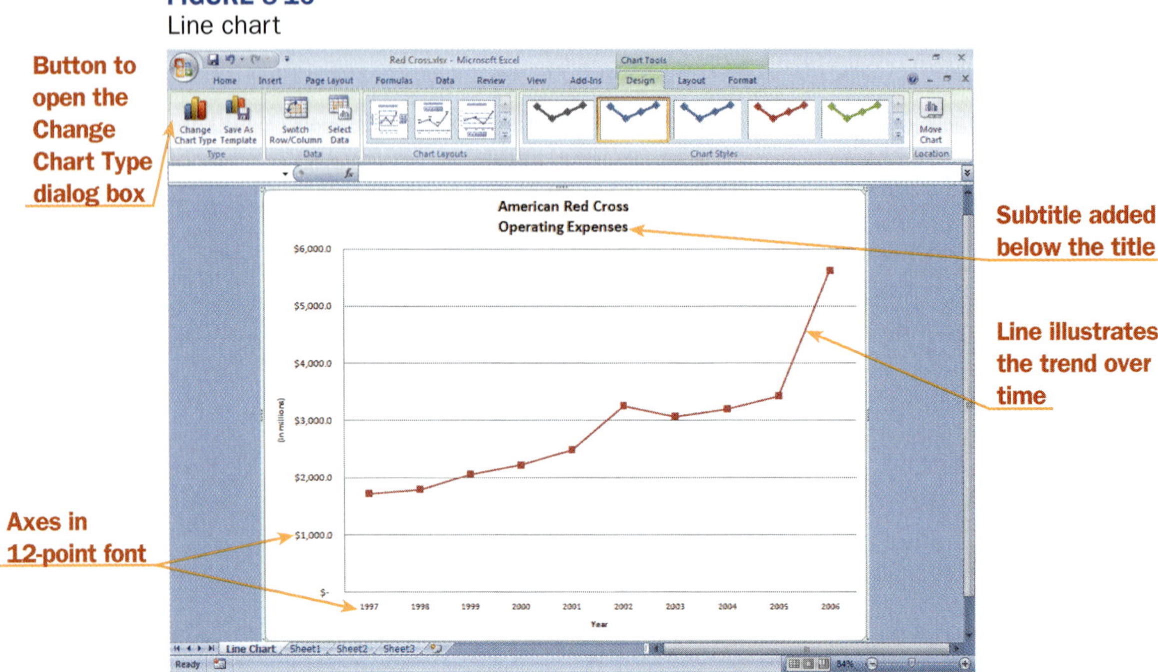

6. Insert a header with your name and the current date, and then print the chart sheet.

7. Save and close the workbook.

> **Extra Challenge**
>
> Convert the line chart you just created to a column chart. Save the workbook as **Red Cross Column** followed by your initials.

SUMMARY

In this lesson, you learned:

- A chart is a graphical representation of data. You can create several types of worksheet charts, including column, line, pie, and scatter charts.

- Charts can be embedded within a worksheet or created on a chart sheet.

- The process for creating a chart is the same for all chart types. Select the data for the chart. Select a chart type. Move, resize, and format the chart as needed.

- Any changes made to a data source automatically appear in the chart based on that data.

- Charts are made up of different parts, or elements. You can apply a chart layout and a chart style to determine which elements appear in the chart, where they appear, and how they look.

- If the data in a chart's data source is changed in the worksheet, the chart is automatically updated to reflect the new data.

■ You can fine-tune a chart by clicking a chart element and then opening its Format dialog box. You can also edit and format the chart text, using the standard text formatting tools.

■ You can change the type of chart in the Change Chart Type dialog box.

VOCABULARY *Review*

Define the following terms:

Axis	Data label	Legend
Chart	Data marker	Line chart
Chart area	Data series	Pie chart
Chart layout	Data source	Plot area
Chart sheet	Data table	Scatter chart
Chart style	Embedded chart	Selection box
Column chart	Exploded pie chart	Sizing handles

REVIEW *Questions*

TRUE/FALSE

Circle T if the statement is true or F if the statement is false.

T   F   **1.** Charts are a graphical representation of data.

T   F   **2.** Pie charts are the best way to represent data that are parts of a whole.

T   F   **3.** Scatter charts are good for representing trends over a period of time.

T   F   **4.** When the data source changes, charts created from that data also change.

T   F   **5.** After you create a chart, you cannot change the chart type or subtype.

FILL IN THE BLANK

Complete the following sentences by writing the correct word or words in the blanks provided.

1. A(n) __________ chart is represented by a circle divided into portions.

2. A(n) __________ chart is inserted on the same sheet as the data being charted.

3. In a chart, the __________ shows the patterns or symbols that identify the different types of data.

4. A(n) __________ formats the chart based on the colors, fonts, and effects associated with the workbook's theme.

5. Charts are made up of different parts, or __________.

PROJECTS

PROJECT 8-1

1. Open the **Populations.xlsx** Data File. Save the workbook as **Populations of Large Cities** followed by your initials.

2. Select the data in the range A5:B14, and then insert a column chart using the 2-D clustered column subtype.

3. Move the chart to a chart sheet named **Column Chart**.

4. Apply Layout 6 and Style 30 to the chart. Delete the Series 1 Data Labels from the chart if it appears over the Jakarta column.

5. Enter the chart title as **World's 10 Largest Cities**.

6. Enter the vertical axis title as **Population in Millions**.

7. Insert a header with your name and the current date, and then print the chart sheet. Save and close the workbook.

PROJECT 8-2

1. Open the **Running.xlsx** Data File. Save the workbook as **Running Times** followed by your initials.

2. Using the data in the range A5:B14, insert a line chart with markers embedded in the worksheet.

3. Apply chart Style 39.

4. In the range A5:A14, delete the word *Week*, leaving only the week number.

5. Add a horizontal axis title below the axis with the text **Week**.

6. Add a rotated vertical axis with the text **Time in Minutes**.

7. Do not include a chart title. Do not include a legend in the chart.

8. Resize and move the chart to fill the range C4:H18.

9. Insert a header with your name and the current date. Print the worksheet with the embedded chart, and then save and close the workbook.

PROJECT 8-3

1. Open the **McDonalds** Data File. Save the workbook as **McDonalds Restaurants** followed by your initials.

2. Using the data in the range A3:B5, create a pie chart using the Pie in 3-D subtype.

3. Apply the Layout 6 chart layout and the Style 26 chart style.

4. Enter the chart title **Total Restaurants**.

5. Show the legend above the chart.

6. Move the chart to a chart sheet named **Pie Chart**.

7. Format the font sizes of the chart title to 28 points, the slice percentages to 18 points, and the legend to 12 points.

8. Insert a header with your name and the current date. Print the chart sheet. Save and close the workbook.

 PROJECT 8-4

1. Open the **Family** Data File. Save the workbook as **Family Expenses** followed by your initials.

2. Using the data in the range A6:B13, create a pie chart using the Pie in 3-D subtype.

3. Move the chart to a chart sheet named **3-D Pie Chart**.

4. Choose the chart layout that includes a chart title and data labels with percentages, but does not include a legend.

5. Change the chart title to **Where Our Money Goes**.

6. Apply the Style 10 chart style.

7. Change the font size of the chart title to 24 points.

8. Change the font size of the data labels to 14 points.

9. Based on the chart, in what area(s) does the family spend the most?

10. Insert a header with your name and the current date. Print the chart sheet. Save and close the workbook.

 PROJECT 8-5

1. Open the **Study.xlsx** Data File. Save the workbook as **Study and Grades** followed by your initials.

2. Using the data in the range B4:C21, create a scatter chart with only markers.

3. Move the chart to a chart sheet named **Scatter Chart**.

4. Apply the Layout 4 chart layout to the chart.

5. Add the following chart title above the chart: **Relationship Between Exam Grades and Study Time**.

6. Add the following horizontal axis title below the axis: **Hours of Study**.

7. Add the following rotated vertical axis title: **Exam Grades**.

8. Change the font size of the chart title to 20 points.

9. Change the font size of the axis titles to 14 points.

10. Delete the legend.

11. Format the vertical axis so its minimum value is fixed at 50.

12. What relationship, if any, does the chart show between exam grades and study time?

13. Insert a header with your name and the current date. Print the chart sheet. Save and close the workbook.

PROJECT 8-6

1. Open the **Concession.xlsx** Data File. Save the workbook as **Concession Sales** followed by your initials.

2. Using the data in the range A4:E9, create a 2-D clustered column chart.

3. Move the chart to a chart sheet named **Column Chart**.

4. Apply the Layout 1 chart layout to the chart.

5. Apply the Style 26 chart style to the chart.

6. Change the chart title to **Concession Sales**. Change the font size of the chart title to 24 points.

7. Add the following rotated vertical axis title: **Sales in Dollars**. Change the font size of the axis title to 14 points.

8. Change the font size of the horizontal and vertical axis labels to 12 points and make them bold.

9. Move the legend above the chart.

10. Change the font size of the legend to 12 points.

11. Right-click the plot area of the chart, and then click Format Plot Area on the shortcut menu. In the Format Plot Area dialog box that appears, click the Solid fill option button. Click the Color button arrow, and then click White, Background 1, Darker 15% (the first color in the third row). Click the Close button.

12. Which product has decreased in sales over the last four games? Which product has increased in sales over the last four games?

13. Insert a header with your name and the current date. Print the chart sheet. Save and close the workbook.

PROJECT 8-7

1. Open the **Triangle.xlsx** Data File. Save the workbook as **Triangle Growth** followed by your initials.

2. Using the data in the range A5:F7, create a 2-D line chart with markers.

3. Move the chart to a chart sheet named **Line Chart**.

4. Apply the Layout 1 chart layout to the chart.

5. Apply the Style 26 chart style to the chart.

6. Change the chart title to **Triangle Software Revenue and Income**.

7. Change the vertical axis title to (**Dollars in Thousands**).

8. Show the legend at the top of the chart.

9. Have the company's sales decreased, increased, or remained stable?

10. Insert a header with your name and the current date. Print the chart sheet.

11. Press and hold the Ctrl key as you drag the Line Chart tab to the right to make a copy. Rename the copied chart sheet **Clustered Column Chart**.

12. Change the chart type to a clustered column chart.

13. Print the chart sheet. Save and close the workbook.

PROJECT 8-8

1. Open the **Chico.xlsx** Data File. Save the workbook as **Chico Temperatures** followed by your initials.

2. Using the data in the range A3:M5, create a 2-D line chart with markers.

3. Move the chart to a chart sheet named **Line Chart**.

4. Apply the Layout 5 chart layout to the chart.

5. Apply the Style 34 chart style to the chart.

6. Change the chart title to **Temperatures for Chico, California**.

7. Change the vertical axis title to **Temperatures in Fahrenheit**.

8. Under Chart Tools on the Ribbon, click the Layout tab. In the Current Selection group, use the Chart Elements box to select Series "High" in the chart.

9. Click the Format Selection button to open the Format Data Series dialog box. Make the following changes:
   A. Click Marker Fill to display the options. Click the Solid fill option button. Click the Color button, and then click Dark Red in the Standard Colors section.
   B. Click Line Color to display the options. Click the Solid line option button. Click the Color button, and then click Dark Red in the Standard Colors section.
   C. Click Marker Line Color to display the options. Click the Solid line option button. Click the Color button, and then click Dark Red in the Standard Colors section.

10. Click Close to close the Format Data Series dialog box.

11. On the Layout tab under Chart Tools on the Ribbon, in the Current Selection group, use the Chart Elements box to select Series "Low" in the chart.

12. Click the Format Selection button to open the Format Data Series dialog box. Make the following changes:
    A. Click Marker Fill to display the options. Click the Solid fill option button. Click the Color button, and then click Blue in the Standard Colors section.
    B. Click Line Color to display the options. Click the Solid line option button. Click the Color button, and then click Blue in the Standard Colors section.
    C. Click Marker Line Color to display the options. Click the Solid line option button. Click the Color button, and then click Blue in the Standard Colors section.

13. Click Close to close the Format Data Series dialog box.

14. Insert a header with your name and the current date. Print the chart sheet. Save and close the workbook.

CRITICAL *Thinking*

 **ACTIVITY 8-1**

 For each scenario, which chart type would be the most appropriate to illustrate the data? Justify your answer.

Scenario 1. A scientist has given varying amounts of water to 200 potted plants. Over 35 days, the height of the plant and the amount of water given to the plant are recorded in a worksheet. What is the best chart type to illustrate the connection between water and plant growth?

Scenario 2. A corporation developed a new product last year. A manager in the corporation recorded the number of units sold each month. He noticed that sales in summer months were much higher than sales in the winter months. What chart type can he use to illustrate this to other sales managers?

Scenario 3. Students entering a high school come from five middle schools. The principal has recorded the name of the middle school and the number of students from each middle school. What chart type can she use to show which middle schools supply significantly more students than other middle schools?

 **ACTIVITY 8-2**

You recently opened a store that buys and sells used CDs. As a small business owner, you are responsible for budgets and inventory. Initially, you tracked the inventory and budget data by hand in a paper notebook. Now that the business is growing, this method has become too cumbersome. You decide to transfer the data into an electronic format.

Create a new workbook and save it as **Sounds Good** followed by your initials. Create and format one worksheet to track inventory and one worksheet to track the budget. Both worksheets should contain the name of your store—Sounds Good CDs—and a title describing the data.

For the inventory worksheet, include (a) the title of the CD or DVD, (b) the artist, (c) the quantity of each, and (d) the cost per item. Enter the data shown in Figure 8-17 in the worksheet. Rename the worksheet as **Inventory**.

FIGURE 8-17

Title	Artist	Quantity	Cost
Nerve Net	Brian Eno	4	$ 6.95
Thursday Afternoon	Brian Eno	2	$ 7.95
Geometry	Robert Rich	3	$ 5.95
On This Planet	Steve Roach	3	$ 8.95
Possible Planet	Steve Roach	5	$ 6.95

The budget worksheet records the expected income and expenses for the month. Include rows for (a) sales revenue, (b) purchases of used CDs, (c) rent expense, (d) utilities expense, (e) tax expense, and (f) net income. Include columns for (a) budgeted amounts and (b) actual amounts. Then, enter the data shown in Figure 8-18.

FIGURE 8-18

	Actual	Budgeted
Sales Revenue	$ 12,875	$ 11,950
Purchases of CDs	5,500	4,800
Rent	575	575
Utilities	350	350
Taxes	817	667
Net Income		

For the Actual Net Income, enter a formula that subtracts the purchases and expenses from revenue. For the Budgeted Net Income, enter a formula that subtracts the purchases and expenses from revenue. Rename the worksheet as **Budget**.

Using the data you entered in the Budget worksheet, create a chart that compares the actual and budgeted values in each category. Use an appropriate chart type. Choose which chart elements to display, where they should be located, and how the chart is formatted.

For all worksheets, insert a header with your name and the current date, and then print the worksheets. Save the workbook as **Sounds Good** followed by your initials.

MICROSOFT EXCEL

REVIEW *Questions*

TRUE/FALSE

Circle T if the statement is true or F if the statement is false.

T F **1.** The active cell reference appears in the Name Box.

T F **2.** To select a group of cells, you must click each cell individually until all cells in the range are selected.

T F **3.** The Save As dialog box appears every time you save a worksheet.

T F **4.** The formula =$B$4+C9 contains mixed cell references.

T F **5.** After you edit the data source in the worksheet, the chart is also updated to reflect the changes.

MATCHING

Match the description in Column 2 with the text position function in Column 1.

Column 1	Column 2
___ **1.** Wrapping	**A.** Moves the text several spaces to the right or left
___ **2.** Orientation	**B.** Aligns the text to the right, left, or center
___ **3.** Indenting	**C.** Combines several cells into one and places the contents in the middle of the cell
___ **4.** Alignment	**D.** Displays cell contents on multiple lines
___ **5.** Merge and Center	**E.** Displays text at an angle, vertically, up, or down

FILL IN THE BLANK

Complete the following sentences by writing the correct word or words in the blanks provided.

1. A(n) __________ cell reference changes when copied or moved.

2. __________ formatting is used to highlight cells that meet specific criteria.

3. The __________ function adds a range of numbers in a worksheet.

4. A(n) __________ chart uses vertical rectangles to represent values in a worksheet.

5. The __________ is information that will appear at the top of every printed page.

MATCHING

Match the correct result in Column 2 to the formula in Column 1. Assume the following values appear in the worksheet:

Cell	Value
B2	5
B3	6
B4	4
B5	7

Column 1	Column 2
___ 1. =12+B5	A. 22
___ 2. =B2*B4	B. 5
___ 3. =(B3+B4)/B2	C. 20
___ 4. =AVERAGE(B3:B4)	D. 19
___ 5. =SUM(B2:B5)	E. 2

PROJECTS

PROJECT 1

1. Open the **Gas.xlsx** Data File. Save the workbook as **Gas Sales** followed by your initials.

2. Format cell A1 with the Title cell style. Format the range A2:A3 with bold.

3. Change the width of column A to 15. Change the widths of columns B through D to 12.

4. Merge and center the range A1:D1.

5. In cell B2, enter the current date, and then apply the Long Date format.

6. Merge and center the range A2:D2.

7. In cell B3, enter 7:55 PM for time, and then apply the Time format.

8. Merge and center the range B3:D3.

9. Format the text in the range A2:D3 in 12-point Cambria.

10. Wrap the text in cell C5.

11. Format range A5:D5 with the Accent 1 cell style, and then bold and center the cells.

12. Format the range B6:B9 in the Number format with a comma separator and no decimal places.

13. Format the range C6:D9 in the Currency format with 2 decimal places.

14. In cell B10, use the SUM function to add the total number of gallons sold, and then format the cell with the Total cell style.

15. In cell D10, use the SUM function to add the total sales, and then format the cell with the Total cell style. Compare your worksheet to Figure UR-1, which shows the completed worksheet.

FIGURE UR-1

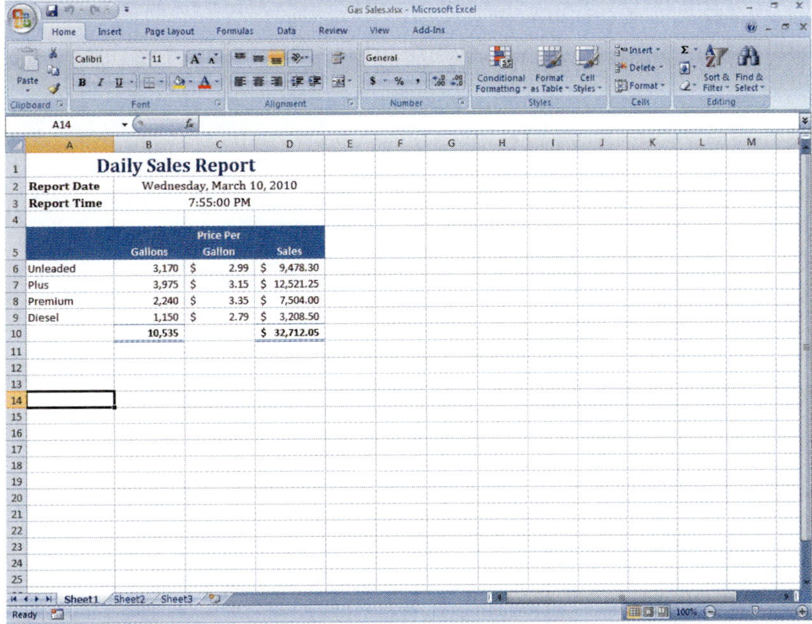

16. Insert a header with your name and the current date. Save, print, and close the workbook.

PROJECT 2

1. Open the **Organic.xlsx** Data File. Save the workbook as **Organic Financials** followed by your initials.

2. Format the company name and other headings in bold and in a larger font than the items in the body of the financial statement.

3. Merge and center each of the first four rows across columns A and B.

4. Separate the headings from the body of the financial statement by one row.

5. Resize the columns so you can view all of their contents, wrapping text as appropriate.

6. Format the first (revenue) and last (net income) numbers in the financial statement to display dollar signs and thousands separators, but no decimal places.

7. Format all the other numbers to include a thousands separator but no dollar sign and no decimal places. Compare your worksheet to Figure UR-2.

FIGURE UR-2

	A	B
1	**Organic Food Company**	
2	CONSOLIDATED STATEMENT OF INCOME	
3	For the Year Ending December 28, 2010	
4	(in thousands)	
5		
6	Revenue	$ 4,892,073
7	Cost of products sold	3,677,738
8	Gross margin	1,214,335
9	Selling, marketing and administrative expenses	402,890
10	Operating income	811,445
11	Interest income	18,945
12	Other expense - net	4,961
13	Earnings before interest and taxes	825,429
14	Interest expense	80,890
15	Income from continuing operations before income taxes	744,539
16	Income tax expense	53,798
17	Income before cumulative effect	690,741
18	Cumulative effect of an accounting change	119,917
19	Net income	$ 570,824

8. Format the worksheet to make it visually attractive and appealing, such as by adding borders, font colors, fill colors, alignments, cell styles, and so forth as appropriate.

9. Insert a header with your name and the current date. Save, print, and close the workbook.

 **PROJECT 3**

1. Open the **Club.xlsx** Data File. Save the workbook as **Club Members** followed by your initials.

2. Sort the range A2:B20 by the values in column B in order from largest to smallest.

3. Resize the columns as needed to so that all the content is displayed.

4. Format the worksheet title with the Title cell style to distinguish it from the other text in the workbook.

5. Enter the title **Exceptional and Outstanding Members** above William Griffin's name, and then format the title in bold italics and in a font larger than the other text in the worksheet.

6. Enter the text **Exceptional Members** above William Griffin's name and bold it.

7. Enter the text **Outstanding Members** above Matthew Carcello's name and bold it.

8. Add the subtitle **Other Active Members** above Mohamed Abdul's name and bold it.

9. Format the service points in the Number format with a thousands separator and no decimal places. Compare your worksheet to Figure UR-3.

FIGURE UR-3

	A	B
1	**Computer Science Club**	
2	*Exceptional and Outstanding Members*	
3	**Exceptional Members**	
4	Griffin, William	1,150
5	Atiase, Allen	1,020
6	**Outstanding Members**	
7	Carcello, Matthew	980
8	Anderson, George	970
9	Santos, Jose	970
10	Hill, Debra	950
11	Smith, Marsha	920
12	Davis, John	890
13	Witt, Terry	870
14	**Other Active Members**	
15	Abdul, Mohamed	780
16	Doan, Arlette	740
17	Porter, Sandra	680
18	Mullin, Richard	630
19	Vinson, Rhonda	630
20	Squires, Judith	610
21	Estes, Susan	570
22	Tse, Allen	530
23	Kermit, Paul	480
24	Edwards, Alice	470
25		
26	Exceptional members have earned 1,001 or more service points.	

10. Format the worksheet using cell styles, alignments, font styles, colors, and so forth to make the worksheet visually appealing.

11. Insert a header with your name and the current date. Save, print, and close the workbook.

PROJECT 4

1. Open the **CompNet.xlsx** Data File. Save the workbook as **CompNet Expenses** followed by your initials.

2. Create a pie chart in 3-D based on the data in the range A12:B18. Move the chart to chart sheet named **Expenses Chart**.

3. Apply the chart layout that includes a chart title above the chart and labels and percentages on the slices.

4. Apply the Style 10 chart style.

5. Enter **Expenses for 2010** as the chart title, and then change the font size to 24 points.

6. Change the font size of the data labels to 12 points. Compare your worksheet with Figure UR-4.

FIGURE UR-4

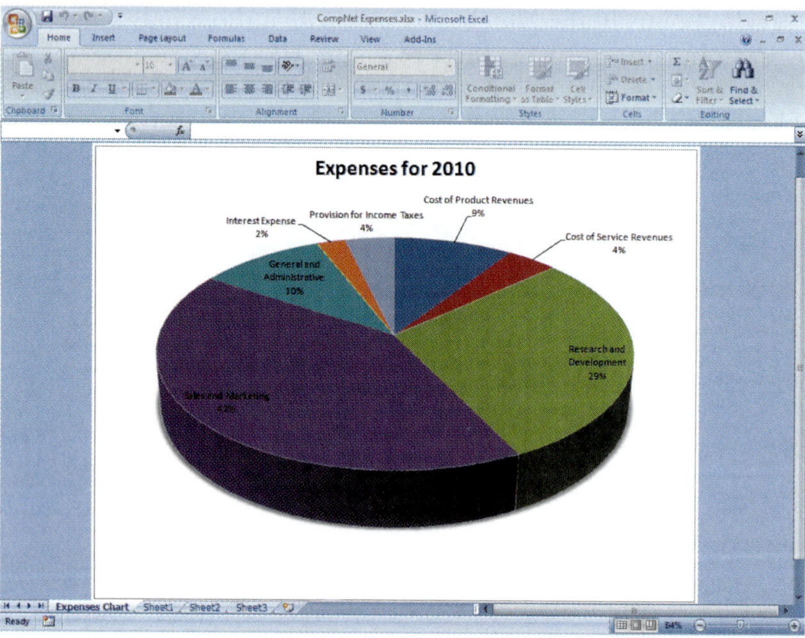

7. Based on the chart, what is the largest expense category? What is the smallest expense category?

8. Insert a header with your name and the current date. Save, print, and close the workbook.

SIMULATION

You work at the Java Internet Café, which has been open only a few months. The café serves coffee, other beverages, and pastries, and offers Internet access. Seven computers are set up on tables along the north side of the store. Customers can come in, have a cup of coffee and a pastry, and explore the World Wide Web.

Your manager asks you to create a menu of coffee prices and computer prices. You will do this by integrating Microsoft Excel and Microsoft Word.

 **JOB 1**

1. Create a new workbook. Save the workbook as **Coffee Prices** followed by your initials.

2. Enter the data shown in Figure UR-5 in the worksheet.

FIGURE UR-5

	A	B	C	D	E
1			Coffee Prices		
2					
3	House coffee	$1.00		Café latte	$3.50
4	Refills	$0.50		Cappucino	$3.50
5	Espresso	$2.00		Café breve	$3.25
6	Extra shot	$0.55		Café con panna	$3.75
7					

3. Change the widths of columns A and D to 20. Change the widths of columns B and E to 10. Change the width of column C to 4.

4. Left-align data in columns B and E.

5. Indent the text in cells A4 and A6.

6. Change the font of all data to Arial, 11 points.

7. Format the data in columns B and E as Currency with two decimal places.

8. Merge and center the range A1:E1. Change the font of the text in the merged cell A1 to Arial, 14 points. Format the merged cell A1 with a bottom border.

9. Hide the Gridlines from view. Copy the data in the range A1: E6. Save the workbook.

10. Start Word and open the **Java.docx** Data File. Save the document as **Java Menu** followed by your initials.

11. Insert one blank line below the *Menu* heading, center the blank line, and then paste a link to the worksheet data you copied. On the Home tab, in the Clipboard group, under the Paste button, click the arrow to open the Paste menu, and then click Paste Special. The Paste Special dialog box appears. In the Paste Special dialog box, click the Paste link option button, and then click Microsoft Office Excel Worksheet Object, as shown in Figure UR-6. Click OK.

FIGURE UR-6

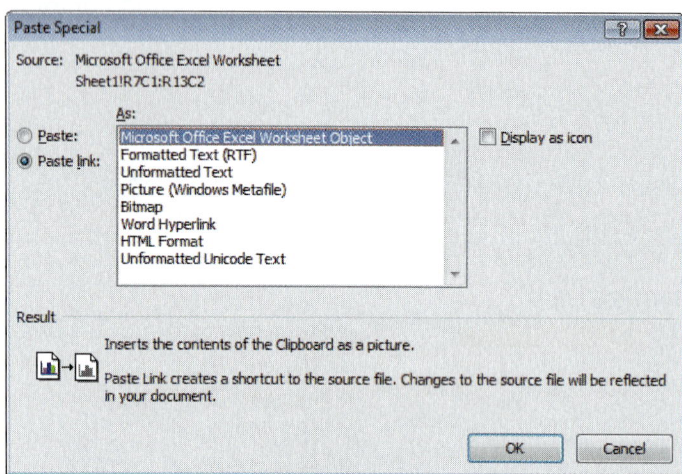

12. Switch to Excel, and then open the **Computer.xlsx** Data File. Save the workbook as **Computer Prices** followed by your initials.

13. Copy the data in the range A1:B13.

14. Switch to the **Java Menu** document.

15. Insert one blank line after the Coffee Prices menu items, center the line if it is not already centered, and then paste a link to the worksheet data you copied. On the Home tab, in the Clipboard group, under the Paste button, click the arrow to open the Paste menu, and then click Paste Special. In the Paste Special dialog box, click the Paste link option button, click Microsoft Office Excel Worksheet Object, and then click OK.

16. Insert your name and the current date in the blank line of the footer.

17. Preview the document. Adjust the placement of data if necessary so that all data fits on one page.

18. Save, print, and close the **Java Menu** document.

19. Close the **Coffee Prices** and **Computer Prices** workbooks without saving changes.

 **JOB 2**

The menu you created has been very successful. However, your manager asks you to make a few changes.

1. Open the **Coffee Prices** and **Computer Prices** workbooks you saved in Job 1.

2. Edit the **Coffee Prices** and **Computer Prices** workbooks as shown in Figure UR-7.

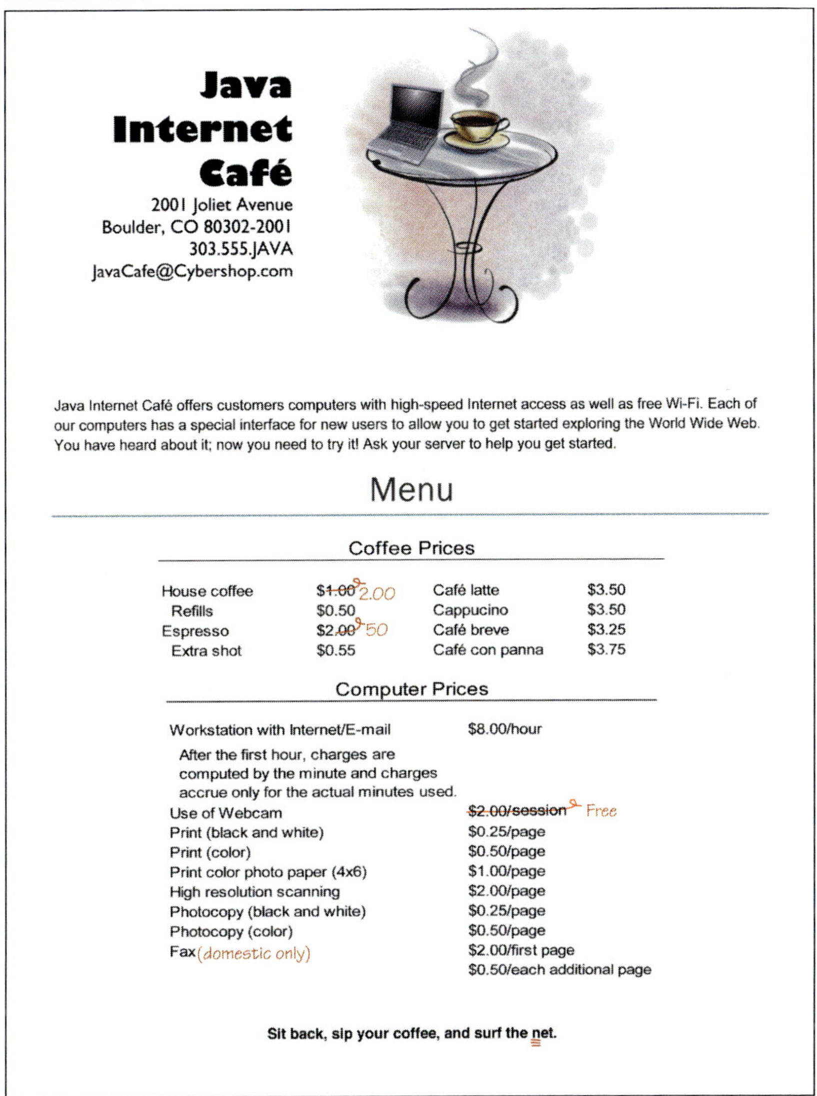

3. Save and close the **Coffee Prices** and **Computer Prices** workbooks.

4. Open the **Java Menu** document you created in Job 1.

5. Update the document when prompted because you revised the linked files since you saved and closed the Java Menu document.

6. Make the correction in the footer, as shown in Figure UR-7.

7. Save the document as **Java Menu Revised** followed by your initials.

8. Print and close the document.

APPENDIX A

COMPUTER CONCEPTS

What Is a Computer?

A computer is a machine that is used to store, retrieve, and manipulate data. A computer takes **input**, uses stored instructions to **process** and store that data, and then produces **output**. You enter the data into the computer through a variety of input devices, such as a keyboard or mouse. The processor processes the data to produce information. Information is output or presented in many ways such as an image on a screen or a monitor; printed pages from a printer, or sound through speakers. Computer **software** is the stored instructions or programming that runs the computer. **Memory** inside the computer stores the programs or instructions that run the computer as well as the data and information. Various **storage devices** are used to transfer or safely store the data and information.

A **computer system** is made up of components that include the computer, input, and output devices. Computer systems come in many shapes, sizes, and configurations. The computer you use at home or in school is often called a **personal computer**. See Figure A-1. **Desktop computers** often have a 'computer case' or a **system unit**, which contains processing devices, memory, and some storage devices.

FIGURE A-1
Example of a computer system

Input devices such as the mouse and keyboard are attached to the system unit by cables or wires. Output devices, such as the monitor, speakers, and printer are also attached to the system unit by cables or wires. **Wireless technology** makes it possible to eliminate wires and use the airwaves to connect devices. **Laptop** or **notebook** computers have all the essential parts in one unit.

The **operating system** is the main software or **system software** that runs a computer and often defines the type of computer. There are two main types or platforms for personal computers. The Macintosh computer, or Mac, is produced by Apple Computer, Inc. and runs the Mac operating system. The PC is a Windows-based computer produced by many different companies, but which runs the Microsoft Windows operating system.

Hardware

The physical components, devices, or parts of the computer are called **hardware**. The main parts are the central processing unit (CPU), the monitor, the keyboard, and the mouse. Peripherals are additional components, such as printers and scanners. Peripherals are not essential to the computer but enhance the computer.

Input Devices

There are many different types of input devices. You enter information into a computer by typing on a keyboard or by pointing, clicking, or dragging a mouse. A **mouse** is a hand-held device used to move a pointer on the computer screen. Similar to a mouse, a **trackball** has a roller ball that turns to control a pointer on the screen. Digital tracking devices, such as a **touchpad**, are an alternative to the trackball or mouse. Situated on the keyboard of a laptop computer, they allow you to simply move and tap your finger on a small electronic pad to control the pointer on the screen.

Tablet PCs allow you to input data by writing directly on the computer screen. Handwriting recognition technology converts handwritten writing to text. Many computers have a microphone or other **sound input device** which accepts speech or sounds as input and converts the speech to text or data. For example, when you telephone a company or bank for help and have the option to say your requests or account number, this is **speech recognition technology** at work!

Other input devices include scanners and bar code readers. You can use a **scanner** to convert text or graphics from a printed page into code that a computer can process. You have probably seen **bar code readers** being used in stores. These are used to read bar codes, such as the UPC (universal product code), to track merchandise or other inventory in a store. See Figure A-2.

Examples of input devices

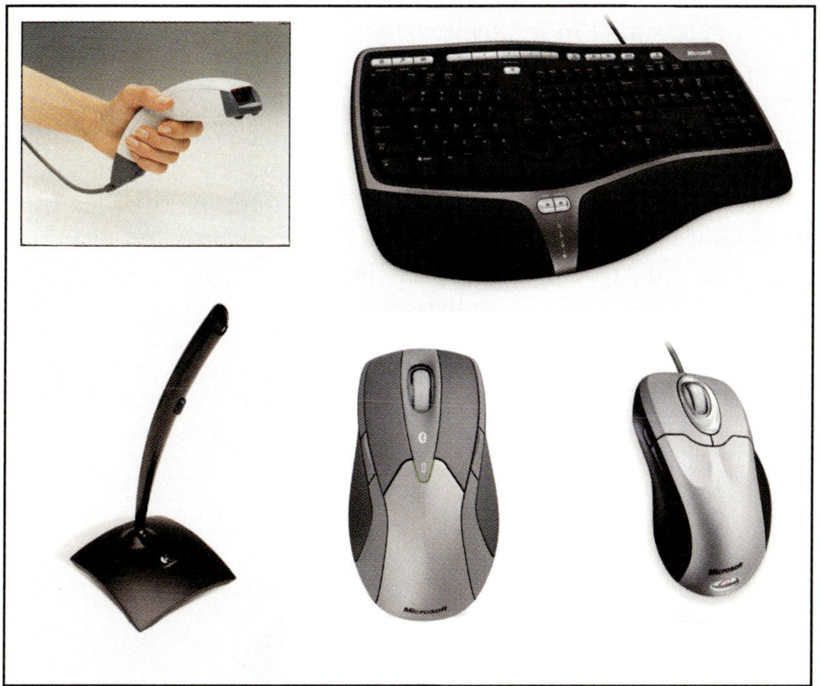

Processing Devices

Processing devices are mounted inside the system unit of the computer. The **central processing unit (CPU)** is a silicon chip that processes data and carries out instructions given to the computer. The **data bus** includes the wiring and pathways by which the CPU communicates with the peripherals and components of the computer. The CPU is stored on the motherboard of the computer. The **motherboard** is where the computer memory and other vital electronic parts are stored. See Figure A-3.

A motherboard

Storage Devices

A storage device is used to store data on a computer. Storage devices are both input and output devices. Most computers have more than one type of storage device. The main storage device for a computer is the hard disk drive that is usually inside the system unit. See Figure A-4. It is fixed storage, not removable from the computer. External and removable hard disk drives are available that can plug into the USB port on the system unit. The hard disk drive reads and writes data to and from a round magnetic platter, or disk. The data is digitally encoded on the disk as a series of 1s and 0s. A byte stands for a single character of data. At the time this book was written, typical hard drives for a computer system that you might buy for your personal home use range from 80 gigabytes (GB) to 250 gigabytes. The prefix "giga" means a billion. A gigabyte (GB or Gbyte) is approximately one billion bytes.

FIGURE A-4
A hard disk drive

The floppy disk drive is an older technology that is no longer available on new computers. Some older computers still have a floppy disk drive which is mounted in the system unit with access to the outside. A floppy disk is the medium that stores the data. You put the floppy disk into the floppy disk drive so the computer can read and write the data. The floppy disk's main advantage was portability. You can store data on a floppy disk and transport it for use on another computer. A floppy disk can hold up to 1.4MB (megabytes) of information. A Zip disk is similar to a floppy disk. A Zip disk is also a portable disk contained in a plastic sleeve, but it will hold 100MB or 250MB of information. A special disk drive called a Zip drive is required to read and write data to a Zip disk.

Another storage device is the **CD drive** or **DVD drive**. These drives are typically mounted inside the system unit, although external versions of these devices are also available. Most new computers are equipped with CD/DVD burners. That means they have read and write capabilities. You use a CD/DVD drive to read and write CDs and DVDs. A **CD** is a compact disc, which is a form of optical storage. Compact discs can store 650MB. These discs have a great advantage over other forms of removable storage as they can hold vast quantities of information—the entire contents of a small library, for instance. They are also fairly durable. Another advantage of CDs is their ability to hold graphic information, including moving pictures, with the highest quality stereo sound. A **DVD** is also an optical disc that looks like a CD. It is a high-capacity storage device that can contain up to 4.7GB of data, which is a seven-fold increase over a CD. There are two variations of DVDs that offer even more storage—a 2-layer version with 9.4GB capacity and double-sided discs with 17GB capacity. Newer versions store even more data. These highest-capacity discs are designed to store large databases. A DVD holds 133 minutes of data on each side, which means that two two-hour full-length feature movies can be stored on one disc. Information is encoded on the disk by a laser and read by a CD/DVD drive in the computer.

Solid state storage is another popular storage technology. A **USB flash drive** is a very portable small store device that works both as a drive and medium. It plugs directly into a USB port on the computer system unit. You read and write data to the flash drive. **Solid state card readers** are devices that can read solid state cards. Solid state storage is often used in cameras.

Magnetic tape is a medium most commonly used for backing up a computer system, which means making a copy of files from a hard drive. Although it is relatively rare for a data on a hard drive to be completely lost in a crash (that is, for the data or pointers to the data to be partially or totally destroyed), it can and does happen. Therefore, most businesses and some individuals routinely back up files on tape. If you have a small hard drive, you can use DVDs or CD-ROMs to back up your system. Figure A-5 shows removable storage media and devices.

FIGURE A-5
Removable storage

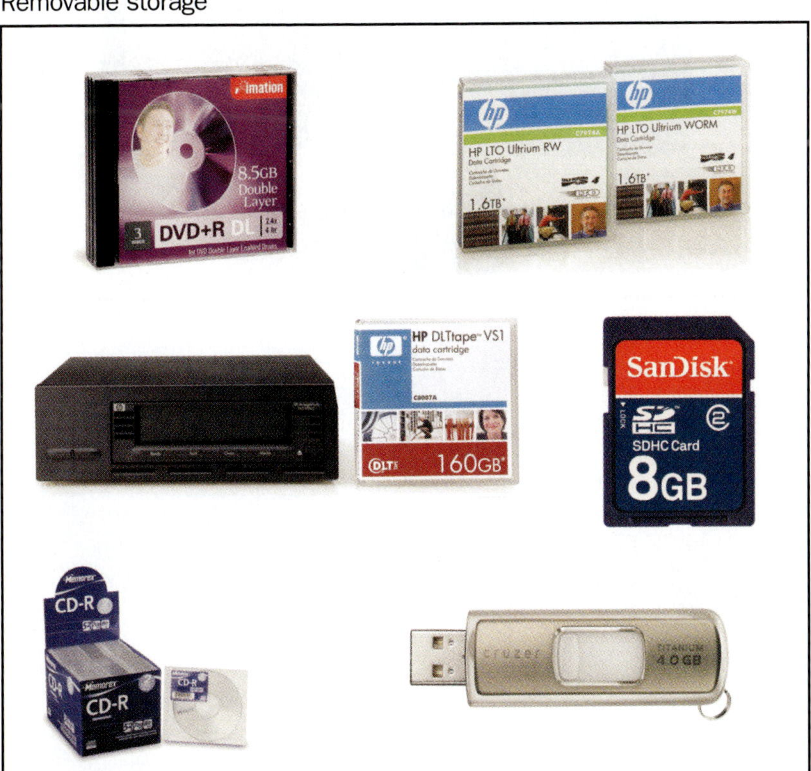

Output Devices

The **monitor** on which you view your computer work is an output device. It provides a visual representation of the information stored in or produced by your computer. The typical monitor for today's system is a flat-screen monitor similar to a television. See Figure A-6. It provides a very sharp picture because of the large number of tiny dots, called **pixels**, which make up the display as well as its ability to present the full spectrum of colors. **Resolution**, the term that tells you how clear an image will be on the screen. is measured in pixels. A typical resolution is 1024 × 768. A high-quality monitor may have a resolution of 1680 × 1050. Monitors come in different sizes. The size of a monitor is determined by measuring the diagonal of the screen. Laptops have smaller monitors than desktop computers. A laptop monitor may be 13", 15", or 17". Desktop monitors can be as large as 19"- 24" or even larger.

FIGURE A-6
A flat screen monitor

Printers are a type of output device. They let you produce a paper printout of information contained in the computer. Today, most printers use either inkjet or laser technology to produce high-quality print. Like a copy machine, a **laser printer** uses heat to fuse a powdery substance called **toner** to the page. **Ink-jet printers** use a spray of ink to print. Laser printers give the sharpest image and often print more pages per minute (ppm) than ink jet printers. Ink-jet printers provide nearly as sharp an image, but the wet printouts can smear when they first are printed. Most color printers, or photo printers for printing photographs, are ink jet printers. Color laser printers are more costly. These printers allow you to print information in a full array of colors, just as you see it on your monitor. See Figure A-7.

FIGURE A-7
Typical printers

Laptop or Notebook Computer

A **laptop computer**, also called a **notebook computer**, is a small folding computer that can literally fit in a person's lap or in a backpack. Within the fold-up case of a laptop is the CPU, data bus, monitor (built into the lid), hard drive (sometimes removable), 3.5-inch floppy drive, CD/DVD drive, and trackball or digital tracking device. The advantage of the laptop is its portability—you can work anywhere because you can use power either from an outlet or from the computer's internal, rechargeable batteries. Almost all laptops have wireless Internet access built into the system. The drawbacks are the smaller keyboard, smaller monitor, smaller capacity, and higher price, though newer laptops offer full-sized keyboards and higher quality monitors. As technology allows, storage capacity on smaller devices is making it possible to offer laptops with as much power and storage as a full-sized computer. See Figure A-8.

FIGURE A-8
A laptop or notebook computer

Personal Digital Assistants (PDA)

A Personal Digital Assistant is a pocket-sized electronic organizer that helps you to manage addresses, appointments, expenses, tasks, and memos. The common input devices for PDAs include touch-senstive screens that accept input through a stylus pen or small keyboards that are either built in to the PDA or available as software on the screen. PDA data and information can be shared with a Windows-based or Macintosh computer through a process called synchronization. By placing your PDA in a cradle or through a USB port attached to your computer, you can transfer data from your PDA's calendar, address book, or memo program into your computer's information manager program and vice versa. The information is updated on both sides, making your PDA a portable extension of your computer. PDAs are becoming more and more functional. Newer PDAs include cameras and have cell phone capability. Depending on the amount of memory in the specific PDA, they can include many of the same programs found on a personal computer.

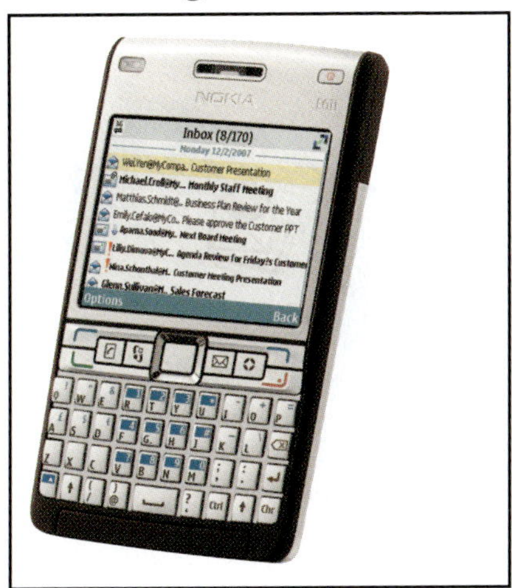

FIGURE A-9
A Personal Digital Assistant

How Computers Work

All of the input, processing, storage, and output devices function together to make the manipulation, storage, and distribution of data and information possible.

Data and Information Management

Data is information entered into and manipulated or processed within a computer. Processing includes computation, such as adding, subtracting, multiplying, and dividing; analysis planning, such as sorting data; and reporting, such as presenting data for others in a chart or graph.

Memory

Computers have two types of memory—RAM and ROM. **RAM,** or **random access memory,** is the silicon chips in the system unit that temporarily store information when the computer is turned on. RAM is what keeps the software programs up and running and provides visuals that appear on your screen. You work with data in RAM up until you save it to a storage media device such as a hard disk, CD, DVD, or solid state storage such as flash drive.

Computers now have sophisticated application programs that tend to include a lot of graphics and data. In order to run these programs, computers require a lot of memory. Therefore, computers have at least 512MB of RAM to start. Many computer systems are expandable and you can add on RAM after you buy the computer. The more RAM available for the programs, the faster and more efficiently the machine will be able to operate. RAM chips are shown in Figure A-10.

FIGURE A-10
RAM chips

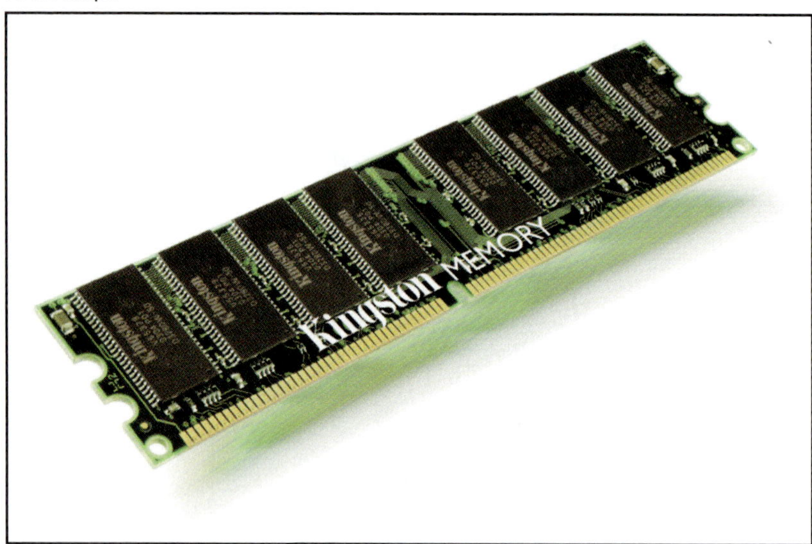

ROM, or read-only memory, is the memory that stays in the computer when it is turned off. It is ROM that stores the programs that run the computer as it starts or "boots up." ROM holds the instructions that tell the computer how to begin to load its operating system software programs.

Speed

The speed of a computer is measured by how fast the computer processes each instruction. There are several factors that affect the performance of a computer: the speed of the processor, or the **clock speed,** the **front side bus speed**—the speed of the bus that connects the processor to main memory—the speed in which data is written and retrieved from the hard drive or other storage media, and the speed of the graphics card if you are working on programs that use a lot of graphic images. These all factor into a computer's performance.

The speed of a computer is measured in **megahertz (MHz)** and **gigahertz (GHz)**

Processors are sold now by name, and each brand or series has its own specifications. Processor manufacturers include Intel, Motorola, and AMD. When you research processors and computers you might see names such as Intel® Core™2 Extreme Processor QX6800, Intel® Core™2 Duo Processor E6700, Pentium® 4 Processor Extreme Edition supporting Hyper-Threading Technology for PCs, or AMD Mobile Athelon or Turion 64 X2. For Macs you might see PowerPC G5 or Xeon 5300.

Networks

Computers have expanded the world of communications. A **network** is defined as two or more computers connected to share data. **LANs (local area networks)** connect computers within a small area such as a home, office, school, or building. Networks can be wired or wireless. The **Internet** is the largest network in the world connecting millions of computers across the globe. Using the Internet, people can communicate across the world instantly.

Networks require various communication devices and software. **Modems** allow computers to communicate with each other by telephone lines. Modem is an acronym that stands for "MOdulator/DEModulator." Modems convert data in bytes to sound media in order to send data over the phone lines and then convert it back to bytes after receiving data. Modems operate at various rates or speeds. **Network cards** in the system unit allow computers to access networks. A **router** is an electronic device that joins two or more networks. For example, a home network can use a router and a modem to connect the home's LAN to the Internet. A **server** is the computer hardware and software that "serves" the computers on a network. Network technology is sometimes called "client-server." A personal computer that requests data from a server is referred to as a **client**. The computer that stores the data is the **server**. On the Internet, the computer that stores the Web pages is the **Web server**. Figure A-11 shows a network diagram.

FIGURE A-11
Diagram of a network

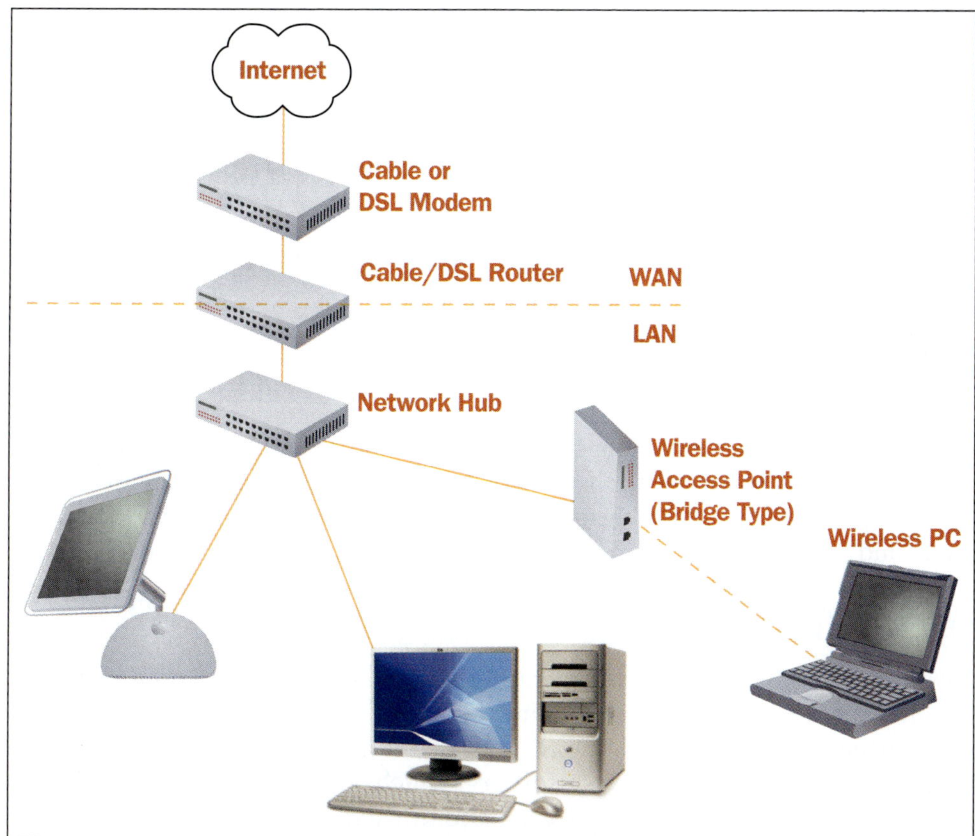

Networks have certain advantages over stand-alone computers: they allow communication among the computers; they allow smaller capacity computers to access the larger capacity of the server computers on the network; they allow several computers to share peripherals, such as one printer; and they can make it possible for all computers on the network to have access to the Internet.

Connect to the Internet

To connect to the Internet you need to subscribe to an **Internet Service Provider (ISP)**. There are several technologies available. Connection speeds are measured in bits per second. Upload speeds are slower than download speeds. **Dial-up** is the oldest, and the slowest, Internet access technology and offered by local telephone companies. To get access to the Internet, your computer has to dial out through a phone line. Many people have moved to **always-on connection technologies**. The computer is always connected to the Internet if you turn the computer on, so you don't have to dial out. These always-on faster technologies, known as **Digital Subscriber Line (DSL)**, include cable connections, satellites, and fiber optic. They are offered by telephone companies, cable television companies, and satellite service providers. It can be noted that satellite Internet access is the most expensive, dialup is the cheapest. Table A-1 shows a brief comparison of these technologies.

TABLE A-1
Comparing Internet access options

FEATURE	DSL INTERNET	CABLE INTERNET	SATELLITE INTERNET	FIBER OPTIC (FIOS)
Max. High Speed	Up to 1.5 Mbps	Up to 3 Mbps	Up to 1 Mbps	Up to 20 Mbps
Access is through	Existing phone line	Existing TV cable	Satellite dish	Fiber optic phone lines
Availability	Generally available in populated areas	Might not be available in rural areas	Available in all areas; note that satellite service is sensitive to weather conditions	Might not be available in all areas as fiber optic lines are just being installed in many areas

Software

A **program** is a set of instructions to the computer. **Software** is the collection of programs and other data input that tells the computer how to operate its devices, how to manipulate, store, and output information, and how to accept the input you give it. Software fits into two basic categories: systems software and applications software. A third category, network software, is really a type of application.

Systems Software

Systems software refers to the operating system (OS) of the computer. The OS is a group of programs that is automatically copied in from the time the computer is turned on until the computer is turned off. Operating systems serve two functions: they control data flow among computer parts, and they provide the platform on which application and network software work—in effect, they allow the "space" for software and translate its commands to the computer. The most popular operating systems in use today are the Macintosh operating system, MAC OS X and several different versions of Microsoft Windows, such as Windows 2000, Windows XP, or Windows Vista. See Figure A-12 and Figure A-13.

The Windows Vista operating system

The Mac OS X operating system

Since its introduction in the mid-1970s, Macintosh has used its own operating system, a graphical user interface (GUI) system that has evolved over the years. The OS is designed so users "click" with a mouse on pictures, called icons, or on text to give commands to the system. Data is available to you in the WYSIWYG (what-you-see-is-what-you-get) format; that is, you can see on-screen what a document will look like when it is printed. Graphics and other kinds of data, such as spreadsheets, can be placed into text documents. However, GUIs take a great deal of RAM to keep all of the graphics and programs operating.

The original OS for IBM and IBM-compatible computers (machines made by other companies that operate similarly) was DOS (disk operating system). It did not have a graphical interface. The GUI system, Windows™, was developed to make using the IBM/IBM-compatible computer more "friendly." Today's Windows applications are the logical evolution of GUI for

IBM and IBM-compatible machines. Windows is a point-and-click system that automatically configures hardware to work together. You should note, however, that with all of its abilities comes the need for more RAM, or a system running Windows will operate slowly.

Applications Software

When you use a computer program to perform a data manipulation or processing task, you are using applications software. Word processors, databases, spreadsheets, graphics programs, desktop publishers, fax systems, and Internet browsers are all applications software.

Network Software

Novell™ and Windows NT are two kinds of network software. A traditional network is a group of computers that are hardwired (connected together with cables) to communicate and operate together. Today, some computer networks use RF (radio frequency) wireless technology to communicate with each other. This is called a **wireless network**, because you do not need to physically hook the network together with cables. In a typical network, one computer acts as the server, which controls the flow of data among the other computers, called nodes, or clients on the network. Network software manages this flow of information.

History of the Computer

Though various types of calculating machines were developed in the nineteenth century, the history of the modern computer begins about the middle of the last century. The strides made in developing today's personal computer have been truly astounding.

Early Development

The ENIAC, or Electronic Numerical Integrator and Computer, (see Figure A-14) was designed for military use in calculating ballistic trajectories and was the first electronic, digital computer to be developed in the United States. For its day, 1946, it was quite a marvel because it was able to accomplish a task in 20 seconds that normally would took a human three days to complete. However, it was an enormous machine that weighed more than 20 tons and contained thousands of vacuum tubes, which often failed. The tasks that it could accomplish were limited, as well.

From this awkward beginning, however, the seeds of an information revolution grew. Significant dates in the history of computer development are listed in Table A-2.

TABLE A-2
Milestones in the development of computers

YEAR	DEVELOPMENT
1948	First electronically stored program
1951	First junction transistor
1953	Replacement of tubes with magnetic cores
1957	First high-level computer language
1961	First integrated circuit
1965	First minicomputer
1971	Invention of the microprocessor (the silicon chip) and floppy disk
1974	First personal computer (made possible by the microprocessor)

The invention of the silicon chip in 1971 and the release of the first personal computer in 1974 launched the fast-paced information revolution in which we now all live and participate.

The Personal Computer

The PC, or personal computer, was mass marketed by Apple beginning in 1977, and by IBM in 1981. It is this desktop device with which people are so familiar and which, today, contains much more power and ability than did the original computer that took up an entire room. The PC is a small computer (desktop size or less) that uses a microprocessor to manipulate data. PCs may stand alone, be linked together in a network, or be attached to a large mainframe computer. See Figure A-15.

FIGURE A-15
Early IBM PC

Computer Utilities and System Maintenance

Computer operating systems let you run certain utilities and perform system maintenance to keep your computer running well. When you add hardware or software, you make changes in the way the system operates. With Plug and Play, most configuration changes are done automatically. The **drivers**, software that runs the peripherals, are installed automatically when your computer identifies the new hardware. When you install new software, many changes are made to the system automatically that determine how the software starts and runs.

In addition, you might want to customize the way the new software or hardware works with your system. You use **utility software** to make changes to the way hardware and software works. For example, you can change the speed at which your mouse clicks, how quickly or slowly keys repeat on the keyboard, and the resolution of the screen display.

Virus and Spyware Protection

Certain maintenance should be performed regularly on computers. **Viruses** are software programs that can damage the programs on your computer causing the computer to either stop working or run slowly. These programs are created by people, called **hackers**, who send the programs out solely to do harm to computers. Viruses are loaded onto your computer without your knowledge and run against your wishes. **Spyware** is also a form of a program that can harm your computer. There are utilities and programs that protect your computer from spyware and viruses.

You should install and update your antivirus and spyware protection software regularly, and scan all new disks and any incoming information from online sources for viruses. Some systems do this automatically; others require you to install software to do it.

Disk Maintenance

From time to time, you should run a program that scans or checks the hard drive to see that there are not bad sectors (areas) and look for corrupted files. Optimizing or defragmenting the hard disk is another way to keep your computer running at its best. Scanning and checking programs often offers the option of "fixing" the bad areas or problems, although you should be aware that this could result in data loss.

Society and Computers

The electronic information era has had global effects and influenced global change in all areas of people's lives. With the changes of this era have come many new questions and responsibilities. There are issues of ethics, security, and privacy.

Ethics

When you access information—whether online, in the workplace, or via purchased software—you have a responsibility to respect the rights of the person or people who created that information. Digital information, text, images, and sound is very easy to copy and share, however, that does not make it right to do so. You have to treat electronic information with respect. Often images, text, and sound are copyrighted. **Copyright** is the legal method for protecting the intellectual property of the author—the same way as you would a book, article or painting. For instance, you must give credit when you copy information from the Web or another person's document.

If you come across another person's personal information, you must treat it with respect. Do not share personal information unless you have that person's permission. For example, if you happen to pass a computer where a person left personal banking information software open on the computer, or a personal calendar available, you should not share that information. If e-mail comes to you erroneously, you should delete it before reading it.

When you use equipment that belongs to your school, a company for which you work, or others, here are some rules you should follow:

1. Do not damage computer hardware.

2. Do not add or remove equipment without permission.

3. Do not use an access code or equipment without permission.

4. Do not read others' e-mail.

5. Do not alter data belonging to someone else without permission.

6. Do not use the computer for play during work hours or use it for personal profit.

7. Do not access the Internet for nonbusiness related activities use during work hours.

8. Do not install or uninstall software without permission.

9. Do not make unauthorized copies of data or software or copy company files or procedures for personal use.

10. Do not copy software programs to use at home or at another site in the company without permission.

Security and Privacy

The Internet provides access to business and life-enhancing resources, such as distance learning, remote medical diagnostics, and the ability to work from home more effectively. Businesses, colleges and universities, and governments throughout the world depend on the Internet every day to get work done. Disruptions in the Internet can create havoc and dramatically decrease productivity.

With more and more financial transactions taking place online, **identify theft** is a growing problem, proving a person's online identity relies heavily upon their usernames and passwords. If you do online banking, there are several levels of security that you must pass through, verifying that you are who you claim to be, before gaining access to your accounts. If you divulge your usernames and passwords, someone can easily access your accounts online with devastating effects to your credit rating and to your accounts.

Phishing is a criminal activity that is used by people to fraudulently obtain your personal information, such as usernames, passwords, credit card details, and your social security information. Your social security number should never be given out online. Phishers send e-mails that look legitimate, but in fact are not. Phishing e-mails will often include fake information saying that your account needs your immediate attention because of unusual or suspected fraudulent activity. You are asked to click a link in the e-mail to access a Web site where you are then instructed to enter personal information. See Figure A-16. Phishing e-mail might also come with a promise of winning some money or gifts. When you get mail from people you don't know, the rules to remember are "you never get something for nothing, and if it looks too good to be true, it's most likely not true."

FIGURE A-16a
Fake e-mails for phishing

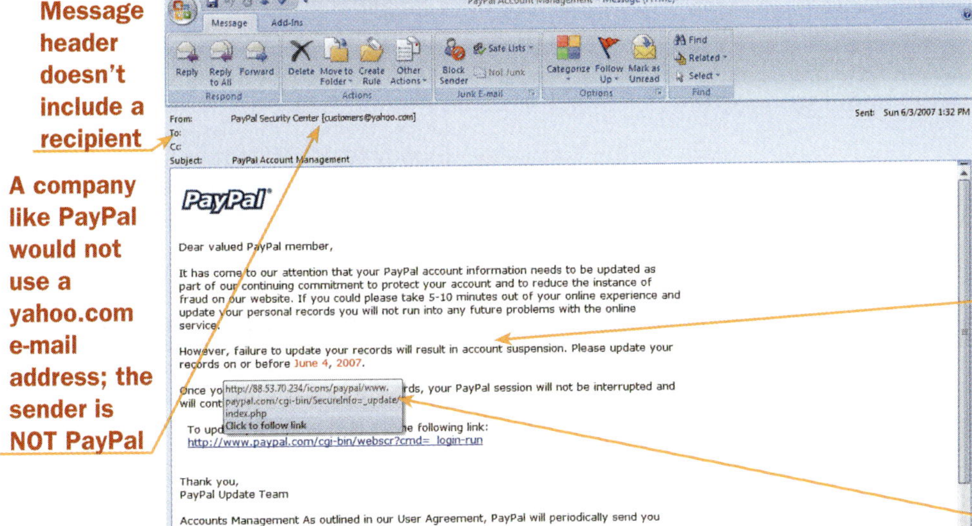

FIGURE A-16b
Fake e-mails for phishing

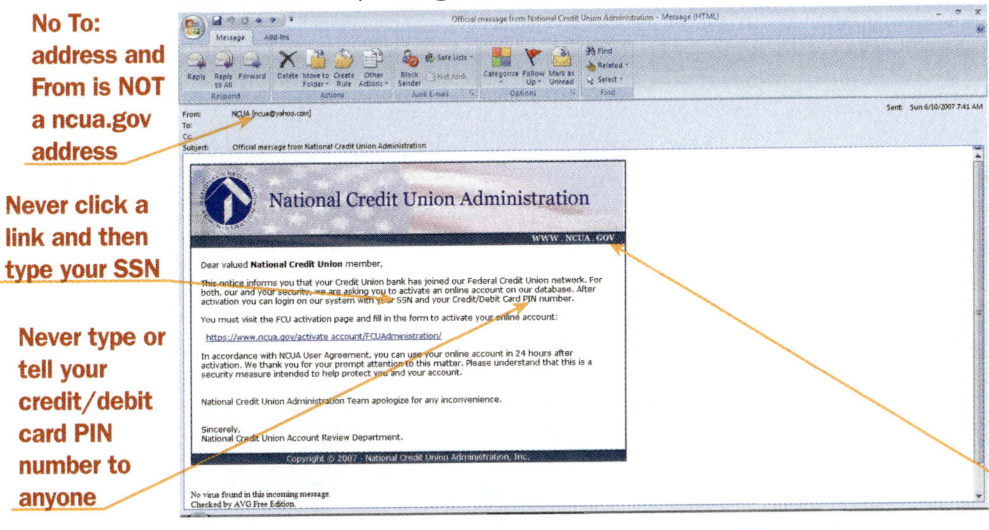

Whatever the ruse, when you click the link provided in the phishing e-mail, your browser will open a Web site that looks real, perhaps like your bank's site, eBay, or PayPal. But, in fact, this is a fake site set up to get you to give up your personal information. Phishing sites are growing. You should never click a link provided in an e-mail to get to sites such as your bank, eBay, or PayPal. Your bank or any other legitimate Web site will never ask you to type personal information on a page linked from an e-mail message. Always type the Web page address directly in the browser. Banks and Web sites have been trying to stop phishing sites through technology. Other attempts to reduce the growing number of reported phishing incidents include legislation and simply educating users about the practice.

Just as you would not open someone else's mail, you must respect the privacy of e-mail sent to others. When interacting with others online, you must keep confidential information confidential. Do not endanger your privacy, safety, or financial security by giving out personal information to someone you do not know.

Ebay is an online auction Web site that provides people a way to buy and sell merchandise through the Internet. PayPal is a financial services Web site that provides a way to transfer funds between people who perform financial transactions on the Internet.

Career Opportunities

In one way or another, all of our careers involve the computer. Whether you are a grocery store clerk using a scanner to read the prices, a busy executive writing a report that includes charts, graphics, and detailed analysis on a laptop on an airplane, or a programmer writing new software—almost everyone uses computers in their jobs. Most scientific research is done using computers.

There are specific careers available if you want to work with computers in the computer industry. Schools offer degrees in computer programming, computer repair, computer engineering, and software design. The most popular jobs are systems analysts, computer operators, and programmers. Analysts figure out ways to make computers work (or work better) for a particular business or type of business. Computer operators use the programs and devices to conduct business with computers. Programmers write the software for applications or new systems. There are degrees and jobs for people who want to create and maintain Web sites. Working for a company maintaining their Web site can be a very exciting career.

There are courses of study in using CAD (computer-aided design) and CAM (computer-aided manufacturing). There are positions available to instruct others in computer software use within companies and schools. Technical writers and editors must be available to write manuals on using computers and software. Computer-assisted instruction (CAI) is a system of teaching any given subject using the computer. Designing video games is another exciting and ever-growing field of computer work. And these are just a few of the possible career opportunities in an ever-changing work environment. See Figure A-17.

FIGURE A-17
Working in the computer field

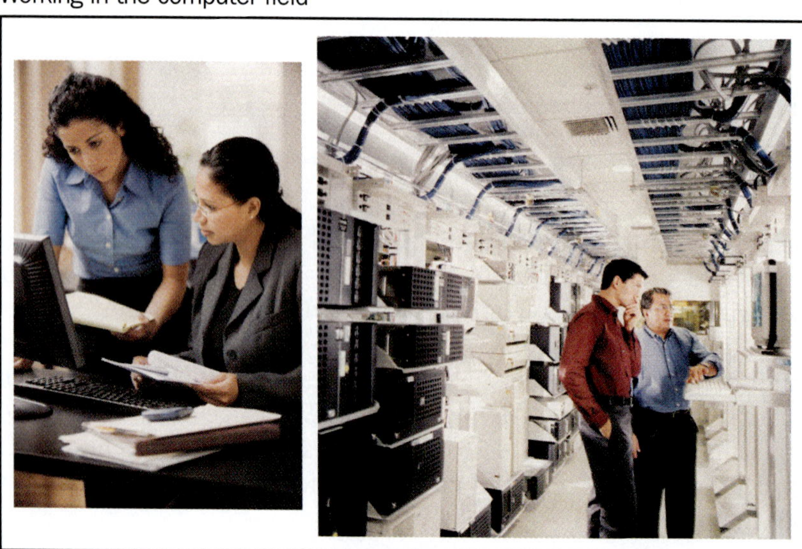

What Does the Future Hold?

The possibilities for computer development and application are endless. Things that were dreams or science fiction only 10 or 20 years ago are now reality. New technologies are emerging constantly. Some new technologies are replacing old ways of doing things; others are merging with those older methods and devices. Some new technologies are creating new markets. The Internet (more specifically, the Web), cell phones, and DVD videos are just a few inventions of the past decades that did not have counterparts prior to their inventions. We are learning new ways to work and play because of the computer. It is definitely a device that has become part of our offices, our homes, and our lives.

Social networking has moved from the streets and onto the Web. People meet and greet through the Internet using sites such as myspace.com and facebook.com.

Emerging Technologies

Today the various technologies and systems are coming together to operate more efficiently. Convergence is the merging of these technologies. Telephone communication is being combined with computer e-mail and Web browsing so users can set a time to meet online and, with the addition of voice technology, actually speak to each other using one small portable device.

The Web, now an important part of commerce and education, began as a one-way vehicle where users visited the Web to view Web pages and get information. It has evolved into sites where shopping and commerce takes place and is now evolving into a technology where users create the content. Web 2.0 and sites such as facebook.com, flickr.com, wikipedia.com, and youtube.com have content generated by the people that visit the Web sites. See Figure A-18.

FIGURE A-18
Content generated by the people that visit Web sites

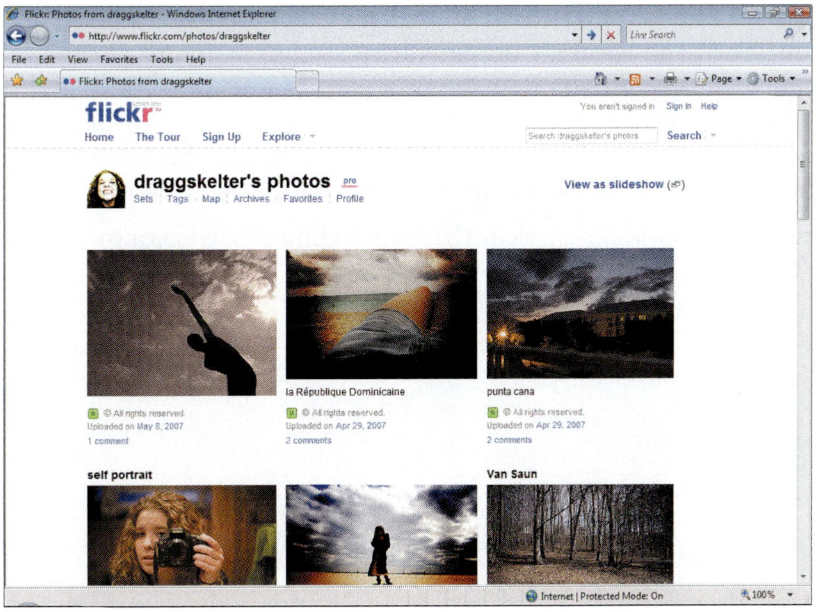

Used with permission by Emily C. Bunin

Computers have radically changed the way the medical profession delivers health care. Through the medical community, computers have enhanced medicine and healthcare throughout the world.

Trends

There are many trends that drive the computer industry. One trend is for larger and faster storage. From megabytes, to gigabytes, to terabytes, storage is becoming less an issue as the cost of storage is also dropping. RAM today is increasing exponentially. The trend is to sell larger blocks of RAM with every new personal computer. Newer processors also operate at speeds that are faster than the previous generation processors.

The actual size of computers is decreasing. Technology is allowing more powerful components to fit into smaller devices—laptops are lighter, monitors take up less space on the desktop, and flash drives can fit in your pocket and store gigabytes of data.

Home Offices

More and more frequently, people are working out of their homes—whether they are employees who are linked to a place of business or individuals running their own businesses. Telecommuting meets the needs of many industries. Many companies allow workers to have a computer at home that is linked by network to the office. Employees can use laptop computers to work both at home and on the road as they travel. A laptop computer, in combination with a wireless network, allows an employee to work from virtually anywhere and still keep in constant contact with her or his employer and customers.

Business communication is primarily by e-mail and telephone. It is very common for serious business transactions and communications to occur via e-mail rather than through the regular mail. Such an arrangement saves companies workspace and, thus, money.

Home Use

More and more households have personal computers. The statistics are constantly proving that a computer is an essential household appliance. Computers are used to access the Internet for shopping, education, and leisure. Computers are used to maintain financial records, manage household accounts, and record and manage personal information. More and more people are using electronic banking. Games and other computer interactions also offer a more reasonable way of spending leisure dollars. The convergence of television, the Internet, and the computer will find more households using their computers for media such as movies and music.

The future is with computing. It's clear that this technology will continue to expand and provide us with new and exciting trends.

APPENDIX B

KEYBOARDING TOUCH SYSTEM IMPROVEMENT

Introduction

- *Your Goal – Improve your keyboarding skills using the touch system so you are able to type without looking at the keyboard.*

Why Improve Your Keyboarding Skills?

- To be able to type faster and more accurately every time you use the computer

- To increase your enjoyment while using the computer

Did You Know?

You will type faster and more accurately when using the touch system instead of looking from the copy and then to the keyboard and pressing keys with one or two fingers—the "hunt and peck" system.

Getting Ready to Build Skills

In order to get ready you should:

1. **Prepare your desk and computer area.**
   a. Clear your desk of all clutter, except your book, a pencil or pen, the keyboard, the mouse, and the monitor.
   b. Position your keyboard and book so that you are comfortable and able to move your hands and fingers freely on the keyboard and read the book at the same time.
   c. Keep your feet flat on the floor, sit with your back straight, and rest your arms slightly bent with your finger tips on the keyboard.
   d. Start your Word processor, such as Microsoft Office Word, or any other text editor. You can use any simple program such as the Microsoft Works word processor or WordPad that is part of the Windows operating system. Ask your teacher for assistance.

2. Take a two-minute timed typing test according to your teacher's directions.

3. Calculate your words a minute (WAM) and errors a minute (EAM) using the instructions on the timed typing progress chart. This will be your base score you will compare to future timed typing.

4. Record today's Date, WAM, and EAM on the Base Score line of the writing progress chart.

1

5. Repeat the timed typing test as many times as you can.

6. Record each attempt on the Introduction line of the chart.

Skill Builder 1

Your Goal – Use the touch system to type the letters j u y h n m and to learn to press the spacebar.

Keys (J) (U) (Y) (H) (N) (M) (SPACEBAR)

What to Do

1. Place your finger tips on the home row keys as shown in Figure B-1.

FIGURE B-1
Place your finger tips on the Home Row keys

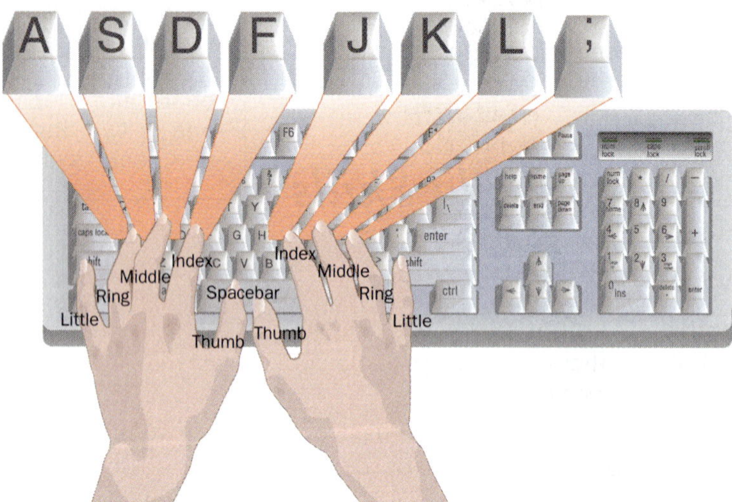

2. Look at Figure B-2. In step 3 you will press the letter keys j u y h n m. To press these keys, you use your right index finger. You will press the spacebar after typing each letter three times. The spacebar is the long bar beneath the bottom row of letter keys. You will press the spacebar with your right thumb.

Did You Know?

There are two forms that you will complete as you work though this appendix to improve your typing skills: the **Timed Typing Progress Chart** and the **Keyboarding Technique Checklist**. Both forms are printed as the last two pages at the end of this Appendix.

Computer Concepts

The home row keys are where you rest your finger tips when they are not typing. The index finger of your right hand rests on the j key. The index finger of your left hand rests on the f key. Feel the slight bump on these keys to help find the home row keys without looking at the keyboard.

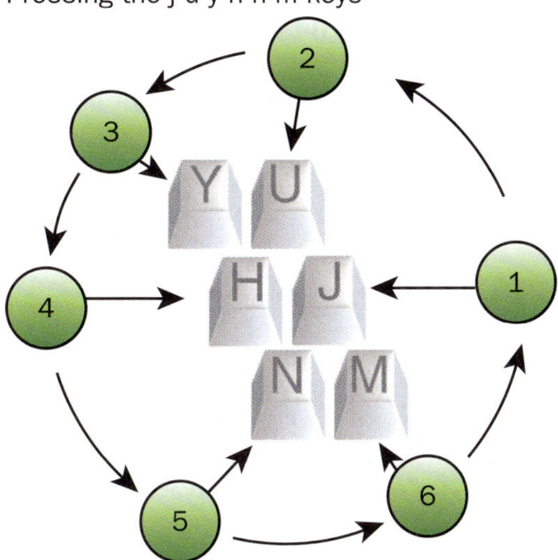

3. Look at your keyboard. Repeat the letters silently to yourself as you move your right index finger from the j key to press each key three times, then press the spacebar. Start typing:

jjj uuu jjj yyy jjj hhh jjj nnn jjj mmm

jjj uuu jjj yyy jjj hhh jjj nnn jjj mmm jjj

4. Repeat the same drill as many times as it takes for you to reach your comfort level.

jjj uuu jjj yyy jjj hhh jjj nnn jjj mmm

jjj uuu jjj yyy jjj hhh jjj nnn jjj mmm jjj

5. Close your eyes and visualize each key under each finger as you repeat the drill in step 4.

6. Look at the following two lines and type:

jjj jjj jjj juj juj juj jyj jyj jyj jhj jhj jhj jnj jnj jnj jmj jmj jmj

jjj jjj jjj juj juj juj jyj jyj jyj jhj jhj jhj jnj jnj jnj jmj jmj jmj

7. Repeat step 4, this time concentrating on the rhythmic pattern of the keys.

8. Close your eyes and visualize the keys under your finger tips as you type the drill in step 4 from memory.

Did You Know?

- Ignore errors.
- To complete the following exercises, you will type text that is bold and is not italicized and looks **like this**.
- If you have difficulty reaching for any key, for example the y key, practice by looking at the reach your finger tips make from the j key to the y key until the reach is visualized in your mind. The reach will become natural with very little practice.
- You may want to start on a new line by pressing the Enter key.

9. Look at the following two lines and type these groups of letters:

j ju juj j jy jyj j jh jhj j jn jnj j jm jmj j ju juj j jy jyj j jh jhj j jn jnj j jm jmj

jjj ju jhj jn jm ju jm jh jnj jm ju jmj jy ju jh j u ju juj jy jh jnj ju jm jmj jy

10. You may want to repeat Skill Builder 1, striving to improve typing letters that are most difficult for you.

Skill Builder 2

The left index finger is used to type the letters f r t g b v. Always return your left index finger to
the f key on the home row after pressing the other keys.
Your Goal – Use the touch system to type f r t g b v .

Keys (F) (R) (T) (G) (B) (V)

What to Do

1. Place your finger tips on the home row keys as you did in Skill Builder 1, Figure B-1.

2. Look at Figure B-3. Notice how you will type the letters f r t g b v and then press the
spacebar with your right thumb.

FIGURE B-3
Pressing the f r t g b v keys

3. Look at your keyboard. To press these keys, you use your left index finger. You will press
the spacebar after typing each letter three times. The spacebar is the long bar beneath the
bottom row of letter keys. You will press the spacebar with your right thumb.

After pressing each letter in the circle, press the home key f three times as shown. Don't
worry about errors. Ignore them.

fff rrr fff ttt fff ggg fff bbb fff vvv

fff rrr fff ttt fff ggg fff bbb fff vvv fff

4. Repeat the same drill two more times using a quicker, sharper stroke.

    fff rrr fff ttt fff ggg fff bbb fff vvv

    fff rrr fff ttt fff ggg fff bbb fff vvv fff

5. Close your eyes and visualize each key under each finger as you repeat the drill in step 4.

6. Look at the following two lines and key these groups of letters:

    fff fff fff frf frf frf ftf ftf ftf fgf fgf fgf fbf fbf fbf fvf fvf fvf

    fff fff fff frf frf frf ftf ftf ftf fgf fgf fgf fbf fbf fbf fvf fvf fvf

7. Repeat step 6, this time concentrating on a rhythmic pattern of the keys.

8. Close your eyes and visualize the keys under your finger tips as you type the drill in step 4 from memory.

9. Look at the following two lines and type these groups of letters:

    fr frf ft ftf fg fgf fb fbf fv fvf

    ft fgf fv frf ft fbf fv frf ft fgf

10. You are about ready to type your first words. Look at the following lines and type these groups of letters (remember to press the spacebar after each group):

    jjj juj jug jug jug rrr rur rug rug rug

    ttt tut tug tug tug rrr rur rub rub rub

    ggg gug gum gum gum mmm mum

    mug mug mug hhh huh hum hum hum

11. Complete the Keyboarding Technique Checklist.

Skill Builder 3

Your Goal – Use the touch system to type k i , d e c.

Keys ⓚ ⓘ ⟨ , ⟩ *(comma)*

What to Do

1. Place your finger tips on the home row keys. The home row key for the left middle finger is d. The home row key for the right middle finger is k. You use your left middle finger to type d, e, c. You use your right middle finger to type k, i, , as shown in Figure B-4.

Did You Know?

The keyboard has letters, punctuation marks, and symbols. You can refer to these all as 'characters'.

Teamwork

Ask your classmate to call out the letters in random order as you type them with your eyes closed. Do the same for your classmate. Ask your classmate or your teacher to complete the Keyboarding Technique Checklist.

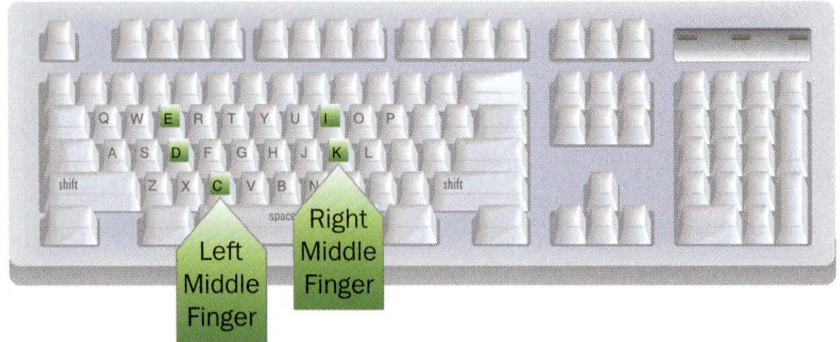

FIGURE B-4
Pressing keys k i , d e c

2. Look at your keyboard and locate these keys: k i , (the letter k key, the letter i key, and the comma key).

3. Look at your keyboard. Repeat the letters silently to yourself as you press each key three times and put a space between each set of letters and the comma to type:

   kkk iii kkk ,,, kkk iii kkk ,,, kkk iii kkk ,,, kkk iii kkk ,,, kkk iii kkk ,,, kkk

4. Look at the characters in step 3 and repeat the drill two more times using a quicker, sharper stroke.

5. Close your eyes and repeat the drill in step 3 as you visualize each key under each finger.

6. Repeat step 5, concentrating on a rhythmic pattern of the keys.

Keys ⓓ ⓔ ⓒ

1. Place your finger tips on the home row keys.

2. Look at your keyboard and locate these keys: d e c (the letter d key, the letter e key, and the letter c key).

3. Look at your keyboard. Repeat the letters silently to yourself as you press each key three times and put a space between each set of letters to type:

   ddd eee ddd ccc ddd eee ddd ccc ddd eee ddd ccc ddd eee ddd ccc ddd

4. Look at the letters in step 3 and repeat the drill two more times using a quicker, sharper stroke.

5. Close your eyes and repeat the drill in step 3 as you visualize each key under each finger.

6. Repeat step 5, concentrating on a rhythmic pattern of the keys.

7. Look at the following lines of letters and type these groups of letters and words:

   fff fuf fun fun fun ddd ded den den den

   ccc cuc cub cub cub vvv vev vet

   fff fuf fun fun fun ddd ded den den den

   ccc cuc cub cub cub vvv vev vet

8. Complete the Keyboarding Technique Checklist.

Skill Builder 4

*Your Goal – Use the touch system to type l o . s w x
and to press the left Shift key.*

Keys ⬜L ⬜O ⬜. *(period)*

What to Do

1. Place your finger tips on the home row keys. The home row key for the left ring finger is s.
   The home row key for the right ring finger is l. You use your left ring finger to type s w x.
   You use your right ring finger to type l o . as shown in Figure B-5.

FIGURE B-5
Pressing keys l o . s w x

2. Look at your keyboard and locate the following keys: l o . (the letter l key, the letter o key,
   and the period key).

3. Look at your keyboard. Repeat the letters silently to yourself as you press each key three
   times and put a space between each set of letters and the periods to type:

   lll ooo lll ... lll ooo lll ... lll ooo lll ... lll ooo lll ... lll ooo lll ... lll ooo lll ... lll

4. Look at the line in step 3 and repeat the drill two more times using a quicker, sharper stroke.

5. Close your eyes and repeat the drill in step 3 as you visualize each key under each finger.

6. Repeat step 5, concentrating on a rhythmic pattern of the keys.

Keys ⬜S ⬜W ⬜X

1. Place your finger tips on the home row keys.

2. Look at your keyboard and locate the following letter keys: s w x

3. Look at your keyboard. Repeat the letters silently to yourself as you press each key three
   times and put a space between each set of letters to type:

   sss www sss xxx sss www sss xxx sss www sss xxx sss www sss xxx sss

4. Look at the line in step 3 and repeat the same drill two more times using a quicker, sharper stroke.

5. Close your eyes and repeat the drill in step 3 as you visualize each key under each finger.

6. Repeat step 5, concentrating on a rhythmic pattern of the keys.

Key SHIFT (*Left Shift Key*)

You press and hold the Shift key as you press a letter key to type a capital letter. You press and hold the Shift key to type the character that appears above the numbers in the top row of the keyboard and on a few other keys that show two characters.

Press and hold down the left Shift key with the little finger on your left hand while you press each letter to type capital letters for keys that are typed with the finger tips on your right hand. See Figure B-6.

FIGURE B-6
Using the Shift keys

1. Type the following groups of letters and the sentence that follows.

   jjj JJJ jjj JJJ yyy YYY yyy YYY nnn NNN nnn NNN mmm MMM

   Just look in the book. You can see well.

2. Complete the Keyboarding Technique Checklist.

Skill Builder 5

*Your Goal – Use the touch system to type a q z ; p /
and to press the right Shift key.*

Keys (;) *(semi-colon)* (P) (/)

What to Do

1. Place your finger tips on the home row keys. The home row key for the left little finger is a. The home row key for the right little finger is ;. You use your left little finger to type *a q z* . You use your right little finger to type *; p /* as shown in Figure B-7.

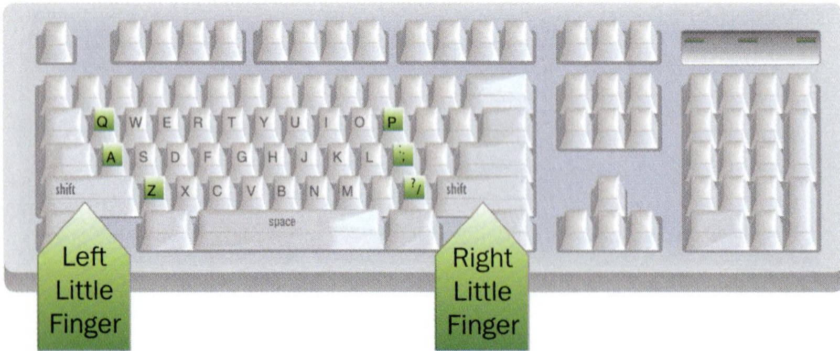

FIGURE B-7
Pressing keys a q z ; p / and the right Shift key

2. Look at your keyboard and locate the following keys: ; p / (the semi-colon, the letter p, and the forward slash).

3. Repeat the letters silently to yourself as you press each key three times and put a space between each set of characters to type:

   ;;; ppp ;;; /// ;;; ppp ;;; /// ;;; ppp ;;; ///

   ;;; ppp ;;; /// ;;; ppp ;;; /// ;;; ppp ;;; /// ;;;

4. Look at the lines in step 3 and repeat the drill two more times using a quicker, sharper stroke.

5. Close your eyes and repeat the drill in step 3 as you visualize each key under each finger.

6. Repeat step 5, concentrating on a rhythmic pattern of the keys.

Keys (A) (Q) (Z)

1. Place your finger tips on the home row keys.

2. Look at your keyboard and locate the following keys: a q z (the letter a, the letter q, and the letter z).

3. Look at your keyboard. Repeat the letters silently to yourself as you press each key three times and put a space between each set of letters and type:

   aaa qqq aaa zzz aaa qqq aaa zzz aaa qqq aaa zzz aaa qqq aaa zzz aaa

4. Look at the line in step 3 and repeat the same drill two more times using a quicker, sharper stroke.

5. Close your eyes and repeat the drill in step 3 as you visualize each key under each finger.

6. Repeat step 5, concentrating on a rhythmic pattern of the keys.

Key (SHIFT) *(Right Shift Key)*

Press and hold down the right Shift key with the little finger on your right hand while you press each letter to type capital letters for keys that are typed with the finger tips on your left hand.

1. Type the following lines. Press and hold down the right Shift key with the little finger of your right hand to make capitals of letters you type with the finger tips on your left hand.

   sss SSS rrr RRR

   Press each key quickly. Relax when you type.

2. Complete the Keyboarding Technique Checklist.

Skill Builder 6

You will probably have to type slowly at first, but with practice you will learn to type faster and accurately.
Your Goal – Use the touch system to type all letters of the alphabet.

What to Do

1. Close your eyes. Do not look at the keyboard and type all letters of the alphabet in groups of three with a space between each set as shown:

   aaa bbb ccc ddd eee fff ggg hhh iii jjj

   kkk lll mmm nnn ooo ppp qqq rrr sss

   ttt uuu vvv www xxx yyy zzz

2. Repeat step 1, concentrating on a rhythmic pattern of the keys.

3. Repeat step 1, but faster than you did for step 2.

4. Type the following sets of letters, all letters of the alphabet in groups of two with a space between each set as shown:

   aa bb cc dd ee ff gg hh ii jj kk ll mm nn oo pp qq rr ss tt uu vv ww xx yy zz

5. Type the following letters, all letters of the alphabet with a space between each letter as shown:

a b c d e f g h i j k l m n o p q r s t u v w x y z

6. Continue to look at this book. Do not look at the keyboard, and type all letters of the alphabet backwards in groups of three with a space between each set as shown:

zzz yyy xxx www vvv uuu ttt sss rrr

qqq ppp ooo nnn mmm lll kkk jjj iii

hhh ggg fff eee ddd ccc bbb aaa

7. Repeat step 6, but faster than the last time.

8. Type each letter of the alphabet once backwards:

z y x w v u t s r q p o n m l k j i h g f e d c b a

9. Think about the letters that took you the most amount of time to find the key on the keyboard. Go back to the Skill Builder for those letters, and repeat the drills until you are confident about their locations.

Timed Typing

Prepare to take the timed typing test, according to your teacher's directions.

1. **Prepare your desk and computer area.**
   a. Clear your desk of all clutter except your book, a pencil or pen, the keyboard, the mouse, the monitor, and the computer box if it is placed on the desk.
   b. Position your keyboard and book so that you are comfortable and able to move your hands and finger tips freely.
   c. Keep your feet flat on the floor, sitting with your back straight, resting your arms slightly bent with your finger tips on the keyboard.

2. Take a two-minute timed typing test according to your teacher's directions.

3. Calculate your words a minute (WAM) and errors a minute (EAM) scores using the instructions on the timed typing progress chart in this book.

4. Record the date, WAM, and EAM on the Skill Builder 6 line.

5. Repeat the timed typing test as many times as you can and record each attempt.

Skill Builder 7

Your Goal – Improve your typing techniques—which is the secret for improving your speed and accuracy.

What to Do

Did You Know?

You may want to ask a classmate or your teacher to record your scores.

1. Rate yourself for each item on the Keyboarding Technique Checklist.

2. Do not time yourself as you concentrate on a single technique you marked with a "0." Type only the first paragraph of the timed typing.

3. Repeat step 2 as many times as possible for each of the items marked with an "0" that need improvement.

4. Take a two-minute timed typing test. Record your WAM and EAM on the timed typing progress chart as 1st Attempt on the Skill Builder 7 line. Compare this score with your base score.

5. Looking only at the book and using your best techniques, type the following technique sentence for one minute:

   .   2   .   4   .   6   .   8   .   10   .   12   .   14   .   16

Now is the time for all good men and women to come to the aid of their country.

6. Record your WAM and EAM on the 7 Technique Sentence line.

7. Repeat steps 5 and 6 as many times as you can and record your scores.

Skill Builder 8

Your Goal – Increase your words a minute (WAM) score.

What to Do

You can now type letters in the speed line very well and with confidence. Practicing all of the other letters of the alphabet will further increase your skill and confidence in keyboarding.

1. Take a two-minute timed typing test.

2. Record your WAM and EAM scores as the 1st Attempt.

3. Type only the first paragraph only one time as fast as you can. Ignore errors.

4. Type only the first and second paragraphs only one time as fast as you can. Ignore errors.

5. Take a two-minute timed typing test again. Ignore errors.

6. Record only your WAM score as the 2nd Attempt. Compare only this WAM with your 1st Attempt WAM and your base score WAM.

Get Your Best WAM

1. To get your best WAM on easy text for 15 seconds, type the following speed line as fast as you can, as many times as you can. Ignore errors.

   .   2   .   4   .   6   .   8   .   10

   Now is the time, now is the time, now is the time,

2. Multiply the number of words typed by four to get your WAM (15 seconds x 4 = 1 minute). For example, if you type 12 words for 15 seconds, 12 x 4 = 48 WAM.

3. Record only your WAM in the 8 Speed Line box.

4. Repeat steps 1-3 as many times as you can to get your very best WAM. Ignore errors.

5. Record only your WAM for each attempt.

Skill Builder 9

Your Goal – Decrease errors a minute (EAM) score.

What to Do

Did You Know?

How much you improve depends upon how much you want to improve.

1. Take a two-minute timed typing test.

2. Record your WAM and EAM as the 1st Attempt.

3. Type only the first paragraph only one time at a controlled rate of speed so you reduce errors. Ignore speed.

4. Type only the first and second paragraphs only one time at a controlled rate of speed so you reduce errors. Ignore speed.

5. Take a two-minute timed typing test again. Ignore speed.

6. Record only your EAM score as the 2nd Attempt. Compare only the EAM with your 1st Attempt EAM and your base score EAM.

Get Your Best EAM

1. To get your best EAM, type the following accuracy sentence (same as the technique sentence) for one minute. Ignore speed.

   Now is the time for all good men and women to come to the aid of their country.

2. Record only your EAM score on the Accuracy Sentence 9 line.

3. Repeat step 1 as many times as you can to get your best EAM. Ignore speed.

4. Record only your EAM score for each attempt.

Skill Builder 10

Your Goal – Use the touch system and your best techniques to type faster and more accurately than you have ever typed before.

What to Do

1. Take a one-minute timed typing test.

2. Record your WAM and EAM as the 1st Attempt on the Skill Builder 10 line.

3. Repeat the timed typing test for two minutes as many times as necessary to get your best ever WAM with no more than one EAM. Record your scores as 2nd, 3rd, and 4th Attempts.

> **Did You Know?** 
>
> You may want to get advice regarding which techniques you need to improve from a class-mate or your teacher.

Assessing Your Improvement

1. Circle your best timed typing test for Skill Builders 6-10 on the timed typing progress chart.

2. Record your best score and your base score. Compare the two scores. Did you improve?

	WAM	EAM
Best Score	____	____
Base Score	____	____

3. Use the Keyboarding Technique Checklist to identify techniques you still need to improve. You may want to practice these techniques now to increase your WAM or decrease your EAM.

Timed Typing

Every five strokes in a timed typing test is a word, including punctuation marks and spaces. Use the scale above each line to tell you how many words you typed.

```
        .       2        .        4       .        6         .
If you learn how to key well now,  it
  8       .    10       .     12      .       14    .       16
is a skill that will help you for the rest
        .    18     .       20      .       22     .      24       .
of your life.  How you sit will help you key
 26    .        28      .      30       .     32     .      34       .
with more speed and less errors.   Sit with your
 36        .     38     .      40      .      42      .         44
feet flat on the floor and your back erect.
        .      46     .      48      .      50     .      52
To key fast by touch, try to keep your
        .      54     .       56     .      58      .       60
eyes on the copy and not on your hands or
       .    62     .     64      .        66    .      68      .        70
the screen.   Curve your fingers and make sharp,
       .      72     .
quick strokes.
        74    .       76      .       78      .       80      .
Work for speed first. If you make more
     82     .       84      .       86      .       88     .        90
than two errors a minute, you are keying too
       92    .      94       .      96      .     98     .     100
fast. Slow down to get fewer errors. If you
        .     102      .        104      .     106      .     108
get fewer than two errors a minute, go for
   .      110
speed.
```

Timed Typing Progress Chart

Timed Writing Progress Chart

Last Name: ________________   *First Name:* ________________

Instructions

Calculate your scores as shown in the following sample and footnotes (a) and (b). Repeat timed writings as many times as you can and record your scores for each attempt.

Base Score: Date ____   WAM ____   EAM ____   Time ____

		1st Attempt		2nd Attempt		3rd Attempt		4th Attempt	
Skill Builder	**Date**	**(a)** **WAM**	**(b)** **EAM**	**WAM**	**EAM**	**WAM**	**EAM**	**WAM**	**EAM**
Sample	9/2	22	3.5	23	2.0	25	1.0	29	2.0
Introduction									
6									
7									
8					-----				
9				-----					
10									
7 Technique Sentence									
8 Speed Line			-----		-----		-----		-----
9 Accuracy Sentence		-----		-----		-----		-----	

(a) Divide words keyed (44) by 2 (minutes) to get WAM (22)

(b) Divide errors (7) by 2 (minutes) to get EAM (3.5)

Keyboarding Technique Checklist

Last Name: ___________________   *First Name:* ___________________

Instructions

1. Write the Skill Builder number, the date, and the initials of the evaluator in the proper spaces.

2. Place a check mark (✔) after a technique that is performed satisfactorily. Place a large zero (0) after a technique that needs improvement.

Skill Builder Number:	Sample									
Date:	9/1									
Evaluator:	SL									
Technique										
Attitude										
1. Enthusiastic about learning	✓									
2. Optimistic about improving	✓									
3. Alert but relaxed	✓									
4. Sticks to the task; not distracted	✓									
Getting Ready	✓									
1. Desk uncluttered										
2. Properly positions keyboard and book	✓									
3. Feet flat on the floor	✓									
4. Body erect, but relaxed	0									
Keyboarding										
1. Curves fingers	0									
2. Keeps eyes on the book	✓									
3. Taps the keys lightly; does not "pound" them	0									
4. Makes quick, "bouncy," strokes	0									
5. Smooth rhythm	0									
6. Minimum pauses between strokes	✓									

GLOSSARY

3-D reference A reference to the same cell or range in multiple worksheets that you use in a formula.

A

Absolute cell reference A cell reference that does not change when copied or moved to a new cell.

Active cell The cell in the worksheet in which you can type data.

Active worksheet The worksheet that is displayed in the work area; also called *active sheet*.

Address bar An area in a window that contains the path to the current folder.

Alignment The position of data in a cell.

Argument The value a function uses to perform a calculation, including a number, text, or a cell reference that acts as an operand.

Ascending sort A sort order that arranges data with letters in alphabetical order (A to Z), data with numbers from lowest to highest, and data with dates from earliest to latest.

AutoFilter A menu that opens when you click a filter arrow. The menu lists all the values that appear in that column along with additional criteria and color filtering options.

AutoFit An automatic determination of the best width for a column or the best height for a row, based on its contents.

Automatic page break A page break that Excel inserts whenever it runs out of room on a page.

Axis A horizontal or vertical line that establishes the relationship between data in a chart.

B

Border A line around the edges of a cell.

Button An icon that, when clicked, gives the program instructions about what you want to do.

C

Cell The intersection of a row and a column in a worksheet.

Cell reference A unique identifier for a cell, which is formed by combining the cell's column letter and row number.

Cell style A collection of formatting characteristics you apply to a cell or range of data.

Chart A graphical representation of data.

Chart area The entire chart and all other chart elements.

Chart layout An arrangement that specifies which elements are included in a chart and where they are placed.

Chart sheet A separate sheet in a workbook that stores a chart.

Chart style Formatting applied to a chart based on the colors, fonts, and effects associated with the workbook's theme.

Clear To remove all of the formatting applied to a cell or range of cells.

Close button Window button that closes the open window or application.

Column A vertical stack of cells in a worksheet; identified by letters at the top of the worksheet window.

Column chart A chart that uses bars of varying heights to illustrate values in a worksheet.

Column heading The letter at the top of a column that identifies that column.

Comment A note that is attached to a cell.

Computer folder In Windows Vista, provides access to hard disk drives, removable drives and media, CD and DVD drives, network locations, and other removable media such as cameras and scanners.

Contextual tab Tabs that appear on the Ribbon only when you select certain items in a file, and that contain commands related to that item.

Conditional formatting Formatting that highlights worksheet data by changing the look of cells that meet a specified condition.

Control Panel The command center for configuring Windows settings.

Copy To duplicate a cell's contents without affecting the original cell.

Cut To move cell contents from the original position and place in the new location.

D

Data label Text or numbers that provides additional information about a data marker.

Data marker A chart symbol (such as a bar, line, dot, slice, and so forth) that represents a single data point or value from the corresponding worksheet cell.

Data series A group of related information in a column or row of a worksheet that is plotted on a chart.

Data source A range of cells in a worksheet that stores the data plotted on a chart.

Data table A grid that displays the data plotted in a chart.

Date and time functions Functions that convert serial numbers to a month, a day, or a year, or that insert the current date or the current date and time.

Descending sort A sort order that arranges data with letters from Z to A, data with numbers from highest to lowest, and data with dates from oldest to newest.

Desktop The main screen and workspace that opens with Windows is started.

Destination The location where data will appear.

Dialog box An interactive message window that appears when more information is required before the command can be performed.

Disk Cleanup A Windows Vista utility that deletes temporary files from the hard disk and improves computer performance.

Documents folder Stores the files you use for your projects, such as documents, presentations, spreadsheets, and other files.

E

Editing mode The mode in which the insertion point is placed within the cell contents, so you can edit and format text directly in the cell.

Embedded chart A chart that is inserted in a worksheet.

Excel *See* Microsoft Office Excel

Exploded pie chart A pie chart with one or more slices pulled away from the pie to distinguish them.

Explorer windows Vista windows that are used to modify computer settings and navigate to items.

F

File extension A series of letters added to the end of a file name that identifies the program in which that file was created.

Fill The background color of a cell. The process of copying a cell's contents and/or formatting into an adjacent cell or range.

Fill handle The black square in the lower-right corner of the active cell or range that you drag over the cells you want to fill.

Filter To display a subset of the data that meets certain criteria and temporarily hide the rows that do not meet the specified criteria.

Filter arrow An arrow that appears in a column heading cell that opens the AutoFilter menu.

Financial functions Functions that are used to analyze loans and investments.

Folder An electronic directory containing files or other folders.

Font size The height of characters.

Font style Emphasis added to cells, such as bold, italics, and underlining.

Font The design of text.

Footer Text that prints in the bottom margin of each page.

Format Painter A tool used to copy formatting from one worksheet cell to another without copying the cell's contents.

Formula An equation that calculates a new value from values currently in a worksheet.

Formula AutoComplete A feature to help you enter a formula with a valid function name and arguments.

Formula Bar The box to the right of the Name Box that displays a formula when the cell of a worksheet contains a calculated value (or the results of the formula).

Freeze panes To keep selected rows and/or columns of the worksheet visible on the screen as the rest of the worksheet scrolls.

Function A shorthand way to write an equation that performs a calculation.

G

Gadget A tool available on the Windows sidebar.

Gallery A window that shows the options available for a command.

Group A collection of related command buttons on a tab.

H

Header Text that prints in the top margin of each page.

Help and Support The Windows system where information can be found using topic lists or by searching using keywords.

Home page The first page that opens when you start your browser.

Hyperlink A cell in a worksheet that opens another file or page when you click it.

I

Icon A small graphic image that represents a file, folder, program, or program shortcut.

Indent To shift data within a cell and insert space between the cell border and its content.

Insertion point Shows where text will appear when you begin typing.

L

Landscape orientation A page or worksheet rotated so it is wider than it is long.

Legend A list that identifies patterns, symbols, or colors used in a chart.

Line chart A chart that uses points connected by a line to illustrate values in a worksheet.

Link Text (often colored and underlined) or a graphic that you click to move to another location or Web page.

Live Preview The results of the formatting options displayed in the worksheet.

Logical functions Functions that display text or values if certain conditions exist.

M

Manual calculation   The option that lets you determine when Excel calculates formulas in the worksheet.

Manual page break   A break you insert to start a new page.

Margins   Blank spaces around the top, bottom, and sides of page.

Mathematical functions   Functions that manipulate quantitative data in a worksheet.

Maximize button   Window sizing button that enlarges a window to the full size of the screen.

Menu   An option list of commands for initiating certain actions or tasks.

Merge   To combine multiple cells into one cell.

Microsoft Office 2007 (Office) A collection of software programs that can be used together. **Office Excel 2007 (or Excel)**   The spreadsheet program in Microsoft Office 2007.

Microsoft Office Help button   Opens the Help window for the program.

Mini toolbar   A toolbar that appears in the work area that contains related to the selected text.

Minimize button   Window sizing button that reduces the window to an icon on the taskbar.

Mixed cell reference   A cell reference that contains both relative and absolute references.

N

Name Box   The cell reference area located below the Ribbon, which displays the cell reference of the active cell.

Navigation pane   An area in a window that contains links to favorite folders, saved searches, and an expandable list of folders.

Normal view   The worksheet view best for entering and formatting data in a worksheet.

Number format   The formatting option that changes the way data looks in a cell.

O

Object   Anything that appears on the screen that you can select and work with as a whole, such as a shape, picture, or chart.

Office Button   Contains commands for working with files, including commands for opening, saving, printing, and creating new files.

Office Clipboard (or Clipboard)   A temporary storage area for up to 24 selections you copy or cut.

Operand   A number or cell reference used in a formula.

Operating system   Software such as Windows Vista that controls the basic operations of a computer.

Operator   A symbol that indicates what mathematical operation to perform on the operands such as a plus sign (+) for addition.

Order of evaluation   The sequence used to calculate the value of a formula.

Orientation   The rotation of cell contents at an angle or vertically.

P

Page Break Preview   The worksheet view for adjusting page breaks in a worksheet.

Page Layout view   The worksheet view that shows how the worksheet will appear on a printed page.

Paste   To place the last item from the Clipboard into the cell or range selected in the worksheet.

Personal folder   Stores your most frequently used folders and is labeled with by the computer user account name.

Picture   A digital photograph or other image file.

Pie chart   A chart that shows the relationship of a part to a whole.

Plot area   The graphical representation of all of the data series.

Point-and-click method   In a formula, to click a cell rather than type its cell reference.

Point   The measurement unit for font size.

Pointer   The tip of a pointing device as it appears on the screen.

Pointing device   A device that allow users to navigate and interact with a computer.

Portrait orientation   A page or worksheet rotated so it is longer than it is wide.

Print area   The cells and ranges designated for printing.

Print title   Designated rows and/or columns in a worksheet that print on each page.

Program window   The rectangle that contains the open program, tools for working with the file, and the work area.

Public folder   Used to store the files you want to share with other users on the same computer or who are connected through a network.

Q

Quick Access Toolbar   Provides access to commonly used commands.

R

Range   A group of selected cells.

Range reference   The unique identifier for a range, which is the cell in its upper-left corner and the cell in its lower-right corner, separated by a colon.

Recycle Bin   Wastebasket icon on the Windows Vista desktop where items are deleted and from which they can be restored before the Recycle Bin is emptied.

Relative cell reference   A cell reference that adjusts to its new location when copied or moved.

Research task pane   A task pane that provides access to information typically found in references such as dictionaries, thesauruses, and encyclopedias.

Restore Down button Window sizing button that returns the window to the size it was before the Maximize button was clicked.

Ribbon Contains tabs from which you can choose a variety of commands.

Row The horizontal placement of cells in a worksheet; identified by numbers on the left side of the worksheet window.

Row heading The number at the left of a row that identifies that row.

S

Scale To resize a worksheet to print on a specific number of pages.

Scatter chart A chart that shows the relationship between two categories of data; sometimes called an XY chart.

ScreenTip A box that appears when you point to a button that contains the button's name, a description of its function, and sometimes a link to more information or a keyboard shortcut.

Scroll arrows Located at either side of a scroll bar; used to move the window contents up or down.

Scroll bar A bar that appears on the edge of a window when there is more content than can appear in the window at its current size.

Scroll box A slider that can be dragged to change position in a scroll bar.

Selection box The marker that surrounds a selected chart element.

Sheet tab The worksheet identifier that appears at the bottom of the workbook window.

Shortcut menu A list of commands that appear when you right-click something in the program window.

Sizing buttons Used to change the size of the program window and exits the program.

Sizing handles Black dots at the corners and sides of the selected chart used to resize the chart.

SmartArt graphic A graphic diagram that visually represents information and ideas.

Sort To rearrange data in a more meaningful order.

Source The location data is being transferred from.

Split To divide the worksheet window into two or four panes that scroll independently.

Spreadsheet A grid of rows and columns in which you enter text, numbers, and the results of calculations.

Statistical functions Functions that are used to describe large quantities of data.

Status bar Provides information about the current file and process.

Style A combination of formatting characteristics, such as alignment, font, font size, font color, fill color, and borders, that are applied simultaneously.

Sum button A button on the Ribbon that insert the SUM function to add long columns or rows of numbers.

T

Tab Area on the Ribbon that organizes the commands into related tasks.

Task pane A pane that opens on the right or left side of the program window, from which you can choose additional tasks.

Taskbar A bar on the bottom of the Windows Vista desktop that includes icons for open or background programs.

Template A predesigned workbook file that you can use as the basis or model for new workbooks.

Text functions Functions that are used to format and work with cell contents.

Theme A preset collection of design elements, including fonts, colors, and other effects.

Title bar The bar at the top of the window that contains the name for that window.

Toolbar An area in a window that contains buttons used to execute a function or open a command menu.

Trigonometric functions Functions that manipulate quantitative data in a worksheet.

Truncate To hide text that does not fit in a cell from view.

U

Uniform Resource Locator (URL) The location of a Web page on the Internet.

V

View buttons Used to change how a file is displayed in the workspace.

W

Web browser Software used to view Web pages; for example, Internet Explorer.

Window A work area in Windows Vista containing a user interface.

Windows Aero Windows Vista graphic interface that includes transparent windows and dialog boxes.

Windows Security Center Windows Vista utility that monitors the status of a computer's security components.

Windows Sidebar A transparent panel attached to one side of the Vista desktop screen that contains gadgets.

Work area Displays the document you are working on.

Workbook The file used to store worksheets; usually a collection of related worksheets.

Worksheet A computerized spreadsheet in Excel.

Worksheet range A group of adjacent worksheets.

World Wide Web (Web) A system of computers that share information by through links on Web pages.

Wrap text To move data to a new line when the cell is not wide enough to display all the contents.

INDEX